PERSONAL CAUSATION

PERSONAL CAUSATION

The Internal Affective Determinants of Behavior

RICHARD DE CHARMS

WASHINGTON UNIVERSITY
ST. LOUIS, MISSOURI

ACADEMIC PRESS New York and London   1968

ACADEMIC PRESS INC.
111 Fifth Avenue, New York, New York 10003

United Kingdom Edition published by
ACADEMIC PRESS INC. (LONDON) LTD.
Berkeley Square House, London W.1

LIBRARY OF CONGRESS CATALOG CARD NUMBER: 68-14650

PRINTED IN THE UNITED STATES OF AMERICA

Preface

This book is primarily intended to make a theoretical contribution, to suggest a somewhat novel way of approaching the problems of human motivation, to break from tradition. I have tried to show that a break is necessary because traditional treatments of motivation are constrained by several philosophical presuppositions which, when carefully analyzed, appear to have a restricting and, in some cases, a trivializing effect on research in motivation.

A break is not a breakthrough. In this age of sonic booms and supersonic breakthroughs, some seem to feel that psychology is on the brink. In my opinion progress comes in small cumulative steps, and although I speak of a break, I think of it as a break with a way of thinking but not with the results that have been produced by that way of thinking. I hope that my contribution builds on rather than detracts from what exists.

At times I have had to fight the temptation to rail against some of the more dogmatic proponents of objectivism in psychology. I hope I have succeeded in overcoming this urge because the objectivist's revolt in psychology has had a commendable rigorizing effect on thinking. But now, after having learned from the discipline of objectivism, we can afford to bring our increased knowledge to bear on other aspects of human behavior. I still recommend the discipline of operational analysis as training for careful thinking. In fact, my greatest fear is that this book may be taken by some as an invitation to reject completely the tough-minded approach and used as an excuse for undisciplined thinking.

The aim of this work is to stimulate the reader to think on a broad scale about big problems and to temper these thoughts with the detailed facts of empirical investigations. I see the book as a proper major source in a course where the aim is that of intensive analysis of some broad theoretical problems. I have allowed myself the luxury of dealing primarily with the things that seem important to me, and only to the extent that these things seem important to others will the book be useful and challenging to them.

In writing this book I have experienced a conflict between my desire to make a theoretical contribution and the necessity to present material as in an advanced text. I have tried to speak to the student who has some background in general psychology and an interest in relating basic concepts of learning and motivation to the behavior of human beings in social interaction. I have not covered the waterfront nor even given complete literature surveys in selected areas. This is not a work for a survey course. In short, my resolution of the text versus scholarly contribution has been to provide enough basic material so that the reader can consider with me a few of the aspects of the outer reaches of our knowledge. I have recorded some of my own speculations and have encouraged the reader to take up the challenge of applying both rational and empirical tools to the understanding of human behavior.

The book developed out of, and was first intended for, my advanced graduate seminar in motivation. Over the past ten years these students have come from a variety of fields and subfields, from physiological to social and clinical psychology and from sociology and education. At first I drafted separate papers based on the readings from original sources that were assigned to the seminar. As a result, an early draft of the book was more a series of essays than an integrated unit and the completed work may still have vestiges of this lack of unity.

The three major sections are related to the historical development of my own thinking. In my early seminars I developed intensively the "legacy of learning theory," discussing in detail Hull and Neo-Hullians. An attempt to integrate this body of literature with the concept of affective determinants of behavior and the relationship of affect to stimulation led me to the speculations about the discrepancy hypothesis and mediating mechanisms presented in Chapters 3, 4, and 5.

A lingering uneasiness about mediation and reinforcement theory became a major preoccupation primarily as the result of discussions with Dr. Peter Ossorio who introduced me to recent philosophic debates concerning causes and motives and to the contributions of the everyday language philosophers. This rekindled my interest, stemming from undergraduate days at Swarthmore, in philosophical presuppositions. I claim no expertise in this area but felt compelled to report the conclusions of an extensive excursion into it. I was faced with the dilemma of having developed a position under the heading of mediating mechanisms that seemed to represent only one level of discourse and could apparently never satisfy my desire for some broader conception of motivation. The result of this reading in philosophy was a radical change in my own rather para-mechanical thinking about causation and motivation as well as a start on a reconceptualization of the basic problems of the relationship between thoughts and action, attribution of motives, and intrinsic aspects of motivation. I have retained Part II where I have tried to push the para-mechanical conception as far as possible, and have discussed why I find it inadequate. In Parts III and IV, I have attempted to broaden the concept of motivation by introducing the idea of personal causation.

An author who writes a book over a period of six or seven years gains advice from many sources. My primary sources of help and encouragement were Professors David C. McClelland and John W. Thibaut. Professor McClelland molded my interest in motivation in my first two years of graduate study at Wesleyan University. Later, in 1965, he provided the opportunity for me to spend a year at Harvard University at which time he read and commented on early drafts of many of the chapters of the book. Professor Thibaut broadened my interests in social psychology when I was finishing my graduate studies with him, and, more recently, he read the entire manuscript and made many suggestions that have made it a better and more unified book. One cannot express thanks adequately for such help. I assume personal responsibility, of course, for the shortcomings of the work.

At some point all of the following read parts of the developing manuscript and provided valuable comments and criticism: J. Aronoff, J. W. Atkinson, R. E. Callahan, W. W. Charters, Jr., Nina de Charms, O. J. Harvey, E. E. Jones, H. H. Kelley, P. Ossorio, A. W. Wirth, and probably others whom I have forgotten.

The intellectual crucible of the graduate seminar has been an invaluable place to discuss ideas, and my debt to my students is inestimable. I owe a special debt to Drs. Thomas E. Johnson and Carl E. Pitts for hours of stimulating discussions. Others who stand out because they have contributed empirical evidence are W. J. Bridgeman, Virginia Carpenter, P. N. Davé, K. Dougherty, H. S. Gall, A. Kuperman, G. Moeller, R. Schaub, D. Schmidt, R. Walker, E. J. Wilkins, and Sally Wurtz.

Much of my own and my students' research has been supported by a contract from the Office of Naval Research ONR 816 (11) through the Social Science Institute at Washington University. At the same time the Graduate Institute of Education at Washington University has provided the freedom and the intellectual climate of inquiry that has made research and writing possible. A semester at the University of Colorado gave me extra time to develop Part II of the book and the sabbatical from Washington University that I spent at Harvard really brought completion of the work into view.

Many have helped with the manuscript. My secretary, Mrs. Lola Latta, has successfully kept things relating to the manuscript in order despite all my propensities to lose and confuse. Lois Blackwell, Alison Ullman,

Vera Costain, Mary Hughey, Tedi Zweig, Nancy Sachar, Dennis Shea, and Sue Garcia have all aided in the preparation of the manuscript. They all have my sincere thanks.

At home my wife, Nina, and son, Christopher, have given help and encouragement and tolerated my obsession.

Permission to reproduce figures and to make quotations were granted by individual authors and their work is credited in each instance as a citation to the list of references. Permission to quote and reproduce figures was also granted by Harvard University Press; University of Nebraska Press; Humanities Press, Inc.; Harcourt, Brace and World, Inc.; Barnes and Noble, Inc.; Basic Books, Inc.; Edmund R. Brill; Hogarth Press Limited; Liveright Publishing Co.; Aristotelian Society; Duke University Press; American Psychological Association; University of Chicago Press; Academic Press, Inc.; Holt, Rinehart and Winston, Inc.; *Psychological Reports;* Appleton-Century-Crofts; The American Sociological Association; *Journal of Personality and Social Psychology;* McGraw-Hill Co.; D. Van Nostrand Books Co., Inc.; *Journal of Abnormal and Social Psychology; Psychological Review; Journal of Experimental Psychology;* W. W. Norton and Co., Inc.; John Wiley and Sons, Inc.; and Harper and Row.

RICHARD DE CHARMS

St. Louis, Missouri
March, 1968

Contents

Chapter 5. The Acquisition of Affective Relationships

PART III
THOUGHT SAMPLING AND ACHIEVEMENT MOTIVATION

Chapter 6. Thoughts, Actions, and Achievement Motivation

Chapter 7. Achievement Motivation Training Courses

PART IV
PERSONAL CAUSATION

Chapter 8. Motivation, Objectivity, and Personal Causation

Chapter 9. **The Attribution Process and Inferred Motivation**

Chapter 10. **Personal Causation and the Internal Determinants of Behavior**

Chapter 11. **We Can Know More Than We Can Tell**

PERSONAL CAUSATION

PART I

BASIC PROBLEMS AND PRESUPPOSITIONS

Chapter 1

SOME BASIC PROBLEMS OF MOTIVATION

The psychology of motivation is beset by a paradoxical situation arising from the fact that "motives" are concepts devised by men to help them explain or predict behavior. Scientifically trained psychologists have developed a concept of motive that is radically different from the everyday notion of motive as used by a layman and applied to his fellow human beings. The layman assumes that a human being, under normal circumstances and within limits, chooses to act in the way he does. If you want to know why a man did something, you look for an explanation that is uniquely associated with him as a person. More often than not a person's behavior can be explained in terms of psychological aspects of him as a person. The scientifically trained psychologist looks for explanations in terms of physical things often external to the person or physical events within his body but often not what the layman would call "psychological."

The layman seems to have a concept of "mental" events that precede and direct behavior and of a unique "person" within which the events occur. The psychologist, on the other hand, deals primarily with "physical events" and physical organisms with no apparent unique characteristics that cannot be explained in terms of physical characteristics of the organism or physical events in the past that have affected the organism. Put in everyday language the question "Why did he behave that way?" is most often translated by the layman into "What led him to *choose* to do that?" It is more often translated by the psychologists to "What conditions *made* him do that?" The first interpretation implies that something within the person was free to choose; the second interpretation implies that something other than the person himself forced or determined his behavior. The first interpretation assumes that the individual is a person who controls his own behavior; the second interpretation assumes that physical forces control his behavior. In terms of causes, the layman takes it for granted that a person *causes* his own behavior, a psychologist

3

assumes that a person's behavior is *caused;* for the layman, a person *is* a cause, for the psychologist, a person is *not* a cause.

The basis of the layman's explanation is a "mind" or "person" that is not any specific physical part of the human organism but some "essence" of the individual. It is natural to assume something of this nature because we all experience it in ourselves. However, the psychologist has found no physical basis for "mind" and has great difficulties with the concepts of "self" or "person"; he has made great strides in understanding behavior without such concepts. Modern psychology viewed as the science of behavior has accepted the assumption that ultimately *it will be possible to explain human as well as animal behavior in terms of the basic principles already known from the other physical sciences by studying in detail the physical, chemical, biological, and physiological events surrounding particular behavioral acts.*[1]

The enormous value of a program of research designed to explain behavior in terms of physical events has been proved in the last fifty years of psychology. Psychologists no longer accept pseudo-explanations in terms of some "essence" or "mind" within the physical organism that guides and directs it; they no longer appeal to a ghost in the machine. Rather, they look for physical events that regularly precede specific behaviors. The layman's concept has proved to be of little help and to be misleading in many instances. The trouble with the layman's notion is that it can explain anything after it has happened by saying that the "mind" caused the behavior, but it leaves the "mind" of the individual as a completely unpredictable agent. Since no two "minds" are thought to be alike and each one is free to choose its own behavior, we are forced to the conclusion that ultimately behavior is unpredictable. Such a conclusion is unacceptable either to the layman or the psychologist for both are attempting to understand and predict behavior and both are, in fact, capable of doing it.

Implicit in the layman's thinking is the notion that the "mind" *causes* the body to act. The psychologist, accepting a different concept of cause, assumes that only physical events can cause other physical events or have any influence on them. Since there is no evidence that "mind" is physical, the psychologist rejects the notion that the "mind" causes behavior.

The crux of the problem of the two types of explanation of behavior seems to lie in two nineteenth century philosophical debates, one known as the "Mind-Body Problem" and the other involving specification of the meaning of the word "cause." We will accept the psychologists' position

---

[1] Later this statement will be referred to as the thesis of the sufficiency of atomic description following Bridgman (1959).

and reject the concept of "mind" as an explanation of behavior. In doing this, we reject the notion that "mind" conceived of as a nonphysical "essence" can cause behavior. We will go further and reject the word "cause" even as a description of the relationship between two physical events. *The concept "cause" implies more than is ever empirically demonstrated to occur in the physical world between two objects or two events.*

For the author of a book entitled *Personal Causation* to reject the word "cause" may come as a surprise. It is the result of a futile attempt to find any empirical meaning in the word. In the company of many psychologists and philosophers, we have arrived at the position that as an empirical description of observed relationships between physical events the word has no meaning. As Bertrand Russell says: "The law of causality . . . like much that passes muster among philosophers, is a relic of a bygone age, surviving, like the monarchy, only because it is erroneously supposed to do no harm" (Russell, 1918).

We reject the word "cause" as most often used because it does do harm, we believe. Nevertheless, we use it in our title because the concept does having meaning, a very important meaning, that is implicit in the layman's conception, but has misled him to attribute causes to the "mind." The source of meaning of "cause" cannot be demonstrated empirically. The meaning comes from a source of knowledge that is available to everyone personally but comes to him privately from his own feelings and behavior. Such knowledge is to be called "personal knowledge" (cf. Polanyi, 1958). A type of personal knowledge is the knowledge of personal causation.

The concept of causation is crucial in what follows, but the way we use it here may be quite different from that with which the reader may be accustomed. A complete explication of the last two paragraphs cannot be given without laying some preliminary groundwork. In doing this we shall attempt to define "personal causation" and show its relation to the more common concept of motivation. We shall investigate the concept of cause most often associated with motivation and note the possible harm that this conception can bring to the psychology of motivation. We shall ask and try to answer the question "Where does the concept of causation come from?" and, as a result, propose that the psychology of motivation must accept from the physical sciences a program based on the ultimate reduction of psychological phenomena to physical events, and at the same time must account for the persistent fact that human beings believe themselves to be "causes" and this belief affects their behavior. From this perspective we shall review some current approaches to the concept of motivation and conclude our introduction with an overview of the rest of the volume.

PERSONAL CAUSATION DEFINED

Personal causation is the initiation by an individual of behavior intended to produce a change in his environment. The concept is basically a motivational one, but the term "motive" has come to be used in a way that often excludes some of the major aspects of personal causation. In order to bring a little more precision to the idea of motivation and at the same time broaden its scope, we have chosen the phrase personal causation.

MOTIVES AND CAUSES

Motives are often considered the causes of behavior and the two concepts have much in common. Science is sometimes defined as a search for causes and, although the concept has apparently been very useful in the physical sciences, an empirical basis for the idea of causation itself has not been found. As the philosopher David Hume argued, the causal inference is extremely persuasive, but it is impossible to isolate an empirical referent in the phenomena of apparently causal sequences that uniquely indicates the presence of causal necessity. Phenomenologically causes seem to "exist," but they cannot be reduced to an empirical aspect of physical events. As a result of this paradoxical situation, while the philosophers argue about the epistemological status of the concept of cause, the less philosophically minded scientists use the concept in one guise or another to help them to understand physical phenomena.

If we accept the notion that motives are the causes of behavior, we are propelled into the controversy over the meaning of the concept of causation. Phenomenologically we have very little trouble with causation and, if we do not try to define it too precisely, we get along quite well using the term and communicating with others. In order to avoid unnecessary complications, let us look at the simplest case of a causal sequence involving only physical objects and try to develop a parallel example of motivation by using the basic assumptions from the physical objects example.

In the time-honored billiard ball example when the cue ball strikes the eight ball on a billiard table the explanation of the movement of the eight ball is sought in terms of physical laws of mechanics. The object that makes a unique contribution to the movement of the eight ball is the cue ball. We are wont to say that the cue ball *causes* the eight ball's movement. The word "cause" may, in this instance, be taken to mean that we are in the habit of attributing causes (the precise meaning of the word "wont" in the previous sentence). If we probe the empirical evidence for the source of attribution of causation as Hume did, we find that it lies in observed situations of (a) concomitant variation (if the cause occurs, then the effect always occurs) or (b) temporal sequence (the cause must precede the event). Yet we can conceive of situations in which both of these criteria are met but in which we would not attribute causation (the rooster crows and the sun rises). This is because we usually resort to a third criterion that demands that there be a *necessary connection* between the cause and the effect, that the cause can be assumed to produce the effect in an efficient way that implies some intrinsic conjunction between cause and effect. Hume found no empirical referent for a necessary connection in any single instance of a causal sequence, and hence attributed this last and most stringent criterion to an inference process resulting from habit. We have seen A precede B so often that we infer that A has some necessary connection with B because of a propensity of the human being to learn by repeated experience.

As a result of this analysis, Hume is interpreted as saying that causes do not exist, but what he actually said was that he could find no physical basis for the crucial element, namely necessary connection. It is often overlooked that Hume started with the assumption that cause is a phenomenological given, that we do attribute causes and that the causal inference is often very useful in science (Lamprecht, 1925). There is something more than mere contiguity and temporal sequence. We can find no empirical referent for the "more," but it is certainly phenomenologically present when we observe a causal sequence. If we could find some empirical basis for the apparent necessary connection, we might feel that we understood and could explain the movement of the eight ball better; but as it stands even without this we can do a good job of predicting its movement.

There are several assumptions that are basic to this analysis of causation that may be found in instances of motivated behavior. The eight ball is assumed to be normally stationary until some external source of energy impinges upon it. This statement contains three assumptions: (a) the normal state of physical objects is *static equilibrium;* (b) the cause of the change from the normal state is a *source of energy;* (c) the cause is *external* to the object in which it produces the change or effect. In addition to these it is implied that (d) the effect is *movement.* If we accept the most important aspect of the Humian position, we will assume further that (e) the attribution of causation is *learned* and (f) the causal concept helps us *predict* future events but cannot be accepted as an explanation.

Now let us apply these assumptions to a motive sequence. A rat is standing on the right side of a Miller-Mowrer shock box that has an electric grid for a floor and a low barrier separating the right and left sides of the box. Electricity is applied to the grid on the right side where the rat is and he quickly leaps over the barrier into the left side where the grid is not charged. This is clearly an example of motivated behavior. Do all the assumptions fit? (*a*) The rat is relatively still; (*b*) the shock or cause is a *source of energy;* (*c*) it is *external* to the rat; (*d*) the effect is *movement* of the rat; (*e*) after several experiences both the rat and the observer have *learned* about the relationship between shock and behavior so that (*f*) in the future the behavior may be *predicted*.

The example derives from an analysis of motivated behavior (Miller, 1951) that takes "drive" as its central concept, assumes that it is an energizing source, and defines drives as "strong stimuli which impel action" (Dollard & Miller, 1950, p. 30). This is one of the most consistent and most valuable versions of drive theory, the drive-stimulus-reduction theory.

The example given makes the analogy between a causal sequence and a motive sequence seem very close and demonstrates the seductiveness of attempting to understand motivation by using the concept of causation. There is great value in stripping the two sequences to their bare essentials, however, because it shows that the closeness of the analogy is more apparent than real. Furthermore, it clarifies the basis for some of the basic problems of motivation theory. If we question whether the normal state of the organism is to be motionless, we question the assumption of static equilibrium. If we question whether a motive provides the force to start behavior, we question the assumption that a motive is a source of energy as well as that of static equilibrium. Having gone this far we may question whether the "cause" of behavior is always external to the motivated object (the organism). Further, we have been using the term "behavior" as if it implied only movement of organisms and we may question whether "behavior" does not mean more than physical movement. What we are saying so far is that with regard to assumptions (*a*) through (*d*), there are reasons for questioning the accuracy of the analogy between causes and motives, and these reasons lead us to most of the current controversies in motivation theory.

Assumptions (*e*) and (*f*) (learning and predicting) are of a different stripe, and bring us to a problem that must be confronted before we can really make judgments about the other assumptions because the problem is the most central one, namely: Where does the concept of causation come from? If we cannot arrive at some position of agreement on this problem, we might as well not even discuss the others since they only arose because we were attempting to use the causal concept to help us understand motivation.

WHERE DOES THE CONCEPT OF CAUSATION COME FROM?

The answer to this question is a critical point of departure in this book. Simply stated our answer to the question is: *We get our knowledge of causation from our knowledge of motivation.* Up to now we have been trying to clarify our knowledge of motivation by using causation. It is the major proposition stated here that this approach is just backwards. The first "cause" that any of us knows is ourselves. When we are motivated, we cause things to happen. We have immediate knowledge of our "motives" prior to any knowledge of physical causes. What we all know from childhood is that we do things and something happens in our surrounding environment — *we* cause effects in the physical world. The most important *thing* in the world for a newborn child is his own body. He learns about it first and what it can do in relation to other things. He learns that he is a causal agent. Only later does he become concerned about what one non-self object can do to another. By that time he has learned that he himself is a cause that has effects and that he is motivated to cause effects. It is therefore only natural to assume that other things are motivated to cause effects and that there are meaningful reasons why another person acts as he does; reasons that are similar to his own, i.e., motives. It is even natural, although incorrect, for the child to assume that physical objects are like himself and therefore have motives like his to cause effects. As Piaget (1929) has shown, the child must learn not to make what we call "magical" attributions to things as if they were people. Human beings, and probably animals too, know without learning about their own simple motives or reasons for acting, and they soon learn to act in a way to satisfy these motives, and along the way they learn that things are caused because *they cause them!* If a child does not learn to cause things to happen he cannot live.

Seen in this light, it is not surprising that the causal inference is very persuasive. We have all learned to make the inference in one of the most important and most ubiquitous learning experiences of our life. At the same time, it is not surprising either that we cannot find external empirical evidence for it. It is not learned in the way that Hume suggested, by the simple repetition of contiguous events in the external world, but by the much more powerful repetition of observing ourselves cause effects in the physical world.

The implications of this analysis are far reaching for both of the concepts under consideration, causation and motivation. For one thing, it should be clear that if we are right about the origin of the concept of causation in personal experiences of motivation, then seeking to explicate motivation by analogy to the concept of causation is like trying to "reduce" an explanation of atoms to a discussion of molecules. The former (motivation) is primary and more fundamental than the latter (causation).

Recognizing motivation as the more fundamental involves us in one of the most difficult problems of psychology and philosophy; namely the validity of knowledge derived primarily from our own private experiences. This type of knowledge is sometimes called subjective knowledge and is considered scientifically to have a lower status, that is, to be less valid, than so-called objective knowledge. We shall try to show, following the work of P. W. Bridgman (1959) and Michael Polanyi (1958), that *personal* knowledge can be a valid source of scientific insight since, in fact, all scientific knowledge derives ultimately from individual private experiences of the sort engaged in by the scientist when he observes the results of an experiment. The problem is not to make science "objective" by taking all individual experiences out of it. This, in fact, is impossible because ultimately the scientist must experience and then interpret the results of his experiment. No, the problem is to systematize these experiences so that they may be communicated to others so that they too can experience them personally, i.e., to verify the personal experience and hence personal knowledge of their colleagues.

For the time being, we will propose without further justification that science is based on personal knowledge and that one form of this knowledge, which is common to all men, is the knowledge of oneself as a causal agent. One type of personal knowledge, learned in childhood by all human beings when the baby learns to distinguish himself from others and other things, is the knowledge of personal causation. Personal causation is, then, the knowledge of oneself as a causal and motivated person, and, in addition, personal causation forms the basis upon which all men learn to attribute motives to other people and ultimately to attribute causes in the physical world.

Accepting this premise involves us in several apparently logically opposed or contradictory propositions, reminiscent of Immanuel Kant's logical antinomies. The most obvious is the subjective-objective distinction, already mentioned, that has most often been resolved in the physical sciences by accepting "objective" knowledge as valid and by rejecting "subjective" knowledge as invalid. Up to a point, this is quite reasonable in the physical sciences in which the "things" to be investigated are "objects." But is it reasonable in psychology in which the "things" to be investigated are not only "objects" in the physical world but also "subjects" in the psychological world, i.e., persons? Following the precepts of physical science, psychologists have tried to resolve the subjective-objective antinomy by rejecting the subjective. We will maintain that in psychology we cannot solve the problem this way. We are really impaled on the horns of the dilemma, since in dealing with persons we are at one and the same time dealing with a physical object in time and space and with a psychological subject who has personal knowledge and intentions.

This problem never becomes more apparent than when we attempt to explain motivational phenomena. We may know all the objective facts in the situation, for example, a murder; we may know the cause of death, the person who committed the act, all the necessary information about his temporal and spatial position and his physical capability to perform the act, and yet we may lack a legal "motive" or what we might prefer to call the reason or explanation for his act. Legal evidence attempts to present the facts, but the physical facts never pass judgment on a man. It is the jury that passes sentence, and the jury is made up of persons who have personal knowledge and put their knowledge together with the physical facts in order to arrive at a verdict that is the result of attributing a motive to the accused person. Once the facts are in, it is the responsibility of the jury to establish "intention."

Juries are required to attribute motives and establish intention, but psychologists have resigned from this responsibility and attempt to establish only the physical facts in the situation. This is because they have chosen to emulate the physical sciences and to rule out subjective aspects such as "intentions" and have reduced "motives" to physical states of biological deficiency or to external physical sources of energy.

Basically, psychology has pursued in detail one level of analysis attempting to treat a person (or animal) as a physical object. Knowledge deriving from this level of analysis is abundant and is basic to the understanding of motivated behavior. But it is not enough; it does not answer all the questions we have to ask about behavior; it leaves us with predictions about physical movement but without explanations of behavior that stem from truly psychological aspects of the person. We must complement our knowledge of persons as objects with another level of knowledge of persons as animate beings possessed of the capacity for personal causation. A complete science of behavior must face the subjective-objective dilemma and investigate and weld together phenomena from both levels, i.e., physical sources of energy that produce movement of the body as a physical object, and psychological sources that also result in bodily effects; it must also simultaneously view the person as a subject who is the personal cause of his own behavior, who has intentions and carries them out within the boundaries of his physical limitations. Behavior is a function not only of physical events but also of personal causes. It is not enough to know what a person did, we need to know about his intentions as well in order to explain his behavior completely. We have thus raised the most basic problem for a psychology of motivation.

Let us try to be as clear as we can about what we are suggesting. We are not proposing a substitute for what now exists under the heading of the psychology of motivation. What we know about motivational phenomena is necessary, and further investigations using present techniques and theories are also necessary to the understanding of the psychology of motivation. Rather we are emphasizing something that is widely accepted, namely, that present theories are not sufficient to account for human motivation. We propose that the analysis of first-person aspects of a human being as a subject be added to the third-person aspects stressed by Behaviorism that treats the person as a physical object.

Having set our sights for something more than what exists at present, let us look briefly at what exists.

Current Approaches to the Concept of Motivation

There is no good way to categorize simply current motivation theories. One set of polar concepts, however, may be useful if we try to understand in advance some of the complexities of the dimension for which the concepts are the end points. The concepts refer to the locus relative to the organism where variables are sought to explain behavior. At the crudest level this locus may be within the organism (internal locus of explanation) or outside the organism (external locus).[2] For example, in the previous discussion of the layman's concept of motivation, we said that he looks for explanations of behavior from within the person. This may be taken as the extreme internal pole of the bipolar dimension. At the other extreme, we may place Behaviorism in the most rigorous form as proposed by Watson (1913), the so-called "empty-organism" or "sawdust" psychology, that assumes that nothing within the organism need be considered.

Neither of these extreme positions is tenable, but current approaches to motivation may be seen as attempts to reconcile the obvious advantages of dealing with observable physical events such as stimuli and responses

---

[2] The dimension derives from Heider's (1958) concept of "locus of causality."

with the nagging fact that human beings appear to be motivated from within.

If the proposed dimension were as simple as external-internal all would be well, but it isn't. To a certain extent, since extreme external Behaviorism has proven inadequate, all theories must take into account variables within the organism. Thus, pure stimulus-response (SR) theories have become stimulus-organism-response (S-O-R) theories. The critical problem then becomes what is meant by "within the organism" and how far "in" does the theorist go? Those most resistant to penetrating the organism attribute to it "reinforcement histories" and, using this one internal-type notion, go on to try to predict behavior and account for the reinforcement histories in terms of external events. Such a position we shall call an Empirical Reinforcement theory (Skinner, 1953, is the outstanding example) and place it near the external end of our continuum.[3]

A cautious step toward "internal" analysis is made by physiological psychologists who may be said to pursue the thesis of the sufficiency of atomic description most rigorously. In its purest form, physiological psychology accepts only physiological facts as explanations of behavior, but, as a matter of fact, we are far from a complete explanation of behavior in physiological terms.

A bolder step along the same line, often given the opprobrious name "physiologizing," constitutes an attempt to bridge the gap between what is known physiologically and what is known behaviorally with hypothetical constructs. This speculative bridge building has resulted in many testable hypotheses and some major advances. Theorists may be seen as starting their bridge from the side of the gorge nearer to the molar facts of behavior or from the side nearer to the molecular facts of physiology. Behavior theorists who have sought to define reinforcement in terms of physiological deficits or their concomitants [a priori reinforcement theorists such as Hull (1943)] are near the behaviorist side, while theorists who have developed physiological models (such as Hebb, 1949) are nearer the other side.

A priori reinforcement theorists, those who look for a response-independent definition of reinforcer, often take a rather strong position concerning the driving (or motivational) force behind behavior. This force may be a stimulus (shock) that is actually external or an internal stimulus (pain) that is the result of external events (shock or deprivation). Although attempts are made to account for internal stimuli, their source is sought in external events. The next step "into" the organism is the

---

[3] In one sense it does not belong on the continuum at all because implicit in the empirical definition of reinforcement is a denial of any motivational force.

postulation of "affect" in affective arousal theories (e.g., McClelland, Atkinson, Clark, & Lowell, 1953; Young, 1961). Affect is another gap-bridging construct, but the gap here is between the physical or physiological and the psychological or phenomenological. Affect may be treated as a physiological response, but it often carries connotations of "feeling." It is here that we first encounter the subjective-objective dilemma discussed earlier. Although it may creep in to reinforcement theories when reinforcement is erroneously allowed to take on the subjective connotation of "reward," the concept affect is often used in arousal theories precisely because it has both subjective and objective connotations.

Once the subjective aspect is raised, we are closer to the internal end of the dimension if we make the arbitrary assumption that theories that deal with a subjective "self" or "person" are more "internal" than those which deal primarily with physiological phenomena within the organism.[4] The postulation of an entity such as a "self" or a "person" within which motivational phenomena are sought opens new vistas for the theorist. The "person" can be thought of as active [as in White's (1959) concept of competence, Goldstein's (1939) self-actualization, Maslow's (1962) "growth-motivation," or Allport's (1955) "Becoming"] whereas an organism is primarily reactive. In the former an internal psychological entity is postulated within which we may assume the locus of motivation for behavior lies.

Heider (1958) has made a distinction between perceiving the locus of causality for behavior as external or as internal to the person. The "self" theorists clearly look for an internal locus, all others mentioned previously look for something less central (in our sense) as the source of behavior, and often these "more external" theorists seem to assume many of the aspects noted earlier of para-mechanical explanations. Motion (behavior) of a naturally immobile object (organism) is produced by an external force (drive-stimulus). Crude as this analogy is, it is at least more precise than present concepts of "self," "person," or "mind." But to attempt a full explanation in terms of only one type of theory is a mistake because both types of explanation are necessary.

In the present volume we will be most concerned with the behaviorally oriented theories. For this reason we have chosen the major examples for further elaboration.

---

[4] We have included this different type of "internal" on our dimension, despite the fact that it may seem forced, because the arbitrary separation of objective and subjective phenomena stands in the way of progress in the motivation area. It is precisely the bringing together of these two that is needed, and in Chapter 2 we shall see that their separation is the result of a category mistake stemming from false assumptions inherited from the philosophic discussions of the mind-body problem.

REINFORCEMENT THEORIES

One of the basic problems confronted by reinforcement theories is the definition of a reinforcer. A definition is an attempt to make communication about the concept possible. At the most fundamental level, a reinforcement theory assumes that the prediction and control of behavior must rely on stimuli outside the organism, and reinforcers are seen as such stimuli. This approach to the problem of motivation is characterized by reductionism. The concepts are most often derived from behavioral observations in the animal laboratory and definitions attempt to reduce all terms to operations and/or quantifiable observed behavior. Stimuli and responses are the basic elements of study. The reader need hardly be told that the major figures contributing to this approach are Skinner at Harvard, and Hull and other learning theorists most of whom were associated in some way with Yale University in the 1930's and 1940's. The development of the concept of reinforcement forms the *most important cumulative effort of relevance* to the psychology of motivation. This development will be discussed in detail in later chapters.

Phenomenologically the term *reinforcement* has taken on some of the connotations of pleasure and pain, and some theorists are willing to talk about positive and negative reinforcement. This may seem an odd turn of events in view of the original meaning of the term which can be recaptured if one thinks of the meaning of "reinforce" in the phrase "reinforced concrete." Originally an event was seen to be reinforcing in the sense that it *strengthened* the bond between a stimulus and a response. Obviously, at this simple level the notions are outmoded, but the surplus meaning which reinforcement has taken on tends to give the illusory satisfaction of an explanation. Meehl (1950) has clearly pointed out, in his discussion of the circularity of the law of effect, the absolute necessity of some external definition of reinforcement which is independent of the response under study.

A Priori *Reinforcement Theories*

The earliest reinforcement theories attempted to give an *a priori* answer to the question "What is a reinforcer?" Under the influence of Darwinian notions of survival, an early contender for the primary criterion for explaining motivated behavior was the reduction of basic psychological needs. Obviously, if these needs were not reduced, the organism would ultimately die. Therefore, it was logical to assume that the surviving species were those with some built in connection between responses and need-reduction.

Under the influence of attempts to explain the learning of new responses, however, it became obvious that many responses persisted which were not associated with primary need-reduction, and that new responses were often acquired when the evidence for primary need-reduction was minimal. The concepts of primary and secondary drive and primary and secondary reinforcement were *invented* to account for these phenomena.

The notion of reinforcement, although first used primarily by associationists to connote the strengthening of a bond between a stimulus and a response, carried with it a strong implication of something pleasant, good, or satisfying. This hedonistic connotation persisted despite great philosophical controversy over psychological hedonism—the postulate that human beings seek pleasure and avoid pain. Thorndike (1913) laid the cornerstone of reinforcement theory with his enunciation of the Law of Effect. His statement used the terms "satisfaction" and "dissatisfaction." Despite his careful behavioral definition of a satisfying state of affairs (a reinforcer) as something which the animal tended to approach or did nothing to avoid, the hedonistic flavor was transmitted through the term "satisfaction." Behavioristically oriented learning theorists avoided the connotations of satisfaction with the notions of need, drive, or tension reduction.

Empirical Reinforcement Theory

Skinnerian (1953) reinforcement theory solves the problem of what response will be chosen of those possible by assuming, as did *a priori* theorists, that the criterion involved is past reinforcement. His definition of a reinforcer, however, is completely empirical and firmly tied to responses. Stated in terms of probabilities, *any response which is reinforced will tend to increase in probability of occurring. A reinforcer is defined as anything that increases the probability of a response.* This completely tautological couplet is, in fact, extremely valuable in learning theory. Given something, X, which has been shown to increase the probability of a response in the past, we can predict that X, used in conjunction with a desired response, will increase its probability, i.e., produce learning.

The pursuit of *reinforcement,* although it has given us some of the best experiments and theorizing relevant to motivation, has also led in another direction. Paradoxically, the development has been carried by more empirically zealous psychologists down the road of reductionism to one logical conclusion about the concept of motivation—*reductio ad absurdum.* In a behaviorist tradition that eschews theorizing and subjective states, shuns first-person explanations, embraces third-person analysis of the organism as a physical object, and defines a reinforcer as anything that will increase the probability of a response, the concept of motivation is not needed and the only consistent position is to drop it entirely. In this respect, Skinner's analysis of behavior in terms of reinforcement is most consistent. Much of the evidence customarily cited as demanding the use of the motivation concept can be handled by the deft use of a Skinnerian definition of reinforcement, and the concept of motivation turns out to be excess baggage. In this sense, the Skinnerian approach constitutes a *reductio ad absurdum* of motivational concepts. Skinner (1953) refers to many motivational concepts such as hunger, thirst, interest, a sense of achievement, incentive, goal, and intent as "explanatory fictions." The inference contained in the phrase is that they do not explain or that they in turn need explanation. As such, they may be discarded.

Affective Arousal Theories

For emphasis we may say that the affective arousal approach is primarily characterized by the often unstated assumption that motivational phenomena have as their ultimate referents hedonistic states of pleasure and pain. The basic concept for such an approach is *affect;* a term which must be defined as the experiencing of these states. The basic problem for such a position is to make communication about such states possible. At the most fundamental level, the affective arousal approach assumes that the understanding of behavior must take into account states within the organism, that is, explanation from "within." Although the emphasis lies "within," the importance of outside influences is not denied.

The concept of affective arousal was integral to the position taken by Young (1936). He, as well as McClelland *et al.* (1953), assumed that stimuli are characterized by positive, neutral, or negative hedonic tone. Positive stimuli are sought out; negative stimuli are avoided when possible. The question naturally arises—What stimuli produce affect? As in the case of the question—What is a reinforcer?—one can take an empirical approach, as Young (1961) did, or one can attempt to find a theory which will tell in advance what types of stimuli will produce positive, neutral, or negative affect as McClelland *et al.* (1953) did.

The basic criticism of affective arousal theories is their inherent reductionism: the stress on "the stimulus" which produces affect. It is difficult to conceive of one specific type of stimulus which ultimately will turn out to be associated with all motivated behavior and hence form the criterion which is the quest of a motivation theory. The philosopher, Gilbert Ryle

(1949) probably makes this criticism most clear. Basically, Ryle is rele-
gating affect to the category of a "para-mechanical myth." To say that a
"thrill," "glow," or "tension" impels the animal to action is an over-
simplification based on the notion of para-mechanical causation that some
outside source of energy must strike the individual and produce action or
at least goad him into it. This criticism may be met by postulating two
aspects of affect.

Affect as the result of a specific stimulus is the easiest way for us to
conceive of it, probably because of the pervasive influence of stimulus-
response psychology. Although probably an oversimplified conception,
it raises the important question of what stimuli produce affect. Despite
Ryle's criticism, it is obvious that some behavior is the result of affective
stimuli, the best example being the avoidance of noxious stimuli. The antic-
ipation of specific positive stimulation is also clearly a determinant of
some behavior. Such a conception of affect, therefore, need not be dis-
carded. It is clear, however, that exploratory behavior, play, and things
such as growth, competence, and self-actualizing behavior are probably
not accompanied by any specific stimulus elements which may be
isolated.

*Affect as a result of broader aspects of experience which guides and
directs behavioral sequences* such as play and exploration is a concept
that we must entertain, though it is much more difficult to grasp and to
make explicit. In this connection, we must investigate the relationships
between affect and behavior over and beyond affect produced by specific
stimuli. We must broaden the concept beyond the notion of a specific
stimulus that goads behavior and consider affect as the result of general
sequences of behavior.

What can be said about reinforcement and affective arousal theories
in general? First, they are both attempts to reduce motivational concepts
to stimulus and response events conceived of as physical phenomena
in the world. Second, both positions treat the subject of a psychological
experiment as a physical object. These approaches stress objectivity and
supply us with the physical restrictions within which behavior occurs.
They are striving to reduce all psychological phenomena to physical,
chemical, and possibly biological determinants. In dealing with motivated
behavior the implication is strong that what is to be explained is move-
ment and that it is to be explained in terms of physical forces impinging
on the organism. Pushed to the extreme, both positions imply that psy-
chological behavior is to be explained in the same terms as physical move-
ment of objects, i.e., the laws of physical mechanics. Although the flavor
of para-mechanical explanation is strong, it is obvious to everyone that

the explanation of human behavior demands more than laws based on a para-mechanical myth.

A priori reinforcement theories as well as affective arousal theories seek to explain behavior apparently originating from within the organism by means of para-mechanical forces (stimuli such as drives or affect) which impel motion. Can it be said that drive-stimuli or affect cause behavior? Certainly not in any mechanical sense similar to the cue ball "causing" the eight ball to move. At best, these approaches try to explain psychological phenomena by a loose analogy to physical mechanics. At worst, they lead us to think of behavior as simple physical movement of an object and of motivation as a physical force.

Bridgman, the father of operationism in physics, points out that the positions derive from the basic thesis of the sufficiency of atomic description.

> This attitude may be formulated in a very general way in the statement that it is not necessary to assume any new principles not already operative in the physics and the chemistry of non-living matter in order to explain the functioning of living matter. It may alternatively be given a more specific and sharpened formulation . . . . "Given a complete description in physical terms of any organism, then there is nothing more to give, in the sense that all the present behavior of the organism and its future behavior in a completely specified environment is fixed" (Bridgman, 1959, p. 201).

As Bridgman says, this thesis may, in fact, be correct in physics and even in psychology; but "in the present state of technology we are fantastically far from being able to implement such a thesis to the extent even of being able to specify the state of all the atoms in the brain, to say nothing of deducing the future unrolling of such a system" (pp. 201–202).

Empirical reinforcement theory is assumed by Bridgman to accept the thesis of the sufficiency of atomic analysis, but it seems to us that Skinner has proposed a concept unique to psychology that may in fact be reducible to atomic description, but that at first appears more amenable to present day technology. The concept is contained in the phrase "reinforcement histories." Skinner has resigned from the position of trying to explain motivated behavior and takes as his burden the prediction of behavior from knowledge of past histories of reinforcement. This position may be called "the thesis of the sufficiency of reinforcement histories" for the prediction of behavior. Like the atomic description thesis, the reinforcement history thesis has been useful as a program to guide research; but, ultimately, the postulate that the prediction of behavior must depend on complete knowledge of the reinforcement history of human beings is equally as "fantastically far" from the capability of present day techniques as is complete atomic description.

Neither the atomic analysis thesis nor the reinforcement history thesis has to be abandoned in order to broaden the concept of affect to something more than a specific anticipation that cues off behavior. But the more general concepts that have been proposed lack the apparent clarity that results from the more mechanistic conception of affect.

The Concept of Competence —
Mastery and Control of the Environment

White (1959) in a seminal article proposes the concept of competence as a crucial element bringing together the diverse evidence cited in criticism of drive theories.

> I now propose that we gather the various kinds of behavior just mentioned, all of which have to do with effective interaction with the environment, under the general heading of competence. According to Webster, competence means fitness or ability, and the suggested synonyms include capability, capacity, efficiency, proficiency, and skill. It is therefore a suitable word to describe such things as grasping and exploring, crawling and walking, attention and perception, language and thinking, manipulating and changing the surroundings, all of which promote an effective — a competent — interaction with the environment. . . . I shall argue that it is necessary to make competence a motivational concept; there is a *competence motivation* as well as competence in its more familiar sense of achieved capacity   (White, 1959, pp. 317–318).

After asking whether the behaviors cited might be accounted for by specific intrinsic motives or a limited number of broader motives, he says: "I believe that the idea of a competence motivation is more adequate than any of these alternatives and that it points to very vital common properties which have been lost from view amidst the strongly analytical tendencies that go with detailed research" (p. 318).

Effectance is the name given by White to the basic motivational aspect of competence. The affective side of effectance is the "feeling of efficacy," the behavioral manifestations are "the fixing of some aspect of the stimulus field so that it stays relatively constant — and it also involves the focalizing of *action* upon this object" (p. 322). Behavior resulting from competence motivation is "directed, selective, and persistent, and it is continued not because it serves primary drives, which indeed it cannot serve until it is almost perfected, but because it satisfies an intrinsic need to deal with the environment" (p. 317).

The major examples given are drawn from Piaget's (1952) descriptions of his own children and how they emphasize play in a contented state.

Competence motivation is not something that overcomes strong bodily urges, but is a "need to deal with the environment" under conditions in which intense hunger, pain, or fear are absent. On the other hand, "there are plenty of instances in which children refuse to leave their absorbed play in order to eat or visit the toilet" (p. 321).

The concept of competence is an excellent example of recent trends away from notions of specific behavior-prodding stimuli toward a more inclusive analysis of trends in the flow of behavior. What White sees as the most essential aspect of playful exploratory behavior is "the continuing transaction which gradually changes one's relation to the environment" (p. 322). In order to capture this essence, one must forego the apparent clarity achieved through analysis of individual transaction with the environment. This poses a critical and unresolved problem. In order to predict a specific act, we look for a criterion that differentiates this act from other possible acts. Such a criterion may be the presence of a drive or a stimulus or affect. It could be the "feeling of efficacy" in some anticipatory form. But if we follow White's argument, there may not be any such criterion available for each individual act. The analysis takes on a broader, more comprehensive explanatory aspect but loses its specific predictive ability.

White is not proposing *the* motive of human behavior, but suggesting one which is important. "It does not include behavior in the service of effectively aroused drives. It does not even include activity that is highly random and discontinuous, though such behavior may be its most direct forerunner" (p. 323). One of the conditions for competence motivation to appear is apparently contentment or at least low drive state. This is reminiscent of the proposal by Maslow (1954, 1955) of a hierarchy of motives. According to Maslow, drives, such as hunger, thirst, and sex, must be dealt with in a satisfactory manner before higher motives come into play. Maslow makes a distinction between deficiency motivation and growth motivation. The notion of growth motivation has its roots in Goldstein's (1939) concept of self-actualization and is similar to Allport's (1955) "Becoming" as opposed to "Being."

In this sketch of major trends, we have chosen to present White's position in some detail to stand as a representative of a general trend emphasizing the striving, outgoing aspect of behavior rather than the defensive essentially passive nature. This trend with its strong supporters in Maslow, Goldstein, and Allport among others, seems to us at once immensely important in its attempt to capture neglected aspects of motivation with an analysis of larger units of behavior, and, at the same time, frustratingly imprecise. In this day of strong reductionistic influence, we find it difficult to deal with these larger hunks, but are increasingly convinced that such a level of analysis is necessary.

Summarizing our discussion of current approaches to motivation, let us emphasize the following distinctions. Research dealing with motivational phenomena has been primarily under the influence of reinforcement theory. The major proposition is the thesis of the sufficiency of *reinforcement histories* in predicting behavior. In general, theorists have defined reinforcement in terms of increased probability of a response leading to an *empirical* specification of what is a reinforcer, or they have attempted to analyze organismic states and come up with an *a priori* definition of a reinforcer.

Some considerations deriving from attempts to specify the theoretical aspects of a reinforcer have led to the suggestion of *affective arousal* theories. *Affective arousal theory* has concentrated effort on the problem of what stimuli produce affect. More general experiential states such as *competence, achievement, self-actualization* have been proposed as determinants in the organization of broader sequences of behavior.

Program for a Complete Explanation of Human Motivation

Accepting the necessity for a *program* based on the atomic description analysis and the reinforcement history thesis, what is needed for a complete explanation of motivation is something based on a first-person analysis of personal knowledge and personal causation. Accepting the fact that man is a type of animal, we are proposing to take advantage of the fact that, since man is being studied by man in psychology, there is a unique source of knowledge applicable to this situation that is not applicable when man studies other animals or physical objects. This unique source derives from the fact that being a man gives the scientist more insight into the private world of another man than of another animal. If I make inferences about a stone based on my own personal experiences I will surely be wrong, and the same is probably true if I make inferences about other animals. But in my own personal experiences, I have a valuable source of knowledge from which to make inferences about other men. The inferences may not always be correct, to be sure, but they clearly give me an edge in dealing with other men as compared to dealing with physical objects. In short, to attempt vigorously to avoid anthropomorphism in dealing with physical objects is only sensible. Objectivity is the goal. But to extend this aspect of physical science to the study of human psychology is absurd. In psychology we can afford to be anthropomorphic and this does not make us necessarily anthropocentric.

Sources of Knowledge

The source of knowledge about most of the motivationally or affectively toned concepts such as hunger is available to all, but it is essentially a private affair. A feeling of hunger, an incentive, an intention, that is, one of Skinner's "explanatory fictions," would be accepted far more readily by a layman as psychological phenomena than would the number of hours of deprivation or an orienting response. In fact, these "explanatory fictions" are used by the layman as if they were valid explanations. They have been rejected for the most part by psychologists for two reasons: (1) they appear to be inadequate as explanatory concepts, and (2) they are subjective states.

The first reason is perfectly valid if true. The second can no longer be accepted. The purging of psychology of all subjective phenomena has served an important function in exposing pseudoexplanations. In addition, strict adherence to behavioristic analysis has most often resulted in parsimony. When behavioristic zeal leads to ignoring psychological phenomena, simply because they are subjective or private, without investigating their importance first, then the procedure is arbitrarily limiting the field (see Koch, 1964, for an elaboration of this).

Skinner has ruled out subjective and, hence, motivational concepts, not because they are private events but because they are inadequate explanations. "The objection is not that these things are mental but that they offer no real explanation and stand in the way of a more effective analysis" (1964, p. 80). Such a statement is based upon the historical fact that mentalistic philosophies have hindered the advancement of behaviorism. The present state of sophistication in psychology, however, will help to avoid the old pitfalls and there are reasons for turning to an analysis of some of the subjective phenomena in their own right.

Clear understanding of the behaviorists' reservations may be used as a backdrop to insure caution against using subjective states as terminal data. The mere fact that these states are originally private, however, is no deterrent to studying them. As Skinner points out, the private-public controversy boils down to the success in communication within the verbal community. An experimenter who observes a rat turning right in a maze is experiencing a private event. The fact that it can be more adequately communicated through the verbal community does not make it essentially different from other private events which are less easily communicated although it may make it more useful scientifically. What is needed is an adequate means of communication about so-called subjective states, not the rejection of them. Skinner himself says, "The extraordinary strength of a mentalistic interpretation is really a sort of proof that in describing a private way station one is, to a considerable extent, making use of public information" (1964, p. 91).

The problem with personal knowledge is to convert it from the private realm to the public realm. Bridgman (1927) gave science a tool for making scientific concepts public through operationism, i.e., the technique of defining concepts in terms of physical operations that can be reproduced by any scientist. Some of the difficulties inherent in a pure operationism will be discussed in Part IV of this book, but the value of attempting to operationalize psychological concepts should be obvious throughout the book. Furthermore, it should be clear that defining concepts in terms of physical operations is the result of a programmatic position that accepts the thesis of the sufficiency of atomic analysis.

On the face of it, operationism may appear to be useless as an approach to establishing the validity of private concepts that constitute some of the content of personal knowledge, especially the knowledge of personal causation, and one might well hesitate to suggest that operationism of any type is applicable to personal knowledge. It was Bridgman (1959) himself, however, who suggested the type of operation that may be applicable to personal knowledge. In order to understand this bold step, we must investigate in some detail Bridgman's presentation. This will be done in Chapter 2. For the present, we need only note that we believe that psychology has a technique for applying operational analysis to concepts derived from personal knowledge. This technique, known as content analysis and applied to thought sampling, will be discussed and criticised in detail in Part III of this book.

An Overview

In this first chapter we have raised many problems, but the reader may be asking himself, "What are the basic problems of motivation theory?" We have not provided a conventional list such as, What is a motive? Is all behavior motivated? Is a motive a directing or an energizing agent? These are not the basic problems. In fact, they may be pseudoproblems growing out of specific orientations to science. The most basic problem derives from the fact that motivation is a concept invented by men to help understand behavior. The concept is not forced on us by experimental data or empirical observations publicly communicated, and a science of behavior based on presuppositions that preclude anything but objective evidence is fooling itself if it uses the motivation concept. Motivation is something we know from within ourselves, from personal causation, and we know it in a different way from the way we know observable facts in the physical world of objects. The most basic problem, then, is to reconcile this type of knowledge with the vast store of more objective knowlege already at hand.

Inevitably, we must try to understand the presuppositions that we take with us in our attempts to explain behavior and this involves us in some very old philosophical debates. In Chapter 2, we try to uncover some of the presuppositions by presenting three basic dilemmas under the headings of the Mind-Body Problem, Causation, and Hedonism.

The first must be unearthed because Descartes and the philosophers have bequeathed to us a conception that supports not only the rejection of the concept of Mind but has promoted a conception of psychology that cannot include the very evidence upon which the concept of motivation is based. We do not have to postulate a "mind," but we must include in our psychology such eminently psychological concepts, which occur only to one individual and are not objectively observable, as thoughts, perceptions, affect, and ultimately motives. The controversy over causation is unearthed in order that we may realize the problems involved in using the concept and may avoid the attractive but erroneous approach to explaining motives in terms of "physical causes" as well as the trap of explaining behavior as caused by thoughts or affect, for instance. The philosophical debate over hedonism forms the roots of explanations of behavior in terms of pleasure or pain, i.e., affect.

All three dilemmas are considered so that we may build upon firm ground and a solid understanding of the past. All three bear on the central problem for motivation, that of reconciling objective with personal knowledge, of investigating the human being as a physical object in third-person terms, and, at the same time, as a psychological subject in first-person terms.

Once we have confronted these problems, we can go on to the more conventional problems. In Part II of the book, we pursue the rather mechanical notion that affect spurs behavior. On the assumption that certain stimuli arouse affect within the organism, and the postulate that behavior will be directed toward maximizing positive and minimizing negative affect, a very general theory of motivation can be developed. Two basic questions are posed by the affective arousal position. The first is: What stimuli in the world produce affect? The second is: How do stimuli acquire the capacity to produce affect? We draw these questions from arousal theory, but we cite evidence from many diverse sources. By the simple gambit of assuming that drive-stimuli produce affect, we are enabled to include an enormous literature which is important to any treatise on motivation. This literature is primarily the result of attempts to answer the question: What is reinforcement? It forms the most solid empirical foundation upon which to build a motivation theory. We have attempted to ask the question in a way that will integrate this reinforcement literature with evidence stemming from affective arousal theories.

At the conclusion of the discussion of stimulation and affect it appears that a specific state of fear or hopeful anticipation may precede some motivated behavior, but apparently it cannot account for all motivated behavior. A more general concept of affect or ultimately of the motivated state appears needed. In Part III, we consider a development in motivation theory that was originally based on the specific concept of affect but broadened to include investigating motivated states through the analysis of thoughts. Here the problem of the relationship of thoughts to behavior is raised in the context of the achievement motive, the human motive measured by thought samples about which most is known. Part III attempts to present and critique the research produced by this technique as well as to elucidate the basic question of the relationship of thoughts to action. Careful analysis of thought samples is presented as the most advanced (yet still very crude) technique of operational analysis of first-person subjective states. An attempt is made to shed some light on the problem of intrinsic motivation from this perspective using the concept of personal causation.

Up to Part III in the book, we shall be concerned with the concept of motivation as it was developed in the theories of psychologists—the results of psychologists' attempts to understand human beings. This may make it appear that they are the only ones in this game or that they do it in a unique way. In fact, all men gain knowledge of their fellow men through observations in interaction with them—all men develop concepts that help them understand their fellow men. Psychologists, generally of the social variety, have studied the process by which men form impressions of other men and attribute to them traits, intentions, and motives. In Part IV, we present the evidence from these studies under the headings of the perception and knowledge of persons, the attribution process, and inferred motives. The data derive from studies in the area of person perception and shed some light on the phenomenology of motivation.

In Part IV, it appears that an important aspect of the attribution process is the inference that behavior originates from the person's own intentions as compared with the inference that behavior is done because he was forced by someone or something else to behave in the way he did. Apparently the perception of motivation in another person affects the behavior of the observer. This raises the question: What about the perception of motivation in self—does this affect behavior? This is the basic question for a theory of Personal Causation. The last section of Part IV of the book attempts to elaborate the concept of Personal Causation and to present some evidence indicating the effects of personal causation on behavior.

In writing the book, our thinking has been most influenced by two concepts. The first, as is evident in Parts II and III, is the concept of affect. We took as a working definition of motive the one presented by Mc-Clelland *et al.* (1953) in which affect is primary, namely, *"A motive is the redintegration by a cue of a change in an affective situation"* (p. 28). We do not take this as "the ultimate definition." In fact, we will not present such a definition. The concept of motivation is not something that can be defined in one sentence. Our concept is presented in the entire book.

The second seminal concept that influenced our thinking, as may be seen most clearly in Part IV, is Heider's (1958) concept of the perceived locus of causality for behavior. Attributing to the self rather than to others the distinction between the perception of an internal or an external locus for causality helped us to reconcile the objective-subjective or first-person–third-person dilemma. This was further clarified for us by Polanyi's (1958) discussion of personal knowledge and resulted in our eventual acceptance of the word "causation" in the special sense of "personal causation."

Chapter 2

SOME PHILOSOPHICAL PRESUPPOSITIONS

"The curious thing is that we have no clear knowledge of what our presuppositions are and when we try to formulate them they appear quite unconvincing" (Polanyi, 1958, p. 59).

The Three Dilemmas

In philosophical terms we face the following formidable problems: (*a*) the mind-body problem, (*b*) the problem of causation, and (*c*) hedonism. The mind-body problem derives from the dualistic assumption (Descartes) that the mind and mental phenomena are distinct from the mechanically operated body and physical phenomena. The problem arises in attempting to discuss the relationship or interaction between the two; for example, can mental events affect bodily actions? The problem of causation at the most general level is the problem of what a cause is and how we know one when we encounter it. Hedonism is the name for the position that human actions are the result of the desire to gain pleasure and avoid pain.

These dilemmas may seem a far cry from modern psychology of motivation, so we must state the problems in our terms. It is superficial to consider the three problems as completely separate and distinct since almost any motivational proposition presupposes some position on all three. Any definition of a motive presupposes a position on the interrelationships between mental and physical events. Using motive as an explanatory concept involves some position on the role of the concept of causation in science. If both mental and physical events are discussed, the question of causal connection arises. A motivation theory that uses concepts such as pleasure, affect, or even reinforcement is faced with

29

the problem of hedonism. A position that assumes that pleasure is a mental state that causes physical behavior events is beset with all three problems.

On the face of it, the simplest approach seems to be to avoid all three problems by ruling out mental events. With one stroke of the theoretical scalpel, such discussions are made unnecessary. Behaviorism is thought by many to have performed this excision with resultant clarification of the problems. Being purely physical events, behavior involves nothing which is mental. Mental events are demonstrated to be a function of other physical events (stimuli) in the environment and functional relationships between stimuli and responses constitute the entire domain of psychology. Troubles arise, however, because behavior is not completely predictable from physical stimuli. There are demonstrable individual differences that force us to take into account something within the organism. One solution is to assume that these differences are residues from past physical stimuli (reinforcement histories). In this way the mind-body problem is dealt with by discarding the mind.

The problem of causation of physical events by mental events is neatly avoided by the same technique—but not *all* the problems of the causal principle. Physical events may be assumed to cause other physical events. Does a perfect correlation between two physical events imply causation? No. Are psychologists dealing primarily with perfect correlations between stimuli and responses? No. Where, then, do we stand on the problem of causation?

Aside from the difficulties involved in obtaining it, is a reinforcement history an adequate explanation of behavior? If we mean by adequate, necessary and sufficient for probabilistic prediction, we may say it is *in principle,* i.e., the principle of the sufficiency of reinforcement history analysis. In practice, however, we can never obtain a complete reinforcement history. Does the reinforcement history *cause* the behavior? In short, how do we use the word *cause?*

Furthermore, obtaining a reinforcement history involves some definition of a reinforcer. A definition in terms of the change in the probability of a response may be useful, though tautological, but it commits the theory to the logical position that all such changes in response are a function of (caused by?) reinforcement. Thus (by one definition) reinforcement is a necessary condition for learning to occur. This implies (since all organisms show at least rudimentary learning) that all organisms will behave in a way that will maximize reinforcement. Substitute pleasure for reinforcement and we have a statement of *psychological hedonism!* Is the reinforcement statement any better than the hedonistic statement?

Only if some definition which is independent of responses can be obtained for reinforcement.

The Mind-Body Problem

The basic problem identified as the mind-body problem is usually associated with Descartes and Cartesian Dualism. With the advances in understanding physical phenomena, especially mechanics, the doctrine of the superiority of mind over matter, the spiritual over the natural was in difficulty. A categorical distinction between mental and physical events with specific laws for each realm promised analytical power. Thus, the Cartesian Dualism which set the stage for the problem of the relationship between the two realms.

In *The Concept of Mind,* Ryle (1949) called this the official doctrine which he presents as follows:

> The official doctrine, which hails chiefly from Descartes, is something like this. With the doubtful exceptions of idiots and infants in arms every human being has both a body and a mind. Some would prefer to say that every human being is both a body and a mind. His body and his mind are ordinarily harnessed together, but after the death of the body his mind may continue to exist and function.
>
> Human bodies are in space and are subject to the mechanical laws which govern all other bodies in space. Bodily processes and states can be inspected by external observers. So a man's bodily life is as much a public affair as are the lives of animals and reptiles and even as the careers of trees, crystals, and planets.
>
> But minds are not in space, nor are their operations subject to mechanical laws. The workings of one mind are not witnessable by other observers; its career is private. Only I can take direct cognizance of the states and processes of my own mind. A person therefore lives through two collateral histories, one consisting of what happens in and to his body, the other consisting of what happens in and to his mind. The first is public, the second private. The events in the first history are events in the physical world, those in the second are events in the mental world. . . .
>
> Even when "inner" and "outer" are construed as metaphors, the problem of how a person's mind and body influence one another is notoriously charged with theoretical difficulties. What the mind wills, the legs, arms and the tongue execute; what affects the ear and the eye has something to do with what the mind perceives; grimaces and smiles betray the mind's moods and bodily castigations lead, it is hoped, to moral improvement (Ryle, 1949, pp. 11–12).

As Ryle points out, such a theory does not derive solely from Descartes, but was among other things an attempt to reconcile early scientific discoveries with the stress of the times on the mental and spiritual aspects of men.

> Descartes was reformulating already prevalent theological doctrines of the soul in the new syntax of Galileo. The theologian's privacy of conscience became the

philosopher's privacy of consciousness, and what had been the bogy of Pre-
destination reappeared as the bogy of Determinism (Ryle, 1949, p. 23).

Ryle's terminology is probably repellent to most psychologists who
have banished such words as "mind" and "soul" as meaningless. Mental
phenomena, or what Ryle calls "mental-conduct concepts," are some-
times admitted as proper data for psychologists although there is no
implication that they derive from something called "the Mind."

The history of modern psychology demonstrates that the relationship
between private and public events is at the crux of most of the contro-
versial issues in psychology. The fact that Weber was concerned with
the mind-body problem is often noted in the psychological history books,
but his Law can be used without falling into the error of assuming a
"mind." Although introspection (the careful inspection of private sub-
jective states) fell into disrepute after Titchener, subjective report is a
vital part of any study of perception from Berkeley's (1709) New Theory
of Vision to Gibson (1950) or even Attneave's (1954) study of informa-
tion processes in perception. The whole problem of the relationship
between perception and sensation is involved.

Closer to home in the motivation area, the sticky problem of the effects
of motivation on perception implies some internal, subjective process
affecting our very perception of physical reality (cf. Bruner & Postman,
1947, 1948) and the effects of awareness on learning (Eriksen, 1962).
In older or more philosophical terms, we are confronted with the prob-
lems of intention, attention, and volition, all of which are relegated to the
area of motivation.

The problem, although no longer stated in terms of mind and body, still
involves polarities such as objective-subjective, public-private, internal-
external, intentional-unintentional, aware-unaware, goal-directed-random,
conscious-not-conscious-unconscious, or in a recent outgrowth of cyber-
netics "man vs. machine." The problem is basic to a discussion between
adherents of the current most accepted view of behaviorism and a grow-
ing number who espouse a position which is not new, most often called
Phenomenology (cf. Wann, 1964). As we shall try to show, understand-
ing of the problem is important to an understanding of both the rein-
forcement-history and the affective-arousal theories.

The obvious success of the strategy of rejecting mentalistic concepts
in psychology with its resultant stress on the analysis of behavior often
leads to the implicit acceptance of a type of materialism that may have
unfortunate consequences. If one accepts the postulates that human
behavior must be studied empirically with methods that are publicly
reproducible, and even that concepts concerning subjective states should

be approached with a healthy skepticism, one has taken the best of the rigorizing effects of behaviorism, logical positivism, and operationism on psychology. Very few investigators would now deny, in principle, the possible value of studying some concepts which have been proscribed in the past, especially if they are closely related to verbal behavior. Most current day writers are willing to liberalize their interpretations of operationism and redefine the unit of behavior to fit almost any conception. The harmful effects of the more doctrinaire behaviorist approach cannot be dealt with as the straw man of the earlier bolder and obviously indefensible statements. What Koch (1964) sees as a "restricting" and "trivializing" effect on psychology of the behaviorists' "methodic proposals" results from generally held but only vaguely perceived orientations imparted mainly in graduate training in psychology. Given the view that ultimately all the principles of human behavior will be reduced to law-like physical relationships between a few simple variables (the atomic analysis thesis), the relationships which are apparently most satisfying are those which come to us from physical mechanics. No one will admit that he expects to find such simple relationships, but many psychologists go about their work in the laboratory as if they had such expectations. This may be especially true in dealing with motives since the analogy to simple mechanical notions of causation is very seductive.

In effect, much of our thinking verges on simple materialism (the position that talking about feelings or desires is useless because they do not exist) or analytic materialism (the position that talking about feelings or desires is useless since they can ultimately be reduced to bodily and material facts). The latter position has the positive attribute of encouraging the search for such "facts." But in too many cases it results in the implicit assumption that these facts will be of the type physicists deal with and too often these conceptions are even more restricted to oversimplified mechanical models.

The basic programmatic statements of behaviorism are unassailable, but their major negative effects derive not from the direct attempt to follow the model but from the subtle restricting of the concept of what psychology ought to be concerned with and from the unintentional constriction of the vision of the results of psychological research.

This latter influence is difficult to verbalize. Ryle (1949) presents an analogy which comes close to communicating the type of subtle restriction involved:

> A scientifically trained spectator, who is not acquainted with chess or any other game, is permitted to look at a chessboard in the intervals between the moves. He does not yet see the players making the moves. After a time be begins to notice

certain regularities. The pieces known to us as "pawns" normally move only one square at a time and then only forwards, save in certain special circumstances when they move diagonally. The pieces known to us as "bishops" only move diagonally, though they can move any number of squares at a time. Knights always make dog-legged moves. And so on. After much research this spectator will have worked out all the rules of chess, and he is then allowed to see that the moves of the pieces are made by people whom we know as "players." He commiserates with them upon their bondage. "Every move that you make," he says, "is governed by unbreakable rules; from the moment that one of you puts his hand on a pawn, the move that he will make with it is, in most cases, accurately predictable. The whole course of what you tragically dub your 'game' is remorsely preordained; nothing in it takes place which cannot be shown to be governed by one or another of the iron rules. Heartless necessity dictates the play, leaving no room in it for intelligence or purpose. True, I am not yet competent to explain every move that I witness by the rules that I have so far discovered. But it would be unscientific to suppose that there are inexplicable moves. There must therefore be further rules, which I hope to discover and which will satisfactorily complete the explanations which I have inaugurated." The players, of course, laugh and explain to him that though every move is governed, not one of them is ordained by the rules. "True, given that I start to move my bishop, you can predict with certainty that it will end on a square of the same colour as that from which it started. That can be deduced from the rules. But that, or how far, I shall move my bishop at this or that stage of the game is not stated in, or deducible from, the rules. There is plenty of room for us to display cleverness and stupidity and to exercise deliberation and choice. Though nothing happens that is irregular, plenty happens that is surprising, ingenious and silly. The rules are the same for all the games of chess that have ever been played, yet nearly every game that has ever been played has taken a course for which the players can recall no close parallels. . . . The rules prescribe what the players may not do; everything else is permitted, though many moves that are permitted would be bad tactics.

"There are no further rules of the game for you to discover and the 'explanations' which you hope to find for the particular moves that we make can, of course, be discovered, but they are not explanations in terms of rules but in terms of some quite different things, namely, such things as the player's consideration and application of tactical principles. Your notion of what constitutes an explanation was too narrow. The sense in which a rule 'explains' a move made in conformity with it is not the same as the sense in which a tactical principle explains a move, for all that every move that obeys a tactical principle also obeys a rule. Knowing how to apply tactical principles involves knowing the rules of the game, but there is no question of these principles being 'reducible' to rules of the game" (pp. 77–78).

Psychologists are now primarily concerned with investigating the physical "rules of the game." This is especially true in physiological psychology and in sensation. When the psychologist confronts problems of perception, learning, and especially motivation, it makes good sense to assume that different techniques and principles may be involved. These must not be incompatible with the physical rules, but they will not involve the same kinds of relationships.

In motivation, this is exemplified by discussions of the distinction between energizing and directing concepts of motivation. Physical rules may tell us the origin and amount of energy available, but they will never tell us the probable behavior in which the energy will be expended.

It is time to ask if it is possible to extend the behavioristic structure beyond the analysis of simple responses; it is past time to extend it beyond simple materialism and simple mechanical explanations in motivation; it is time to move slowly and cautiously into an analysis of certain phenomena which recommend themselves first because they have resisted molding into the present views and yet remain as persistent problems.

It is not the job of a book devoted primarily to motivation to solve the problems involved in psychophysical dualism. But it would be well to have "clearly in mind" a position which is at least compatible with the study of motivation and such concepts as affect and locus of causality.

We shall accept the value of the position that all psychological phenomena that can be reduced to physical or physiological facts should be. This is in agreement with analytical materialism and the atomic analysis thesis. We will not accept it as proven or even demonstrable that all such phenomena are ultimately reducible to physical or physiological facts. As a consequence, some subjective states will be allowed the scrutiny of psychological investigation. Physical and physiological evidence will be welcomed as one aspect, but will not be accepted as ultimate terminal data. In fact, so-called psychological states will be held up for analysis with some attempt to avoid the temptation of "physiologizing."

In summary, the mind-body problem is raised here to show how the Cartesian Dualism has led through Behaviorism to a thoroughgoing analytic materialism. Complete understanding of behavior from knowledge of objective facts about human beings treated as physical objects is postulated. But to assume that thoughts, intentions, motives, and other not immediately observable phenomena are not to be included within the domain of Psychology, is to make a category mistake. The mind-body problem for the twentieth century psychologist is to understand the relationship between these aspects of personal knowledge and behavior and to reconcile the third-person objective with the first-person subjective analysis.

Privileged Access and the Way Things Are

Phenomenologically it appears that we have a different source of knowledge about our own feelings and actions than we do about the feelings and actions of others. "I cannot feel your hurt, but I can feel mine."

To some, this distinction means that the "privileged access" of the individual to his own states must make his judgment about himself more accurate than his judgment about others.

Granted that private states provide the individual with some knowledge including the very feeling of existence (*cogito ergo sum*), and the distinguishing of "self" from "other," what constitutes the difference between my knowledge of me and my knowledge of you? There are three possible sources of knowledge: (*a*) events that the individual can observe only in himself (feelings, affect, etc.); (*b*) events that the individual can observe in himself and in others (behavior); and possibly (*c*) events that the individual can observe in others but not in himself (it is sometimes assumed that one is blind to certain self-aspects). Events that I can only observe in myself must clearly distinguish my knowledge of me from my knowledge of you.

Although we shall emphasize the private and apparently "immediately given" personal knowledge, it is not to be assumed that we are saying that *all* personal knowledge is private and immediately given. As stressed by Behaviorism, we learn a great deal about ourselves by actually observing our own behavior. *Feelings* associated with emotional arousal may be immediately given, but the *interpretation* of what emotional arousal means for the individual may be the result of his learning to label his own felt emotional states. The complications involved in my experiencing signs of emotional arousal (such as a pounding heart) and understanding what they indicate in me are receiving attention in ingenious experiments by Schachter and Singer (1962), Valins (1966), and others to be discussed in Chapter 5. These studies make it clear that before appropriate labeling occurs, I may be immediately experiencing a pounding heart and not know why. After I have learned to label my emotional states, I may *experience* a pounding heart and an *interpretation* that I am emotionally aroused because of imminent danger *both* as immediately given and as personal knowledge, despite the fact that the latter (interpretation) is based on learning.

A person may also acquire knowledge by experiencing his own behavior and by observing his own and others' behavior. In fact, a strict Behaviorism would attempt to derive all self-knowledge from observations of behavior (cf. Bem, 1965). Ryle puts it this way: "The sorts of things I can find out about myself are the same as the sorts of things that I can find out about other people, and the methods of finding them out are much the same" (Ryle, 1949, p. 155).

In stressing the concept of personal causation, we are not denying that we learn from our own and others' behavior, although we are giving priority to the personal and ultimately private aspects of knowledge about our feelings and motives. A person starts with these private aspects and then he may learn to label and infer things about his own and others' behavior. He does not start with observations of others' behavior and then learn to infer things about his own feelings and motives.

The concept of personal knowledge emanating from private first-person subjective states opens up the possibility of a practically untouched area that might be called the phenomenology of motivation, i.e., the study of aspects of human behavior that lead to the inference or perception of motivation in others based on private sources of knowledge about our own motivation. Some research beginnings in this direction, largely growing out of the work of Heider (1958), will be presented in Chapter 9 of this book.

But to return to the problem at hand, we must point out in passing that accepting subjective states into the scientific arena is not as radical as it may seem, especially to operationists following Bridgman (1927). More and more subjective phenomena are being accepted into scientific philosophy.

"Although many of the alleged results of introspection were indeed questionable, a person's awareness of his own state of imagining, feeling, etc., must be recognized as a kind of observation, in principle not different from external observation, and therefore as a legitimate source of knowledge, though limited by its subjective character" (Carnap, 1956, pp. 70–71).

Although we may question whether thoughts and feelings are "observed" in the same way as external events [see reference to Malcolm (1964) in what follows], nevertheless, thoughts, affect, and motives are not outside the realm of scientific concepts and are not categorically different from more observable facts of behavior. Although they are less amenable to objective observation, they are basically similar and can be studied by techniques available to the psychologist. It takes training to learn to use words and concepts in any realm with fairly precise meaning. The physical sciences have helped us be more precise in dealing with objects by the use of operational definitions and the training that is necessary to help us to use concepts from personal knowledge more precisely is not different in kind from training to use physical concepts although it is more difficult. Once we realize that no meaning is absolute, we can see that approaching meaning from either objective facts or personal knowledge is a matter of approximation.

For if it be granted that the language community cannot always be *universalized* with respect to *all* significant terms, the question of whether the referent be located in direct experience or in the "public" world becomes a relatively minor matter. In both cases, the fact of communication (thus "checkability") will be contingent on relevant observer sensitivities – which later are, in principle at least, open to specification. In both cases, communication will often not be all or none, but rather a matter of degree. For both cases, the history of mankind and of science gives overwhelming evidence that high degrees of inter-observer agreement are attainable. Moreover, terms having both "types" of referent *can and do* enter into stable predictive relationships (Koch, 1964, pp. 29–30).

OPERATIONAL ANALYSIS OF PERSONAL KNOWLEDGE

Bridgman (1927), the champion of operationism, has argued more recently (Bridgman, 1959) for the central role of individual observations and the private aspect of scientific pursuits. In doing so, he has discussed the operational analysis of "introspectional words in the private mode" (p. 216).

Bridgman (1959) uses two words that may lead to misunderstanding among psychologists: "introspection" and "projection." For the psychologist, introspection is identified with Titchener and the psychology of Structuralism. The introspectionism of the structural school was the ultimate in attempts to "objectify" perception by means of removing all possible personal content and involvement. This could not be further from the meaning implied by Bridgman's phrase which refers to words such as "conscious," "pain," "think," "motive," "intention," and "desire." These are introspectional words for Bridgman. They refer primarily to the private mode although they may have public components. In order to avoid the implications that history has attached to "introspection," we prefer to refer to these words as descriptive of personal knowledge.

When Bridgman uses the term "projection" in the phrase "the operation of projection," he means simply that one person can imagine himself in another's place and hence "project" himself into the other's circumstances. There is no implication, however, that the person projects characteristics onto another person that he rejects in himself as in the psychoanalytic use of the term. A word that captures Bridgman's meaning in this context is "empathy" when used purely in the sense of imagining another's situation and without overtones of sympathy.

With these clarifying concepts in mind, let us look at Bridgman's proposal for validating introspectional words in the private mode (personal knowledge) by means of the operation of projection (empathy). In his chapter "On the fringes of psychology," Bridgman has done something rare and refreshing. He has actually confronted epistemological problems with psychology as the main focus. It is typical for physical scientists and philosophers of science to develop their epistemological concepts in the realm of physics and chemistry and then imply the importance of using similar concepts in psychology. This leaves the psychologist frustrated, wondering exactly how the philosophers would apply their epistemological concepts to psychological problems. Bridgman, on the other hand, apparently through discussions with Skinner at Harvard and other psychologists, has seen the central importance of the human individual in any scientific research. This has led him to a direct confrontation with the theory of knowledge as derived from psychological theory and evidence.

He first notes that most current American psychologists are essentially "materialists" and "non-vitalists" and hence accept the thesis of the sufficiency of atomic analysis. At one level and as a programmatic approach that may never be realized in fact, he accepts this. The impossibility of ever specifying exactly "the configuration of all the atoms in *any* material system, whether living or dead" (as pointed out by Niels Bohr) is a serious criticism, but Bridgman sees even more serious problems in reducing introspectional words to a purely public basis by means of the program implied by the thesis.

Now I suspect that this first part of his discussion is not entirely clear to some behavioral psychologists primarily because they may have been following a program that entails the atomic analysis thesis without clearly understanding its implications. The physiological psychologist is most consistent in assuming that behavior may be explained by reduction to such atomic events that underlie neurophysiological phenomena. The behaviorist may look to the day when the answers will come from physiology, but in the meantime he works with grosser units of behavior and accepts the thesis of the sufficiency of reinforcement histories as the programmatic basis of his work. Neither the physiological psychologist nor the Behaviorist deals with the realm of first-person knowledge, i.e., introspectional words in the private mode. For the well-trained behaviorist, there appears to be no problem in getting the private and the public sources of knowledge on common ground because they see no need to consider the private sources of personal knowledge.

Having recognized that all so-called "objective" knowledge, i.e., communicable knowledge in the public mode, has its basis in a private experience, Bridgman insists that we must confront the first-person introspectional words directly as the ultimate source of any knowledge.

My solution is somewhat similar to that of Skinner in that I also recognize that the introspectional words are in a special class, but my solution differs from his in that instead of discarding these words altogether I retain many of them, but with a restricted meaning. The special nature of the introspectional words becomes obvious when one tries to give an account of what is involved operationally in using these words on both the public and the private level. These words are a subclass of the more general class of words the operational meaning of which depends on who it is that is performing the operations. . . . In the case of the intro-spectional words the operational heterogeneity is especially obvious: one is tempted to say — especially aggravated. Consider, for example, what is involved in carrying out the injunction "Verify that individual X has a toothache." The operational verification is entirely different depending on whether the Individual X is myself or another. When it is I that have a toothache my operation of verifica-tion is direct, immediate, and so elemental that it is well-nigh impossible to des-cribe to another how I do it. Whereas if I have to verify that some other individual has a toothache, my operations are complex, roundabout, and I can never be sure that I may not be mistaken — the unreliability of the lie detector is notorious. If it is not I that am enjoined to verify that X has a toothache but someone else, let us call him A, then as I observe A making his verification I see that he goes about it with much less fuss and feathers when the individual X happens to be A himself than when X is another. The operational dichotomy in these situations is so inti-mately involved with everyday experience that it seems to me I can ignore it only at my peril. It is not enough that the operational dichotomy can be played down, as does the behaviorist, by saying that X's toothache is accessible only to X; I want to empahsize the dichotomy. In fact, I believe, as will appear in detail later, that serious social consequences follow the ignoring of the dichotomy (Bridgman, 1959, pp. 216–217).

It thus appears that the difference between private and public may be clarified by distinguishing between two distinct classes of operations of which one class applies directly to the private mode.

The class of operations performable by only one person may very well have a calculus of its own, and part of the task of the behaviorist is to investigate what this calculus may be. In investigating these operations the psychologist may, if he chooses, remain on the public behavioristic level, the uniquely performable opera-tion being described in public behavioristic terms, the same for all of us. To this extent I can act as does the behaviorist. But I want to push the matter further. In the class of operations performable by only one person there is a subclass which is so sharply set off from all the others that I think it demands special treatment — this is the subclass of operations which only I can perform. The dichotomy between the operations by which I decide that I am having a toothache and any of my neighbors is having a toothache is so sharp and spectacular that it is to be em-phasized by every means in my power. This dichotomy is the most insistent and uncompromising of the characteristics of my world — I do not see how I can neglect it and possibly hope to give an adequate description of what happens to me, or to adapt myself to living in the world (p. 217).

Emphasizing the importance of the operational dichotomy, Bridgman restricts his use of important introspectional words such as conscious, motive, intention, etc., to the private mode entirely. "In particular, I propose to use such words only in my private aspect. Such usage is consistent with the vision that I cannot get away from myself. Because of this, any 'ultimately true' account that I can give of the world has to be from myself as center—any valid report has to be reducible to the first person singular if it is not actually already in the first person" (pp. 217–218).

He makes it clear that he could translate all first-person statements into "words of solely public import" as the behaviorist does. This, however, would involve operational circumlocutions that would constantly have to report that the person using the operations was the only one capable of making them (e.g., person A verified that he had "pain," was "conscious," had an "intention" and was the only one who could verify this by this type of operation). Bridgman feels that this is too high a price to pay and wants to bridge the gap between "my consciousness" and my knowledge of "your consciousness" by the special "operation of projection."

Before we move on to the special operation, however, we may note that this type of argument concerning two types of operations is implicit in a critique of Behaviorism by Malcolm (1964). A few lines from Malcolm capture the essence of Bridgman's argument so far.

> The Achilles' heel of this doctrine [Behaviorism] lies in its treatment of psychological sentences in the first-person-present tense (p. 149).
>
> The notion of verification does not apply to a wide range of first-person psychological reports and utterances. Another way to put the point is to say that those reports and utterances are *not based on observations*. The error of introspectionism is to suppose that they are based on observations of inner mental events. The error of behaviorism is to suppose that they are based on observations of outward events or of physical events inside the speaker's skin. These two philosophies of psychology share a false assumption, namely, that a first-person psychological statement is a report of something the speaker has, or thinks he has, observed (Malcolm, 1964, p. 151).
>
> Man's puzzling status as a subject and a person is bound up with these first-person utterances, having the two striking characteristics I have tried to point out: First, that for the most part, they are not made on the basis of any observation; second, that they are "autonomous" in the sense that, for the most part, they cannot be "tested" by checking them against physical events and circumstances, other than the subject's own testimony. If we want to know what a man wants . . . the man himself is our best source of information (p. 154).[1]

Malcolm says that first-person-present experiences are unverifiable in the sense that no two people can experience *exactly* the same thing. But in this sense *any* experience, concept, or knowledge is unverifiable. The crucial problem is not whether you can ever experience my exact sensa-

---

[1] Before pointing to "the Achilles' heel" of behaviorism, Malcolm had cogently discussed its advantages in dealing with third-person analyses, so the above quotes must not be assumed to come from an entirely negative context.

tions, but whether we two can, by a series of approximations, come to communicate about the private mode through operations that give meaning to introspectional words. It is for this purpose that Bridgman introduces the operation of projection.[2]

> It seems to me that the operation by which I give meaning to your use of "conscious" is a simple one in the sense that everyone uses the operation. I shall call it the operation of "projection," I "project" myself into your position, that is, I imagine myself in your position, and I ask myself what I would be saying or doing in such a position. If I can imagine that I myself would be using the same word in that position, then I understand the meaning of your word and you have been successful in your communication. For present purposes it is not necessary to attempt to analyze the operation of projection further. Simple observation shows that it is an operation which I continually perform without hesitation, and I believe that you also perform the same operation . . . .
>
> The operation of projection thus serves a much broader function than merely to give meaning to the private words which we use in talking to each other. In its general social context, as an operation by which we anticipate the actions of our fellows and adapt ourselves to them generally, it is what a physicist would call a first approximation. We know that our fellows do not act exactly as we would under all circumstances. In coarse outline all human beings are alike, but in finer detail they differ. We correct the operation of projection by using the specific knowledge that we have acquired of the particular individual with whom we are dealing (Bridgman, 1959, p. 220).

Up to this point, Bridgman may be interpreted as saying that people in general engage in the operation of projection and that it helps them to understand their fellow men. What has this to do with science and psychology? The answer is that psychologists also engage in this practice and the question is: How can it be made more precise?

The Scientific Use of the Operation of Projection

Bridgman describes briefly a seminar that he conducted at Harvard the purpose of which was to demonstrate "that a consistent and detailed use of operational analysis would provide a technique by which agreement could be reached with regard to at least the meanings of some of the more important terms of primarily social import" (p. 244).

The seminar consisted of seven doctoral candidates in areas ranging from engineering to social philosophy, and they considered such words as "community," "society," "rights," etc. Bridgman reports:

> The one outstanding impression that I got from the experience was of the unfathomed complexity of the verbal background of each one of us and the fact that no two backgrounds were alike. . . .

---

[2] In reading the following, forget the psychoanalytic connotations of projection and read it to mean "imagining another's experiences."

> With regard to the operational method of attack I am, if possible, more convinced than ever of its value as a tool for the analysis of meanings. . . . It is, however, very difficult to discover what is the actual operational structure of the meaning system of any individual at any fixed epoch. . . . Neither does use of the tool of operational analysis put agreement on an almost automatic basis, as I had hoped. The situation revealed by detailed analysis is so complex and individuals differ so widely that agreement is to be expected, even with the aid of this powerful tool, only after long and serious effort. In particular, seven people is by far too large a group to permit a sufficiently detailed analysis of what each has in the back of his head to justify the expectation of agreement in the time available. Moderate success might be hoped for with only one other member, but even with one, I would never be sure that I had caught all the implications of his ostentions (Bridgman, 1959, pp. 244–246).

By now the reader may be asking: "What is this tool of operational analysis as applied to words like society?" Operational definitions usually connote to psychologists a specific description, in terms of physical objects and apparatus, of the conditions set up by an experimenter to produce a specific phenomenon. The description constitutes the operational definition of the phenomenon. The emphasis given by the term "operational" is on the hardware, but the hardware is actually secondary. The aim is to attain concrete, *communicable meaning* for the concept. It seems reasonable to attempt to assign communicable meaning to introspectional words in the private mode, but how can it be done through operational analysis?

> Speaking roughly, the locus of the most important part of whatever it is that gives a word identity and meaning is in the brains of the people that use the word. . . . From this point of view it is not the word as it stands in isolation on the printed page which means something, but I who read the word, or you who wrote the word, who mean something. Emphasis on the activity aspect of the word demands that this not be lost sight of. A simple verbal trick is helpful in this connection. Never ask, "What does word X mean?" but ask instead "What do I mean when I say word X?" or "What do you mean when you say word X?" . . . . I shall say that I know the meaning of a word if I can state the conditions which dictate use of the word by you or by me (Bridgman, 1959, pp. 17–19).

Operational analysis, then, means an attempt to specify in what activities I must engage in order to arrive at the situation described by the word under consideration, the result of the question, "What do I mean when I use it?" In short, what are the conditions for its use.

Used for words restricted to the private mode, the analysis can be difficult because I am the only one who can testify to my operation, but I can compare mine with yours. As such, operational analysis touches on two related philosophical approaches, namely (*a*) "ordinary language" analysis as practiced by Austin (1962), and called by some, Linguistic

Phenomenology, and *(b)* the technique, used in workshops on phenomenology (Spiegelberg, 1965) called *sym-philosophein* or co-subjectivity and consisting of philosophizing together "in the genuine Platonic sense" (p. 9). All of these attempts seem to lack something in specificity: they seem to use a blunt instrument to split hairs. The instrument (discussion) is blunt because it is not focused, the subject seems like splitting hairs because the goal of reaching agreement on introspective words is unclear.

Psychologists have wrestled with a similar problem and have devised a method that allows a check on the reliability of communication about words that have in them a component of the private mode. This method has been developed specifically with regard to words relevant to social motivation such as achievement, affiliation, etc. The result of the method is the technique of content analysis. The content of any written document can be analyzed for the incidence of any words or meanings that can be specified carefully enough so that their occurrences can be simply counted. The technique of counting based on a manual that defines what is to be counted is simple enough. The method of developing the manual, i.e., the definitions of the things to be counted, is the crucial aspect. The method of developing a series of definitions to be included in the manual has been successfully used by McClelland and his associates (McClelland *et al.,* 1953; Atkinson, 1958) for definitions of several words indicative of motivational states. More is said about the use of the manual than about its development, but the latter involves all the elements of Bridgman's operational analysis of introspective words, and Spiegelberg's co-subjectivity and linguistic phenomenology. Developing a manual, however, adds two crucial elements, namely *(a)* specificity, and *(b)* a technique for testing the reliability of communication. Specifically, a manual is developed for one concept such as "achievement." The definitions are constantly checked and refined in the heads of two or three persons by a process of approximation. Starting with an overall definition, they search separately for instances of the concept in the same written productions of other people. To the extent that they agree when they compare their results, it can be said that they are using the same concept. When disagreements occur, they are in a position to improve their precision by refining their definition and rechecking on more written material. They are not merely discussing their concepts but constantly checking them in the crucible of thoughts produced by other people.

This technique is long and arduous (typically two persons working together need spaced trials of two or three hours a day for a period that often extends to a month before reliability of approximately 90% can be obtained), but after the hard labor has been accomplished the result is as close an approximation to complete agreement as can be attained in this realm.

It appears that we have a foothold in the area of operational analysis of motivational concepts that derive at least partially from personal knowledge and hence are at least partially in the private mode. The development of careful definitions to be used in content analysis adds the dimensions of focus and checks of reliability of communication. Its great merit, as compared to more philosophical approaches, is that it has a specific goal—explaining motivated behavior in human beings. Measures derived from content analysis have been found to be extremely useful in this respect, and evidence from this area tends to confirm validity of the concepts thus clarified even if it cannot be said that the evidence directly verifies the results of the operational analysis of the private experience ultimately involved. In Part III of this book, a detailed discussion of the research dealing with achievement motivation will be presented. The technique devised for content analysis of thought samples is to us the closest approximation yet devised to what Bridgman has proposed for the operational analysis of concepts derived from personal knowledge. It is a tentative and as yet very crude technique for solving the 20th Century mind-body problem, i.e., bridging the gap between subjective-objective or first-person and third-person analyses.

Causation

The word "cause" and the phrase "causal explanation" are, of course, very solemn expressions. They remind us at once of those unheard impacts of those little invisible billiard-balls which we learned to fancy, erroneously, were the truly scientific explanation of everything that goes on in the world. So when we hear the promise of a new scientific explanation of what we say and do, we expect to hear of some counterparts to these impacts, some forces or agencies of which we should never ourselves have dreamed and which we shall certainly never witness at their subterranean work. But when we are in a less impressionable frame of mind, we find something unplausible in the promise of discoveries yet to be made of the hidden causes of our own actions and reactions (Ryle, 1949, pp. 324–325).

The problems posed for motivation theory by the concept of causation derive from the same dilemmas encountered with the mind-body problem. If motive is considered to be the "cause" of behavior, we are confronted with the problem of explicating what we mean by cause. Furthermore, motives must be a specific type of cause, and if we lean too heavily on subjective states of intention and volition in our conception of motives we are impaled on the mental-physical dilemma, whereas if we conceive of "cause" too mechanistically ("those little invisible billiard balls") we tend to restrict our conception of what a motive may be. "That there should be any causal transactions between minds and matter conflicts with one part, that there should be none conflicts with another part of the theory" (Ryle, 1949, p. 66). The dilemma here again derives from *(a)* the implicit dualism imposed by conceiving of intentions, volitions, etc. as things which are completely separate and distinct from behavior, and *(b)* from the implicit mechanistic interpretation of causation.

To put this discussion in perspective briefly before proceeding, we must note that modern science, especially since Darwin, has been consistently attacking the conception of man as a separate and distinct (and superior) being. The doctrine that man is not subject to the same physical laws as inanimate objects and animals is the origin of the mind-body problem. In reducing the concept of man, first to an animal, and ultimately to a machine operating through cybernetic feedback mechanisms, science has found much that is useful.[3] However, the fact that men are somehow different from physical objects is usually acknowledged. Whether the difference is one of degree or kind is in contention. One can at least note immediately that the most obvious observable difference between human beings and physical objects is contained in the word "animate." Human beings are seen as an origin of motion, as internally motivated, sometimes as a center of consciousness. That is, they are seen as having an *internal locus of causality*. The distinction is basically a motivational one.

This distinction remains despite great strides in reducing many of the mysteries of human and animal behavior to physical facts and mechanical laws. A very useful technique has been developed of purging all words of their more ghostlike vitalistic connotations and reducing scientific vocabulary to physical objects and events. For instance, one feels greater security in discussing with Ryle "mental-conduct-concepts" rather than "thoughts," "feelings," and "desires." But the laws of mechanical causal chains are based on the assumption that the locus of causality for any movement (behavior) of a physical object will be found external to that object. We have, therefore, two alternatives: *(a)* we can apply this principle to human (and animal) behavior and give up the notion of an internal locus; or *(b)* we can investigate the ubiquitous phenomenologically supported conception of human beings (and animals) as originators of causal sequences and as having loci of causation internal to themselves, i.e., as motivated. Pursuing the latter alternative, as we shall do here, does not commit us to assuming that no behavior may be attributed to external loci of causation, but it does commit us to attempting to distinguish between internal and external loci. Our source of knowledge of the distinc-

---

[3]For a full discussion see "Men and Machines," *Proceedings of the Aristotelian Society,* 1952, Supplementary Vol. 26.

tion, which is ultimately a personal event, involves us in the problem of privileged personal access to knowledge.

The first alternative (giving up the notion of internal locus and motivation) may reduce ultimately to semantic distinctions. Essentially, we may stick to words concerned with physical objects and events but the language cannot be identical to the language of physics. It must be adapted. We have at the very least to distinguish between inanimate and animate objects. Brentano (1874) maintained that it was impossible to deal with certain concepts without referring to "intentional language." Chisholm (1955–1956) points to the possibility that the distinction above may ultimately be semantic in the following passage:

> Let us say (1) that we do not need to use intentional language when we describe non-psychological, or "physical," phenomena; we can express all that we know, or believe, about such phenomena in language which is not intentional. And let us say (2) that, when we wish to describe thinking, believing, perceiving, seeing, knowing, wanting, hoping, and the like—either (a) we must use language which is intentional, or (b) we must use a vocabulary which we do not need to use when we describe non-psychological, or "physical," phenomena (p. 129).
>
> The easiest way to construct a non-intentional language for psychology is to telescope nouns and verbs. Finding a psychological verb, say "expects," and its grammatical object, say "food," we may manufacture a technical term by combining the two. We may say that the rat is "food-expectant" or that he "has a food-expectancy." . . . But this way of avoiding intentional language has one serious limitation. If we wish to tell anyone what our technical terms mean, we must use intentional language again (p. 133).

If we are to take the obvious distinction between animate and inanimate objects seriously, we must investigate the origin of animism. This will necessarily involve some solution to the problem of intentional language. The step that we hope to take in this direction is through the use of the concept of perceived locus of causality and its relationship with affect. The use of the word "cause" in the phrase "perceived locus of causality" may be misleading. The phrase derives originally from phenomenological description (Heider, 1958), but the word may be misplaced (in Ryle's sense of a category error) in a phrase which applies to subjective (perceived) phenomena. We must clarify the use of the word "cause."

Three positions have been distinguished with regard to causation (Bunge, 1959), namely: *(a)* causalism, *(b)* semi-causalism, and *(c)* acausalism.

CAUSALISM

In its traditional form, causalism is the assumption that determinism and causation are coextensive and that science is the discovery of causality and scientific laws are all causal. In rationalistic form (Kant, Leibniz), causalism assumes that the causal principle is an *a priori* principle of thought. "It is ... the belief of Kantians, who assert that the causal bond is synthetic, in the sense of being verifiable *in* experience, but not derivable from it nor further analyzable" (Bunge, 1959, p. 28).

SEMICAUSALISM

This form recognizes causation as one principle of lawful relationships. As advanced by Bunge (1959), semicausalism holds that causation is one form of the more general category of determinism. Deterministic sequences in science may be of a causal or of some other form.

ACAUSALISM

This position may derive from radical empiricism in which case causation is reduced to external connection, succession, and concomitance. In this view, the causal concept soon becomes excess baggage and is seen as of decreasing importance in science.

Acausalism may also take the form of "indeterminism," which denies the existence of lawful relationships. We need not detain ourselves with this form despite the recent interest generated in microphysics by the celebrated Heisenberg Principle of Indeterminacy (cf. Cassirer, 1956).

It is difficult for a behavioristically oriented psychologist to deny the persuasiveness of acausalism as derived from empiricism.[4] But, if we take the step of discarding the word *cause,* have we made the first step toward the undoing of motivation theory? If "cause" must go, can "motive" be far behind? Actually, as hinted in the footnote, it is probably of no great import what language we choose to adopt. We will eventually come face to face with the problem of the predictability of behavior from events reported to us by the subject, e.g., affect states and perceived responsibility for behavior.

Ultimately, acausalism involves a radical empiricism which, in the extreme, denies us the luxury of logical constructs and theories. Having no taste for this type of asceticism, and at the same time wishing to avoid the alternative of pure rationalism, we propose that all three forms of the causal concept are attempts to find a physical empirical basis for causa-

---

[4] In fact, the author was long persuaded that this was the simplest solution and could be reconciled with a theory of motivation. It appears that reducing causal phenomena to external connections, etc., may be ultimately another form of the technique, discussed in connection with intentional language, of developing a new vocabulary with the sole purpose of avoiding the word "cause."

tion and therefore overlook the origin of the concept in personal knowledge. The causal principle must not be conceived of in simple macrophysical terms—we must avoid what Ryle (1949) has called the "bogy of mechanism."

CAUSES AND GERMS

A slightly more sophisticated position which is persuasive for people dealing with motivation is to conceive of a cause as it is often conceived of in microbiology, i.e., the cause of a disease is a germ. It is very satisfying to be able to attribute the "cause" of a disease to a specific germ; but if we restrict our notion of cause to this level, it does not apply to motivation. Clearly, no one will ever discover a microorganism that will be identified as the origin of motivation.[5]

This example, however, helps clarify the situation if we inquire why a germ can be identified as a cause. There may be many conditions that contribute to an infection in a specific individual. In the individual, the elimination of any one of the conditions could prevent the disease. In short, many factors contribute and might be seen as causal. In epidemiology, the one which is isolated and considered in some sense "more causal" is the one that is constant across many cases in which other conditions vary. Identifying this type of cause originally is impossible with a single case. The first step is classifying "disease" by noting similar physical effects or symptoms across cases. This is by no means a simple process. Only when it is done, however, can a single source be sought.

The first step is still only vaguely envisioned in motivation although it is most often assumed to be the isolation of regularities in behavior. Simple taxonomies may be useful, but the ultimate goal is the identification of some factor or factors that are uniquely associated with one class of behavioral regularities. Any insights as to what form these predictive factors may ultimately take will help in the classification task and hasten the acquisition of knowledge.

A germ-type conception of the role of science in discovering causes is oversimplified; all causes are not germs. But the general technique, that of identifying unique factors associated with specific classes of events, is based on the ultimate assumption that events (in the case of psychology, behavioral events) are organized and related in meaningful ways, i.e., understandable. The underlying assumption is a deterministic faith. Such

---

[5] Although such things as a hunger hormone (Luckhardt & Carlson, 1914), blood sugar level (Grossman, 1955), or plasma-free fatty acid level (Bogdonoff, Klien, Estes, Shaw, & Back, 1961) may be related to motivated states.

determinism must be accepted by the science although it cannot be demonstrated empirically. The study of natural phenomena must be based upon empirical evidence *plus* the thought processes of the investigator: radical empiricism is impossible in principle. The investigator must constantly be humbled by the fact that the strength of his work comes down to his ability to impose order on the empirical data, and the imposition of order is a logical thought process. Order is constructed and imposed, not given to him by the data. Whether one accepts some notion of an ultimate order or not, it is clear that no one can hope to approach an order at such a level of magnitude. At best, our schemes must be seen as poor approximations. We cannot be so grandiose as to assume that what we "discover" at a theoretical level is anything more than a constructed scheme which roughly fits some of the empirical evidence as we now know it. We must never forget that the way we see it is a function of our tools (both logical and technical).[6] Both a cause and a motive are constructed concepts which we attempt to impose on data. An inadequate understanding of such basic concepts will ultimately hamper the quest. An oversimplified assumption that "the cause" is out there to be found may be fatal. It is our contention that assuming that the goal of science is to search for causal relationships is misguided, especially if it is accompanied by an oversimplified concept of cause.

PRODUCTION, OCCASION, AND ELICITATION

We may proceed by taking a more definite stand on certain issues and examining the implications. First, let us note that we have ruled out a notion of cause as the unique factor which *produces* the effect. A motive is a concept which may be said to *contribute* to the production of a behavioral effect. Thus a motivational state may be said to occasion and, in some cases, elicit a behavioral effect.

We are concerned with the interaction between physical events (a lighted cigarette applied to the skin, i.e., a physical stimulus) and psychological events (pain, i.e., the phenomenological experience). In what sense can a causal connection be drawn between the two? Following Wisdom (1934), we shall say that event E_1 produces event E_2, if we can satisfy ourselves that E_1 constitutes a complete explanation of E_2. On the

---

[6] The basic problem of epistemology and scientific methodology is that of setting forth a system that facilitates the transition from empirical data to rational concepts. The two basic components are contained in the name of the philosophical position Logical-Empiricism (see Feigl & Scriven, 1956–1958). A cogent attempt to spell out a general approach to relating data and concepts will be found in Margenau (1950).

other hand, most psychologists would admit a relationship between the physical stimulus (lighted cigarette) and the phenomenological stimulus (pain). Few, if any, would wish to leave it at that and not investigate at least intervening neuro-physiological events. None would be willing to admit that E_1 constitutes a complete explanation of E_2. Thus on our definition, E_1 does not produce E_2. As Wisdom (1934) points out, E_1 does not create E_2 "out of nothing." Many other factors are necessary for a complete explanation.

The establishment of a correlation (concomitant variation) between physical stimuli and psychological stimuli is an empirical affair. We shall assume that some such relationships are accepted even by the most rigorous empiricist. Interpretation of these relationships remains in contention as does their establishment at more complicated levels which involve affect — the answer to the question, "What stimuli produce affect?" (see Part II).

We may use the less rigorous term "elicit" for the observed connection between events. A complete explanation of an event involves both (a) a previous change (or changes) in conditions, and (b) necessary circumstances which remain unchanged. Thus, the event pain (E_2) is contingent both upon the cigarette stimulus (E_1) and the presence of an intact organism (O). We would define the word "elicit" to relate E_1 to E_2 but not to relate O to E_2. Thus, the cigarette stimulus elicits pain, but the necessary conditions in the organism do not.

The situation becomes more complex when typical instances of motivated behavior occur. Typically, an environmental change must be coordinated with an organismic state to produce so-called motivated behavior. But, if left at this stage of analysis, the organismic state (motive) cannot be seen to "elicit" the behavior, and in this sense a motive cannot be said to have a causal relationship with behavior. If an internal change or stimulus (e.g., a drive-stimulus) is assumed (or demonstrated), the difficulty is reduced. We shall return to this problem shortly.

The ability to distinguish between an event (E_1) which actually elicits E_2 and conditions or events which must be obtained for the sequence to occur, constitutes the crux of the problem in the area of causation. In simple cases, the distinction seems to be obvious to all observers. But the criterion upon which one selects the "obviously" critical event is far from obvious.

As both Hume (1740) and Kant (1781) pointed out, justification for a causal connection must be extra-empirical. Apparently, no unique indicator in empirical data reveals the presence of a causal relationship. The concept is imposed on the data by the investigator. Certain logical restrictions help to isolate the critical events, but the establishment of a so-called "causal relationship" calls on both empirical evidence and so-called "logical canons."

The philosophers have bequeathed to us canons that can be useful in developing methodologies, but they are not empirically foolproof. We must establish (a) concomitant variation, (b) temporal sequence, and possibly (c) co-presence and co-absence of cause and effect. Concomitant variation may be established empirically. Temporal sequence is based on the logical assumption that an effect cannot be attributed to an event which follows it, i.e., cause must precede effect. Although this is a logically prescribed step, it can often be determined empirically or required experimentally [cf. the distinction between a "projected experimental" design which controls temporal sequence and an "ex post facto" design which does not (Selltiz, Jahoda, Deutsch, & Cook, 1959)].

Absolute co-presence and co-absence (if A then B, and if not A then not B) is rare in science and rarer still in psychology. When it can be established, it is usually at a level which is relatively unimportant theoretically. The relationship between light intensity and pupil dilation might be given as an example, although even this is complicated by other variables (see, e.g., Hess & Polt, 1960). The achievement of such a relationship is the result of the sophistication of the concept of light intensity, on the one hand, and sophistication as to anatomical arrangements in the eye, on the other. Such facts may be extremely useful in psychology but they do not constitute relationships in which at least one variable is behavioral in the sense most often considered in psychology, i.e., not merely reflexive.

The logical, rational, or mental aspect involved in postulating causal relationships cannot be overstressed since it constitutes the most elusive and yet compelling attribute of the concept. It is here that the analogous concept "motive" is similar. Ultimately, we appeal to some extra-empirical criterion in assigning causes and motives. Paradoxically, we may have better access to the source of our concept of motive than to that of cause. An analysis of the source of both concepts is uniquely psychological.

Analysis of the source of the causal concept has been thought to involve either (a) the empirical assertion that it is the result of repeated observation (Locke) or (b) the notion that it involves a synthetic a priori mental category of thought (Kant). Neither alternative is, at present, appealing, but any resolution apparently must involve both empirical and logico-rational components. The best attempts to study the problem by modern experimental techniques will be found in Michotte's (1963) series of strikingly original experiments. Development of the concept in children has been studied by Piaget (1930). Both of these approaches, which have roots in the writing of Maine de Biran (see Michotte, 1963), will be discussed in detail in later sections and taken as basic to any discussion of the concept of motive.

Having briefly reviewed the philosophical controversy about causation, we may now reaffirm the position taken in Chapter 1. We reject *any* concept of cause that implies some notion that the efficacy or necessary connection between two events is something inherent in the events or something that may be empirically demonstrated. Thus, we accept the Humian empirical argument, and yet attribute to "cause" meaning as a concept that does not derive from observations of physical objects or events. We do not look to "innate ideas" as the origin of the concept as Kant did. The concept of cause derives from experiences of ourselves as causes, from the personal knowledge of personal causation.

There is a nice distinction that we must make here. Personal knowledge, although based on experience, is not necessarily based on observations. Following Malcolm's (1964) argument presented previously, we must not make the mistake of assuming that personal knowledge derives only from observation of the self that are similar to observations of some other person. As Bridgman (1959) has pointed out, the operation involved in *my* verifying that *I* am motivated is quite different from the operation involved in *my* inferring that *you* are motivated. In verifying my own motivational state, I need not make any specific "observations" at all. This is not to say that I do not *sometimes* make observations of my own behavior, feelings, etc., but merely that I do not *always*. In fact, more direct knowledge, not based on specific observations, is more common. This distinction is important in relating the position presented here to similar positions now to be discussed.

The notion that the concept of cause originates in motives was probably first presented in the early 19th Century by the philosopher Maine de Biran, as pointed out by Michotte (1963). In fact, our presentation could be said to be a restatement of Biran's except for the distinction, noted previously, between "experience" and "observation."

Biran postulated that we have direct experience of our own causality through the feeling or perception of effort. From this feeling of effort comes our idea of causation.

"A being who had never made an effort would not in fact have any idea of power, nor, as a result, any idea of efficient cause. He would see one movement succeed another, e.g. one billiard ball bump into another and push it along; but he would be unable to conceive, or apply to this sequence of movements, the idea of efficient cause or acting force, which we regard as necessary if the series is to begin and continue" [quoted in Michotte (1963), p. 11].

The idea of causation for Biran derives from the feeling of effort, a concept similar to our notion of personal causation. The basic experience, however, is characterized as a feeling that was observed within one's self. This feeling of effort is similar to Munsterburg's (1888) and Wundt's (1863) "feeling of innervation" that was so severely criticized by James (1890). James' argument is that rarely is a movement preceded by the observation of a feeling. The feeling comes after the movement. We shall encounter this same problem in postulating affect that precedes motivated behavior. Apparently, it is a mistake to postulate any conscious observation of effort or affect[7] that immediately precedes behavior. We have tried to clarify this by the distinction between experience itself and observing experience. The experience of personal causation is not the observation within one's self first of a feeling of innervation and of affect and then of an act that has effects in the physical world. It is the immediate experience, often not consciously noted, of the total bundle all at once. In fact, the "self-conscious" observation of the various aspects may destroy the total experience. To attempt to isolate affect or the feeling of innervation as the "cause" of behavior is to attempt a para-mechanical explanation. In some cases of motivated behavior the analogy may help, but not in all.[8]

Hedonism

The theory that human action is the result of the desire to gain pleasure and avoid pain is what is meant by hedonism. Some postulate relating behavior to pleasure and pain is invariably found in theories of motivation. The simple assumption that all behavior is an attempt to attain pleasure or avoid pain was the major tenet of motivational theories of philosophers of the 18th and the 19th Centuries.

---

[7] With regard to affect see the section to follow on Affect, Twinges, and Motives.

[8] In passing, two things may be noted. First, Piaget (1930) presents a similar idea of the child's conception of causality that will be discussed in the last section of this book. Second, Michotte (1963) feels that his data comparing "live movement" of caterpillars and frogs with "dead movement" of objects indicate that Biran's "immanent activity" from which he derives the notion of "causality" is actually qualitatively different from physical causality. Hence, physical causality cannot be derived from immanent activity or the feeling of force. We still believe, however, that the idea of physical causation has its roots in personal causation, but even if Michotte is right that physical causation is distinct from personal causation, it does not prejudice our major argument, namely, that to look for an explanation of motivation in physical causes is a mistake.

Wholehearted acceptance of hedonism, however, raised both psychological and ethical problems. On the one hand, a controversy raged over the psychological nature of man. Could man's hedonistic tendencies be assumed to be a function of man's psychological makeup? Was it the psychological nature of human beings always to seek pleasure and to avoid pain? Such a position was labeled Psychological Hedonism and was repudiated with arguments involving incidents of renunciation of pleasure and even examples of masochism. The classic argument involved voluntary martyrdom in which it was maintained that psychological hedonism was disproved by the case of martyrs who seek a painful demise in preference to a more pleasurable life.

Moral philosophy faced the problem of reconciling the assumption that seeking pleasure, although natural, was evil, with some notion of the perfectability of mankind to become a creature who would seek the "good" rather than the "pleasurable." Attempts were made to equate the good and the pleasurable as early as the Greek philosophers Aristippus and the Cyrenaics. Troland (1928) has labeled this position: Hedonism of the Present. Immediate pleasure is the consummate good of human action.

The realization by the Epicureans that immediate pleasure might be renounced for a greater gain in the future led to Hedonism of the Future. Renunciation in favor of the future rather than immediate indulgence was combined with notions of the greatest good for the largest number to form several approaches to Ethical Hedonism (Hobbes, Bentham, and the Mills, father and son). Bentham's hedonistic calculus involved a calculation of the *quantity* of pleasure for the largest number of people. John Stuart Mill raised the problem of the *quality* of pleasure as well as the role of conscience. Could the pleasure gained by a pig wallowing in mud be equated with the pleasure of intellectual or morally "good" pursuits? Can "poetry" be compared with "pushpin" (a contemporary game)?

Herbert Spencer resolved Mill's hedonistic utilitarianism with evolution, arguing that with the evolution of man different things became pleasurable. This is the antecedent of the survival model of reinforcement, which assumes the postulate that the species that derive pleasure from what is good for them have survived. Thus, the resolution of "the good" and "the pleasurable."

Boring (1950) points out that Freud's pleasure principle is essentially a hedonism of the future. This was rejected, however, by experimentalists, such as Thorndike, and modern reinforcement theorists in favor of a *hedonism of the past* epitomized by the Law of Effect. This law "is the principle that action which leads immediately to pleasure is impressed and remembered and so repeats itself as habit" (Boring, 1950, p. 706). Past pleasure (reinforcement) determined present (habitual) behavior.

The Nature of Affect (Pleasure-Pain) and Its Relation to Behavior

At least two basic problems lie at the heart of these earlier philosophical discussions. These problems still plague motivational psychology, but the modern techniques of research and analysis promise to give greater purchase on them. At the most basic level is the question: "What is the nature of pleasure and pain?" Without some answer to this question, it is not very fruitful to ask the second question: "In what way is behavior affected by pleasure and pain?" Modern psychological questions that descend directly from these dilemmas are: "What is a reinforcer? Is all behavior motivated? Is reinforcement necessary for learning?" The contingency between a definition of pleasure-pain and its relationship to behavior was clearly indicated in Thorndike's statement of the Law of Effect. Learning of responses was made contingent upon reinforcement. Reinforcement was conceptually defined in terms of pleasure ("a satisfying state of affairs"). A satisfying state of affairs was operationally defined as "one which the animal does nothing to avoid, often doing things which maintain or renew it" (Thorndike, 1913, p. 2).

This statement of the Law of Effect is conceptually hedonistic and has the characteristic of many conceptual statements of psychological hedonism; namely, it is circular. Behavior aims toward pleasure, and pleasure is defined in terms of behavior. The only way out of this circularity is to break the cycle empirically with an independent demonstration of the pleasurable component (reinforcer, affect, hedonic tone). As Meehl (1950) has pointed out, this may be done empirically by establishing that a reinforcer is "trans-situational," i.e., leads to approach behavior in other situations (with the same organism), and hence can be assumed as a general reinforcer for this organism. Thus, the definition of a reinforcer as something which increases the probability of a response may be empirically useful, although it is formally circular.

Theoretically, it may be possible to designate a set of objects, stimuli, or experiences that may be assumed *a priori* to be satisfying or pleasurable. Such an approach would have greater explanatory power, since it would be based upon some central concept which could be used to distinguish all "things" which are "pleasurable," "satisfying," "reinforcing," or lead to positive affect. This approach would be of enormous value. It would give us direct access to the criterion to apply to any situation to tell us which behavior in that situation would tend to be repeated. Such a criterion would form the core of a theory of motivation of learned behavior if it could be assumed that anticipatory affect always precedes behavior.

Unfortunately, no such "criterion" has as yet been discovered. In fact, philosophers following Ryle (1949) have argued that it is fruitless to pursue such a will o' the wisp because it is no more than a fiction. Ryle feels that the probability of finding something which is common to all pleasurable experiences is very small. Furthermore, the fact that such a possibility ever occurred to anyone is the result of a category mistake — that of assuming that pleasure is a unique "feeling" (analogous to the feeling of innervation) that accompanies all pleasurable experiences and precedes motivated behavior.

HEDONISM OF THE PAST AND FUTURE

We must now confront one of the most difficult problems in relating affect and behavior. Is behavior controlled by past experiences of affect (hedonism of the past, e.g., the law of effect) or by the anticipation of affect (hedonism of the future, e.g., purposivism)? The organization of goal-directed behavior is apparently centered around a future event — the goal. It is, however, inadmissible to assume that a future event influences (or causes) a prior event.

The learning theorists' resolution of this problem using the law of effect concentrates on past events and assumes a learned relationship between the behavior and the consequent affect (reinforcement). In Chapter 5, we shall review Hull's (1931) ingenious resolution of this problem and see the inadequacies found in it by Mowrer (1950) and others in the explanation of avoidance conditioning. Extensive work in learning theory involving mediation seems to demand a theory of motivation that postulates some immediately antecedent affective event that influences the probability of responses. Such a position (to be discussed in detail in Chapters 3, 4, and 5) would combine demonstrated relationships between affect and stimuli, with learned anticipations of affect that organize behavior. The concept of affective mediating mechanisms may be used to pin down the acquired relationships between affect and behavior. The details of the development of the concept of mediation will be left until we have reviewed other proposed resolutions. At present we must deal with the possibility that a major assumption of such a position may be untenable.

The position that derives from the definition of motive presented at the end of Chapter 1[9] rests on the assumption that the anticipation of affect which organizes and directs behavior is an identifiable event that occurs immediately prior to the behavior. This antecedent affective event may be said to elicit the behavioral event. Since this antecedent affective

[9]"A motive is the redintegration by a cue of a change in an affective situation" (Mc-Clelland *et al.,* 1953, p. 28).

event is the result of an acquisition process developing out of past events that produced a change in affect, the assumption is made that many different events have one characteristic in common, namely, affect or a similar change in affect. In dealing with the question, What is this "similar characteristic"?, i.e., What is affect?, we are tempted to assume that it is a consciously experienced feeling. If this were the case, we might expect to find some physiological correlates of the experience and thereby solve the problem of measurement. Evidence such as the discovery of the "pleasure centers" in the brain (Olds & Milner, 1954) tends to encourage this assumption. But philosophically and phenomenologically, the assumption is tenuous.

Affect, Twinges, and Motives

In developing the case against category mistakes resulting from Cartesian Dualism, Ryle discusses motives and emotions and presents his much discussed analogical example of brittleness of glass as a dispositional property (see, for instance, Anscombe, 1957; Gosling, 1962; Peters, McCracken, & Urmson, 1952). He identifies brittleness as the dispositional property of glass, which leads to "shattering" when a stone hits it. An analogy is then drawn to the "motive" vanity in a human being.

> I shall shortly argue that to explain an act as done from a certain motive is not analogous to saying that the glass broke, because a stone hit it, but to the quite different type of statement that the glass broke, when the stone hit it, because the glass was brittle. Just as there are no other momentary actualizations of brittleness than, for example, flying into fragments when struck, so no other momentary actualizations of chronic vanity need to be postulated than such things as boasting, daydreaming about triumphs and avoiding conversations about the merits of others (Ryle, 1949, pp. 86–87).

Ryle would consider the concept of affect one of the "momentary actualizations" which he is ruling out. He argues that inclinations (motives) are not based on "thrills, twinges, pangs, throbs, wrenches, itches, prickings, chills, glows, loads, qualms, hankerings, curdlings, sinkings, tensions, gnawings, and shocks" (pp. 83–84). The road taken by Ryle defines "vanity" in terms of the behaviors associated with it ("boasting," "daydreaming," etc.). Psychologists would see this as a response-response definition of motivation (J. S. Brown, 1953) that is commensurate with behaviorism. In fact, Ryle encourages the association of his position with behaviorism (Ryle, 1949, Chapter 10), although he does not wholeheartedly embrace it.

His position would not rule out "twinges" of affect if he found them, but he argues that they do not occur. Thus, he says:

But before expanding this argument I want to show how intrinsically unplausible
the view is that, on each occasion that a vain man behaves vaingloriously, he ex-
periences a particular palpitation or pricking of vanity. To put it quite dogmatically,
the vain man never feels vain (p. 87).

A consistent affective arousal theorist, one who assumes that motivated
behavior is elicited by an anticipated change in affect, which is itself a
state of affect (e.g., McClelland *et al.,* 1953), would reply quite as dog-
matically: "The vain man does experience *affect.*" The distinction hinges
on the same problem we met previously, namely, the definition of "feel-
ing" or the distinction between *immediate experience* and the ability to
report having *observed* an experience. Ultimately, this too reduces to an
attempt to convert a subjective experience available originally at the first-
person level to a third-person description of "objectively" observed
behaviors.

The affective arousal position and Ryle's attempt to infer a dispositional
property from behavioral concomitants of motivated states highlight the
inadequacies of present accounts of the relationship between affect and
behavior. The affective arousal theory, deriving much of its empirical
support from studies involving strong affective states (pain, fear) induced
through the manipulation of external stimuli (shock),[10] proposes a simple
solution to the prediction of motivated behavior. If it is assumed that one
component of every motivated state is affect and that the affect is what
directs behavior, then all that is needed is a precise measure of affect
from which the behavior may be predicted. Thus, in the avoidance con-
ditioning situation in which shock has been paired with the black side of
the box (Miller, 1951), if we could measure the affect aroused by the black
box, we could predict avoidance behavior without requiring any knowl-
edge of the past history of pairing shock with the black box.[11] Or, in the
positive case, if we could measure the affect (anticipation of success)
aroused by a challenge, we could predict achievement responses in
McClelland's sense (McClelland *et al.,* 1953).

The affective-arousal model has great potential, assuming a general
measure of affect could be developed to account for behavior that is pre-
ceded by a state of affect. The deficiency in the model, however, is that it
presupposes a para-mechanical interpretation of the relationship between

---

[10] Although this research comes primarily from the laboratories of Miller (1959) and
Mowrer (1950) and is based on negative stimuli, McClelland *et al.* (1953) developed the
affective arousal model (stimulus→affect→response) to include positive anticipatory states.
Subsequently, Mowrer (1960a) added "hope" and "relief" to his theory, and even Miller
(1963) has suggested a "go" mechanism.

[11] Of course, we would have to know something of the animal's learning response repertory
to know what form the avoidance response might take.

affect and behavior. Basically, affect must *precede* behavior and *cause* it, almost in the sense of energizing it or at least directing it. Ryle's view presents the possibility that much behavior that is apparently motivated does not appear to be preceded by a "twinge" of affect. In fact, the affect may be a component part of the whole event that cannot be extracted from the other components such as behavior. Much so-called intrinsically motivated behavior does not appear to be "driven" or even specifically "directed" by affective states. Examples crop up most often in "free" situations of play or creative activity.

A broader definition of affect, relieving it of the connotation of an observed experience or feeling, may help resolve this problem, and we have tried to show the value of postulating affect in Part II of this book. Ultimately, however, we are forced to postulate the concept of personal causation (Part IV) and to avoid all implications of a mechanical analogy. This may be a start in the direction of a solution, but the problem still remains. It is basically the problem of Hedonism. In its 20th Century form, the problem of Hedonism is the problem of the relationship between stimulation and affect and between affect and behavior.

PART II

AFFECT, STIMULATION, AND BEHAVIOR

Chapter 3

AFFECT AND STIMULATION I:
THEORETICAL PROBLEMS

> . . . *"painful feelings are connected with an increase and pleasurable feelings with a decrease in stimulation. Let us, however, be careful to preserve this assumption in its present highly indefinite form, until we succeed, if that is possible, in discovering what sort of relation exists between pleasure and 'pain,' on the one hand, and fluctuations in the qualities of stimuli affecting mental life, on the other (Freud, 1915a, p. 64).*

In this second section of the book, we will investigate some of the underlying aspects of motivation using the assumption that affect is of central importance. *Affect is to be understood as an emotional response with physiological and phenomenological correlates aroused or elicited by certain stimulus conditions in the environment.* This level of analysis attempts to reduce the basic units to specifiable stimuli and responses and is most easily understood by assuming a temporal sequence such that a stimulus arouses affect, which in turn elicits an instrumental response.

$$S \longrightarrow \text{Aff} \longrightarrow R$$

The first link in this chain may result either from the way the organism is built, i.e., the fact that the organism is equipped with receptors that respond to certain stimuli, or it may be the result of a process of acquisition or learning. In the first case, the relationship between stimulus and response is *required* by the structure of the organism; in the second case, it is *acquired* as a result of some process of adaptation or learning. In either case the first and most critical question (as raised by Freud in the opening quote) is: What stimuli produce affect?

What Stimuli in the World Produce Affect?

Most of the attempts to classify stimuli affectively seem to be inadequate from one point of view or another. On the face of it, there seems to be no hard and fast rule that a certain stimulus *always* produces affect. This is especially true for stimuli that (sometimes) produce positive affect. We feel safest in predicting that a stimulus will produce affect when the stimulus is intense, and in almost every case the prediction is for negative affect. Even with strong stimuli, however, we may be incorrect in predicting negative affect under some circumstances. Thus a laceration of the skin of the arm will almost invariably produce reportable pain, especially if the damage is extensive. Under extreme conditions, however, such as the exigencies of combat, a soldier may sustain a serious wound in the arm and may discover it only later. From this, we are led to infer the absence of reportable pain.

The example of extreme conditions (in the environment and the organism) makes it clear that an adequate theory to predict what stimuli will produce affect cannot concentrate on the stimuli alone. Account must be taken of surrounding stimuli as well as of the state of the responding organism. Second, it is clear that measurement as well as theoretical problems are raised as soon as we introduce the term "reportable." In addition, the fact that strong stimuli most reliably lead to negative affect suggests a relationship between intensity of stimuli and production of affect.

The most important point is that we must take into account some interaction between the incoming stimuli and the state of the perceiving organism. To a certain extent, reinforcement theorists may be said to have done this although typically they were merely trying to find some reinforcers so that they could proceed with problems more related to learning. They clearly assume that food will be a reinforcer only when the organism is hungry. They also assume that the effectiveness of the reinforcer may be a function of the intensity of hunger as well as of the quantity and quality of the reinforcer. However, rather than start with drive-stimuli, we shall attempt a systematic presentation of possible relationships between any stimuli and the general concept of affect.

In the present chapter, we present six more-or-less dichotomous concepts under which research and theory dealing with stimulation and affect can be organized. We then present three basic models that deal with the relationships between stimulation and affect and look for the roots of these models in the writings of Sigmund Freud.

SOME ORGANIZING CONCEPTS

Physiological vs. Psychological Emphasis

Research in motivation can be characterized by its relative emphasis on underlying physiological mechanisms, or on its emphasis on more psychological aspects. The former is more "respectable" and "tough-minded" while the latter is forced to deal with subjectively reported data and experience. The difference is analogous to a distinction between sensation and perception, between the sensory phenomena of the neurons and the subjective experience of a feeling of happiness.

Drives and Affect

Closely allied to the physiological-psychological distinction is a distinction between emphasis on drives *vs.* emphasis on affect. Psychologists investigating the physiological origins of strongly motivated behavior postulated that motivated behavior is a result of a physiological deficit or need. As we shall see in more detail later, however, behavior could not be predicted directly from knowledge or physiological deficit. Apparently, some intervening construct was needed and this was called "drive." Drive was postulated to be some nonlinear function of physiological deficit and behavior, in turn, was a function of level of drive. The intervening construct of drive sometimes carries with it surplus meaning concerning the subjective states of the organism although in its purest form as an intervening variable (MacCorquodale & Meehl, 1948) no such surplus meaning is implied.

The postulation of affect as a needed concept stems from subjective states that are psychological in character. Thus, need defined as a physiological deficit occupies one end of the physiological-psychological continuum, and affect, thought of in the phenomenological sense, occupies a position at the other end. Drive lies somewhere in between taking on more of the first (physiological) aspect, if the theorist conceives of it as an hypothetical construct with physiological concomitants, and more of the second (psychological) aspect, if it is conceived of as a felt drive within the organism. The notion of a drive as a stimulus is a step toward the psychological side, especially if an attempt is made to measure the perception of the drive stimulus.

Internal vs. *External Stimulation*

The stimuli associated with motivated behavior may be classified as originating either from within or from outside the organism. Emphasis on needs directs attention to internal determinants, and, when the drive concept is separated from the concept of need, the stress is primarily upon the internal stimuli associated with drives. This is because the drives most often studied are primarily derivatives of the need for food and the need for water, namely, hunger and thirst.

Despite this emphasis, it had always been realized that external stimuli play an important role, especially with respect to pain, since pain is obviously a motivator and pain can be inflicted by shock. Shock studies make it clear that it is necessary to take into account external stimuli as well as internal stimuli associated with drives. As a result drive-stimuli are postulated that may be either internal or external.

Negative vs. *Positive Stimuli*

External stimuli have often been conceived of as positive or negative incentives. A rough classification of such stimuli could be made through observation of approach *vs.* avoidant responses, e.g., stimuli that lead to approach-behavior may be said to be positive and stimuli that lead to avoidance-behavior may be said to be negative. But, the very words positive and negative carry subjective connotations. Obviously, the referent is some positive or negative subjective state such as pleasure-pain or positive and negative affect. This relationship between the behavioral concomitants and the subjective states was apparent in Thorndike's (1913) original postulation of satisfying and annoying states as states that the animal will attempt to maintain (satisfying) or states that it will attempt to terminate (annoying). Reinforcement theory as an outgrowth of Thorndike's statement of the Law of Effect has tended to equate reinforcement with reward (stressing the positive aspect) although, of course, the term "reinforcement" itself refers only to strengthening. This has led to some curious twists such as the use of positive and negative reinforcement.

Empirical approaches to the defining of a reinforcer (Skinner, 1953) place no positive or negative evaluation on a reinforcer. *A priori* attempts to designate what stimuli will be reinforcers, however, have leaned heavily on need and drive theories of motivation. As such, they have stressed that a reinforcer is the reduction of a negative or noxious stimulus.

Reduction vs. *Arousal Theories*

Emphasis on internal drive stimuli or noxious external stimuli has led to theoretical formulations that stress the reduction of such stimuli. Thus, drive-stimulus reduction or tension reduction is said to be reinforcing. Apparently, however, organisms can learn to anticipate both negative and positive affect, and since anticipation is affectively laden itself, it has been postulated that learning can lead to an arousal effect. Formerly neutral stimuli may acquire the capacity to arouse both positive and negative affect (anticipation). The notion of arousal and anticipation shifts the emphasis from events that follow the response to events that precede it.

Consequent vs. Antecedent Events

Arousal is a phenomenon that occurs before a behavioral act; reduction is the possible result of a behavioral act. Thus, if the theorist stresses arousal, he is more apt to consider stimuli antecedent to the behavior to be explained. On the other hand, if it is postulated that behavior is initiated in order to reduce a state of the organism and is reinforced (strengthened) as a function of the adequacy of the reduction, then the theorist must emphasize the consequences of the behavior in order to determine its adequacy.

In general, the first concept in each of the headings given above was stressed first historically. As more data became available, theorists were forced to take into account the second concept in each of the above headings. Thus, stress on physiological aspects alone has proven inadequate and psychological aspects had to be brought in; drive theories have been forced to look at affect; internal determinants proved inadequate when external stimuli were ignored; theories stressing only the negative aspect of stimulation needed to add the recognition of positive aspects; reduction theories that stress consequent events are being confronted with the importance of arousal and antecedent events. Clearly, we are not saying that theorists have completely ignored positive stimuli, antecedent events and even arousal; it was a matter of emphasis. We are advocating the vigorous investigation of these aspects and of affect, not to the exclusion of the others, but because theory and research in this area have neglected them until recently.

Some Theoretical Relationships between Stimuli and Affect

STIMULUS-INTENSITY-REDUCTION THEORIES

What stimuli in the world produce affect? The answer to this question has been slow in coming from experimental data. One approach has concentrated on the biological aspects and has associated affect with the change in bodily needs. Thus, presumably, an increase in a state of need results in pain or negative affect; while a decrease in a state of need results in pleasure or positive affect. The internal drive that results from the need is a stimulus or tension of differential intensity but external stimuli (e.g., shock) can have drive qualities also. Internal drive stimuli usually arise slowly through deprivation and induce behavior that has in the past tended to reduce the deprivation. External drive stimuli often are characterized by sudden onset, as in the case of shock. In their purest form, stimulus-intensity-reduction theories postulate that all stimulation is associated with negative affect (pain), and that the amount of negative affect is an increasing function of the intensity of stimulation.

Diagrammatically, the stimulus-intensity-reduction theory can be presented on a hedonic continuum as shown in Figure 3.1. Figure 3.1 is the first of three schematic diagrams, all of which have the hedonic continuum on the ordinate. The hedonic continuum is schematized as running from extreme negative affect (pain), through decreasing negative affect to zero affect (neutral), through increasing positive affect, to intense pleasure.

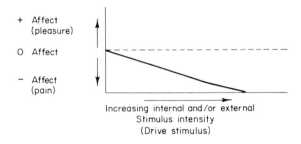

FIG. 3.1. The schematic relationship between affect and stimulus intensity as postulated by an absolute stimulus-intensity-reduction theory.

The three major theoretical approaches to the relationship between stimulation and affect (namely, stimulus-intensity-reduction, arousal-jag, and arousal) will all be schematized along the hedonic dimension, for comparison purposes. Figure 3.1, for instance, shows that for a drive-stimulus-reduction theory strong stimulation produces strong negative affect (pain), moderate stimulation produces moderate negative affect, and lack of stimulation produces no affect. This figure points up one of the difficulties of drive-stimulus-reduction theories in their crudest representation. If affect is taken to be a function of the absolute level of stimulus-intensity, as implied by the figure, then there is no possibility of positive affect or pleasure. This we shall refer to as an absolute stimulus-intensity-reduction theory, implying that affect is a function of the absolute value of the intensity of stimulation.

A relative stimulus-intensity-reduction theory might postulate that affect is a function of the relative change in the level of stimulus intensity. Thus, if the intensity is changing, a decrease in stimulus intensity over time would lead to a decrease in negative affect; an increase in stimulus intensity would lead to an increase in negative affect. Still we have no absolute level associated with positive affect, but it might be held that pleasure is the result of a decrease in negative affect and that pain is the result of an increase in negative affect. Essentially, however, all of these possibilities might be referred to as negative theories since they deal only with different levels of negative affect.

The Arousal-Jag Theory

The question always arises in connection with stimulus-intensity-reduction theories as to why animals and humans apparently sometimes seek out increased stimulation as if it were pleasurable. The notion of the arousal jag is essentially meant to answer this question, while still retaining the basic negative aspect of the reduction theories.

"Arousal jag" is the name for the concept that increased intensities of stimulation are tolerated — indeed, sought out — because of the anticipated pleasure associated with the subsequent decrease that follows. Such a postulate seems to necessiate at least two assumptions: (*a*) the assumption of a learned anticipation, i.e., that the subject has learned from the past that submitting to the increased stimulation (presumably accompanied by negative affect) will with high probability be shortly followed by decreased stimulation, and (*b*) that the decrease in stimulation from a higher level is more "rewarding" in some sense than the increase is "punishing." In other words, it is tolerable to endure the negative aspects of increased stimulation when one knows that the subsequent decrease will occur almost immediately and that the pleasure of decrease will outweigh the pain of increase. Derogatorily, this theory may be said to refer to the phenomenon of the child who bangs his head against the wall because it feels so good when he stops.

Such a statement is unfair, since the theory has much to recommend it. Apparently there must be postulated an accelerated functional relationship between stimulation and affect. It is probably necessary to postulate a relative theory in which production of affect is proportional to the relative speed of increase or decrease in the intensity of stimulation. If increase in stimulation is slow (as in increasing hunger), the concomitant negative affect is minimized; if the decrease in stimulation is fast (as in eating), the resulting positive affect is maximized. As a result the net amount of positive exceeds the net amount of negative affect. The arousal jag might, in this sense, be analogous to some well-known physical phenomena such as the slow buildup of kinetic energy that is to be suddenly released or the electrical induction coil that stores energy for a sudden discharge. Such analogies all involve the conservation and utilization of energy, and are basic to Freud's discussion of the economy of psychic energy in wit and play-pleasure. (See section entitled "Freud and Arousal Phenomena.")

Basically, the notion involved in the arousal jag can be diagrammed as shown in Figure 3.2. Here affect is assumed to be an absolute function of intensity of stimulation as well as a function of the rate of change in

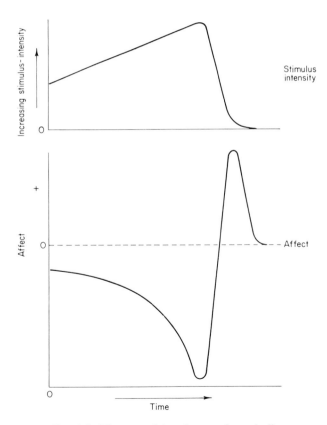

FIG. 3.2. The arousal jag shown schematically.

intensity. Thus if the stimulus-intensity (see top figure) starts out at a moderate level, affect (see bottom figure) is negative. As the stimulus intensity increases, negative affect increases at an accelerated rate. When the stimulus-intensity levels off at its highest point, the level of negative affect recovers to a point above its minimum since the acceleration produced by a change in stimulus intensity no longer obtains. However, since stimulus intensity is greater than at the beginning of the cycle, the affect correspondingly is more negative than at the beginning. As stimulation is reduced suddenly to zero, affect peaks at maximum positive affect, again because of the acceleration produced by the changing level of stimulus intensity. Then, when stimulation settles at zero (or a low level), affect returns to zero.

The assumption that affect is a function not only of the absolute level of stimulus intensity, but also of the rate of change, is plausible in view of the evidence on sensory adaptation. A slowly changing level of stimulus intensity allows the organism more time to adapt to the change, and this could be related to the amount of affect produced. With gradual changes in stimulation, adaptation will produce a damping of affect whereas sudden shifts in stimulus intensity minimize the possibility of adaptation and maximize affect.

Introducing the notion of adaptation suggests two further complications. If affect is a function of the speed of change of stimulus intensity because of the adaptation effect, then, when adaptation effects are minimized, affect should revert to an absolute function of stimulus intensity. This may be the case with stimulus intensities so extreme that the organism is unable to adapt. This deduction apparently is plausible since it would appear that there are extreme levels of stimulus intensity where the arousal jag would not be applicable. This is probably because extreme stimulus intensity results in permanent tissue damage and hence pain. The increase in stimulus intensity is not immediately followed by sudden pleasurable reduction (as is necessary for the arousal jag) because although the external stimulus (for instance a loud noise) may be reduced, if the eardrum has been permanently damaged painful stimulation may continue. Thus the arousal jag should apply to small or moderate levels of stimulus intensity but not to extremely strong stimuli. This situation might be seen as analogous to metal fatigue. Up to a certain point, a resilient metal can quickly recover from stress especially if the stress builds up slowly. Beyond this point, however, structural damage occurs and the metal cannot completely recover. Considering the fact that different sense modalities have different rates of adaptation suggests the possibility that the sense modalities that adapt most quickly need the most rapid rate of change to produce affect. This possibility will be raised again in Chapter 4.

The notion of adaptation raises another point. If, within certain limits, the organism can adapt to different levels of stimulus intensity, the perceived level of stimulus intensity may be zero although the actual physical level is above zero. The organism may be said to be adapted to the stimulus intensity and therefore to perceive it as zero. This possibility leads us to the consideration of arousal theories and theories based on the notion of optimal stimulation.

Arousal Theories

As we have seen, the fact that increases in stimulation are at times sought out raises difficulties for the stimulus-intensity-reduction theories. In arousal-jag theories, this difficulty is averted by postulating that moderate increases are sought out because of the subsequent reduction. Arousal theories postulate that certain types of stimulation lead to positive affect and are sought for their own sake. Again, we may theoretically separate the discussion into theories that treat affect (*a*) as a function of the absolute level of stimulus intensity or (*b*) as a function of the level of stimulus intensity relative to an immediately prior state, or, as we have said previously, as a function of the relative rate of change of stimulus intensity.

In arousal theories, we encounter a further complexity. Stimulus intensity is assumed to be a unidimensional variable acting within one sense modality, but a more molar approach to stimulation is evident in some arousal theories. In these theories, variations in the complexity of patterned stimulation are assumed to be related to affect. Such a step forces the researcher out of the realm of easily quantifiable intensity variables and into attempts to measure variables such as complexity, novelty, etc. It is clear that stimuli that lead to different aesthetic judgments can be said to arouse different amounts of affect. Furthermore, aesthetic objects vary along other dimensions than stimulus intensity, and attempts to include new dimensions in arousal theories increase their scope but also augment the measurement difficulties encountered.

For the sake of simplicity, we have divided our discussion of arousal theories into what we shall call sensory theories and aesthetic theories. This is probably an oversimplification, but we use "sensory" for theories relating affect to stimulus intensity in one sense modality; whereas we use "aesthetic" to refer to theories relating affect to sensory patterning, perceptual configuration, or combinations of sense modalities.

The basic paradigm for all of these types of arousal theory seems to be the discrepancy hypothesis. In general terms, the discrepancy hypothesis is difficult to state because it must be stated in terms of discrepancies from something and the "something" differs with the type of theory. If we let the "something" be called X for the time being, then we can say that in general the discrepancy hypothesis states that affect is a curvilinear function of the magnitude of discrepancy of a sensory or perceptual event from X. Specifically, a small discrepancy from X produces positive affect and a large discrepancy from X produces negative affect. This statement is obviously exquisitely imprecise, both because X and "a perceptual event" are left undefined and because "large" and "small" are undefined.

Absolute Stimulus Arousal Theory

If we now define X as zero stimulus intensity (or at least a point below the sensory threshold), then we can say that any stimulus (perceptual event) in that modality that is a small discrepancy from zero intensity, i.e., of moderate intensity, should produce positive affect; whereas any stimulus that is a large discrepancy, i.e., of extreme intensity, should produce negative affect. This is the statement of an absolute sensory arousal theory. Arousal refers to the elicitation of positive or negative affect within the organism. The term "arousal" in this sense could also apply to the elicitation of negative affect by strong stimulation in stimulus-intensity-reduction theory. According to reduction theories, however, behavior is thought to be initiated to reduce stimulus intensity, whereas according to arousal theories behavior may be initiated to increase stimulus intensity. Thus, reduction theories consider changes in negative affect to be primary; arousal theories, although they include changes in negative affect, also consider the arousal of positive affect.

To return to our example above of an absolute sensory arousal theory, we may diagram such a theory as shown in Figure 3.3.

Relative Stimulus Arousal Theory

The concept of adaptation that was important in explaining the arousal jag is also important in arousal theories based on the discrepancy hypothesis. Absolute stimulus arousal theories seem to account best for evidence from experiments in which the effects of adaptation are minimal, either because they are controlled or because they are carried out in sense modalities in which adaptation occurs slowly.

In order to state the relative stimulus arousal form of the discrepancy hypothesis, the concept of adaptation level is substituted for X in the general statement. It then reads: small discrepancies of stimulus intensity from the adaptation level of the organism produce positive affect; large discrepancies produce negative affect. The schematic diagram is essentially the same as that reproduced in Figure 3.3, except that the discrepancies along the abscissa are now relative to the level of adaptation of the organism, which corresponds to the zero point in Figure 3.3. In physical terms, the absolute levels of stimulation that produce either positive or negative affect may vary considerably depending on the state of adaptation of the organism. The abscissa in Figure 3.3, therefore, must be changed from absolute to relative levels of stimulation — relative to the adaptation level. The predictive power of the model should be increased

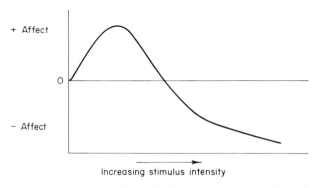

Increasing stimulus intensity

Fig. 3.3. Schematic presentation of an absolute-sensory-arousal theory based on the discrepancy hypothesis.

by assuming that affect from a specific stimulus is a function of the state of the organism as well as of the characteristics of the stimulus since it seems quite plausible that affect is dependent on the state of the organism. It is a commonplace observation that what is pleasant to me today may be boring or unpleasant tomorrow.

Again we are faced with a possible increase in the power of a model that is dependent on the solution of difficult measurement problems. In a relative stimulus arousal theory, the direct correlates of affect are to be sought in the perceptual realm rather than in the domain of physically measured quantities such as stimulus intensity. First, it is necessary to determine the adaptation level of the organism; second, it is necessary to determine perceived discrepancies from it. In most sense modalities the approximate relationship between physical measures and perceived differences is known. Using the Weber-Fechner Law, one can assume a logarithmic function and thus avoid the psychophysical measurement of perceived differences. The determination of the adaptation level can be done using Helson's (1959) definition, namely, the stimulus "which calls forth the neutral response can be regarded as the stimulus to which the organism is attuned or adapted, and its value is said to be the *adaptation level*" (p. 356).

In at least one sense modality, the relative sensory arousal model based on the discrepancy from an adaptation level so defined takes on a slightly different form from the one shown in Figure 3.3. When temperature is considered—the perception of heat and cold—the organism is adapted to a certain temperature, and discrepancies from that temperature diverge in two directions: namely, warmer and colder than the adaptation level. This produces what has been called the "butterfly curve," which is made up of two curves of the type presented in Figure 3.3. The schematic diagram of this is presented in Figure 3.4.

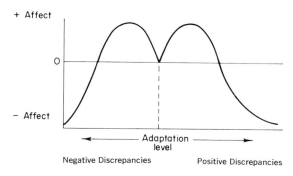

FIG. 3.4 The "butterfly curve" of the discrepancy hypothesis.

Perceptual and Cognitive Complexity Theories

The most general statement of the discrepancy hypothesis could apply to any experience of an organism. Moderate discrepancies along any dimension of experience, either singly or in combinations of several dimensions, might lead to positive affect; while large discrepancies might lead to negative affect. This should be so if the discrepancy hypothesis is a basic and general law that applies in general to single sense modalities and the numerous combinations that make up experience. The saying "variety is the spice of life" might be said to be the layman's interpretation of the relationship between varied experience and affect. Phenomenologically, the discrepancy hypothesis appears to have some validity in the broader realm of experience, especially aesthetic experience. The theme and variations is a common device in music, as is syncopation of rhythm. Both of these examples may arouse positive affect, and could be seen as small discrepancies from expectations. Similar examples might be drawn from the areas of literature, poetry, and painting. At this general level, the discrepancy hypothesis takes the following form: small discrepancies in (perceptual or cognitive) complexity (of the stimulus configuration which forms the immediate experience of the person) from the expectation level of the person produce positive affect; large discrepancies produce negative affect. The concept of expectation level is assumed to be analogous to that of the adaptation level. However, the expectation level is apparently a learned phenomenon, and is presumably conscious in the sense that it can be verbally reported. The adaptation level, although built up by experience, cannot be said to be "learned" in the same sense, and consciousness is more or less irrelevant to the adapting of sense organs.

The measurement difficulties encountered in attempting to test the discrepancy hypothesis at the aesthetic level are formidable. The criteria for an exact determination of the expectation level are vague although the problem could be attacked using some of the techniques developed for measuring the level of aspiration. (It should be noted that the apparent close parallel between the concepts of aspiration level and expectation level may be misleading. We are using expectation level here purely in terms of expected stimulus configurations, as in the case of a well-known and hence highly predictable melody. This is in the aesthetic realm. As we shall see later, the aspiration level has a strong component of self reference; it is an expectation about how I will perform, with a prejudged evaluation of what is a good and what is a poor performance.)

In addition to the problems encountered in attempting to establish the expectation level, the scale along which discrepancies are to be measured is highly ambiguous. Using the distinction between absolute and relative theories, we can conceive of two different possibilities, and, as in the case of stimulus arousal theories, some combination of the two will probably give the best approximation. If absolute configurational, or cognitive, complexity is taken as the relevant dimension, then it seems plausible that extreme stimulus simplicity could be boring, moderate complexity pleasing, and extreme complexity displeasing. This statement has some validity, but we can easily think of some art works that might be said to be elegant in their simplicity, i.e., extreme simplicity is the most pleasing. Obviously, simplicity-complexity may have to be defined in a relative way, and again, it seems most important that it be defined relative to the past experience of the perceiving organism.

Assuming that past experience leads to expectations, the relative form of the configurational-complexity or cognitive-complexity theory forces us to measure some residue of past experience and to compare present experience with it. The absolute qualities of the experience are useful only insofar as the relationship between them and perceived experience is known. Expectation carries with it the connotation of prediction. If I expect an event to occur, I am implicitly predicting it. If the event does not occur or does not occur in the way that I predicted (expected) it, then my prediction is disconfirmed. To the extent that my prediction is disconfirmed, the event has been discrepant from my expectation level. Thus the predictability (deviation from randomness) of events might be a way to approach the measurement problems raised here. Recent advances in the field of information theory present a technique for measuring the predictability or randomness of stimulus events and, as we shall see in Chapter 4, some attempts have been made to use this technique in assessing the discrepancy hypothesis in the realm of complex stimuli such as music.

Three differences between adaptation level and expectation level. There is, apparently, a need for greater clarity about the distinction between adaptation level and expectation level. We will, therefore, digress briefly to record three possible differences that may help in clarifying this distinction.

Investigation of physiological adaptation level seems to lead to the conclusion that, although past experience is extremely important in determining the physiological adaptation level, we should not conclude that this past experience leads to learning with respect to adaptation level. We would not say that a physiological adaptation level is learned, for instance, in the case of dark adaptation or temperature adaptation. On the other hand, when we turn to psychological expectation levels, we are struck by the importance of past experience in a way that is somehow analogous to past experience with regard to the adaptation level. However, with expectation levels learning seems to be clearly indicated. This, then, may be the first and biggest distinction between adaptation levels and expectation levels. (Parenthetically we might add that this distinction may be very important in the origin of motives. Motives, which are theoretically the result of expectation levels, are themselves assumed to be learned. Thus, if we base the learning of motives on the changes of physiological adaptation level, we have only one type of learning involved, that is, the learning of the response and the cues which are associated with affect produced by a change in adaptation level. However, with expectation levels, we have the added complication that the expectation level is based on a probability learning phenomenon that itself forms the basis for the learning of motives.)

Other differences that occur to us, but that may not be as important, are that apparently the adaptation level changes quite slowly, whereas the expectation level may change quickly or instantaneously. Furthermore, physiological adaptation levels are probably based only on past experience of a very recent period in the history of the organism and always include the immediate past for that sense modality. By comparison the expectation level must be defined in terms of a subjective schematization of a stimulus class, and the important past experiences refer only to this ill-defined stimulus class. The relevant experiences may have occurred over a long history of the organism's interaction with the environment, and the immediate past experience of the organism may be irrelevant to this particular stimulus class.

Reduction and Arousal Aspects of Freud's Theory of Motivation

In the writings of Sigmund Freud, we find discussions of almost all the basic problems of motivation. However, it is difficult to make categorical statements about Freud's theory. This is because of Freud's voluminous writings and his perfect willingness, apparently, to change his position without informing the reader that his present position may be quite different from the one presented in earlier writings. It is well known that "early" Freud is quite different from "middle" or "late" Freud in many respects. This, plus the fact that Freud never set himself the formal task of writing his theory of motivation as such, makes it impossible to present "Freud's theory of motivation." However, a perusal of some of Freud's ideas with regard to motivation reveals that he has addressed himself, at one time or another, to most of the basic problems of motivation. The concepts used by many later theorists can be traced to Freud's pioneering statements.

It is not the intent of this section to be complete either in presenting Freudian theory or even in presenting all of Freud's ideas on motivation. Rather we shall raise what appear to us to be the most important problems discussed by Freud that have been reflected in the more modern theories to be discussed in Chapter 4. Thus, we are using Freud as the background against which to present certain problems with the hope that seeing their origin in his writings will clarify the use made of the concepts by later theorists. For this purpose, we shall concentrate, primarily, on Freud's writings on metapsychology, specifically his discussion of "The Instincts and their Vicissitudes" (1915).

The basic motivational concept that Freud uses is expressed by the German word *Trieb,* or *Naturtrieb.* In most translations this is rendered "instinct" in English. As Fenichel (1945) has pointed out *Trieb* might have been rendered "drive" or "motive," thus avoiding the difficulties that have been encountered with the word "instinct."

> However, the expression *Trieb* which Freud uses does not signify exactly the same thing as the English expression *instinct,* as it is customarily translated. Inherent in the concept of instinct is the idea that it represents an inherited and unchangeable pattern; in the German concept of *Trieb* this unchangeability is by no means implied. On the contrary, the *Triebe* obviously are changed in aim and object under influences stemming from the environment, and Freud was even of the opinion that they originated under the same influence. This incorrect equating of *instinct* and *Trieb* has created misunderstandings" (Fenichel, 1945, p. 12).

As is well known in psychology, the word "instinct" came to be a catch-all for explanation and fell into disrepute (cf. Beach, 1955). Unfortunately, the same pitfall is inherent in drive or motive as an explanatory concept. Simply stated, the pitfall involves explaining specific behavior by the instinct that may be named for the behavior, but which gives no further insight into the conditions that lead to the behavior. Instinct may be seen as "human nature," and the term carries the connotation of being a natural or innate aspect. This is also the connotation of *Naturtrieb.*

FREUD AS A STIMULUS-INTENSITY REDUCTION THEORIST

Freud set out in "The Instincts and their Vicissitudes" to give more meaning to his concept that is translated "instinct." He points out that this is not a clear and sharply defined concept of the type which might be seen as necessary as a basic concept. He says: "In actual fact no science, not even the most exact, begins with such definitions. The true beginning of scientific activity consists rather in describing phenomena and then in proceeding to group, classify and correlate them. Even at the stage of description it is not possible to avoid applying certain abstract ideas to the material in hand . . ." (p. 60). Such an idea, says Freud, is that of an instinct. "Let us try to ascertain what is comprised in this conception by approaching it from different angles."

> First, from the angle of *physiology.* This has given us the concept of a "stimulus" and the pattern of the reflex arc, according to which a stimulus applied to living tissue (nervous substance) *from* the outside is discharged by action *to* the outside. This action is expedient in so far as it withdraws the stimulated substance from the influence of the stimulus, removes it out of its range of operation.

What is the relation of "instinct" to "stimulus"? There is nothing to prevent our subsuming the concept of "instinct" under that of "stimulus" and saying that an instinct is a stimulus applied to the mind. But we are immediately set on our guard against *equating* instinct and mental stimulus. There are obviously other stimuli to the mind besides those of an instinctual kind, stimuli which behave far more like physiological ones. For example, when a strong light falls on the eye, it is not an instinctual stimulus; it *is* one, however, when a dryness of the mucous membrane of the pharynx or an irritation of the mucous membrane of the stomach makes itself felt.

We have now obtained the material necessary for distinguishing between instinctual stimuli and other (physiological) stimuli that operate on the mind. In the first place, an instinctual stimulus does not arise from the external world but from within the organism itself. For this reason it operates differently upon the mind and different actions are necessary in order to remove it. Further, all that is essential in a stimulus is covered if we assume that it operates with a single impact, so that it can be disposed of by a single expedient action. A typical instance of this is motor flight from the source of stimulation. These impacts may, of course, be repeated and summated, but that makes no difference to our notion of the process and to the conditions for the removal of the stimulus. An instinct, on the other hand, never operates as a force giving a *momentary* impact but always as a *constant* one. Moreover, since it impinges not from without but from within the organism, no flight can avail against it. A better term for an instinctual stimulus is a "need." What does away with a need is "satisfaction." This can be attained only by an appropriate ("adequate") alteration of the internal source of stimulation.

Let us imagine ourselves in the situation of an almost entirely helpless living organism, as yet unoriented in the world, which is receiving stimuli in its nervous substance. This organism will very soon be in a position to make a first distinction and a first orientation. On the one hand, it will be aware of stimuli which can be avoided by muscular action (flight); these it ascribes to an external world. On the other hand, it will also be aware of stimuli against which such action is of no avail and whose character of constant pressure persists in spite of it; these stimuli are the signs of an internal world, the evidence of instinctual needs. The perceptual substance of the living organism will thus have found in the efficacy of its muscular activity a basis for distinguishing between an "outside" and an "inside."

We thus arrive at the essential nature of instincts in the first place by considering their main characteristics — their origin in sources of stimulation within the organism and their appearance as a constant force — and from this we deduce one of their further features, namely, that no actions of flight avail against them. In the course of this discussion, however, we cannot fail to be struck by something that obliges us to make a further admission. In order to guide us in dealing with the field of psychological phenomena, we do not merely apply certain conventions to our empirical material as basic *concepts;* we also make use of a number of complicated *postulates.* We have already alluded to the most important of these, and all we need now do is state it expressly. This postulate is of a biological nature, and makes use of the concept of "purpose" (or perhaps of expediency) and runs as follows: the nervous system is an apparatus which has the function of getting rid of the stimuli that reach it, or of reducing them to the lowest possible level; or which, if it were feasible, would maintain itself in an altogether unstimulated condition. Let us for the present not take exception to the indefiniteness of this idea and let us assign to the nervous system the task—speaking in general terms—of *mastering stimuli*. We then see how greatly the simple pattern of the physiological reflex is complicated by the introduction of instincts. External stimuli impose only the single task of withdrawing from them; this is accomplished by muscular movements, one of which eventually achieves that aim and thereafter, being the expedient movement, becomes a hereditary disposition. Instinctual stimuli, which originate from within the organism, cannot be dealt with by this mechanism. Thus they make far higher demands on the nervous system and cause it to undertake involved and interconnected activities by which the external world is so changed as to afford satisfaction to the internal source of stimulation. Above all, they oblige the nervous system to renounce its ideal intention of keeping off stimuli, for they maintain an incessant and unavoidable afflux of stimulation. We may therefore well conclude that instincts and not external stimuli are the true motive forces behind the advances that have led the nervous system, with its unlimited capacities, to its present high level of development. There is naturally nothing to prevent our supposing that the instincts themselves are, at least in part, precipitates of the effects of external stimulation, which in the course of phylogenesis have brought about modifications in the living substance.

When we further find that the activity of even the most highly developed mental apparatus is subject to the pleasure principle, i.e. is automatically regulated by feelings belonging to the pleasure-unpleasure series, we can hardly reject the further hypothesis that these feelings reflect the manner in which the process of mastering stimuli takes place—certainly in the sense that unpleasurable feelings are connected with an increase and pleasurable feelings with a decrease of stimulus. We will, however, carefully preserve this assumption in its present highly indefinite form, until we succeed, if that is possible, in discovering what sort of relation exists between pleasure and unpleasure, on the one hand, and fluctuations in the amounts of stimulus affecting mental life, on the other. It is certain that many very various relations of this kind, and not very simple ones, are possible.

If now we apply ourselves to considering mental life from a *biological* point of view, an "instinct" appears to us as a concept on the frontier between the mental and the somatic, as the psychical representative of the stimuli originating from within the organism and reaching the mind, as a measure of the demand made upon the mind for work in consequence of its connection with the body.

We are now in a position to discuss certain terms which are used in reference to the concept of an instinct—for example, its "pressure," its "aim," its "object" and its "source."

By the pressure [*Drang*] of an instinct we understand its motor factor, the amount of force or the measure of the demand for work which it represents. The characteristic of exercising pressure is common to all instincts; it is in fact their very essence. Every instinct is a piece of activity; if we speak loosely of passive instincts, we can only mean instincts whose aim is passive.

The aim [*Ziel*] of an instinct is in every instance satisfaction, which can only be obtained by removing the state of stimulation at the source of the instinct. But although the ultimate aim of each instinct remains unchangeable, there may yet be different paths leading to the same ultimate aim; so that an instinct may be found to have various nearer or intermediate aims, which are combined or interchanged with one another. Experience permits us also to speak of instincts which are "inhibited in their aim," in the case of processes which are allowed to make some advance towards instinctual satisfaction but are then inhibited or deflected. We may suppose that even processes of this kind involve a partial satisfaction.

The object [*Objekt*] of an instinct is the thing in regard to which or through which the instinct is able to achieve its aim. It is what is most variable about an instinct and is not originally connected with it, but becomes assigned to it only in consequence of being peculiarly fitted to make satisfaction possible. The object is not necessarily something extraneous: it may equally well be a part of the subject's own body. It may be changed any number of times in the course of the vicissitudes which the instinct undergoes during its existence; and highly important parts are played by this displacement of instinct. It may happen that the same object serves for the satisfaction of several instincts simultaneously, a phenomenon which Adler has called a "confluence" of instincts [*Triebverschränkung*]. A particularly close attachment of the instinct to its object is distinguished by the term "fixation." This frequently occurs at very early periods of the development of an instinct and puts an end to its mobility through its intense opposition to detachment.

By the source [*Quelle*] of an instinct is meant the somatic process which occurs in an organ or part of the body and whose stimulus is represented in mental life by an instinct. We do not know whether this process is invariably of a chemical nature or whether it may also correspond to the release of other, e.g. mechanical, forces. The study of the sources of instincts lies outside the scope of psychology. Although instincts are wholly determined by their origin in a somatic source, in mental life we know them only by their aims. An exact knowledge of the sources of an instinct is not invariably necessary for purposes of psychological investigation; sometimes its source may be inferred from its aim.

Are we to suppose that the different instincts which originate in the body and operate on the mind are also distinguished by different *qualities,* and that that is why they behave in qualitatively different ways in mental life? This supposition does not seem to be justified; we are much more likely to find the simpler assumption sufficient—that the instincts are all qualitatively alike and owe the effect they make only to the amount of excitation they carry, or perhaps, in addition, to certain functions of that quantity. What distinguishes from one another the mental effects produced by the various instincts may be traced to the difference in their sources. In any event, it is only in a later connection that we shall be able to make plain what the problem of the quality of instincts signifies (Freud, 1915b, pp. 118–123).

In this quote, Freud discusses each of the problems posed by the sets of concepts we presented at the beginning of this chapter. He is clearly attempting to put together the physiological and the psychological as he says ". . . instinct is a borderland concept between the mental and the physical . . . ." The concept of instinct itself is seen as a drive or stimulation that constitutes a persistent force. He takes the stand that the important stimulation for the concept of instinct is internal to the organism from which no flight is possible. He does, however, discuss briefly the effects of external stimulation. The concept of affect is contained within his notion of pleasure and pain, and he postulates that mental apparatus is automatically regulated by feelings of pleasure and pain, and that these reflect the process of mastering stimuli. He stresses pain (negative affect) and correlates it with increases in stimulation, while pleasure (positive affect) is associated with decreases in stimulation. The connection between stimulus mastery and the consequent change in pleasure-pain is similar to the emphases of more recent theorists on events consequent to the behavior being studied. The section dealing with the nervous system as an apparatus whose function it is to reduce stimulation is a classic statement of the general position of tension-reduction theories, especially, the drive-stimulus-reduction theory of Dollard and Miller (1950).

Freud and Arousal Phenomena

This magnificent statement from Freud speaks for itself and certainly is the forerunner of many of the theories that we shall examine in the next chapter. From it we might conclude that Freud was a thoroughgoing drive-stimulus-reduction theorist. Within this very quote, however, Freud shows some apprehension in assuming a simple relationship between pleasure and pain and stimulation. This, as we shall see, has developed into an extremely controversial problem, since *(a)* Freud's rough statement implies that the most pleasurable condition of mankind should be a state of minimal stimulation, and *(b)* the relationship between the pleasure-pain continuum and stimulation is highly ambiguous. For instance, is the decrease of an extremely intense (painful) stimulus pleasurable or merely less painful? Is it not possible that increasing stimulation under some conditions may be pleasurable? Freud makes it particularly clear that he feels it necessary to account for the apparent pleasurable aspects of increasing stimulation in his account of sexual forepleasure. He depends primarily on the ultimate reduction of tension for his explanation, but it is clear that the contradiction of the theory implicit in evidence that some tension is sought out and apparently pleasurable bothered him. In dealing with these phenomena, he comes close to an arousal-jag-type position.

> The fact that sexual excitement possesses the character of tension raises a problem the solution of which is no less difficult than it would be important in helping us to understand the sexual process. If the tension of sexual excitement is counted as an unpleasurable feeling, we are at once brought up against the fact that it is also undoubtably felt as pleasurable. In every case in which tension is produced by sexual processes, it is accompanied by pleasure; even in the preparatory changes in the genitals a feeling of satisfaction of some kind is plainly to be observed (Freud, 1905a, p. 209).

There are then two sources of "pleasure," one apparently the result of tension increase, the other the result of tension decrease.

This distinction between the one kind of pleasure due to the excitation of the erotogenic zones and the other kind due to the discharge of the sexual substances deserves, I think to be made more concrete by a difference in nomenclature. The former may be suitably described as "forepleasure" in contrast to the "end-pleasure" or pleasure of satisfaction derived from the sexual act (Freud, 1905a, p. 210).

We remain in complete ignorance both of the origin and of the nature of the sexual tension which arises simultaneously with the pleasure when erotogenic zones are satisfied (Freud, 1905a, p. 212).

In another place he says:

It will be remembered that we have taken the view that the principle which governs all mental processes is a special case of Fechner's "tendency toward stability," and have accordingly attributed to the mental apparatus the purpose of reducing to nothing or at least of keeping as low as possible, the sum of excitation which flow in upon it. . . . Every unpleasure ought thus to coincide with a heightening, and every pleasure with a lowering, of mental tension due to stimulus; . . . but such a view cannot be correct. It seems that in the series of feelings of tension we have a direct sense of the increase and decrease of the amounts of stimulus, and it cannot be doubted that there are pleasurable tensions and unpleasurable relaxation of tension (Freud, 1924, pp. 159–160).

Freud attributes the pleasure involved in drama, the purpose of which is to arouse "terror and pity" according to Aristotle, to a type of sexual forepleasure. ". . . The consequent enjoyment corresponds on the one hand to the relief produced by a thorough discharge and on the other hand, no doubt, to an accompanying sexual excitation; for the latter, as we may suppose, appears as a by-product whenever an affect is aroused, and gives people the sense, which they so much desire, of a raising of the potential of their psychical state" (Freud, 1905b, p. 305).

Ultimately, however, Freud seems to resort to the tension-reduction that follows excitation to explain forepleasure in a way that reminds one of the arousal-jag. "I am of the opinion that all the aesthetic pleasure we gain from the works of imaginative writers is of the same type as this "fore-pleasure," and that the true enjoyment of literature proceeds from the release of tensions in our minds" (Freud, 1908, p. 183).

In discussing wit and humor, Freud makes a distinction between harmless and tendency wit and play-pleasure and removal pleasure.

The effect of tendency-wit may now be formulated as follows: It enters the service of tendencies in order to produce new pleasure by removing suppressions and repressions. This it does by using wit-pleasure as fore-pleasure. When we now review its development, we may say that wit has remained true to its nature from beginning to end. It begins as play in order to obtain pleasure from the free use of words and thoughts. As soon as the growing reason forbids this senseless play with words and thoughts, it turns to the jest or joke in order to hold to these sources of pleasure and in order to be able to gain new pleasure from the liberation of the absurd. In the role of harmless wit it assists the thoughts and fortifies them against the impugnment of the critical judgment whereby it makes use of the principle of intermingling the pleasure-sources. Finally, it enters into the great struggling suppressed tendencies in order to remove inner inhibitions in accordance with the principle of fore-pleasure. Reason, critical judgment, and suppression, these are the forces which it combats in turn. It firmly holds on to the original word-pleasure sources, and beginning with the stage of the jest opens for itself new pleasure sources by removing inhibition. The pleasure which it produces, be it play-pleasure or removal-pleasure, can at all times be traced to the economy of psychic expenditure, in so far as such a conception does not contradict the nature of pleasure, and proves itself productive also in other fields (Freud, 1916, p. 726).

Removal pleasure is clearly a concept that fits the tension reduction or at least the arousal-jag version of an ultimate reduction theory. Play-pleasure is thought to be reducible to a reduction principle also, but its origin in children's play with words is hard to mold into this rubric. Apparently, children simply enjoy verbal play that has no connection with a potential change in tension or stimulation. Such play-pleasure, as found in harmless wit, may result from the economy of psychic expenditure (a reduction mechanism), but in its most primitive form children's play seems to have an "intrinsically" pleasurable quality. The original "motive" for play may be the exception to the reduction rule, but as nonsense play develops it is taken as an attempt to escape the seriousness of life.

When the child learns to control the vocabulary of its mother tongue it apparently takes great pleasure in "experimenting playfully" with that material . . . it connects words without regard for their meaning in order to obtain pleasure from the rhyme and rhythm . . . .

I believe that *whatever the motive which actuated the child when it began such playings,* in his further development the child indulges in them fully conscious that they are nonsensical and derives pleasure from the stimulus which is interdicted by reason. He now makes use of play in order to withdraw from the pressure of critical reason (Freud, 1916, p. 717, italics added).

Ultimately the explanation depends on a reduction principle, but play, from which the behavior develops, is recalcitrant and resists being subsumed under the principle in its purest form.

More advanced play than that with words leads Freud to another concept of importance to the psychology of motivation and that is the concept of mastery. In the famous discussion of the child seeking to control and master the anxiety produced by his mother leaving him, Freud derived the child's play with a spool from the principle of reduction of anxiety through mastery.

This good little boy, however, had an occasional disturbing habit of taking any small objects he could get hold of and throwing them away from him into a corner, under a bed, and so on, so that hunting for his toys and picking them up was often quite a business. As he did this he gave vent to a loud, long-drawn-out "o-o-o-o" accompanied by an expression of interest and satisfaction. His mother and the writer of the present account were agreed in thinking that this was not a mere interjection but represented the German word *"fort"* [gone]. I eventually realized that it was a game and that the only use he made of any of his toys was to play "gone" with them. One day I made an observation which confirmed my view. The child had a wooden reel with a piece of string tied round it. . . . What he did was to hold the reel by the string and very skillfully throw it over the edge of his curtained cot, so that it disappeared into it, at the same time uttering his expressive "o-o-o-o." He then pulled the reel out of the cot again by the string and hailed its re-appearance with a joyful "da" [there]. This, then was the complete game — disappearance and return. . . .

The interpretation of the game then became obvious. It was related to the child's great cultural achievement — the instinctual renunciation (that is, the renunciation of instinctual satisfaction) which he made in allowing his mother to go away without protesting. He compensated himself for this, as it were, by himself staging the disappearance and return of the objects within his reach. . . . The child cannot possibly have felt his mother's departure as something agreeable or even indifferent. How then does his repetition of this distressing experience as a game fit in with the pleasure principle? (Freud, 1920, pp. 14–15).

This passage is used by Freud to show how play may be used to gain control and security (through mastery or aggression) in an anxiety arousing situation, again a tension reduction explanation in which unpleasure is courted so that it can be mastered. The emphasis is on the resulting security or aggression toward the mother rather than the possible excitement inherent in an uncertain situation. The need of the child for security in this situation, and in the evidence that children demand that stories be repeated endlessly in exact detail was seen by Freud as the origin of the repetition compulsion. Freud saw these phenomena as the result of a need to return to a former and more secure state, a reduction of tension, a result of the principle of inertia, ultimately the manifestation of the death instinct. Schachtel (1959) and Brown (1959) have criticized Freud's accentuation of the negative and pointed to the apparent positive seeking of greater interaction with the environment, an arousal rather than a reduction explanation of mastery.

Thus, much of what impressed Freud as repetition compulsion in the child's need to repeat a story or a play activity over and over again turns out to be neither the result of a desire to return to an earlier state nor the effect of the principle of inertia, but an essential requirement for the gradual exploration of the environment, the world of reality, and the child's relations to it. . . . The enjoyment in doing that which one already masters, as compared with the hazards of any new venture, are ever present competitors in man's life. Their relative strength may result in an empty, fear-conditioned inertia which dreads the new and prefers the familiar, or in the victory of the desire to explore something new and to have significant experiences (Schachtel, 1959, p. 265).

We have presented evidence that Freud encountered problems in the consistent application of the tension-reduction model. This should not obscure the fact that he was attempting to use it as a universal principle. The value of noting exceptions is that we see in them the roots of modern concepts such as *(a)* arousal jag, *(b)* arousal of pleasure as in play, and even *(c)* a positive orientation toward mastery of the environment that is not too different from competence motivation or even personal causation.

Chapter 4

AFFECT AND STIMULATION II:
SPECIFIC MODERN APPLICATIONS

Drive-Stimulus Reduction Theories

Until recently theories of motivation have been dominated by some form of stimulus-intensity reduction. This predominant influence comes from Hullian drive-reduction theory, which in turn developed not only from Freudian postulations but also from such ancestors as the notions that drives are the result of bodily deficits (needs), that the body in its wisdom attempts to correct these deficits by homeostatic mechanisms, and that these phenomena are all bound up with survival of the organism.

We shall not go into the details of these early theories. However, to ·show the extent of their influence, Hunt (1963) traces the roots to Claude Bernard (1859), Walter B. Cannon (1915), and Curt Richter (1922, 1927). Bernard and Richter stressed the importance of humoral influences (chemical or hormonal components in bodily fluids) in motivation. Cannon developed a local-stimulus theory of drives and discussed the homeostatic "wisdom of the body" (Cannon, 1932). Hunt cites all of the following as essentially assuming drive to be some sort of noxious stimulus that impels action—Carr (1925), Dashiell (1925, 1928), Dollard and Miller (1950), Freeman (1934, 1948), Freud (1900, 1915), Guthrie (1938), Holt (1931), Hull (1943), Melton (1941), Miller and Dollard (1941), Moss (1924), Mowrer (1950), Thorndike (1913), and Warden (1931).

So much for an attempt to show the extent of the general notion of drive reduction. Let us note that since about 1930 the emphasis has been on a drive as a stimulus, either internal or external, among learning theorists such as Hull, Miller, and Mowrer. We shall be dealing primarily with drive theories that have sprung up alongside learning theories in the brains of behaviorists.

In this tradition, one might sketch the development as swinging from early emphasis on general internal states (needs), to emphasis on specific stimuli (drives), first produced by bodily deficits (hunger, thirst) and then by external pain-inflicting stimuli (shock). With the relaxation among behaviorists of the proscription of going beneath the skin (into the "sawdust" or the "black box"), we are seeing a return to discussion of internal processes. These processes may be hypothetical, such as mechanisms postulated by Hebb (1949, 1955), the hope, fear, relief, and disappointment mediators of Mowrer (1960a,b), or the "go mechanism" of Miller (1963). Or they may be based on actual findings such as those of Olds and Milner (1954) involving pleasure centers in the brain, or evidence for motivational arousal involving the reticular arousal system (Berlyne, 1960, 1963).

The behaviorist learning theorists of the post-Hullian era are returning to a direction which Morgan (1957) attributes to physiological psychologists of 1930. "Thus it came about that, in the 1930's, the stimulus concept of drive had established a strong foothold in behavior theory. At just this time, however, physiological research on the mechanisms of drive was given new impetus by (a) biochemical advances in the areas of endocrinology and nutrition, which permitted the experimental manipulation of elements in the internal environment, and (b) by the appearance of more refined methods of stimulating and destroying limited regions of the nervous system, which enabled investigators to correlate changes in drive with activity in certain neural centers and systems" (Morgan, 1957, pp. 4–5). Morgan (1943) himself moved toward internal determinants by developing the notion of the "central motive state."

It might be said that nonphysiologically oriented psychologists are belatedly arriving at the conclusion that central states are important. Be that as it may, the notion of the drive as a stimulus has had tremendous value as a spur to research and theorizing. Since this book is more behaviorally than physiologically oriented, we shall trace the notion of drive in the period since 1930.

DRIVE-NEED DISTINCTION

Motivation theory of about this time was faced with a paradox. On the one hand, Cannon (1915) had supplied ample evidence that there were specific stimuli, such as hunger pangs or the dryness of the mouth and throat in thirst, that were associated with bodily needs. From such data, he developed his local theory of hunger and thirst. However, a behaviorist correlating behavior with some underlying motivational state could not be satisfied with these specific stimuli, since it was obvious that consummatory behavior persisted after the dryness of the throat was relieved and after hunger pangs ceased. On the other hand, bodily deficits, although eventually reduced by eating or drinking, were probably not affected by the time eating or drinking had stopped. That is, actual assimilation does not occur immediately upon consumption. Furthermore, there does not appear to be a perfect relationship between physiological need and behavior induced by motivational factors. Thus a moderately hungry organism may appear behaviorally more driven than an extremely hungry one, and an organism that needs oxygen may not appear to be motivated at all.

For these reasons the concept of drive was distinguished from that of need, the latter being used to refer to physiological deficit and the former most often considered to be a construct that is related more closely to behavior than to need, but which is roughly associated with need (see for instance Brown, 1961, p. 67, or Morgan, 1957). Even the two references cited will indicate the fact that agreement on a definition of drive is hard to come by. Brown assumes probably the most prevalent one, namely, that used by the Hullians. Morgan stresses "energy" and says that drive "implies movement, activity, striving, or effort" (p. 2). They both agree that needs frequently, but not always, give rise to drives.

Hull and Drive-Reduction Theory

For Hull (1943), drive is an intervening variable. "It is important to note in this connection that the general concept of drive (D) tends strongly to have the systematic status of an intervening variable or X, never directly observable" (p. 57). He explains his notion of the intervening variable as follows: "Whenever an attempt is made to penetrate the invisible world of the molecular, scientists frequently and usefully employ logical constructs, intervening variables, or symbols to facilitate their thinking. These symbols or X's represent entities or processes which, if existent, would account for certain events in the observable molar world" (p. 21). He then cites habit as an example and stresses the importance of anchoring intervening to observable antecedent and consequent events. He points to hazards involved in using such logical constructs but says: "But once (1) the dynamic relationship existing between the amount of the hypothetical entity (X) and some antecedent determining condition (A) which can be observed, and (2) the dynamic relationship of the hypothetical entity to some third consequent phenomenon or event (B) which also can be directly observed, become fairly well known, the scientific hazard largely disappears" (p. 22).

Chapter 5 of the *Principles of Behavior* is primarily devoted to an attempt to pin down antecedent conditions for drive through manipulation of hunger, thirst, or sex. Thus Hull cites Wada (1922) as showing the relationship between stomach contractions (measured by a small balloon swallowed by the human subjects) and general restless movements. Similar evidence is taken from Richter (1927) and Wang (1923) for sexual variations and activity in rats.

At the end of the chapter, he has a note on the "problems associated with the use of drive (D) as an intervening variable" (p. 66). He points out that two equations are needed to pin down the antecedent and consequent relationships. "In the case of hunger, for example, there must be an equation expressing the degree of drive or motivation as a function of the number of hours food privation, say, and there must be a second equation expressing the vigor of organismic action as a function of the degree of drive (D) or motivation, combined in some manner with habit strength" (p. 66). He goes on to say that it is relatively easy to determine the relationship between hours of deprivation and vigor of the reaction, "but it is an exceedingly difficult task to break such an equation up into the two really meaningful component equations involving hunger drive (D) or motivation as an intervening variable. It may confidently be predicted that many writers with a positivistic or anti-theoretical inclination will reject such a procedure as both futile and unsound. From the point of view of systematic theory such a procedure, if successful, would present an immense economy. This statement is made on the assumption that motivation (D) as such, whether its origin be food privation, electric shock, or whatever, bears a certain constant relationship to action intensity in combination with other factors, such as habit strength. If this fundamental relationship could be determined once and for all, the necessity for its determination for each special drive could not then exist, and so much useless labor would be avoided. Unfortunately it may turn out that what we now call drive and motivation will prove to be so heterogeneous that no single equation can represent the motivational potentiality of any two needs" (pp. 66–67).

This quote shows the thinking behind Hull's theory that drive is a general energizing construct not specific to certain needs. It also shows the necessity for determining independently levels of drive and the effect of these on behavior. As we shall see, the relationship between hunger measured by body weight loss or hours of deprivation, and drive measured in amount of food consumed, turned out to be very complicated; although roughly the more hunger, the more consumption. We see then that even for hunger it is difficult to investigate the underlying equations relating behavior to motivation. Hull recognized the difficulty and proceeded both to attempt to investigate the problem and to build his theory on it.

This problem has been stressed because it became the basic problem of the 1950's when manipulatory, exploratory, and curiosity behavior of animals demanded explanation and drive-reduction theorists took the first step by assuming an underlying drive. The further step of relating it to antecedent conditions becomes extremely complicated and brings up the problem of arousal. With hungry or thirsty rats, antecedent conditions were controlled and emphasis on consequent conditions prevailed, but when consequent learning occurs in the absence of observable antecedent variables it is useless to postulate the reduction of a drive unless the drive can be anchored to something.

In anchoring drive to hunger, complications have arisen. Hull cites a study by Finan (1940) in which rats that were 1, 12, 24, and 48 hours deprived learned to press a bar for 100% reinforcement. Each group received the same number of reinforcements, then after "the food used had been equalized" (p. 82) extinction was carried out. The median number of reactions to produce extinction were 25, 57.5, 40, 41 for 1, 12, 24, and 48 hours deprivation, respectively. Apparently the relationship is not a simple one. This problem has received much attention since Finan's study (see for instance Siegel, 1947; Horenstein, 1951; Heathers & Arakelian, 1941; Saltzman & Koch, 1948). An important factor apparently involves shifting from one level of deprivation for acquisition to another for extinction. Yamaguchi (1951) attempted to control this factor and found monotonically increasing relationships between hours of deprivation and responses to extinction.

Despite problems of relating level of drive to observable antecedent conditions, Hull proceeded to his law of primary reinforcement. *"Whenever an effector activity occurs in temporal contiguity with the afferent impulse, or the perseverative trace of such an impulse, resulting from the impact of a stimulus energy upon a receptor, and this connection is closely associated in time with the diminution in the receptor discharge characteristic of a need, there will result an increment to the tendency for that stimulus on subsequent occasion to evoke that reaction"* (Hull, 1943, p. 80).

The law of primary reinforcement is obviously important as a statement of the relationship between learning and motivation, but what does it have to do with the basic problem of this chapter, namely, stimulation and affect? Implicit in this theorizing is the assumption that "receptor discharge characteristic of a need" is a stimulus the reduction of which leads to reinforcement (strengthening of a bond). Hull never discussed such subjective states as pleasure or affect, but in our terms it may be assumed that the stronger receptor discharges (increased drive) lead to negative affect as a monotonically increasing function. The goal of the organism is to reduce these receptor discharges to a minimum. Hullian theory, then, is an example of drive-stimulus reduction theory as schematized in Figure 3.1, Chapter 3. The affective relationship is most clear with shock, which is a "noxious" stimulus. It was here that Miller (1948a) took up the argument.

Summarizing what we have learned from Hull *(a)* receptor discharges characteristic of a need may be seen as a drive stimulus that the organism will attempt to reduce (by inference we can discuss the relationship between stimulus and affect); *(b)* the relationship between the inferred drive and antecedent conditions must be demonstrated, but the procedure is difficult and the result complicated; *(c)* drive is a general energizing component to be distinctly separated from the directing component of habit.

MILLER AND MOWRER

As learning theorists, Miller and Mowrer went their separate ways in the middle to late 1940's, Miller maintaining the orthodox Hullian one-factor drive-reduction principle[1] while Mowrer (1950) developed his two-factor theory, which demanded contiguity alone for the attachment of emotional reactions to stimuli. From our point of view, however, their positions are similar in assuming that stimulus-intensity reduction is the critical factor in reinforcement. Miller (Miller & Dollard, 1941) gives us the statement of the relationship between drive and stimulus. "A drive is a strong stimulus which impels actions. Any stimulus can become a drive if it is made strong enough. The stronger the stimulus, the more drive function it possesses" (p. 18).

This statement apparently still remains (Miller, 1959) as a fundamental postulate. It fits the paradigm presented diagrammatically in Figure 3.1 of Chapter 3 if we take the liberty of assuming the relationship between high drive and negative affect. Its precision results in little need for clarification, but the brevity of treatment here should not mislead the

---

[1]Miller (1963) has presented a contiguity based alternative with many similarities to Mowrer's (1960a) position.

reader in estimating its importance. This statement is a real milestone in motivation theory. Its relationship to Hull's drive-reduction theory should be obvious, as should its similarity to Freud's (1915b) statement (quoted in Chapter 3) that the function of the nervous system is to reduce stimulation to the lowest possible level. But Miller's statement has the advantage (if interpreted literally) of restricting such stimuli to drive stimuli. The statement has been criticized (McClelland *et al.,* 1953) as implying (as Freud's statement clearly does) that the organism seeks a state of lack of stimulation. However, if drives are distinguished from appetites, which allow for seeking increased stimulation,[2] then the Miller definition as applied to drive stimuli becomes a primary postulate that must be accounted for by all theorists.

Miller's use of drive differs from Hull's in that he sees drive generalization as a function of stimulus generalization. "One deduction from this assumption is that drive generalization should occur as a special case of stimulus generalization" (Miller, 1959, p. 253). This assumption is a direct reference to the notion that drives are strong stimuli. The deduction has led to the research known as irrelevant drive studies, i.e., learning under one drive, testing under another (Miller, 1937, 1948b; Webb, 1949; Grice & Davis, 1957). Experimentally, it is difficult to distinguish between Miller's deduction and Hull's notion that drive is a nonspecific energizer. As we shall see in Chapter 5, the idea of generalization gradients has been invoked in discussions of specific human motives measured in fantasy (Goss & Brownell, 1957). The generalization notion may give one basis for the indentifying of specific human motives.

A further outgrowth of Miller's theorizing is what we have called a relative stimulus-intensity-reduction theory. Up to now, any reduction has been considered reinforcing. Campbell (1955) and Campbell and Kraeling (1953) have shown that the reinforcing effect of noxious stimulus reduction varies if the absolute amount of reduction is constant but the initial intensity varies. Put another way, the amount of reinforcement appears to follow a relationship similar to Weber's Law: in the middle range of initial stimulation an equal ratio of stimulus reduction has approximately the same reinforcing properties; but at the extremes the relationship breaks down.

Mowrer (1960a,b) has revised his earlier (1950) two-factor learning theory. The revision involves shifting to only one type of learning (by contiguity) but to two types of reinforcement (incremental and decre-

---

[2]Tomkins (1962) makes such a distinction. What we called here "appetites" he calls "affects," but the distinction between our use of "affect" and Tomkins' "affects" would lead to confusion here.

mental stimulation). "In short, as far as 'types of learning' are concerned, the current version is 'one factored'; but it remains definitely two-factored as regards reinforcement. This is perhaps not a very good and sufficient basis for deriving a *name* for the present theory; but, for the time being at least, two-factor learning theory can serve as well as any other, provided that it does not imply two kinds, or forms, of *learning,* simply two kinds of reinforcement" (Mowrer, 1960b, p. 15).

It is not our purpose here to go into details of Mowrer's learning theory with its *twelve* kinds of reinforcement (Mowrer, 1960a, see p. 213). By "kinds of reinforcement" he actually means types of stimuli (independent or response-dependent) that may be associated with primary drive (incremental or decremental) or secondary drive (hope and relief under decremental, and fear and disappointment under incremental stimulation). Despite this exhaustive classification, the basic types of drive stimuli are incremental and decremental. Simply stated, incremental stimulation (drive induction) is bad; decremental stimulation (drive reduction) is good. Thus we have at base a stimulus-intensity-reduction theory with much the same characteristics as Miller's. A qualification on this underlying postulate will be discussed in the following section on the arousal jag.

The ingenious use of contiguity theory to account for all twelve types of learning and the derivation of mediation through anticipatory states of hope, fear, disappointment and relief will be discussed in more detail in Chapter 5.

EVIDENCE THAT QUESTIONS THE
DRIVE-STIMULUS-REDUCTION THEORY

Before proceeding to a discussion of theories that incorporate the concept of arousal, we must pause to note the types of experimental data that have called drive-stimulus-reduction theory into question and forced some theorists to consider the concept of arousal. Roughly, these data fall into two categories *(a)* data on exploratory, manipulatory, and curiosity behavior that apparently indicate that learning can occur and behavior be maintained in the absence of any obvious reduction of primary or secondary drives, and *(b)* evidence from studies of sensory deprivation that the human organism seeks stimulation rather than seeks to reduce it to a minimum as implied by Freud's statement quoted in Chapter 3 or by Figure 3.1.

Harlow (Harlow, 1950; Harlow, Harlow, & Meyer, 1950; Harlow & McClearn, 1954) has demonstrated that monkeys will manipulate gadgets placed in their cages without any resultant drive or stimulus reduction. In fact, when the gadgets lead to a food reward, the manipulation *per se* deteriorates. This series of experiments will be discussed in some detail in Chapter 10.

As early as 1925 Dashiell found that rats which were neither hungry nor thirsty would explore an intricate maze with no apparent reinforcement. In the 1950's, Montgomery and his colleagues (Montgomery, 1951, 1953a,b,c, 1954, 1955; Montgomery & Monkman, 1955; Montgomery & Segall, 1955; Zimbardo & Montgomery, 1957 and others) studied in detail the relationships between the so-called primary drives of hunger, thirst, and fear and the exploratory "drive." Their results indicate that exploration has many of the characteristics of a drive, but does not appear to be related to previous states of deprivation, and is, therefore, difficult to account for within a stimulus-intensity-reduction theory.

Berlyne (1950, 1954a,b, 1957, 1962) has demonstrated a phenomenon that he calls "curiosity" in animals and humans. In a typical experiment (Berlyne, 1950), "rats were allowed to explore three identical objects — wooden cubes or cardboard cylinders — for five minutes, and they were then put back into the situation ten minutes later, to find one of the cubes replaced by a cylinder, or vice versa. During this second trial, they spent significantly more time exploring the novel object than exploring the other, familiar objects" (Berlyne, 1960, p. 107). With humans, the typical experiment allows the subject to choose to look at one of two stimulus objects or measures the amount of time he looks at a stimulus. According to Berlyne (1960) the measures indicate intrinsic investigatory responses in humans toward stimuli that are incongruous, complex, and surprising.

Evidence that reduced stimulation is something to be avoided rather than sought out comes from sensory deprivation studies (Bexton, Heron, & Scott, 1954; Heron, Doane, & Scott, 1956; Lilly, 1956). Bexton *et al.* (1954) offered to pay college students twenty dollars a day quite literally to do nothing. Very few of them could tolerate this "ideal" job for more than two or three days. "Doing nothing" consisted of lying on a bed for 24 hours a day in a sound-proof room while wearing translucent goggles and other paraphernalia all devised to reduce sensory stimulation to a minimum. Far from being a pleasant state, this environment was apparently intolerable after an initial period of sleep. Many specific effects were noted in subjects under sensory deprivation, such as deterioration of performance on cognitive and motor tasks, plus phenomena which may be interpreted as seeking or creating stimulation. Hallucinations were common and subjects apparently enjoyed hearing stimuli, such as old stock market reports, which would normally be extremely boring.

Such is a sample of an enormous literature that has accumulated since about 1950. For a more detailed review the reader is referred to Cofer and Appley (1964) or Berlyne (1960). White (1959) and Hunt (1963) have pressed the argument against drive-stimulus-reduction theories using such evidence.

BERLYNE — AN AROUSAL-REDUCTION THEORY

When Berlyne's *Conflict Arousal and Curiosity* (1960) is first encountered, one may expect to find what we have called an arousal theory. A substantial portion of the book can be read without being disabused of this assumption; but basically the theory is a reduction theory. It is, however, a reduction theory with an ingenious difference that allows it to incorporate the research on curiosity, manipulation, exploration, and sensory deprivation, which have been used to criticize more conventional drive-stimulus-reduction theories (White, 1959; Hunt, 1963).

The novel aspect of the theory involves viewing arousal as a central neurological phenomenon that is not a direct result of intensity of stimulation. Here Berlyne draws heavily on research investigating the reticular arousal system (Moruzzi & Magoun, 1949; Lindsley, 1957), and bases his theory on the notion that reduction of arousal in the reticular arousal system (RAS) is the basis of reinforcement. Drive, for Berlyne, becomes arousal, and therefore he has to discuss the relationship of other definitions of drive to his own, and relate drive to arousal. In addition, he has to relate arousal of the RAS to stimulation. Unlike previous theorists, Berlyne uses a concept closer to the hedonic or affective dimension. This concept is attractiveness, which can be measured by preference or approach behavior. Attractiveness must then be related to stimulation and arousal.

Drive, according to Berlyne, is a term that takes on three different meanings in contemporary discussions. These three meanings derive from the energizing (drive$_1$), selecting (drive$_2$), and reinforcing (drive$_3$) emphases placed on drive by various writers. "There is first the notion of drive as a condition that affects the *level of activity*" (Berlyne, 1960, p. 165). "The second notion represents drive as an *internal condition that makes certain overt responses more likely than others*" (p. 166). "The third notion identifies drive as a *condition whose termination or alleviation is rewarding*" (p. 167).

Berlyne postulates that arousal of the RAS can serve the function of all three versions of drive and is especially concerned with drive$_3$. "As for drive$_3$, we shall adopt the hypothesis that *decreases in arousal are*

rewarding" (p. 170). It is because of this that we have referred to Ber-
lyne's theory as an arousal-reduction theory.

Up to this point the theory seems to have little to recommend it over
any stimulus-intensity-reduction theory, and it would seem to be in
trouble in accounting for curiosity and exploratory behavior. But it was
just such behaviors that the theory started out to explain. The crucial
innovation lies in assuming that arousal (of the RAS, which is drive) is
not a simple function of bodily deficit or even of intensity of stimulation.
Arousal is a function of the stimulus properties of the environment, to
be sure, and these properties have "arousal potential" that is something
like stimulus intensity; but here is the innovation. Very low "arousal po-
tential" and very high "arousal potential" both lead to a high RAS arousal,
whereas moderate arousal potential gives low arousal of the RAS. This
somewhat paradoxical postulation is the result of the way arousal poten-
tial is defined, and some evidence showing that boredom (low arousal
potential) actually leads to high RAS arousal, that is, low environmental
stimulation is arousing.

Arousal potential seems a confusing choice in terminology but Berlyne
is obviously avoiding mere "stimulus intensity" because he has de-
scribed stimulus characteristics that apparently lead to stimulus selection,
prolonged inspection, and curiosity. These characteristics are called the
collative variables "since they all depend on the collation, or comparison,
of information from different sources" (Berlyne, 1963, p. 290). The colla-
tive properties of stimuli are *"novelty, surprisingness, change, ambiguity,
incongruity, blurredness,* and the power to induce *uncertainty"* (p. 290).
With these properties in mind (which are probably best summarized by
the term *stimulus-complexity*), we can turn to the definition of arousal
potential. "By arousal potential we mean all those variables, including
collative properties of stimuli, with which arousal, in most conditions,
increases. But although arousal seems on the whole to vary directly with
these properties, the actual relation between arousal and arousal potential
is likely to be curvilinear" (1963, p. 317).

Arousal (of the RAS) is said to be a curvilinear function of arousal
potential of the environmental stimulus properties (see Figure 4.1). It is
this that makes the name "arousal potential" unfortunate. On the surface
of it, the relationship of arousal to arousal potential sounds as if it would
be circular and trivial. Arousal would have to be a direct function of
arousal potential if arousal potential were measured by the amount that a
stimulus potentially arouses the organism. But arousal potential is capa-
ble of independent measurement, as it must be to avoid triviality. Arousal
potential is a result of the collative properties of stimuli, and "All the

collative properties are eminently quantitative. They can all exist in varying degrees, and we shall have to find ways of measuring them and allotting numerical values to them before research can go much farther. But the task of measuring them lands us in all kinds of perplexities from the outset" (1963, p. 291).

In order to simplify this chain of reasoning somewhat and reduce the confusion between arousal of the RAS and arousal potential of stimuli, we shall use "stimulus complexity" as one aspect that (*a*) is a collative variable and hence can exist in varying degrees of arousal potential, and (*b*) comes close to uncertainty, which is measurable by information theory (Attneave, 1957). It seems to us less confusing while at the same time less complete to discuss the relationships between stimulus complexity (as one example of arousal potential) and RAS arousal and attractiveness.

Attractiveness is a monotonically decreasing (linear?) function of increasing arousal (of the RAS). The term "attractiveness" is not explicitly defined, but it seems to have a spurious positive connotation. Apparently, as in earlier reduction theories there is nothing that is absolutely positive. What is attractive is the lessening of something that is negative, namely, RAS arousal. "When arousal stands above its possible minimum, we assume that there will be an aversive state and that anything that serves to bring it down toward its possible minimum will have a reward value. Maintaining the level of arousal near its possible minimum will mean seeking just the right intermediate influx of arousal potential and escaping from environments where arousal potential [stimulus complexity] is too high or too low" (1963, p. 317).[3]

Figure 4.1a clearly places Berlyne in the reduction camp (compare with Figure 3.1). Figure 4.1b allows him to account for the empirical evidence (Bexton *et al.,* 1954) that low levels of stimulation are disturbing. Finally, the consequent relationship between attractiveness and stimulus complexity in our terms and arousal potential in his (Figure 4.1c) is merely a composite of the other two curves. Thus when stimulus complexity (arousal potential) is either high or low, arousal (RAS) is high; and when arousal (RAS) is high attractiveness is low.

We may note here, as does Berlyne, the similarity between Figure 4.1c and the curve generated by theories of optional stimulation or activation and sensory discrepancy theories (Fiske & Maddi, 1961; Hebb, 1955; Engel, 1928; see also Figure 3.3).

---

[3]In another place, Berlyne does however "venture the hypothesis that pleasant emotional excitement and rewarding stimuli also heighten arousal, although probably less sharply than states of distress and punishing stimuli" (1960, p. 174). It is hard to reconcile this with the above statement.

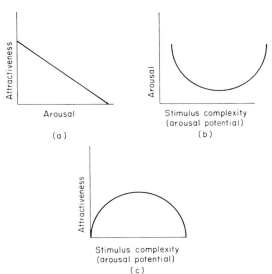

Crucial to the support of Berlyne's hypothesized relationship between arousal in the RAS and arousal potential of stimuli is evidence that situations of low stimulus arousal potential produce high arousal. The evidence is scanty.

> The author has elsewhere (Berlyne, 1960, Chapter 7) put forward the somewhat paradoxical hypothesis that lack of stimulation or monotony is unpleasant, when it is, because it produces a rise rather than a fall in arousal. This hypothesis was offered rather reticently, but a few scraps of experimental evidence and some speculation, derived from neurophysiological findings on the relations between the cerebral cortex and the reticular formation, were offered in support . . . . Since then, further pertinent data have become available. Davis (1959) found that reduction of exteroceptive stimulation below normal levels occasion rises in muscular and circulatory activity accompanied by slower breathing. A number of experiments reviewed by Kubzanski (1961) reveals that, while sensory deprivation is not always experienced as uncomfortable, electrocutaneous, EEG, and circulatory changes indicative of high arousal are apt to appear during periods when motor and verbal signs of emotional disturbance are present (Berlyne, 1963, p. 310).

Arousal-Jag Theories (Mowrer & Berlyne)

As explained in Chapter 3 the arousal-jag notion attempts to account for the apparent seeking of increased stimulation by most animals without simultaneously assuming that increased stimulation is in any way positive or rewarding in its own right. We saw indications of this type of thinking in Freud's discussion of sexual forepleasure and wit. We now intend to look at arousal-jag statements in Mowrer (1960a) and Berlyne (1960), the latter having apparently coined the phrase "arousal jag." It may seem paradoxical to return to these two theorists who have already been characterized as primarily reduction theorists. Let it be emphasized that the main aspects of their theories have already been covered. In each case, as in Freud, they add small sections attempting to account for the seeking of increased stimulation. These are essentially appendages to their theories. It is the present author who stresses the importance of the arousal-jag notion. Berlyne (1960) discusses the theory that he named in only three pages of his 350-page book, and returns to apply it to humor in a mere five more pages. Mowrer (1960a), of course, does not refer to the arousal jag by that phrase, but he discusses the phenomenon in connection with his "reservations" and "complications."

Let us look at Berlyne's statements first and quote more than half of his section on the arousal jag. (What is omitted from the quote comprises two introductory paragraphs setting the problem and one final paragraph suggesting that the neural mechanism underlying the arousal jag may be the "pleasure centers" discovered by Olds, 1956.)

> We can, however, point to many facts contradicting the assumption that aversive or drive$_3$ states are *invariably* avoided and implying that they may even be welcomed in some conditions.
>
> Even in the case of pain, we have masochistic behavior in human beings and experiments like the one by Masserman (1946) in which a cat eagerly presses an electrified lever to obtain food. There have been several experiments with rats in which electric shocks actually strengthen responses that occur simultaneously with, or just before, the shocks (Hamilton and Krechevsky, 1933; Muenzinger, 1934; Gwinn, 1949). Further experiments support the view that the responses in question are reinforced by the subsequent reduction of pain or fear (Farber, 1948; Mowrer, 1950).
>
> As for fear, one has only to visit the nearest fairground to appreciate the economic value of being tossed and flung through the air, and posters advertising the latest horror film will graphically depict the allurements of being scared out of one's wits.
>
> Much the same point can be supported with regard to hunger or thirst. Various devices from a walk to an anchovy are employed to work up an appetite. As for the sex drive, any comment would be supererogatory.
>
> We are far from being in a position to characterize in detail the conditions in which increases in drive are sought and to differentiate them from those in which they are avoided. But as far as we can see at present, the important ones are (1) that the drive is aroused to a moderate extent, and (2) that the arousal is promptly followed by relief.
>
> Both of these conditions have been cited by Hebb (1949, 1955) as those in which

arousal or emotion will be pleasurable, and they are implied by Meyer's (1956) hypothesis that emotion is pleasurable when we feel that the situation is under control.

Some psychoanalytic writers might be inclined to assume that if fear, pain, or other forms of distress are actively courted, it must be for the sake of self-punishment as a means of assuaging guilt feelings. This may conceivably be a contributory condition at times, but the evident importance of quick relief in most of the pertinent cases argues against this view. If mountaineers were habitually suspended over abysses for days on end instead of for a few minutes at a time, their number might well be smaller than it is, although the pastime would, no doubt, still find a few devotees.

There is, however, another psychoanalytic interpretation of apparently self-persecuting behavior that is closer to ours. This is the theory of "belated mastery" (Fenichel, 1945), according to which experiences that originally produced anxiety are repeated as a means of gaining control over them. As Fenichel puts it, "An expenditure of energy is associated with the anxiety or the fearful expectation felt by a person who is uncertain whether he will be able to master an expected excitation. The sudden cessation of this expenditure brings its relieving discharge which is experienced by the successful ego as a 'triumph' and enjoyed as functional pleasure. . . . When a child is tossed in the air by an adult and caught [and] is certain that he will not be dropped, he can take pleasure in having thought that he might have been dropped; he may shudder a little, but then realize that this fear was unnecessary. To make this pleasure possible, conditions of reassurance must be fulfilled. The child must have confidence in the adult who is playing with him and the height must not be too great."

This is precisely the kind of process that we shall assume to occur in connection with arousal. In fact, we shall assume that it is at work whenever a momentary rise in arousal potential, such as a pleasant surprise or a colorful spectacle, is rewarding in the absence of a previous and independently produced spell of severe supraoptimal arousal. Such slight and transitory jumps in arousal will become pleasurable as a consequence of the drop in arousal that quickly terminates them. Consequently, behavior that is regularly followed by such *arousal jags,* as we shall call them, will be learned (Berlyne, 1960, pp. 198–199).

Here we have Berlyne's basic statement and the added bonus of a statement from the psychoanalytically oriented Fenichel.

The notion of arousal in humor that we saw in Freud has prompted Berlyne to apply the notion of the arousal jag to that area.

We may thus look to the arousal jag once again to throw light on the reward value of humor. This means that we must find both factors that provoke arousal and factors that prevent arousal from rising too high or ensure speedy relief.

Whatever other factors may be present to discharge or curb arousal, there is always the influence of the playful mood or atmosphere in which humorous material is sampled. There is a whole assortment of social cues which make it possible to discriminate occasions for taking some event or remark as a joke from occasions for taking it seriously. The wag smiles or nudges his listener to set aside the repercussions that his audacity would otherwise cause — and which it may still

cause if his efforts to have it accepted as a jest do not succeed. Not only the be-
havior of the jester but the whole social and physical context may bring out light-
hearted rather than solemn responses to stimuli having the capacity to evoke both.
The cues involved are comparable to those that enable an animal to distinguish
playful fighting from a dangerous attack and inhibit him from injuring his opponent.
. . . All types of verbal wit or humorous anecdote seem to incorporate a divergence
from the expected, a change in something familiar which leaves enough resemblance
to the familiar for some of its responses to be evoked and yet contains some fea-
ture that frustrates these responses and thus provokes conflict, uncertainty, and
surprise. This constitutes an important source of arousal value, opening the way
to the reward value of an arousal jag, and it also assimilates the formal mechanisms
of humor to those of art (Berlyne, 1960, pp. 259–260).

A similar phenomenon is seen in tragedy. Thus the arousal jag may be
seen as the underlying mechanism of catharsis. Berlyne does not make
this broad a statement, but he does say:

> Tragedy depends on identification. The hero suffers through some fault of char-
> acter, such as we all possess, or through some ferocity of fate to which none of us
> is invulnerable. Any relief of arousal comes, therefore, after the drama has ended
> and its reverberations have faded away (Berlyne, 1960, p. 261).

These examples certainly show instances of slow arousal and sudden
"relief" which fit the arousal jag notion as presented in Chapter 3. How-
ever, one may question whether all the pleasure of tragedy comes with
the relief at the end. One certainly may question whether the pleasure of a
so-called "shaggy-dog" story comes at the end. As I understand them,
"shaggy-dog" stories drag out the arousal period to strengthen antici-
pation, which in the end is usually disappointed. Such stories seem to re-
tain their popularity although the typical reaction at the end is one of a
disappointed anticipation. (Of course the pleasure in such a story may lie
primarily with the teller, who puts something over on the listener.)

Let us now turn to Mowrer's (1960a) analysis of the rise in appetite,
which he associates with parasympathetic arousal. In the following quote
he attempts to resolve the paradox in the arousal jag, saying that an ap-
petitive reaction is something that the organism *has to pass through.* He
says that it is "even punishing." But as the problem is, in his own words,
"intricate," we shall quote him in detail and reproduce a figure from this
work (Fig. 4.2).

> Granted that the evidence on this complicated issue is not yet all in, at least a
> provisional resolution seems possible. A stimulus which has secondary reinforcing
> properties is one which, per hypothesis, is capable of reducing some sort of sec-
> ondary drive, most commonly drive-produced fear. Now fear reduction presup-
> poses a lessening of activity on the part of the *sympathetic division* of the auto-

nomic nervous system. But we know that stimuli associated with primary drive reduction may be not only reassuring and relaxing but also exciting, stimulating, motivating. How are these seemingly contradictory effects possible? May it not be that stimuli which in the past have been associated with consummatory states acquire the capacity *first* to allay fear, i.e., quiet sympathetic arousal, and *then* to activate the parasympathetic nervous system, which mediates the appetites?

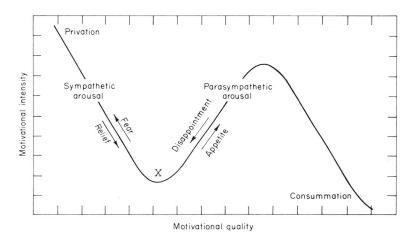

Fig. 4.2. Diagram suggesting a hypothesis concerning the relationship between secondary reinforcement, conceived as fear reduction, and appetite (Mowrer, 1960a, p. 204).

It has often been remarked that the sympathetic and parasympathetic divisions of the autonomic nervous system are antagonistic or reciprocal in their actions; and it is certainly true that fear must subside before one can react appetitively and that one has to stop being appetitively aroused before one can become very fearful. However, there is a good deal more that can be said about this relationship, if it is schematized as indicated in [Fig. 4.2]. Here it is suggested that there is not only a "vertical" (quantitative) but also a "horizontal" (qualitative) dimension of function. This means that a rise or fall in either sympathetic or parasympathetic activity involve a rise or a fall in motivation. But—and this is the point especially to be noted —"movement" along the functional course indicated in [Fig. 4.2] is never directly up or down; there is always a *lateral* component, such that the individual, in becoming either more or less fearful or more or less appetitively aroused, is also moving either from left to right (away from privation toward consummation) or from right to left (away from consummation toward privation). Therefore, although a *decline* in fear and a *rise* in appetite are, from one point of view, antithetical, in another way they represent a *continuous* function: they are two successive steps or stages in the organism's progress from privation to consummation. And, of course, the same holds true, in reverse order, of the relationship between a decline in appetite and a rise in fear.

Classical hedonic theory . . . tended to assume that stimuli are inherently pleasant or unpleasant, quite apart from any factor of intensity; whereas, in homeostatic theory, the tendency is to equate pleasure to drive reduction and the opposite quality to drive increase. It may be that these two systems, in appearing to be contradictory, are really complementary, each referring more particularly to one rather than to the other of the *two* different, but related, dimensions implied in [Fig. 4.2].

Hence we conclude, if this analysis is sound, that a secondary reinforcer, when it *first* impinges upon an organism in a state of strong drive and drive fear (privation), causes a relief (fear reduction) reaction and *then,* very probably, an appetitive (excitement) reaction, as a sort of *detour* which the organism has to pass through, for reasons already indicated, on its way to a state of consummation and satiation. This is not to deny that appetitive arousal is motivating and, in a sense, even punishing. If, for example, an individual in a state of complete satiation and comfort could, merely by wishing (or by pressing a button), suddenly transport himself back to a condition of appetitive arousal (without the normally attendant primary drive also being present), it is unlikely that he would do so. Why, then, when a hungry, thirsty, or otherwise deprived organism is at point X on the curve shown in [Fig. 4.2], does it not *remain* there, instead of moving on through appetitive arousal to consummation? This may, in fact, be exactly what happens in individuals who are said to be shy. But the more confident, more experienced individual is willing to tolerate appetitive arousal because it promises to lead, ultimately, to consummation; whereas the rise in motivation which is produced by fear points in the reverse direction, toward further privation . . . . Or, to put the matter a little differently, movement in either direction from point X on the curve involves a form of "loss," i.e., drive increase; but appetitive arousal also involves a form of "gain," i.e., movement toward consummation, whereas fear arousal involves a "loss" in *both* dimensions.

What then, in simplest terms, may one say of the concept of secondary reinforcement type-2, or of hope? One may say: (a) that whenever an otherwise strongly motivated organism is moving to the *right,* along the curve shown in[Fig. 4.2], that organism is in a state of hope or hopefulness; and (b) that such movement may involve either drive fear decrement (first phase) or appetitive arousal (second phase) followed by the attainment (normally) of a state of consummation, with a general drive level well below anything achieved beforehand, at point X.

It is to be regretted that this hypothesis is somewhat intricate; but so, apparently, are the facts. As of the present, this hypothesis fits the facts rather well and will be accepted as the basis for further theoretical analysis until revision is clearly indicated (Mowrer, 1960a, pp. 202–205).

This hypothesis is indeed intricate. In fact, if looked at closely, it may be seen as undermining the whole edifice developed by Mowrer's theory, starting with his disagreement with Miller over avoidance learning. Was it not a similar situation (arousal of fear from pain or shock) that led him to abandon the secondary-reinforcement explanation of avoidance learning? In this instance he reverses himself and uses it when faced with incremental (appetitive) stimulation that produces learning.

This example makes it clear how close the arousal-jag explanation is to a secondary reinforcement theory. The increase in stimulation (appetite) is minimal compared with the decrease that follows. Thus the minimal increase may itself elicit anticipation. Presumably, however, the anticipation must take on positive elements. The whole problem of anticipation is crucial to motivation and affective arousal. It involves acquired (secondary) relationships between stimuli and affect. This chapter deals primarily with primary relationships. Secondary reinforcement and acquired anticipations will be developed in detail from the notions of fractional anticipatory goal responses and mediation in Chapter 5.

It should be noted, however, that any theory of what we shall call extrinsic incentives must account for the acquisition of behavior that is of itself repugnant, since extrinsic incentives are to be defined as those which are "tied on" to repugnant behaviors to make them tolerable "in order to" attain the incentive. Such is not the case, however, with all learning and behavior. If arousal is thought to be innately positive in some instances, then certain arousing behaviors may be intrinsically motivated. The problem of the intrinsic-extrinsic distinction will be discussed at length in Chapter 10. For the time being, we have reached the point of considering examples of arousal theories.

Affective Arousal Theories

P. T. Young: An Empirical Affective Arousal Theorist

Young has been espousing an affective arousal theory for many years (Young, 1936). He conceives of his position as an experimental hedonism based on the postulate that "affective processes have an objective existence within the organism and that their nature and functions can be discovered" (Young, 1959, p. 104). As to the basic question that we have been investigating in this chapter, namely, the relationship between stimulation and affect, Young takes a clear position. He is at pains to distinguish between sensory and hedonic intensity, citing several studies in support. For instance, Young and Greene (1953) found that preference for pairs of sucrose solutions was directly proportional to the logarithm of the concentration, a finding similar to one reported by Engel (1928). Young and Falk (1956) found a curvilinear relationship between acceptability and concentration of sodium chloride, a finding similar to those of Engel (1928), Bare (1949), and Harriman and MacLeod (1953). Young and Asdourian (1957) compared a preferred concentration of sodium chloride with several concentrations of sucrose and found all sucrose solutions to be preferred. These results indicate the difficulty of relating hedonic intensities.

The studies from Young's laboratory illustrate the type of research upon which his theorizing is based. The rats in these studies are most often satiated on all so-called primary drives and given choices in an ingenious choice apparatus developed for the purpose. Young feels that the data "demonstrate convincingly the necessity of distinguishing between *sensory* intensity and *hedonic* intensity and hence between the sensory and affective aspects of neural excitation" (Young, 1959, p. 107).

Although Young has studied affect and stimulation, he is not willing to state any general proposition about the relationship between the two. Thus he shuns any inclusive principle such as the discrepancy hypothesis. For this reason he may be classed as an *empirical* affective arousal theorist, since he espouses no principle upon which a relationship between a particular sensory input may be related to affect. Presumably he feels that each new sensory modality demands empirical demonstration of a relationship.

Several of Young's studies (Young & Shuford, 1954; Young & Falk, 1956) as well as studies discussed by him (Bare, 1949; Guttman, 1953) provide data demonstrating a curvilinear relationship between sensory intensity and some measure of affect. These studies might be used as evidence for the discrepancy hypothesis. Young, however, takes great care to show that, although they seem to demonstrate a range of optimally preferred concentrations, this range is extremely variable. It is, for instance, changed for sodium chloride by adrenalectomy[4] (Bare, 1949; Young & Chaplin, 1949) or by dietary conditions (Young, 1955). Young concludes, "Although optimal concentrations do exist for sugar, salt, saccharine, and other substances, the attempt to locate *stable* optima has been like a chase for some will-o'-the-wisp" (1955, p. 210). This position does not invalidate the discrepancy hypothesis, but its most damaging evidence is the consistent finding with sweet solutions (Engel, 1928; Young & Greene, 1953) that large discrepancies (high concentrations) do not produce negative affect.

We have in Young an empirical affective arousal theorist who presents data on the relationship between sensory stimulation and affect but draws no general principle from the relationship.

In general, Young presents the following "tentative formulation" of the objective principles of experimental hedonism:

1. *Stimulation has affective as well as sensory consequences....*
2. *An affective arousal orients the animal toward or against the stimulus-object....*

---

[4]It was assumed at one time that adrenalectomy lowered the sensory threshold for sodium chloride in rats. Pfaffman and Bare (1950) have apparently shown this to be untrue. They distinguish between the *sensory threshold* and the *preference threshold*. Adrenalectomy apparently lowers the preference but not the sensory threshold. This fact also is given as support for Young's distinction between sensory and hedonic dimensions.

3. *Affective processes lead to the development of motives....*
4. *The strength of a recently acquired motive is correlated with the intensity, duration, frequency, and recency of previous affective arousals....*
5. *The growth of motives is dependent upon learning as well as upon affective arousals....*
6. *The laws of conditioning apply to affective processes....*
7. *Affective processes regulate behavior by influencing choice....*
8. *Neurobehavioral patterns are organized according to the hedonic principle of maximizing the positive and minimizing the negative affective arousal (Young, 1959, pp. 122–124).*

Data Relevant to the Discrepancy Hypothesis

ABSOLUTE SENSORY DATA

We have already noted that the main theoretical proposition in the area of arousal theory is the discrepancy hypothesis, most forcefully proposed by McClelland *et al.* (1953). As Hilgard points out, "It is of historical interest that Fechner (1873) wrote along the same lines as early as 1873 and was quoted favorably by Freud" (Hilgard, 1963, p. 264). Wundt (1874) presented a curve showing the relationship between stimulus intensity and hedonic tone, which was reproduced and discussed by Ziehen (1914), and which was purely conceptual and not based on data. Wundt pointed out, "As feelings, unlike sensations, are not subject to exact measurement, nothing can be said concerning the detailed form of this curve of feeling" (1874, pp. 311–312). The curve presented, however, resembled Figure 3.3 in this volume.

Empirical evidence for the relationship first came, according to Beebe-Center (1932), in nonquantitative form from an incomplete study by Kiesow (1899) and from a study by Lehmann (1892). Kiesow related intensity of a sweet stimulus in taste to judgements of pleasantness-unpleasantness. Beebe-Center quotes him as saying that the curve "begins at the threshold with a stage of indifference. It then increases very slowly until there is reached another stage of indifference. The curve then inclines towards unpleasantness and decreases rather fast" (Beebe-Center, 1932, p. 167). This apparently follows the Wundtian curve except for the inexplicable second "stage of indifference." The study is of more than historical interest in that it presents one of very few studies that show that increasing sweetness can be unpleasant. Lehmann's (1892) study is a forerunner of a more modern study by Haber (1958) to be discussed later, and as such deals with affective reactions to temperature. Lehmann had two subjects dip two fingers into water at 35°C (slightly above normal skin temperature). The subjects described their feelings while the water was heated to 50°C over a period of two minutes and twenty seconds. The range from 35° to 40° was reported as pleasant, and the reports indicated increasing unpleasantness up to 50°, when pain was reported.

These two early studies are examples of studies using single-sensory dimensions in which measurements are absolute, i.e., not relative to an initial state of the organism. Of all the studies reported in the literature, this classification (absolute single sensory) applies to more than one-half. Table 4.1 is an attempt to classify the studies to be discussed here under the sensory versus aesthetic and absolute versus relative dimensions discussed in Chapter 3. The classifications are sometimes arbitrary. The studies listed under the category of "Single-sensory dimension: Absolute" include many rat studies conducted for various reasons, but not as a test of the discrepancy hypothesis (with the exception of Hunt and Quay, 1961). These rat studies do, however, confirm with rats and rather precise measurement, the earlier findings on humans with salt and sugar solutions. Here we shall concentrate on the human studies.

Saidullah's (1927) study produced curves for salt solutions which fit the Wundt-McClelland hypothesis. However, one factor which has been controversial in the McClelland *et al.* (1953) version was already apparent in Saidullah's results. Very low concentrations of salt are rated as moderately unpleasant (especially at 36°C) rather than as indifferent, as implied by the McClelland formulation. A unique aspect of the Saidullah experiment is the variation of the temperature of the solutions resulting in the general finding that increasing the temperature lowers the curve (reduces pleasantness or increases unpleasantness) at all concentrations of solution.

Engel's (1928) data give a comparison of sweet, sour, bitter, and salt solutions. They show that all substances follow the predicted curve except the sweet solution which never reaches maximum with increasing concentration and never becomes unpleasant or even less pleasant. The curve seems to be monotonically increasing (pleasantness as a function of concentration) to an asymptote. This discrepant finding for sucrose has been found in rats also (Young & Greene, 1953). When rats are given a choice between two sugar solutions they consistently choose the solution with the higher concentration. "This relation held all the way from solutions that were barely perceptible as sweet to thick syrup-like solutions near limit of saturation" (Young, 1955, p. 217).

Young and Greene (1953) report, however, that if the amount ingested over a period of 60 minutes is measured, a 9% solution of sucrose rates higher than a 36% solution. "Certainly we would be justified in concluding from these curves that a 9 percent solution is more highly acceptable

TABLE 4.1
STUDIES RELEVANT TO THE DISCREPANCY HYPOTHESIS

	Investigator	Stimuli	Subjects
I. Single-sensory dimension			
A. Absolute	Kiesow (1899)	Sweet taste	Humans
	Lehmann (1892)	Water temperature	Humans
	Saidullah (1927)	Salt solutions	Humans
	Engel (1928)	Salt, quinine, tartaric acid, sugar	Humans
	Beebe-Center et al. (1948)	Saccharine	Humans
	Bare (1949)	Salt	Rats
	Young and Chaplin (1949)	Salt	Rats
	Weiner and Stellar (1951)	Salt	Rats
	Harriman and MacLeod (1953)	Salt	Rats
	Guttman (1953)	Sucrose	Rats
	Young and Greene (1953)	Sucrose	Rats
	Young and Falk (1959)	Salt	Rats
B. Relative	Warren and Pfaffman (1959)	Sucrose octaacetate	Rats
	Meier et al. (1960)	Flickering light	Rats
	Hunt and Quay (1961)	Vibration	Rats
	Alpert (1953)	Light intensity	Humans
	Haber (1958)	Water temperature	Humans
	McCall (1965)	Light intensity	Rats
II. Aesthetic Dimension (Patterned)			
A. Absolute	Angier (1903)	Division of lines	Humans
	Maddi (1961)	Numbers and sentences	Humans
	Kenny (1955)	Joke endings	Humans
B. Relative	Alpert (1953)	Rhythm	Humans
	Pitts (1963)	Music	Humans
	Terwilliger (1963)	2 inch square patterns	Humans
	Munsinger & Kessen (1964)	Random shapes and approximations to English	Humans

than a 36 percent solution" (Young, 1955, p. 216). Data from Guttman (1953) on bar pressing to receive different concentrations of sucrose show the drop at high concentrations characteristic of the discrepancy hypothesis rather than the asymptotic relationship reported by Engel.

Finally, Beebe-Center, Black, Hoffman, and Wade (1948), using a sweet substance (saccharine solution), report that in a choice situation the preference for the saccharine solution in comparison to water first increases and then decreases to a negative value as concentration increases.

It is thus apparent that different measurement techniques may result in different findings. It will be recalled that the studies discussed previously and others like them led Young to the statement that the search for optimal concentrations was like the search for a "will-o'-the-wisp." Thus he would probably feel that using these studies as evidence for the discrepancy hypothesis is unjustified.

RELATIVE SENSORY DATA

Under this heading, we shall describe three studies. In his Master's thesis, Alpert (1953) presented his subjects with approximately homogeneous stimulation *(ganzfeld)* in the visual field of one eye. His apparatus allowed him to vary the intensity of red light (stimulating primarily one set of receptors, the cones) in the visual field. A comparison of intensities was possible in that he could vary intensity independently in the periphery and in a small fixated spot covering the fovea (about 18° of visual arc). After adapting the subject to a *ganzfeld* of a certain intensity (adaptation level), various comparison intensities were produced in the center spot for approximately two seconds. After the comparison was switched off and the constant switched on, the subject made a hedonic judgement on a seven point scale. Thus hedonic tone could be plotted as a function of discrepancies of the intensity of the spot from the adaptation level (AL). The results of the experiment are summarized by McClelland *et al.* (1953) as follows: "(1) When the *AL* is low, and the receptors are close to the 'resting' state, increases in stimulation produce first positive affect and then negative affect as postulated [according to the discrepancy hypothesis]. . . . (2) When the *AL* is high, well above the resting state, all increases in stimulation tend to produce negative affect and all decreases tend to produce positive affect. . . . (3) There is no marked evidence in these curves either *(a)* for large decreases in stimulation leading to negative affect or *(b)* for stimulation around the *AL* producing a neutral hedonic response" (pp. 51–52). The results from this experiment cannot be taken as an adequate test of the hypothesis. Points (a) and (b) above lead McClelland *et al.* (1953) to consider the no stimulation resting state as a natural adaptation level. Possibly the curve postulated by the discrepancy hypothesis is affected by attempting to adapt the receptors to intensities increasingly far from the natural adaptation level. As applied to this experiment the argument, however, is purely *ad hoc*.

Terwilliger (1963), in a study that will be discussed in more detail, presents conceptual and empirical evidence for assuming that the curve predicted by the discrepancy hypothesis may be a function of both discrepancies from the adaptation level of the moment and from zero on the scale of stimulus variation (in the Alpert study, intensity). The formula presented by Terwilliger results in a slightly asymmetrical "butterfly curve" rather than the symmetrical one as shown in Figure 3.4. Thus McClelland's discussion of the Alpert study has some support.

The best study under the single-sensory dimension (relative) heading is the study by Haber (1958) in which clear butterfly curves were obtained for each subject in the experiment. The stimuli were buckets of water at varying temperatures. The subject dipped both hands into one bucket and held them there until they had adapted (they could no longer feel warmth or cold). The hands were then placed in two other buckets with the instructions to remove the less pleasant hand. After the choice was recorded, the hands were again placed in the adaptation level bucket until adapted, and then another comparison was made. Data from this technique comprised a paired-comparison technique from which preferences could be plotted while such things as left versus right hand, and the spatial position of various buckets could be controlled. Figure 4.3

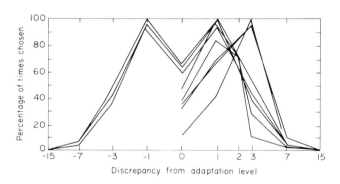

FIG. 4.3. Affect as a function of discrepancies of temperature above and below the *AL* (Haber, 1958, p. 373).

presents the results of this experiment using 33°C as the *AL*. It is clear that the discrepancy hypothesis derives strong support from this experiment. Haber had less success when he attempted to adapt the subjects to temperatures above skin temperatures. Here we confront the possibility of a skewed curve, and again it is possible that the Terwilliger formula with its correction for discrepancy from natural adaptation level might help account for these data.

Probably one of the most sophisticated studies in this area is the rat study by McCall (1965) in which changes in light intensity were made contingent upon bar pressing. Groups of rats experienced a change in illumination subsequent to bar pressing that was one of 3 levels (equal log units) brighter or one of 3 levels duller than the initial level. McCall found a symmetrical curve of increasing bar pressing rate as a function of increased amount of change (either brighter or duller) from initial level. "After the consistent but decidedly less potent effects of the initial and consequent intensities were extracted, a symmetrical curve very much like Haber's (1958) theoretical formulation accounted for 86% of the remaining variance" (McCall, 1965, p. 262).

The next study in this section (Hunt & Quay, 1961) will be touched on only briefly here. It will be discussed in detail under the heading "Discrepant Notes." Hunt and Quay reared rats in vibrating cages and tested them against control rats as to frequency of bar pressing *(a)* to turn vibration off and *(b)* to turn vibration on. The results are interpreted as indicating that vibration is innately negative in reinforcement value, and that rearing rats in vibration does not result in their preferring it but apparently reduces their aversion to it. The authors suggest that these data call into question Hebb's (1949) discrepancy principle[5] as well as the discrepancy hypothesis of McClelland *et al.* (1953).

The two other studies listed in this section (Table 4.1) are used by Hunt and Quay (1961) as further evidence for the proposition that some stimuli are innately negatively reinforcing. Results similar to Hunt and Quay's were found using sucrose octaacetate (an avoided substance) in the water of rats from birth (Warren & Pfaffman, 1959) and rearing rats in flickering light (Meier, Foshee, Wittrig, Peeler, & Huff, 1960).

ABSOLUTE AESTHETIC STUDIES

Angier (1903) studied the aesthetics of unequal division. He confronted his subjects with an apparatus on which they could adjust the division of a 160-mm line. Subjects moved the divider through all positions first and then adjusted it to the most pleasing one. No judgment of equal division was allowed. McClelland *et al.* (1953) reduced Angier's data to graphic form (see Figure 4.4) resulting in a "butterfly curve." Unfortunately, the zero frequency at equal division resulted from the instructions to the subjects. However, the original data demonstrate that

---

[5]Hebb's principle is cited as stressing that large discrepancies from accustomed stimulation (a stable cage for rats reared in vibration) should be disturbing and avoided.

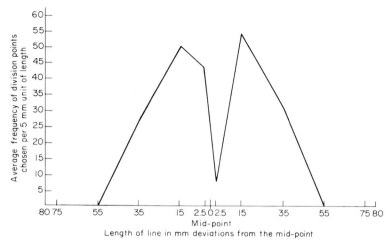

FIG. 4.4 Unequal division points of a straight line chosen as most pleasing (McClelland *et al.,* 1953, p. 49).

both sides of the curve turn down from their maximum points to empirically determined less preferred points close to equality. Nine of ten subjects had lower frequencies of choices close to equality than farther out. This is evidence that the middle point and points around it are less preferred.

Maddi (1961) reports a study in which environmental regularity was varied. Each subject received a booklet, each page of which contained either a number or a sentence-completion item. The booklets were composed in such a way that during the first eight series of pages (24 pages), each set ended by a sentence completion. The order was regular in all sets (number, number, sentence completion) or irregular in all sets. Thus in the regular series, subjects set up an expectancy of regularity, whereas no such expectancy was possible in the irregular series. One-third of the subjects were randomly assigned regular booklets and required to predict after each series the order of the next series; one-third were assigned regular booklets and not required to predict; and one-third were assigned irregular booklets and not required to predict. Thus an incomplete 2×2 design was used. Three of the four possible combinations of regularity-irregularity, prediction-no-prediction were used, omitting the irregularity-prediction cell.

After the eight series that established regularity or irregularity, each subject received a ninth series. Each of the three groups was subdivided and received *(a)* a ninth series that was the same as the regular series (number, number, sentence completion), *(b)* a ninth series that deviated by one degree (either adding or dropping a number), or *(c)* a ninth series which deviated by two degrees (either adding or dropping two numbers). Thus the independent variables constituted environmental regularity-irregularity and within regularity prediction or no-prediction. Orthogonal to these variations deviation from the regular series was varied from zero deviation to 2 degrees of deviation.

The dependent variable consisted of a measure of affective tone derived from a type of content analysis of the sentence completions. Affective tone was scored on a five point scale if the completion being scored fell into one or more of five content dimensions, namely: (1) expected outcome, (2) evaluation, (3) interest, (4) description, (5) expressed feeling. If the completion was not relevant to any of these dimensions it was given the neutral score of three. In short, a careful attempt was made to get a valid and reliable (inter-scorer reliability .91) measure of affective tone from the sentence completions.

Since a sentence completion occurred at the end of each of the nine series, a check on changes in affective tone as the series progressed was available. These results showed that for the prediction group (regularity) affective tone rose from negative to a positive peak (of interest?) at series 3 and then dropped off to a negative rating. For the no-prediction group (regularity), a similar relationship appeared with a peak at series 4. The no-regularity group showed no pronounced peak and was generally lower (always in the negative range) than the other two groups. These results may be seen as indicating that as the regularity of the environment (presented in the booklets) establishes itself, affective tone moves from slightly negative to positive and back to negative. Apparently, expectation is not met at first; but as the series continues, the expectation in the regular series comes closer to the outcome (producing positive affect), then, when the clear expectation is always confirmed late in the series, the affect drops again to slightly negative. There was evidence for this interpretation that involved the percentage of incorrect predictions. This percentage steadily decreased, but when it was still moderately high, affective tone peaked. When the percentage of incorrect prediction had dropped to 6%, the affective tone was negative. Apparently, predicting (paying closer attention?) led to earlier coincidence between expectation and outcome and to an earlier peak in affect as well as an earlier drop off presumably to boredom. All of these results may be interpreted as an expectancy shift in expectation level that changes the discrepancy between expectation level and the outcome, and hence leads to changes in affect—first increase and then decrease—as would be predicted by the discrepancy hypothesis. In this connection, the similarity between these and some results with rhythm (Alpert, 1953) that will be presented below should be noted.

Maddi's results for the three levels of deviation from regularity in series nine are presented in Figure 4.5. The discrepancy hypothesis would predict first an increase and then a decrease in affect as deviations from regularity (expectation level) increase. This prediction is confirmed since both the prediction and no-prediction groups who received environmental regularity (developed an expectation level) show this general trend. The no-regularity group, having developed no such expectation level, would be predicted to show no such relationship, and they did not.

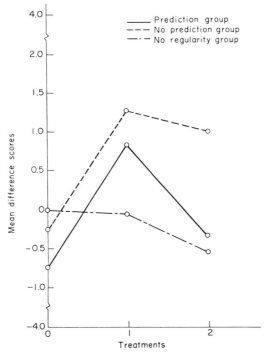

Fig. 4.5. Mean difference scores associated with treatments 0, 1, and 2 (Maddi, 1961, p. 343).

These results, however, do not quite fit the McClelland formulation of the discrepancy hypothesis, since the zero deviation from regularity apparently leads not to neutral affect but to slight negative affect. Maddi, in fact, predicted negative affect with no deviation arguing from data on satiation by Karsten (1928). Maddi's results are consistent with those reported earlier by Saidullah (1927), in which very low concentrations of salt were rated as moderately unpleasant. Apparently, the discrepancy hypothesis may have to be slightly modified, since there is some evidence that zero or very small discrepancies from either a natural adaptation level (in taste) or an expectation level (in environmental regularity) may be slightly negative.

Finally, under this heading we have placed a study on humor in joke endings (Kenny, 1955), which will be discussed in more detail under "Discrepant Notes." In this study subjects were presented with 30 jokes that had been classified as to three degrees of incongruity of ending. The results demonstrated "that the lowest stimulus-expectancy incongruity jokes are rated the most humorous. This result argues strongly against both the incongruity and the discrepancy hypothesis" (p. 647). This result looks more like evidence for stimulus-intensity-reduction theories.

RELATIVE AESTHETIC STUDIES

In his Master's thesis, Alpert (1953) attempted to demonstrate the effects of repetition of rhythms on affect. As mentioned earlier, he found that repetition resulted in affective responses that were at first negative, then positive, and then neutral. These results are similar to Maddi's (1961) findings with successive affective measurement in his series of environmental regularity, and they can be similarly interpreted. If the rhythm is assumed to be strange and unexpected at first, then the distance between the event (listening to the rhythm) and the expectation level is great, resulting in negative affect. Repetition increases the familiarity of the rhythm, that is, it moves the expectation level toward it so that the discrepancy becomes smaller and approaches zero, resulting in positive affect and then in indifference.

This theoretical interpretation involves many untested assumptions, such as the assumption that there is something like an expectation level (which presumably could be measured), that there is some underlying dimension of familiarity of expectedness, and that repetition of a stimulus complex moves the expectation level along the continuum. In a series of studies using musical stimuli, Pitts (1963) set out to test some of these assumptions. He chose complexity as the concept to be scaled and attempted to obtain both an objective (physical) measure and a subjective (psychophysical) measure of complexity of musical stimuli that could be related to a hedonic measure. The goal was to plot the relationship between subjective evaluations of complexity and hedonic evaluations (hypothesizing a butterfly curve) and to demonstrate the effects of repetition of one stimulus on the curve.

Several preliminary studies were conducted attempting to refine an objective measure of complexity, using information theory with its concept of uncertainty (unexpectedness), and to relate this objective physical measure to subjective scaling of complexity. Measurement of music by information theory turned out to be quite complex, and Pitts moved in the direction of tailoring his musical stimuli (specifically written) to a simplified objective measure which was based entirely on probabilities of the occurrence of notes in the melody line of the music. Such things as rhythm, tempo, and mood were held constant. By this means, a series of chordal sequences were composed ranging from a highly predictable one in which dependent probabilities were high, to one sequence in which the chords were assigned by use of a table of random numbers. With such a series of chords, Pitts demonstrated a high relationship between the objective measurement of uncertainty and the subjective scaling of complexity by subjects ($r = +.94$, $N = 42$). However, with these highly controlled stimuli, the subjects' affective responses were not significantly different for the various sequences and were essentially neutral to all stimuli.

In order not to throw out the affect with the information theory, Pitts returned to a set of musical stimuli that were not so severely restricted by the dictates of the objective measurement, i.e., that were more like real music. With these stimuli, using both a paired-comparison and a simple absolute scale technique to measure perceived complexity and affect, Pitts obtained data that showed (1) very high relationships between the more laborious paired-comparisons and the simple scales, (2) a relationship between affect and complexity that could be interpreted as a butterfly curve, and (3) no effect on the curve of 20 repetitions of the most liked musical stimulus. This last result called into question the hypothesis that repetition (increased familiarity) would move the butterfly curve. However, it did indicate the high reliability of both the complexity and affect measures and showed that the obtained curve could be replicated with the same subjects three times with a week intervening between two of the measurements.

Having demonstrated the validity of the simple absolute scales (by comparison to paired-comparisons), Pitts replicated the whole study using different subjects ($N = 32$). This replication had the advantage that the subjects did not listen to a complete paired-comparison matrix for each measure. They merely listened to all stimulus items and scaled each one (on a five point scale) for affect; then heard them all again and scaled them for complexity. The most *disliked* item[6] was then repeated 21 times, after which affect and complexity were again measured in that order.

---

[6]This was assessed from earlier groups and, incidentally, was the item that was rated as most complex.

The results can be seen in Figure 4.6. As in the previous study a butter-fly-like curve is apparent both before and after repetition, and there is apparently no effect of the repetition between the pre- and post-test.

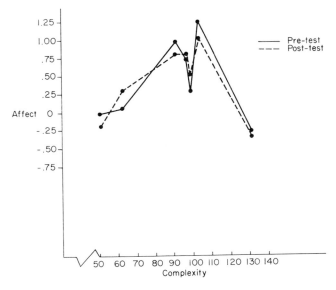

FIG. 4.6. Mean of pre- and post-test measures of affect as a function of complexity of musical selections (Pitts, 1963, p. 44).

Further discussion of this study will appear later in the chapter. The evidence seems to be quite good for the shape of the curve, although there are problems in assessing just where the dip should occur, i.e., where the expectation level can be assumed to be. Statistical techniques, however, did establish that the dip could not be attributed to random fluctuation. In addition, the trough is quite close to the arithmetic mean of judged complexity of all stimuli. This is the point that would be assumed to be the adaptation level in psychophysical judgements such as weight lifting (Helson, 1947).

Another study under this heading (Terwilliger, 1963) used two-inch squares containing various patterns produced by drawing lines parallel to the sides and resulting in rectangles of various sizes in various positions. A technique of measuring these patterns for complexity was developed using information theory, thus generating the underlying dimension. Subjects in two replications were presented with booklets of these patterns, and after familiarizing themselves with the patterns, they chose the most pleasing and the least pleasing pattern. Using these as end points of a seven point scale, they rated all of the patterns (37 patterns in the first replication and 61 in the second).

Terwilliger argued that there were two plausible hypotheses concerning the relationship between complexity and pleasingness. Citing Koffka (1935) he argued that the Gestalt position might posit that the simpler the figure the more pleasing it would be. Thus pleasingness would be a simple negative function of complexity much like the theoretical relationship presented above (Figure 3.1), for the stimulus-intensity-reduction theories. Terwilliger presents the following formula for this hypothesis:

$$Pl = -aC + b$$

Pl stands for pleasingness, C for complexity, and a and b are constants. The second hypothesis is the discrepancy hypothesis, for which the following formula is presented:

$$Pl = a + b \mid D \mid -c \mid D \mid^2$$

where D stands for the discrepancy between the stimulus and the adaptation level. Terwilliger combined the two to give his hypothesis, which predicts a skewed butterfly curve where pleasingness is both a function of the discrepancy between the stimulus and the adaptation level and of the absolute complexity of the stimulus that is at adaptation level, thus:

$$Pl = a + b \mid D_c \mid -c \mid D_c \mid^2 -d \mid D_c \mid$$

where D_c equals the difference between the complexity of the pertinent stimulus, and the complexity of the stimulus at adaptation level.

This is a new and provocative postulation of a skewed form of the discrepancy hypothesis, which predicts that as the adaptation level (or in our terminology as applied to aesthetic stimuli, the expectation level) deviates more and more from some natural adaptation level, the curve will become more and more skewed.

The results of Terwilliger's studies are seen in Figure 4.7, and they tend to support his contentions. The adaptation level was established as the mean complexity value of all patterns. The curve is hand drawn and no statistics of goodness of fit to the theoretical curve were derived.

Munsinger and Kessen (1964) report a series of nine studies relating stimulus variability and meaningfulness to preferences in human subjects. Using random shapes and different sequential approximations to

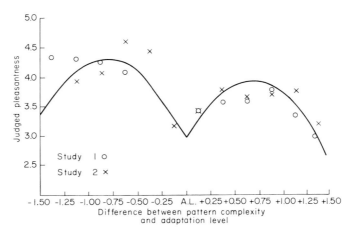

FIG. 4.7. The relationship between pattern complexity and median rated pleasantness of patterns (Terwilliger, 1963, p. 392).

English, they were able to present stimuli that varied from completely redundant to completely random. The approximations to English varied from one word repeated over and over, through prose passages and four orders of statistical approximations, to completely random words. The random shapes were developed by a technique involving a square board with 10,000 points on which polygons with various numbers of exterior angles could be constructed using procedures of random selection of coordinates. Shapes were generated of increasing complexity from 3 turns (or angles) up to 40 turns. Results clearly indicated preferences for the mid-ranges of complexity. Inferring cognitive uncertainty from statistical complexity, Munsinger and Kessen say: "There is an intermediate amount of cognitive uncertainty which is consistently preferred. Cognitive uncertainty is jointly determined by number of independent characteristics of the stimuli and their judged meaningfulness. Preference varies with Ss' experience of variability, whether experience is induced experimentally or is the result of specific professional training" (Munsinger & Kessen, 1964, p. 22).

DISCREPANT NOTES

Hunt and Quay (1961) set out to test some implications of what they conceive to be the discrepancy principle as presented by Hebb. "Hebb (1949, p. 149) claimed that while mild discrepancies in sequences and qualities of inputs from the accustomed sequences or qualities may be pleasurable, large discrepancies will produce the disruptive emotional disturbance" (Hunt & Quay, 1961, p. 149). Assuming that normal rats will learn to press a bar to stop their cage from vibrating, Hunt and Quay go on to say: "Hebb's discrepancy principle suggests that rats reared in a vibrating cage *(a)* will learn to press a bar to reinstate the accustomed vibration once it is removed and *(b)* will fail to learn to press a bar to stop vibration" (p. 149).

Three litters of rats ($N = 20$) were reared from before birth in vibrating cages, and three litters ($N = 21$) were reared normally. These environmental conditions prevailed until the rats were 56 days old, at which time testing began. Each rat was tested individually in a separate cage containing a lever. In the first series of tests the cage was stable, and a bar press produced 30 seconds of vibration. The number of bar presses was measured over a 24-hour period. After most of the rats had been thus tested, the second series was carried out in which the test cage was vibrating and a bar press stopped vibration for 30 seconds. Since each rat was tested individually, it took three months to complete the testing. Table 4.2 presents the results.

TABLE 4.2
MEAN NUMBER OF BAR PRESSES TO TURN VIBRATION
ON OR OFF[a]

		Result of Bar Press	
		Vibration ON	Vibration OFF
Vibrated animals	N	17	20
	$\bar{X}$	9.8	10.1
Controls	N	13	21
	$\bar{X}$	16.8	47.5
	p	<.01	<.001

[a] Material from Hunt and Quay (1961)

These results are interpreted by Hunt and Quay as contradicting "the expectation that the vibrated animals would press the bar more often than the controls to obtain vibration" (p. 151). The results do confirm the expectation "that the control animals did press the bar more often. . . than did the vibrated animals to stop vibration" (p. 151). Thus Hunt and Quay's derivation from Hebb's discrepancy principle does not receive support in the main test with the vibrated animals.

Hunt and Quay go on to say "apparently living with vibration from before birth can *diminish the negative reinforcement value* of vibration. . . but it *fails to give vibration positive reinforcement value*. . . . Although the fact that vibrated pups and control pups had essentially equal weights at 4 weeks of age argues that vibration can hardly be considered to be noxious, this finding suggests that it must be *innately negative in reinforcement value*" (p. 152). They claim that their procedures give an operational definition of innately negative reinforcement value. Citing further evidence from Warren and Pfaffman (1959) using sucrose octaacetate, and Meier *et al.* (1960) using flickering light, Hunt and Quay conclude that "these findings do not deny the discrepancy principle; they merely set a limit upon it beyond that already clearly recognized in stimuli which are painful or organismically damaging. Innately negative reinforcement value may thus be seen to be independent of either pain or noxiousness" (p. 153). In addition to this conclusion, which is obviously relevant to affect theories, Hunt and Quay point out that their results are difficult to reconcile with the McClelland *et al.* (1953) and Haber (1958) statements of the discrepancy hypothesis. Citing Haber's symmetrical butterfly curve (see Figure 4.2), Hunt and Quay point out the impossibility of fitting a symmetrical curve despite the fact that they have very few points to plot.

One bit of data reported by Hunt and Quay, however, is very intriguing and lends some credence to the butterfly-curve notion. Hunt and Quay assumed that vibrated animals would turn on the vibration more than nonvibrated animals, and, when this was not the result found, they assumed that they had made their point against Hebb. But they seem to have slighted a most intriguing finding. The control rats actually turn on the vibration *significantly more often* than do the vibrated rats. (This result is significant at less than the .02 level of probability by either a *t* or the Mann-Whitney *U*.) How can this be explained by assuming that vibration constitutes innately negative reinforcement?

Some more complex hypothesis than the mere assumption that "living with vibration from before birth can *diminish the negative reinforcement value of vibration*" (Hunt & Quay, 1961, pp. 151–152) is needed. If it is assumed that the experimental rearing has moved the adaptation level of the vibrated animals toward vibration and away from no vibration, then these results (of turning vibration on) would be predicted by the McClelland-Haber theory. This is because vibration would be a moderate discrepancy and hence sought out for the control rats, but would be less of a discrepancy for the vibrated animals. How else may the findings be explained?

It is impossible to resolve the problem with data from only two points on the curve, and it is true that a symmetrical butterfly curve cannot be fitted. However, there is no evidence that the butterfly curve is always symmetrical. McClelland *et al.* (1953) in the earliest formulation considered the concept of natural adaptation levels, and it seems quite clear that in a modality such as response to the warm-cold dimension there are points beyond which the organism cannot adapt. If the adaptation level is approaching the point of nonadaptability, the butterfly curve if applicable at all will of necessity be nonsymmetrical. We have seen that Terwilliger (1963) specifically predicted a nonsymmetrical curve.

Assuming that a nonsymmetrical curve could be used, it is then possible to account for Hunt and Quay's data; *but it is probably inappropriate.* This is because the McClelland-Haber theoretical curve is plotted in terms of absolute levels of affect. The Haber data were collected by a paired-comparison technique where the subject was *forced* to choose one and reject the other stimulus (in a sense, avoid one and approach the other). Hunt and Quay's data, on the other hand, are unique in that the rat is free to choose or not. In one situation, he is selecting (or approaching) vibration and rejecting (avoiding) nonvibration; in the other, the reverse is true. The two environmental conditions under which the rats choose are entirely different. The paradoxical result is that control rats apparently approach vibration significantly more than vibrated rats when it is the result of bar-pressing, but they avoid it far more than vibrated rats do when the result of bar-pressing is to stop it.

This paradox reminds the author of a cliche about New York city. The tourist says, "I love to visit the city but I certainly wouldn't want to live there." In a sense the tourist both seeks it out and avoids the city more than the New Yorker does. This paradox and that of the vibrated rats is beyond our theorizing at present. It would seem more promising, however, to attempt to get some further evidence that could clearly be construed in terms of the discrepancy hypothesis (either positive or negative) rather than to assume that vibration is an innately negative reinforcer. One might simply ask, in closing, if Hunt and Quay's conclusions are correct, why has a company found it profitable to put vibrators in motel beds? Why will a traveler put a quarter in a slot for 30 minutes of "relaxing vibration?"

The Discrepancy Hypothesis and Learned Values, Ego Involvement, and Cognitive Dissonance

The discrepancy hypothesis as presented by McClelland *et al.* (1953) was sketched as a very general principle basic to motivation, and little was said about the possible limits of its usefulness. Thus, applying the principle to situations that involve cognitive expectations leads to the consideration of anticipations or hoped for events. Such research as that done on level of aspiration and risk-taking may seem to be explicable in terms of the discrepancy hypothesis. This is probably a misapplication of the principle. The research discussed up to this point demonstrates that some variant of the discrepancy hypothesis derives support in sensory or aesthetic realms *where the subject has no vested interest through learned values or ego involvement in the outcome.*

It makes sense, and we shall see some data that support the necessity, to restrict the discrepancy hypothesis and not try to use it in situations in which the subject has attached affect to certain outcomes. In this chapter, we have been discussing required relationships between stimuli and affect; but similar relationships may not obtain when acquired dispositions are strong. Stimuli that produce one type of affect intrinsically may acquire the capacity to produce a different type of affect extrinsically through learning. What we have covered, up to this point, merely sets the stage for a discussion of more complex relationships, for obviously much behavior in the working life of adult humans involves more than the arousal of affect by sensory stimulation; it involves acquired and extrinsic relationships and self-relevant values.

An example of misapplication of the discrepancy hypothesis to a situation in which stimuli have acquired extrinsic value is in the area of school grades. It seems ridiculous to predict that a student expecting a C would be happy receiving a B (small discrepancy) but unhappy receiving an A (large discrepancy). Grades are extrinsic motivators themselves and have acquired values that are arbitrary and independent of discrepancies between expectations and outcome. There is the possibility that a student expecting a C and receiving an A may feel some discomfort in his inability to predict. However, this is not because of the affect associated with the "good" grade, but because of the unpredictable environment. He may be concerned that if the world is that unpredictable the next time he may receive an F; but such a feeling is not based on the absolute value of the grade.

Van Ostrand (1960) and Harvey and Clapp (1965) have conducted experiments specifically to demonstrate the inapplicability of the discrepancy hypothesis to such situations. Harvey and Clapp dealt with personal evaluations of subjects where they could be assumed to hope for positive evaluations. They predict that deviations toward hope (the good end of the continuum) will lead to positive affect, and deviations away from hope will lead to negative affect.

> Subjects were exposed to controlled feedback which deviated from their expectancies by equal magnitudes toward either the confirmation or refutation of

hope. More specifically, subjects indicated both how they expected and hoped to be rated by a relative stranger on 15 characteristics and, in addition to rating themselves and the stranger on the same scale, they completed a scale aimed at measuring their self-esteem. Following exposure to ratings from the stranger that deviated from subject's expectancy by comparable amounts toward either confirming or refuting hope (which was higher than expectancy), each subject redid the above ratings as well as completing a three-item scale that asked his degree of pleasure-disappointment, and his feelings of positivity-negativity toward himself and the other person as a consequence of the evaluations made of him. This provided eight dependent variables, five relating to change in ratings of expectancy, self, the other person, and self-esteem and three relating to effective consequences of the feedback (p. 46).

Seventy-nine subjects participated in the experiment. Results showed that none of the dependent variables showed a relationship to the independent variable (deviation from expectancy) that would be predicted by the discrepancy hypothesis. Six of the eight dependent variables were significant, showing, in general, increases (in affect) as a function of the size of discrepancy from expectancy in the direction of hope (positive evaluation) and decreases as a function of the size of discrepancy away from hope.

It would seem that these results permit the clear inference that not only the magnitude of the deviation of an input from expectancy but that direction of the discrepancy, toward the confirmation or refutation of hope, also contributes significantly to the affective and behavioral consequences of an event. The fact that equivalent deviations from expectancy produced different effects depending on their relationship to hope indicates that such discrepancy hypotheses as those embodied in the notion of the butterfly curve (McClelland et al., 1953; Haber, 1958) do not hold when aspiration and preferences are called into play (pp. 50–51).

A study by Kenny (1955) presents data dealing with humor that apparently gives another lead in restricting the application of the discrepancy hypothesis. In this study, jokes were rated on the surprisingness of the ending and were classified into three categories of deviation from the expected. Contrary to the discrepancy hypothesis prediction that the moderate category would be judged the most entertaining, the ratings showed the jokes with the most expected endings to be most pleasing and those with the least expected endings to be least pleasing. This experiment was confounded by the use of jokes considered to be examples from both of Freud's types, i.e., harmless wit and tendency wit, and there was a predominance of tendency-wit jokes in the small discrepancy group. We would expect the affect associated with tendency wit to derive from ego orientation, to be stronger than that from harmless wit, and not to follow the discrepancy hypothesis. On the other hand, harmless wit, which involves no self-orientation, should be found to follow the discrepancy hypothesis.

Festinger's (1957) theory of cognitive dissonance results in predictions about deviations from expectancies that differ from those of the discrepancy hypothesis. The theory and results deriving from Festinger's formulations deal most often with situations that are strongly self-relevant rather than with the more sensory or aesthetic areas in which the discrepancy hypothesis applies. However, one study investigating cognitive dissonance deals with discrepancies from expectations and is apparently relevant to the discrepancy hypothesis.

Aronson and Carlsmith (1962) dealt with performance expectancy as a determinant of actual performance. They found evidence for the prediction that "if a person expects to perform poorly in a particular endeavor, a good performance will be inconsistent with his expectancy; he will attempt to reduce dissonance by denying this performance" (p. 182). The results might be seen as confirming the expectation from the discrepancy hypothesis that a student who expects a C and receives an A will be unhappy, although no measure of affect was used. This interpretation has little to recommend it, however, and the cognitive dissonance explanation presented by Aronson and Carlsmith seems more cogent. This experiment is clearly a case in which self-relevance is involved, and thus we would not apply the discrepancy hypothesis. Here, in contrast to the Harvey and Clapp (1965) study, there seems to be more involvement in maintaining a consistent self-image (of poor performance) than in showing good performance.

We have attempted to present some of the evidence for and against the discrepancy hypothesis, and we have found that the type of situation to which it may be applicable apparently needs restriction. Ego-involving level of aspiration situations evidently involve other relationships between affect and stimulation. Let us now return to the sensory and aesthetic realm and speculate about some possible problems and extensions.

Some Speculations about the Discrepancy Hypothesis

McClelland's statement of the discrepancy hypothesis apparently makes sense phenomenologically in some areas. However, despite the extensive data just reported, it can still be questioned whether the hypothesis is an adequate basis upon which to develop a type of affective map of stimuli and further to develop motivational propositions. Inadequacies may be found at two levels: (a) in comprehensiveness of the hypothesis, but (b) more basically in the vagueness of the statement of the hypothesis, which leads to ambiguity as to measurement techniques and operations adequate for experimental tests.

The greatest difficulties arise in attempting to deal with complex stimuli or stimulus patterns. Clearly, many complex stimulus patterns — beautiful paintings or pieces of music — produce affect within the human organism; but along what dimensions can these be scaled? McClelland assumes that the discrepancy hypothesis holds at the sensory level within one sensory dimension. Evidence for this comes from work by Engel (1928) for taste and Haber (1958) for temperature. In both cases, a simple physical dimension is used along which differences of intensity of stimulation may be related to reported affect. In the taste experiment, concentration of solution is used; in the temperature experiment, the logarithm of degrees centigrade. Actually, the discrepancy hypothesis deals with a relationship between affect and perceived discrepancies, not between affect and absolute intensities of stimuli even at the level of one sensory dimension. In other words, the perception of the stimulus and its discrepancy from past stimulus events is what is called for by the hypothesis. A direct test of the discrepancy hypothesis as stated by McClelland demands psychophysical scaling of the perception of differences along the perceptual dimension from some adaptation level. This scale forms the abscissa or independent variable in the typical schematic drawing of the discrepancy hypothesis. In addition, some determination of the adaptation level of the organism is necessary. Neither Engel nor Haber actually measured perceptual differences along the abscissa. They assumed them to be a function of physical measurement of intensity differences. In the Haber experiment, physical measurement of intensity was combined with determination of the adaptation level. Since the general relationship between physical measurement of intensity and perceived differences is known to approximate a logarithmic scale from the adaptation level, Haber was on safe ground in assuming that the perceived differences correspond very well with his physical scale of measurement.

The point that the discrepancy hypothesis calls for a perceptual scale of differences from some adaptation level has been labored because it becomes crucial when an experimenter attempts to test the discrepancy hypothesis with stimuli that vary along some dimension for which no simple physical measure of intensity is available. McClelland apparently feels that the hypothesis applies much more broadly than just to situations in which physical intensity can be measured. Yet, in attempting to apply the hypothesis at the more complex level, measurement difficulties arise, and it would seem that there are conceptual difficulties also.

A case in point is the study by Pitts (1963), described earlier. The study was initiated with the intention of developing a type of physical measure of the complexity of music using information theory and the concept of entropy. This measure was supposed to be roughly comparable to Haber's physical temperature scale. However, Pitts had to determine the relationship between this measure and subjects' perceived differences in complexity, since there was no careful psychophysical experimentation to demonstrate this relationship as there was in the realm of temperature differences. As a matter of fact, it turned out that scaling of music with an entropy measure in itself was a difficult task, and that the perception of music by subjects along a simplicity-complexity dimension was quite complicated.

During the course of several pilot studies designed to develop musical stimuli that would meet the requirements of scaling both by entropy and perceptually with a high degree of comparability, Pitts discovered that his stimuli had to be made simpler and simpler until he was reduced to simple chordal progressions that could be considered music in only a very rudimentary sense. It was clear that complexity of musical stimuli, as perceived by the human ear, involved dimensions not tapped by his measure of entropy. It should not be assumed from this that an entropy measure could not be developed that would account for the subtle distinctions made by the human ear. At present we do not know, although it is clear that Pitt's entropy measure could be refined. Actually, it accounted only for probabilities of the various notes in the melody line. Probabilities of combinations of notes of several orders could be built in, as well as similar probabilities for notes other than the melody. In addition, rhythmic variations ought to be scalable, taking the probability of quarter-notes, half-notes, etc. Rhythm plus pitch of notes might be combined, and so on. The possibilities of developing a more complex entropic measure of music are many, but the computation becomes formidable even with high-speed computers. For this reason, Pitts decided in his pilot studies to tailor the music to his entropy measure, rather than to do the reverse. Thus his chordal sequences forced a relationship between the melody line and notes in the chord, tempo was strictly controlled, and rhythm was not varied. This resulted in increasing the correlation between the entropic measure and the perceived complexity, but as the musical stimuli were simplified over the course of various pilot studies and perceived differences in complexity became more highly related to the entropic measure, the subjects reported fewer differences in affective reactions to the stimuli. As a matter of fact, there were no significant differences between reported affective feelings for the various chordal sequences. For this reason, Pitts abandoned the chordal sequences and the entropic measure and returned to stimuli that were more like music. Is it possible that variations along a simple physical dimension do not produce affect, and that the discrepancy hypothesis applies only when two or more dimensions are present?

Such a proposition at first seems completely untenable. It seems to be refuted by data from Engel and Haber; and if several underlying dimensions are necessary in order to produce affect, it would seem that the problem becomes hopelessly complex. Does the discrepancy hypothesis now imply discrepancies along all dimensions, between two dimensions, or what?

On the other hand, such a proposition clarifies some problems. For instance, why has no one reported a discrepancy curve of affect associated with discrepancies from adaptation levels in the time-honored area of lifted weights? After all, this is the area in which the concept of adaptation level was developed by Helson (1947). If more than one dimension is necessary, then one would not expect to find associated affect. The author does not recall any published study that attempted to relate affect to variations in a lifted-weights study.[7]

Another lead comes from careful consideration of the studies that apparently refute the proposition. Thus, Haber found clear affective relationships with the single dimension of variations in temperature. The measurement technique used by Haber, however, may have been very important in determining his results. He spoke of one adaptation level, but as a matter of fact he adapted both hands to the same level, and then forced a contrast between them by immersing them in water of different temperatures. The important point here is that a contrast was developed between two separate sets of receptors simultaneously. The same was true of Alpert's study using the cones of the retina. It may be that simple change of the stimulations of a given set of receptors along one dimension produces no affect, but that some kind of simultaneous contrast effect does.

McClelland et al. (1953) have hypothesized that receptors such as the cones of the retina that adapt to small changes rapidly should produce little affect, whereas receptors that adapt slowly, such as taste and smell receptors, should produce much affect (see also Chapter 3). We might postulate further that for slow-adapting receptors successive comparison would yield affect, but for fast-adapting receptors simultaneous comparisons would be necessary. One might conclude from this that *contrast* is

---

[7]One of the author's students, R. F. Singer, reports that his subjects ($N=6$) were unable to report affective responses to variations in lifted weights.

the essence of stimuli that produce affect; that simultaneous contrast is effective for quick-adapting receptors; and that successive contrast may be effective only for slow-adapting receptors. If this analysis has any merit, it would be interesting to conduct affect experiments using both simultaneous and successive techniques (methods of single stimuli and paired-comparisons). Could it be, for instance, that if asked to report affective sensations when lifting weights singly the subjects will fail, but if asked to drop the weight that is least preferred when two are lifted after an adaptation level has been produced, the subjects will have consistent instantaneous preferences? Apparently, within a single physical dimension, contrast, especially simultaneous contrast, can produce affect. What about contrast between dimensions? Is such a phrase meaningful? In dealing with stimuli such as music, it is easy to assume that there may be several dimensions involved, and several adaptation levels, but this is very difficult to demonstrate. It is in realms such as these that Mc-Clelland assumes an analogue of the discrepancy hypothesis. The adaptation level becomes an expectation level, and the discrepancies often involve discrepancies along a familiarity dimension that is closely related to expectations.

There are many problems in making the jump from sensory stimuli, which are closely related to one physical dimension and to one type of sensory receptor, to more complex stimuli. Clearly, the notion of "expectation" involves a cognitive element that has not appeared prominently in more purely sensory studies. The concept probably involves us with a learning aspect also, for expectations are learned. It is when these purely psychological aspects — cognition and learning — enter the picture that we seem to be most at a loss as to how to predict the production of affect from physical stimuli. It is just such situations, however, that are apparently the most common in everyday life.

Are there any experiences in everyday life that apparently produce affective responses? "We have a most extremely delicate foreshadowing of the sensory effects. Why else the start of surprize that runs through us if someone has filled the light-seeming box with sand before we try to lift it, or has substituted for the cannon-ball which we know a painted wooden imitation? *Surprize* can only come from getting a sensation which differs from the one we expect. But the truth is that when we know the objects well, the very slightest difference from the expected weight will surprize us, or at least attract our notice" (James, 1890, pp. 501–502). The recent proliferation of light plastic objects has probably made the experience described by James familiar to us all, namely, the lifting of an object such as a plastic toy or wastebasket that has the appearance of being rather bulky, only to have it apparently leap up at us. Such an experience usually results in a mild surprise that has affective connotations, and is the result of a discrepancy between a cognitive expectation based on past experience (learning) and deriving from visual inspection of the object and the kinesthetic event of lifting it, i.e., a discrepancy involving two sensory modalities. The most difficult concept to handle at this level is expectation. Apparently, the major difference between expectation versus stimulus discrepancies and adaptation versus stimulus discrepancies (as in the Haber experiment) is a cognitive one. Adaptation can be said to be a sensory phenomenon and is usually the result of immediate past experience. Expectation is commonly thought of as a cognitive phenomenon and may be the result of more distant past experience. The cognitive element is especially evident in the fact that objects are apparently cognitively categorized, and effects on expectations are often limited to these categories. Thus, D. R. Brown (1953) demonstrated that the Helson adaptation level phenomenon obtained within a class of objects seen by subjects as weights to be lifted in the experiment. When the experiment was apparently interrupted and the subject was asked to hand the experimenter a pack of cigarettes, the immediate past experience in lifting weights had little to do with subject's judgement of the weight of the pack of cigarettes.

The example of surprise at the disconfirmation of an expectation about the weight of an object is already beyond the limits of experimental data and is about as far as we should go in speculation about the discrepancy hypothesis.

To summarize briefly what we have learned in our investigation of the discrepancy hypothesis: *(a)* affect is a function of the discrepancy between simultaneous perceptual events; *(b)* the intensity of the affect may be a function of the speed of adaptation of the sensory receptors; *(c)* the most reliable method of producing affect from discrepancies is by utilizing contrasts between simultaneous perceptual events; *(d)* there is some evidence (Engel, 1928) that contrast between successive perceptual events may produce affect, especially in sense modalities (taste) in which speed of adaptation is slow; *(e)* affect may be the result of contrast between feedback from different receptors of the same sense modality (Haber, 1958), or *(f)* the result of contrast between feedback from different sense modalities although there is no real experimental evidence for this effect.

Conclusions

No attempt will be made at this point to summarize the entire chapter. However, it should be stressed that the data and theories reviewed deal only with innate sources of affect. Having attempted to gain some clarity in this area, we may now move on to build on this foundation some notions of the acquisition of relationships between affect, stimuli and behavior. So far, we have barely scratched the surface of our topic since innate relationships are almost always accompanied by acquired relationships in the organization of adult human behavior.

Before we turn to the question of acquisition, let us try to emphasize the two main points which seem to emerge from the welter of studies reported thus far. Taken as the basic phenomenon under consideration, affect seems to result from two general sources, which can be roughly distinguished conceptually and which seem to follow different principles. One source, for which there is ample evidence, is drives. Apparently drives result in negative affect only, and behavior tends to be organized around the principle of reduction of the negative affect and the drive (drive-stimulus-reduction principle). Drives, as the term implies, may result in "twinges" of affect that energize behavior in a para-mechanical way. In extreme situations of deprivation, drives probably take precedence over other sources of affect, but in everyday life they appear inadequate to account for the affective organization of behavior.

Another general source of affect derives primarily from less extreme and nondrive produced sensory and/or aesthetic stimulation. Such stimulation apparently results in either positive or negative affect, and the most promising principle for the prediction of which kind of affect will result is the discrepancy hypothesis. This hypothesis accounts for results only when past acquisition of evaluative scales and/or ego involvement is minimal, i.e., where innate or intrinsic relationships hold but not where acquired extrinsically developed evaluative dimensions are predominant. Obviously, much more must be said about the development of the acquired evaluative dimensions and the factor of self-involvement.

Chapter 5

THE ACQUISITION OF
AFFECTIVE RELATIONSHIPS

Neutral stimuli that occur regularly in combination with stimuli that produce affect can, by a learning process, come to produce an anticipation of affect that is probably a miniature feeling of affect itself. This fractional anticipatory affect may then come to elicit appropriate behavior that will enhance the affect if positive or reduce it if negative. After learning has occurred, the anticipatory affect may be used as an explanation of behavior — it may be seen as the essence of the motive behind the behavior. The paradigm involved is the one that we started with at the beginning of Chapter 3 (stimulus $\longrightarrow$ affect $\longrightarrow$ behavior), and, despite its paramechanical aspects, it is quite useful in accounting for behavior elicited by strong drives resulting from physiological deprivation, and ego involvement where fear of loss of esteem is at stake — situations in which the anticipatory affect is negative. It may also apply to situations where the anticipatory affect is positive as suggested by McClelland *et al.* (1953).

In this chapter, we shall trace the development of the behavioristic analysis of anticipation in early papers by Hull to the concept of mediation as discussed by Osgood and Mowrer. At the heart of this analysis is the assumption that affect is a distinct stimulus, such as pain, or is associated with a distinct response such as a goal response. As in Chapters 3 and 4, we are here pursuing the molecular and mechanistic approach to its ultimate, despite the reservations stated in Chapters 1 and 2, that a complete analysis of motivated behavior must account for broader aspects than specific stimuli that impel action. After a consideration of "mediating mechanisms," we shall investigate the importance of early learning experiences in the development of affective associations and then consider the question of whether such associations that are crucial to the development of motives are the result of learning or of imprinting.

The acquisition of associations between stimuli and responses is the domain of learning theory, whether it is a reinforcement theory that assumes that reinforcement is necessary for learning to occur or a contiguity theory that assumes that stimuli and responses may become connected merely by occurring together (in contiguity). The acquisition of the capacity of a neutral stimulus to elicit affect may be seen as the problem of secondary reinforcement as posed by learning theorists. Theory and research involving animal learning and primary and secondary reinforcement forms the background for much of the current thinking to be used in the discussion of the basic problem of this chapter.

The Legacy of Learning Theory

Much of what is useful from learning theory concerning affective organizing principles derives originally from a seminal series of papers by Hull (1930, 1931, 1932, 1934). This series forms a *tour de force* of creative thinking. It is a joy to follow a mind such as Hull's in his early attempts to formulate some basic principles of behavior. In order to appreciate and comprehend fully the ideas and the working of this creative man, the reader may find it useful to attempt to forget what he already knows about Hullian theory. He must attempt to place himself in the decade of the 1930's, equipped as it was with evidence from Pavlov, Watson, and Thorndike on conditioning, with the concept of redintegration, and with Hull's original observations of some empirical facts concerning the way rats go about learning a maze. It is a mistake to approach these early papers of Hull with the assumption that they were written to support his later principles of behavior. Rather the reader must realize that Hull is starting with the work of the men mentioned above and with some empirical observations and is attempting tentatively to develop some principles of learning. Indeed, Hull is concerned on the one hand with the inadequacy of Watsonian behavior theory to account for simple behavior of rats, such as the elimination of blind alleys in a maze — behavior, which seems to demonstrate "foresight or purpose." On the other hand, he is concerned with avoiding assumptions about "spiritual or supernatural forces" and with explaining the process by "entirely naturalistic" means.

THE PURE STIMULUS ACT AND THE PRINCIPLE OF REDINTEGRATION

Hull starts with an analysis of a sequence of events and develops the notion of the pure stimulus act, which together with the principle of redintegration tends to account for chaining of actions.[1] The following passage presents this first step.

I

One of the oldest problems with which thoughtful persons have occupied themselves concerns the nature and origin of knowledge. How can one physical object become acquainted with the ways of another physical object and of the world in general? In approaching this problem from the point of view of habit, it is important to recognize that knowledge is mediated by several fairly distinct habit mechanisms. In the present study but one of these will be elaborated.

Let us assume a relatively isolated inorganic world sequence taking place as shown in [Figure 5.1a]. Here S_1, S_2, etc., represent typical phases of a sequential flux, the time intervals between successive S's being uniform and no more than a few seconds each. Let us suppose, further, that in the neighborhood of this world sequence is a sensitive redintegrative organism. The latter is provided with distance receptors and is so conditioned at the outset as to respond characteristically to the several phases of the world sequence. Each S accordingly becomes a stimulus complex impinging simultaneously on numerous end organs. As a result, each phase of the world sequence now becomes a cause, not only of the succeeding phase in its own proper series, but also of a functionally parallel event (reaction) within the neighboring organism. The organismic responses of the series thus formed have no direct causal relationship among themselves. R_1 in itself has no power of causing (evoking) R_2. The causal relationship essential in the placing of R_2 after R_1 is that of the physical world obtaining in the S-sequence; R_2 follows R_1 because S_2 follows S_1. The situation is represented diagrammatically in Figure [5.1b].

Now a high-grade organism possesses internal receptors which are stimulated by its own movements. Accordingly each response (R) produces at once a characteristic stimulus complex and stimuli thus originated make up to a large extent the internal component of the organism's stimuli complexes. Let these internal stimulus components be represented by s's. If we assume, in the interest of simplicity of exposition, that the time intervals between the phases of the world flux selected for representation are exactly equal to those consumed by the $S \rightarrow R \rightarrow s$ sequences, the situation will be as shown in [Figure 5.1c], S_2 coinciding in time with s_1, S_3 with s_2 and so on.

Now, by the principle of redintegration, all the components of a stimulus complex impinging upon the sensorium at or near the time that a response is evoked, tend themselves independently to acquire the capacity to evoke substantially the same response. We will let a dotted rectangle indicate that what is enclosed within it constitutes a redintegrative stimulus complex; and a dotted arrow, a newly acquired excitatory tendency. After one or more repetitions of the world sequence, the situation will be as shown in [Figure 5.1d].

---

[1] It has been the author's experience that a definition of the term "redintegration" should be noted well before continuing to read Hull. It should be noted that the term implies associative learning, but there is no implication that reinforcement is a necessary condition to produce "redintegration." Redintegration is defined in Warren (1934) as "1. The reinstatement of a total presentation, in the form of a memory or idea, upon the appearance of a partial constituent of such (former) presentation; 2. The arousal of a response by a fraction of the stimuli whose combination originally aroused it." The term was introduced by Hamilton (1859).

As a result of the joint operation of the several factors summarized in [Fig. 5.1d], the organismic reactions (*R*'s) which at the outset were joined only by virtue of the energies operating in the outer world sequence of *S's*, are now possessed of a genuine dynamic relationship lying within the organism itself. To make this clear, let it be assumed that the world sequence begins in the presence of the organism, but is at once interrupted. The resulting situation is shown diagrammatically in [Figure 5.1e]. The newly acquired excitatory tendencies, unless interrupted by some potent influence should continue the organismic sequence of responses very much as when they were first called forth as the result of the stimulation by the world sequence.

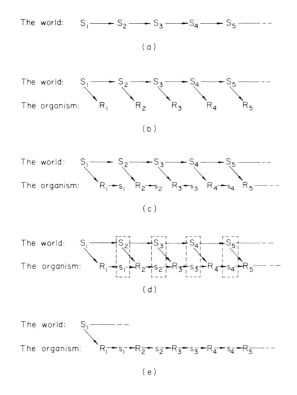

FIG. 5.1 The development of a series of excitatory tendencies (Hull, 1930, pp. 511–513).

In summary it may be said that through the operation of a variety of principles and circumstances, the world in a very important sense has stamped the pattern of its action upon a physical object. The imprint has been made in such a way that a functional parallel of this action segment of the physical world has become a part of the organism. Henceforth the organism will carry about continuously a kind of replica of this world segment. In this very intimate and biologically significant sense the organism may be said to know the world. No spiritual or supernatural forces need be assumed to understand the acquisition of this knowledge. The process is entirely a naturalistic one throughout.

II

Once the organism has acquired within its body this subjective parallel to the ways of the physical world, certain other activity patterns or habit mechanisms at once become operative. One of the more important of these is the power of fore-sight or fore-knowledge. A great deal of mystery has surrounded this problem. Foresight may be defined for our present purpose as *the reaction to an event which may be impending, but which has not as yet taken place.* The difficulty seems largely to have been concerned with the problem of how an organism can react to an event not yet in existence. The reasoning runs: An event not yet in existence cannot be a stimulus; and how can an organism react to a stimulus which does not exist? In terms of our diagram, how can R_5, which is a reaction to the stimulating event s_5, take place before s_5 itself has occurred?

An important circumstance connected with foresight is the fact that the tempo of the acquired subjective parallel to the outer world sequence is not limited to that of the latter. Indeed, there is evidence indicating a tendency for a primary con-ditioned reaction to run off at a higher speed than that of the master world sequence which it parallels. Thus it comes about that, even when both series begin at the same instant, the end-reaction of the subjective series may actually antedate the stimulus in the world sequence which exclusively evoked it previous to the conditioning shown in [Fig. 5.1d]. It is evident that this possibility of the height-ened tempo on the part of the organismic act sequence is intimately connected with the possession by the organism of knowledge of events before they actually take place. . . .

III

A reflective consideration of the habit mechanisms involved in anticipatory defense reactions reveals a phenomenon of the greatest significance. This is the existence of acts whose sole function is to serve as stimuli for other acts. We shall accordingly call them *pure stimulus acts.* Under normal conditions practically all acts become stimuli, but ordinarily the stimulus function is an incidental one. The consideration of the approach of an organism to food may clarify the concept. Each step taken in approaching the food serves in part as the stimulus for the next step, but its main function is to bring the body nearer the food. Such acts are, therefore, primarily instrumental. By way of contrast may be considered the anticipatory defense sequence presented above. R_5, the actual defense reaction, obviously has instrumental value in high degree. R_4, on the other hand, has no instrumental value. This does not mean that it has no significance. Without R_4 there would be no s_4, and without s_4 there would be no R_5 *i.e.,* no defense. In short, R_4 is a pure stimulus act. In the same way R_3 and R_2 serve no instrumental function but, nevertheless, are indispensible as stimulus acts in bringing about the success-ful defense response. . . . The pure stimulus act thus emerges as an organic, physio-logical — strictly internal and individual — symbolism. Quite commonplace instru-mental acts, by a natural reduction process, appear transformed into a kind of *thought* — rudimentary it is true, but of the most profound biological significance.

Thus the transformation of mere action into thought, which has seemed to some as conceivable only through a kind of miracle, appears to be a wholly naturalistic process and one of no great subtlety. Indeed, its obviousness is such as to challenge the attempt at synthetic verification from inorganic materials. It is altogether probable that a "psychic" machine, with ample provision in its design for the evolution of pure stimulus acts, could attain a degree of freedom, spontaneity, and power to dominate its environment, inconceivable alike to individuals unfamiliar with the possibilities of automatic mechanisms and to the professional designers of the ordinary rigid-type machines (Hull, 1930, pp. 511–517).

This type of analysis allowed Hull the luxury of talking about foresight —fore-knowledge and purpose—since the subjective chaining tended to run off ahead of the actual environmental stimuli, antedate them, and hence anticipate them. Up to this point there has been no mention of reinforcement. The principle of redintegration is used to account for acquisition of the pure-stimulus act, i.e., the "organic, physiological symbolism."

THE DRIVE-STIMULUS AND THE GOAL-GRADIENT— THE ADVENT OF REINFORCEMENT

A difficulty arose, however, in the fact that, assuming these mechanisms only, one could not account for the learning of a maze, since the above analysis would predict that the animal would always repeat the same sequence of chained responses that occurred on the first trial, thus never eliminating errors. This was obviously contrary to fact and led Hull to postulate several important mechanisms all of which depend on the importance of primary reinforcement. Hence the importance of reinforcement in the theory.

The mechanisms that he introduced at this point to bring in reinforcement were the drive-stimulus (S_D, called in the first paper S_P) and the goal gradient. He developed the drive-stimulus notion in the following passage, noting in a footnote that the assumed effect of the goal-gradient would be spelled out in a later paper (Hull, 1932).

II

Let it be assumed that a relatively isolated inorganic world flux takes place in time. Characteristic phases of the world sequence, separated from each other by but a few seconds each, are represented by S_1, S_2, S_3, etc., as they appear in [Figure 5.2a]. In the neighborhood of this world sequence is a sensitive redintegrative organism provided with distance receptors and so constituted as to respond characteristically to the several phases of the world flux with a parallel behavior flux. Phases of the response flux corresponding to the world-stimulus flux are represented in [Figure 5.2a] by R_1, R_2, etc., the final or goal reaction being indicated by R_G. Let it be assumed, further, that within the organism there is a source, such as hunger, which produces the continually recurring stimulation represented in [Figure 5.2]by S_D. Now, according to the principle of redintegration, all the components of a stimulus complex which may be impinging on the sensorium at or near the time that a response is evoked tend themselves independently to acquire the capacity to evoke substantially the same response. The stimulus complexes in [Figure 5.2] which fall under this principle are each enclosed within a dotted rectangle. It may be seen from an examination of the diagram that S_D, owing to the fact that it persists throughout the entire behavior sequence, will acquire a tendency to the evocation of R_1, R_2, R_3, and R_G, i.e., to the evocation at any moment of *every* part of the reaction sequence. These newly acquired excitatory tendencies are indicated in the diagram by dotted arrows (Hull, 1931, p. 489).

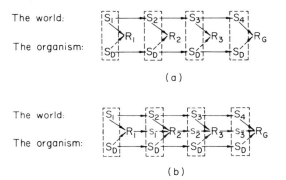

(a)

(b)

FIG. 5.2 The goal-gradient and drive stimulus (Hull, 1931, pp. 489–490).

III

It has been shown elsewhere that under certain conditions, notably when the behavior sequence is made up of symbolic or pure-stimulus acts, the multiple excitatory tendency of the persisting stimulus, S_D, may evoke the final or goal reaction of the series almost or quite at the outset of the movement, thus dropping out the useless and actually wasteful intervening acts formerly leading to the goal. But in cases where the intervening acts are mainly instrumental in nature, as is obviously the case with the locomotor activities involved in maze running, it is physically impossible to drop out any of the acts involved in traversing the *true* pathway and at the same time reach the goal. With the maze remaining constant, the space between the starting point and the goal must, somehow, be gotten over if the food is to be obtained. Consequently, if the anticipatory invasion by the goal reaction of the instrumental behavior sequence normally leading to the goal should result in the interruption of the sequence, the actual goal will never be reached and the episode will be biologically abortive. Such an interruption will inevitably take place either when (*A*) the invading goal reaction is of such a nature that it cannot be performed by the organism at the same time as the antecedent instrumental acts leading up to it, or (*B*) when the execution of the goal reaction results in the removal of the source of the physiological drive stimulus (S_D). . . .

That this abortive anticipatory invasion of the antecedent instrumental sequence by the goal reaction does not take place with as great frequency as does the biologically valuable short-circuiting of pure-stimulus-act sequences raises an important theoretical question. A plausible explanation of this difference is found in the nature of the stimuli complexes operative in the two cases. Except for remote excitatory tendencies, which are here neglected in the interest of simplicity of exposition, the typical stimulus complex of the instrumental sequence leading to a goal is shown in [Fig. 5.2b]. Consider, for example, the stimulus complex immediately preceding R_2. It consists of the external stimulus S_2, the proprioceptive stimulus, s_1, arising from the preceding activity, and the persisting or drive stimulus, S_D. The typical symbolic series, on the other hand, being ordinarily an internal process, characteristically lacks in its stimulus complex the external factor, S_1, at least as a dynamic and coercive component. The significance of this stimulus difference becomes apparent when it is observed that the S_2- and s_1-components operate in the direction of a simple and stable chain-reaction tendency whereas the S_D, in addition to a chaining tendency, may have at the same time a very strong tendency to evoke other reactions, and especially the goal reaction (Hull, 1931, pp. 490–492).

This can account for acquisition and predict a short-circuiting, i.e. elimination of wrong responses in the maze. Hull realized a real problem with his analysis based on the conditioning of the drive-stimulus (S_D) to all S's. The paradox here was that if this were the only mechanism operating, when the organism is no longer reinforced in the goal box, as in extinction, the connection between (S_D) and *all* responses should be extinguished, thus leaving the organism no food-seeking behavior. He states this dilemma as follows:

Specifically, once the drive stimulus (S_D) has suffered experimental extinction as regards its goal reaction, this inhibition might conceivably spread to every other reaction into which S_D enters as a stimulus. But since S_D is present throughout the series the tendency to inhibition would thus spread from the termination of the sequence at once throughout its whole length and might, therefore, produce the generalized disintegration known to exist.

As yet our knowledge of secondary inhibitory tendencies is too meager for us to express an opinion with any confidence as to whether a spread of inhibition would be brought about by the mechanism sketched above, and, if so, whether the tendency would be strong enough to produce the disintegration just referred to. The following consideration makes it seem doubtful: If the inhibitory tendency to reactions emanating from S_D were strong enough to over-ride the chaining excitatory tendencies holding the behavior segments together in the series in which the frustration took place, it should also be strong enough to produce a similar disintegrative tendency in every other sequence which this drive (S_D) enters as a stimulus. This means that if the organism were consistently disappointed in finding food in one accustomed place until it would no longer seek it in that location there would also result in a similar paralysis of all attempts to seek food in any place at all, at least until the inhibitory tendency should have subsided. And in that event the organism would be about as likely to seek food in the place previously proven disappointing as in some alternative place which has consistently yielded food. Since these deductions are obviously contrary to fact, at least in this extreme form, we must seek some further or supplementary mechanism for the explanation of habit disintegration which results from withdrawal of reward (Hull, 1931, pp. 498–499).

THE FRACTIONAL ANTICIPATORY GOAL-RESPONSE

Probably the most important, motivationally relevant mechanism that Hull invented is the extremely ingenious fractional anticipatory (ante-dating) goal-response (r_g) that produces, through proprioceptive stimulation, the anticipatory goal-stimulus (s_g).

> There remains the more likely alternative that a split-off portion of the goal reaction which chances not to be in conflict with the antecedent instrumental series may be so displaced. Unfortunately, little is known experimentally of the dynamics of this fascinating possibility. Observation, however, supporting theoretical expectation, seems to indicate that anticipatory goal reactions appearing in the midst of normally antecedent instrumental act sequences are generally incomplete, fractional, imperfect, and feeble. Fortunately, with pure-stimulus acts, weakness within limits is of no disadvantage (Hull, 1931, pp. 493–494).
>
> ... It is assumed that as learning proceeds, S_D gets conditioned to the several phases of the reaction sequence and with an intensity roughly proportional to the proximity of each to the goal, the goal reaction itself possessing the most strongly conditioned excitatory tendency of all. It is assumed, further, that this tendency, at least occasionally, will be sufficiently strong to evoke a weak r_G-reaction even at the outset of the series. This movement of the fractional goal reaction to the beginning of the behavior sequence together with its subsequent persistence throughout the cycle is indicated diagrammatically in [Figure 5.3a]. The persistence of r_G is due to the parallel persistence of S_D which continuously evokes it.
>
> Like all other movements, r_G causes characteristic proprioceptive stimulations to arise from the muscles involved. This complex of stimulation flowing from r_G may be represented conveniently by s_G, [Figure 5.3b]. It is obvious that since r_G persists throughout the behavior sequence, s_G must also do so. It thus comes about that our dynamic situation is possessed of two persisting stimuli, S_D and s_G. Some of the potentialities of the drive stimulus (S_D), have been elaborated elsewhere. The second persisting stimulus (s_G), by way of contrast, will be called the *goal stimulus* (Hull, 1931, pp. 495–496).

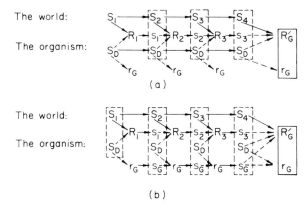

FIG. 5.3 The fractional anticipatory goal response (Hull, 1931, pp. 495–496).

At this early stage he spelled out in some detail the important differences between the drive-stimulus (S_D) and the goal-stimulus (s_g). He says this:

> Despite the very significant similarity of the goal stimulus to the drive stimulus there are equally significant differences which need carefully to be noted. In the first place, the two stimuli differ radically in their source, or origin. The drive stimulus, in the typical case of hunger already before us, evidently has its origin in the *physicochemical* processes involved in nutrition. The goal stimulus, on the other hand, is dependent, in the main at least, upon the existence of the drive stimulus and the conditioning of it to the goal reaction. The drive stimulus thus has an essentially non-redintegrative origin, whereas the goal stimulus is preeminently a redintegrative phenomenon. The drive stimulus is not likely to be greatly disturbed by either the presence or absence of the goal stimulus, but anything which terminates the drive stimulus will automatically bring the goal stimulus to an end.
>
> A second significant difference between the drive stimulus and the goal stimulus arises from the fact that from the single drive stimulus there may evolve many tolerably distinct goals. A rat, for example, will, when hungry, eat many different kinds of food. The eating of each kind of food may become a different goal with the goal reaction in each case presumably in some sense distinct. Moreover, the same kind of food may constitute the goal in many different mazes. It is evident that this possibility of a multiplicity of goal stimuli for each drive stimulus has important dynamic potentialities, especially in view of the small number of drives as contrasted with the immense variety of mammalian goals (Hull, 1931, pp. 496–497).
>
> The drive stimulus accounts very well for the random seeking reactions of a hungry organism, but alone it is not sufficient to produce the integration of complex behavior sequences such as is involved in maze learning. There must always be a reward of some kind. Once the reward has been given, however, the behavior undergoes a marked change most definitely characterized by evidences of actions anticipatory of the goal, which actions tend to appear as accompaniments to the sequence ordinarily leading to the full overt goal reaction.
>
> It is shown how these fractional anticipatory goal reactions could be drawn to the beginning of the behavior sequence and maintained throughout it by the action of the drive stimulus (S_D). The kinaesthetic stimulus resulting from this persistent anticipatory action should furnish a second stimulus (s_G), which would persist very much like S_D. These two persisting stimuli alike should have the capacity of forming multiple excitatory tendencies to the evocation of every reaction within the sequence. They should differ, however, in that the anticipatory goal reaction stimulus would be dependent for its existence upon the integrity of the drive stimulus. A second difference is that a single drive stimulus may generate many distinct goal stimuli.
>
> The general *a priori* probability of the existence of the goal stimulus finds confirmation in the fact that it affords a plausible explanation of a class of experimentally observed facts hitherto inexplicable. It enables us to understand, for example, why withholding the usual reward at the end of an accustomed maze run will cause a disintegration of that particular habit sequence while leaving the organism free to pursue alternative sequences based on the same drive. It offers an explanation of why, during a maze learning process, the substitution of one

reward for another presumably of about the same attractiveness should produce a transitory slump in the learning scores. It throws light on why an animal evidently motivated by the anticipation of one kind of food will leave untouched a different but otherwise acceptable type of food which has been surreptitiously substituted. There is a reason to believe that as the experimental literature on the motivating influence of rewards increases the goal stimulus mechanism will find enlarged application (Hull, 1931, pp. 504–505).

For the sake of definiteness and additional clarity the hypotheses elaborated above may be assembled in brief dogmatic form: Pure-stimulus acts are the physical substance of ideas. Ideas, however, are of many varieties. Among them are goal or guiding ideas. The physical mechanism constituting these particular ideas is the anticipatory goal reaction. This appears to be substantially the same as ideo-motor action. The anticipatory goal reaction seems also to constitute the physical basis of the somewhat ill-defined but important concept of purpose, desire, or wish, rather than the drive stimulus as has sometimes been supposed, notably by Kampf. This interpretation of purpose explains its dynamic nature and at the same time removes the paradox arising under the classical psychology where the future appeared to be operating causally in a backward direction upon the present. This hypothesis also renders intelligible the 'realization of an anticipation' by an organism. It is found in situations where a fractional anticipatory goal reaction as a stimulus has motivated a behavior sequence which culminates in a full overt enactment of a goal-behavior complex of which it is a physical component (Hull, 1931, pp. 505–506).

With this mechanism ($r_g s_g$) we have the behavioristic analogue of anticipation that Hull used to explain learning of the maze through elimination of blind alleys, extinction and later secondary reinforcement.

THE GOAL-GRADIENT HYPOTHESIS

The goal-gradient hypothesis was postulated to account for the fact that errors in maze learning are usually eliminated first near the goal box. The goal-gradient hypothesis states "that the goal reaction gets conditioned the most strongly to the stimuli preceding it, and the other reactions of the behavior sequence get conditioned to their stimuli progressively weaker as they are more remote (in time and space) from the goal reaction" (Hull, 1932, p. 26).

Assuming the goal-gradient, Hull proceeds to demonstrate that a rat placed at the choice-point in a simple maze with two pathways of differing length to the goal will have a stronger reaction potential for the response of entering the short pathway if he has experienced both pathways in the past. The response of entering the short pathway is stronger by the goal-gradient hypothesis because the goal-reaction occurs more quickly after it. Hull deduces the fact that the important quantity in determining which reaction will be prepotent at a choice-point is the ratio of the distances of the two paths, equal ratios leading to equal difficulty of discrimination regardless of absolute length (Yoshioka, 1929). Hull then ventures the fundamental generalization that "the larger the gradient difference between two alternative tendencies, the more perfect the preferential differentiation; whereas the smaller the gradient difference, the less perfect will be the differentiation" (Hull, 1932, p. 34).

The goal-gradient hypothesis is based on the notion of generalization of habit strength by a process of conditioning of S_D and S_g to the various s_g's and r_g's throughout the maze. These concepts explain the elimination of blind alleys as learning proceeds, assuming that the rat has enough variability in his early trials to traverse the several paths to the goal. Of this Hull says: "In this connection it may be pointed out that there appears to be some mechanism within the rat's organism which makes for spontaneous variability of response, and which thus tends to insure the rather full exploration of all possibilities until definite conditioned excitatory tendencies get set up which are strong enough to over-ride the spontaneous tendency to variability. Fortunately the bulk of this spontaneous variability of reaction precedes the setting up of the excitatory tendencies, at which time it should produce a fairly equal distribution of practice. This should enable the goal gradient principle to play an important role in bringing about the elimination of the blind alleys" (Hull, 1932, p. 36).

The goal-gradient hypothesis also is consistent with the facts that (1) long mazes take longer to learn than short mazes and that (2) the rat moves faster the closer he gets to the goal. Further discussion (Hull, 1932) is given of the graphic shape of the goal-gradient.

The Habit-Family Hierarchy

Hull is disturbed, however, by the possibility that the rat may take the long path so much more often than the short path that the long response becomes prepotent. The habit-family hierarchy is postulated to handle this problem. Hull (1934) derived the hierarchy concept from a consideration of convergent and divergent excitatory tendencies. The divergent mechanism (see Figure 5.4a) is a "fan-like series of divergent excitatory tendencies radiating from a single stimulus, each leading to a distinct reaction" (Hull, 1934, p. 33).

The convergent mechanism (see Figure 5.4b) is "the convergence of a number of excitatory tendencies from separate stimuli, all upon a single response" (Hull, 1934, p. 33). The divergent mechanism is used to account for the variability of response in trial-and-error learning. It helps resolve the problem mentioned above, that the first path in a maze is not simply repeated over and over because it was reinforced. It is important to realize that these divergent tendencies are learned and generalized to the maze from other partially similar situations. Hull says further of the divergent mechanism: "Much the same mechanism seems also to be responsible for anticipatory intrusions, particularly of the fractional component of the anticipatory goal reaction which has been supposed to bring about the phenomenon of ideomotor action and its tremendously important functional correlate, guiding or directive ideas. No doubt other and equally important functions performed by this mechanism are yet to be discovered" (Hull, 1934, p. 34).

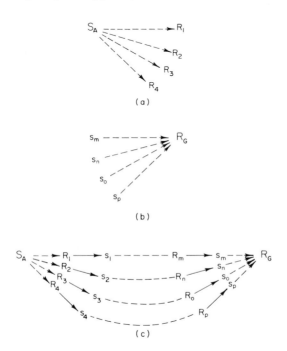

FIG. 5.4 Divergent and convergent excitatory tendencies combining to form the habit-family-hierarchy (Hull, 1934, pp. 33–34, 39).

The convergent mechanism leads to a response equivalence and may account for examples of transfer of training. Hull says: "The functional dynamics of this mechanism have been studied even less than have those of the divergent mechanism, but it is believed that they have far-reaching implications for the explanation of the more subtle forms of mammalian adjustment. In particular there is reason to believe that functional equivalence of stimuli plays an important rôle in bringing it about that habits established under certain stimulus conditions will function with little or no delay in new situations having nothing whatever as *objective* stimuli in common with the conditions under which the habit was originally formed" (Hull, 1934, p. 35). Hull uses the convergent mechanism as a mechanism for mediating transfer in discussing the Shipley (1933) experiment. Since this is the heart of the mediation problem, we shall return to it later in this chapter.

The habit-family hierarchy is constructed by putting the divergent and convergent mechanisms together. Figure 5.4c shows the habit-family associated with S_A and leading to R_G, i.e., several possible pathways or responses that may lead to R_G. "Despite the 'emergent' nature of the habit-family mechanism, it nevertheless retains clear functional evidences of its origin. The individual habit sequences of a particular family are still alternative in that but a single member can be active at once. At the same time they are equivalent in that all are alike in bringing about substantially the same final reaction or adjustment to the problem situation presented by S_A" (Hull, 1934, p. 39).

As Hull points out, the simplest application of the habit-family hierarchy is to separate paths in a maze. "The fact that both of the action sequences begin with the same stimulus (S) and terminate in the same reaction (G) constitutes them a habit family; the fact that one sequence is preferred above the other constitutes them a hierarchy" (Hull, 1934, p. 40).

At this point Hull presents two hypotheses as follows:

> *1. That in the albino rat, habit-family hierarchies based primarily on locomotion are set up very early in life, presumably as the result of locomotion in free space, with the result that the animal at the beginning of a maze experiment is already in possession of a vast repertoire of equivalent but fairly distinct locomotor habits, any one of which, in free space, would mediate a transition of his body from the starting point to the goal.*
> *2. That when one member of a habit-family hierarchy has attained a goal in an objectively novel situation, the learning thus acquired is transferred without specific practice to the remaining members of the hierarchy (Hull, 1934, p. 41).*

In discussing hypothesis 2, he says that it is not presented as an ultimate principle. "On the contrary, it is confidently expected that in case it turns out to be sound, it will be found to be deducible from certain still more general principles" (Hull, 1934, p. 42). In a footnote he states, "This statement also holds for the principle of the goal gradient." As we shall see, the more general principles involved the assumption of reinforcement as a necessary condition for learning, and this assumption leads to some trouble in deducing the goal gradient in his later work. At this point Hull points out that: "There is reason to believe, however, that in case the goal reactions or pre-goal reactions as a whole are in physiological conflict with the sequence properly leading to them, some *portion* of the goal reaction which chances not to be in such conflict will be temporarily detached from the goal aggregate and will move forward in the sequence independently and rather freely" (Hull, 1934, p. 42).

After pointing to the well-known anticipatory salivation effect, Hull states:

> It thus seems probable that the fractional anticipatory goal reaction . . . is the major mechanism which brings about the integration of the habit-family hierarchy. It is this mechanism which appears to be mainly responsible for the important and characteristic phenomenon of the transfer of practice effects from a less preferred member of a habit hierarchy to a more favored one. There is also reason to believe that under certain circumstances the fractional anticipatory goal reaction will be powerfully supported in this action by the drive stimulus . . . in case the latter is the same in the new situation as in the old. Even in cases where the drive may be superficially distinct, there is some reason to believe that there may be an inner core of identity which, if present, would doubtless aid considerably in mediating a transfer. While the inadequacy of our knowledge about these matters is such that we must be very tentative at present as to the precise details of the processes involved, it may be worth while to give an account of how the vicarious transfer under consideration might conceivably take place.
>
> The final or goal reaction is represented as consisting of two components, R_G' and r_G. The latter is assumed usually to be relatively insignificant in absolute magnitude but, because of its supposed ability to move forward rather freely in the behavior sequence, to be of the greatest significance as the physical substance of goal or directive ideas. . . .
>
> Suppose that an organism possessing the combination of excitatory tendencies . . . should find itself in a somewhat novel situation presenting an initial external stimulus S_1', and a different drive (S_D') as well. Suppose, further, that by trial-and-success the organism finds its way to the goal over the route involving the action sequence $R_1, R_2, R_3, R_4, R_5, R_6, R_7, R_G$. Now, if this action sequence is repeated a few times, r_G will become conditioned to S_D' and so will be brought forward to the beginning of the series. By virtue of this fact, r_G *will be brought into the presence of S_1' and will therefore become conditioned to it.* . . . Accordingly, whenever the animal finds himself in the presence of S_1' particularly if there is a pause before the beginning of locomotion, S_1' as a stimulus will evoke r_G, which will bring with it the proprioceptive stimulus s_G. But s_G, by virtue of previous conditioning . . . possesses excitatory tendencies both to R_1 and R_I. Since, assuming a simple goal gradient, R_1 has at this point a strength of 4 units . . . and R_I a strength of 8 units, this competition of excitatory tendencies will eventuate in reaction R_I, *which has never before taken place in this (objective) situation.* We accordingly have here a mechanism adequate to produce the transfer of practice effects which we have been seeking (Hull, 1934, pp. 43, 45–46).

In a further application Hull discusses the problem raised in the earlier paper (1932) of how an overlearned running of a long pathway, which would make this response prepotent, is eliminated. Essentially he uses the classical conditioning mechanism of disinhibition to account for this.

We shall not go into the details here, but they fit rather neatly.

We have followed Hull through his early thinking and found him very ingenious in deriving mechanisms to explain a rather trivial type of serial learning, namely, maze learning in the rat. As he has pointed out, potentially the mechanisms can be applied to many more important situations and can provide a basis for explanation of such phenomena as foresight, purposes, insight, transfer, and what later became known as latent learning and latent extinction.

The Postulate of Primary Reinforcement: A Problem

There is one step in Hull's thinking that is inevitably confusing. When he is integrating the notion of the goal-gradient with the connection between the drive stimulus (S_D) and the fractional anticipatory goal response (r_g), he assumes that initially S_D develops the capacity to evoke the R_g and the fractional component of it the r_g. Once that has happened, at any time that the S_D is present it will tend to evoke r_g. The evocation of specific responses (R_1, R_2, etc.) depends upon the further connection of specific stimuli (S_1, S_2, etc.) to the S_D and to r_g.[2] Apparently the connection between the S_D and r_g does not work back from the goal to the starting box in the maze. Just the connection between the S_D-r_g complex and the specific S's and R's work back slowly, as deduced from the goal-gradient hypothesis.

This interpretation is most consistent with the present series of papers. However, we are left with the principle of redintegration to account for the connections between the various R's, aside from R_g, and the stimulus complexes. In attempting to maintain a consistent reinforcement theory in his later works Hull developed his famous postulate of primary reinforcement:

> When a response (R) is closely associated with a stimulus trace (s) and this stimulus-response conjunction is associated with a rapid decrease in drive-produced stimuli (S_D) there will result an increase in the tendency for that stimulus trace (s) to evoke the response (R).
>
> The rapid decrease in the goal stimulus (s_G) is also reinforcing.[3]

---

[2] Apparently this is what is meant by the statement "S_D gets conditioned to the several phases of the reaction sequence and with an intensity roughly proportional to the proximity of each to the goal." Since he clearly states later that the S_D is of nonredintegrative origin, i.e., is or is not there depending on the organismic state and cannot be elicited by redintegration, the above statement must mean that the capacity of S_D to result in R_1 or R_2, etc., is proportional to their proximity to the goal.

[3] We have used Hilgard's (1956) paraphrasing of the postulate and its corollaries because they emphasize the point we are making.

Corollaries to this postulate were as follows:

> *Corollary i. Secondary drive*
> When a neutral stimulus trace (*s*) has been closely associated with the evocation and rapid decrease of drive-produced stimuli (S_D), the hitherto neutral stimulus trace (*s*) acquires a tendency to bring about these drive stimuli (S_D), so that the previously neutral stimulus trace (*s*) becomes the occasion for a secondary drive (*s* $\longrightarrow S_D$).
>
> *Corollary ii. Secondary reinforcement*
> When a neutral stimulus trace (*s*) has been closely associated with a rapid diminution in drive produced stimuli (S_D), the hitherto neutral stimulus trace (*s*) acquires a tendency to bring about the reduction of S_D, so that the previously neutral stimulus trace (*s*) acquires "the power of acting as a reinforcing agent" (Hilgard, 1956, p. 129).

With these corollaries, we can go back and replace the principle of redintegration with the principle of reinforcement. Rather than attribute the connection between a specific R and the stimulus complex to redintegration, we may attribute it to reinforcement since one of the components in the stimulus complex (s_g) is a reinforcer (corollary ii).

However, as Hilgard (1956) points out, this is not entirely satisfactory, since that same component acquires the tendency to arouse the drive-stimulus, i.e., act as a secondary drive. To quote Hilgard: ". . . it becomes evident that a neutral stimulus trace associated consistently with a reinforcing state of affairs acquires two functions (and both at once!): (1) the power to arouse a secondary drive (Corollary i), and (2) the power to reduce drive stimuli, and hence act as a secondary reinforcing agent (Corollary ii)" (Hilgard, 1956, pp. 129–130).

The details of this paradox have been presented to make it clear that the problem arises only when Hull attempts to make his earlier statements conform to a thoroughgoing reinforcement position. As long as the principle of redintegration was used, all was consistent. This point receives its significance from the fact that apparently one of Hull's primary mechanisms for tying responses to anticipation involves the connection of an anticipatory response to the relevant stimulus by contiguity *only* (redintegration), although the final response may be said to be reinforced. Thus Hull developed a mechanism ($r_g s_g$) that is very useful if one does not demand a consistent reinforcement theory.

Mowrer's Espousal of the Contiguity Principle

When the S_D is internal and slow in onset, as assumed by Hull in the early papers, it is easy to overlook the fact that it may become associated with other stimuli by contiguity. But when a sudden strong external stimulus is assumed to be drive producing, it becomes harder to avoid the conclusion that it alone (an increase in drive stimulation) conditions fear responses to other stimuli present in the environment. The interest in shock as a drive-inducing stimulus (Miller, 1948a; Mowrer & Miller, 1942) led Mowrer (1947, 1950) to espouse a contiguity theory for the learning of "signs."

In what Mowrer (1960a) called the two factor-theory, version two, he pointed to a difficulty in explaining experimental studies of avoidance learning in terms of Hull's reinforcement theory based on drive reduction.

In the Miller-Mowrer box (Mowrer & Miller, 1942), which is composed of a white and a black compartment, a rat is placed in the white compartment and shortly thereafter he is shocked. After many responses he eventually stumbles into the black compartment and finds no shock. After several such experiences the rat begins to react to the white compartment with fear even when the shock is not turned on. He will soon learn to avoid shock by escaping from the white compartment immediately. Such behavior is quite resistant to extinction, and the animal will go on avoiding the white compartment long after he has ceased to be shocked there.

The drive-reduction explanation of this advanced by Miller (1948a) and Mowrer himself at first (see Mowrer & Lamoreaux, 1942) is that the avoidance response is reinforced by the reduction of the drive stimulus (pain from shock). The stimulus of the white box acquired negative properties similar to the shock by association with it, and the acquisition of fear of the white box is also reinforced by the reduction of pain. Thus fear becomes an acquired drive the reduction of which, by escape from the white box, is secondarily reinforcing.

The acquisition of drive properties by the white box was said to be similar to the phenomenon pointed out by Skinner (1938) and Bugelski (1938) with a click that is associated with food. When the presentation of food in a Skinner box during learning is accompanied by a click, and then the click is continued during extinction trials when food is no longer forthcoming, greater resistance to extinction is found than in similar extinction trials when the click is not present. As a result, the click is said to be secondarily reinforcing. A secondary reinforcement explanation of avoidance conditioning assumes that the avoidance situation, where the white box is present both during acquisition and extinction, is analogous to the situation where the click is present in both phases.

This explanation, using Hullian drive-reduction principles, did not satisfy Mowrer, for he pointed out that the acquisition of fear apparently occurs at the sudden onset of the shock, i.e., the white box acquired the ability to arouse fear not because the shock later went off, but because it came on. Mowrer produced evidence (Mowrer, 1950, Chapters 9 and 10; Mowrer & Aiken, 1954; Mowrer & Solomon, 1954) to demonstrate that when the fear-producing stimulus is contiguous with the onset of shock, learning is more facilitated than when it is contiguous with the termination of shock, as would be predicted if fear is learned by contiguity of formerly neutral stimuli with an increase in pain rather than by the subsequent reduction of pain that follows the termination of shock.

In the face of these data, it is difficult to maintain that the learned drive (fear) is acquired according to the principle of drive reduction, since the onset of shock is clearly drive-inducing. Mowrer, therefore, assumed that two principles of learning are needed: contiguity for sign learning and drive reduction for solution learning. As he says:

> Most learning situations are complicated and can be understood only by taking *both* of these forms of learning into account. Active avoidance learning is a case in point. Here, what occurs first is *sign* learning, whereby fear becomes conditioned to a formerly neutral stimulus or signal; then, with the organism now motivated by this secondary drive, trial-and-error behavior occurs and a behavioral *solution* to the fear problem is found. Thus, where Behaviorism restricted itself to the simple, one-step S-R formula, we are here confronted by the necessity of postulating, minimally, a two-step, *two-stage formula:* S-r: s-R, where S is the danger signal, r the response of fear which is conditioned to it, and where s is the fear, experienced as a drive, which elicits (after learning) response, R. Thus, what is elicited as the response to S, namely r (as an internal *response*), becomes the immediate (internal) *stimulus* for R. Miller and Dollard (1941) have usefully characterized fear as a response-produced drive. Fear occurs first as a response, but it is a disagreeable, "painful" response and so possesses motivational properties (Mowrer, 1960a, p.77).

MOWRER AND MEDIATION

The above quote summarizes Mowrer's 1950 resolution of the paradox of the learning of fear. In addition, it is clear that by 1960 he was explicitly considering fear to be an internal response. By 1960 an internal response was for him a mediator between a stimulus and a response, and Mowrer's (1960a,b) more recent version depends heavily upon such mediation.

Mediation by surrogate overt responses was proposed by Hull in the $r_g s_g$ mechanism that developed out of the notion of the pure-stimulus act. He specifically demanded a response that was at least in principle overt and observable. Evidence for mediating responses was produced by Shipley (1933) in an experiment in which he was able to produce a finger flexion by the presentation of a light although the light had never been directly connected with finger flexion. This was done by (*a*) conditioning the light to elicit an eye blink through a tap on the cheek. Then (*b*) the tap and blink were connected with shock and finger flexion. Finally (*c*), the light apparently elicited the blink that elicited the finger flexion by the mechanism of overt response mediation (see Figure 5.5).

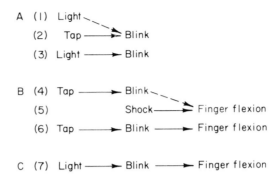

FIG. 5.5 Diagram of Shipley's demonstration of response mediation.

In a replication of the Shipley experiment, Lumsdaine (1939) found that in some cases in Stage c the light elicited the finger flexion *first* and the blink came only afterwards. If the actual motor response is necessary for mediation, this presents a paradox; but, as pointed out by Osgood (1953), if the overt response is itself merely the index of an internal response that is the actual mediator, then the fact that some of Lumsdaine's subjects blinked after the finger flexion merely indicates that the internal mediator elicited the finger flexion even before the blink. Such an explanation may be supported by knowledge of the workings of neural circuits, but the very fact that we must look to such a source for support points up an important difference between the Hullian theorizing about overt mediators and Mowrer's notions of internal responses as mediators. At present any theory using what has come to be known as the "mediation hypothesis" (from Osgood, 1953) is open to the criticism that the mechanism for the explanation for mediation has been buried in the head and demands some "neurophysiologizing" to support it. As long as Hull insisted that the "little r_g's" were actual overt responses that could in principle be observed, he avoided this problem. Osgood (1953), Mowrer (1960a,b) and the later section of this chapter entitled "Toward a Contiguity Theory of the Acquisition of Affective Relationships" are all in danger of having an omnibus explanation that is buried in the head. As we shall see, however, recent "head mining" experiments (cf. Olds & Milner, 1954) have been laying bare some of the secrets that are buried there, and these studies apparently make the mediation hypothesis quite tenable.

In Chapter 4 we saw that Mowrer (1960a) maintains that learning occurs either in the presence of incremental or decremental stimulation, incremental being punishing and decremental being rewarding. The effects of these types of stimulation are to produce the learning of "hope," "fear," "relief," or "disappointment." The fact that fear is included will give the reader not familiar with Mowrer in the original the connecting link between his recent theory and his 1950 two-factor theory (the analysis of avoidance conditioning in terms of fear as discussed at length above). In 1960, hope, relief, and disappointment join fear, and they are all considered mediating internal responses. We must stress two points, although we shall not now go into detail. First, hope and disappointment are here still associated with change in stimulation, and the "best" state is that of lowest stimulation. In terms of affect there is really no positive affect, i.e., "good things" are defined as the lack of negative affect (strong stimulation). An animal that is said to have "hope" does not anticipate the pleasure of the promised food; he anticipates the relief from hunger that food brings. Later in this chapter we will propose that mediation can occur through the anticipation of changes in positive as well as negative affect.

A second important point is that Mowrer apparently continually assumes that the presence of incremental or decremental stimulation is a necessary condition for learning of the mediators. Change in stimulation constitutes an affective component in the learning situation as distinct from a cognitive or verbal component, and yet Mowrer uses his notions of mediation to discuss the learning of language and the development of images in the cognitive realm. It is often difficult to see the presence of the necessary incremental or decremental stimulation in some of the examples of learning discussed in *Learning Theory and the Symbolic Processes* (Mowrer, 1960b).[4]

It is interesting to note that Mowrer's position stresses the learning of emotional mediators and has some trouble accounting for the resultant behavior. He realizes this defect and makes the link to overt behavior depend on response-produced stimulation that regulates further responses. Response-produced stimulation is a mediator that acts like a servo-mechanism. Miller (1963) has criticized this aspect of the theory, saying no less than three times that this is a "fatal weakness" in the theory. It might be said concerning Mowrer's theory [analogously to Guthrie's (1952) comment that Tolman's rat is perpetually "lost in thought"] that

---

[4] Feather (1963) has argued that a motive-expectancy-value model provides an alternative to Mowrer's Revised Two-Factor Theory. In a way not unlike that to be presented in our next section, Feather rejects increments and decrements of fear, but he goes on to stress cognitive aspects (expectations) more than we will in what follows.

Mowrer's rat is perpetually lost in mediation. Be this as it may, Miller (1963), after more than a decade of attempting to defend a pure drive-stimulus-reduction theory [though he maintains (Miller, 1957, 1959, 1963) that the odds are against its correctness], has presented a new alternative. The basic innovation involves what he calls "go" or "activating" mechanisms in the brain. These mechanisms might be seen as mediators, since they "act to intensify ongoing responses to cues and the traces of immediately preceding activities, producing a stronger intensification the more strongly the 'go mechanism' is activated" (Miller, 1963, p. 95). Miller notes that the crucial difference between his new alternative and Mowrer's is in connecting the "go mechanism" directly to responses. Thus, "all responses, including the activation of this 'go mechanism' are subject to conditioning with contiguity being sufficient" (p. 95).

Toward A Contiguity Theory of the Acquisition of Affective Relationships

Affective Mediating Mechanisms

The details of the development of mechanisms for mediation have been presented because mediation is the key concept bequeathed to motivation theory from Neobehaviorism. If it is assumed that reactions to the environment and behavior come to be organized along affective lines, some mechanism must be postulated that allows the organism to anticipate affect. This mechanism we shall call an *affective mediating mechanism.*

Affective mediating mechanisms are convenient constructs that help distinguish the motivational (affective) component from other mental processes. We conceive of some quite specific neurological process that may correspond to the phenomenological experience of affect, and we assume that this neurological component accompanies much stimulation from sources external to the organism and from internal sources such as hunger pangs and response-produced stimulation.

Two types of affect may be postulated—primary and secondary. Primary affect is that which stimuli produce in the organism because of the way the organism with its various receptors is built. Primary affect results from a required relationship between stimulation and an affective response, as discussed in detail in Chapter 3. Thus, in the normal organism, primary negative affect (pain) is elicited by a stimulus of intense heat. Primary positive affect is more subtle but may be the result of such things as a small change (discrepancy) in stimulus conditions. Secondary affect is acquired through a process of contiguity between aroused affect and formerly neutral stimuli. Through acquisition, the organism gains the capacity to anticipate affective states. Affective mediating mechanisms are the result of acquisition and hence constitute secondary affect. They are lesser counterparts elicited by formerly neutral stimuli of the original primary affect that occurred in contiguity with the neutral stimuli. Primary affect may be the result of neural firing in a certain area of the brain produced by specific stimuli. Secondary affect is most probably neural firing in the same area as the corresponding primary affect, but elicited by a formerly neutral stimulus that has become connected with the affective area by neural pathways that have been channeled through contiguous stimulation. This rough "neurologizing" is purely conceptual and draws upon no expert knowledge. Only two assumptions are needed to support it, first, the age-old assumption that acquisition involves some process of connection within the nervous system of two previously unconnected circuits. Second, it is assumed that the firing of some circuits or some portion of the central nervous system produces affect phenomenologically.

Although the previous statements present the underlying thinking concerning affective mediating mechanisms, they tend to overemphasize them as physiologically and psychologically distinct "things." They are, however, a conceptual abstraction, a part of a larger whole that is the total response of the nervous system to stimulation. Most probably primary affect never occurs in isolation, and certainly secondary affect (the affective mediating mechanism) never does. Thus the two types of affect may be conceived of as "ideal types" distinguished for analysis and conceptual clarity but probably not separable within the organism.

With this notion in mind it is necessary to complete the picture by including cognitive and motor aspects of the total response of the nervous system. These further aspects may clarify by contrast our concept of the affective aspects. Any stimulus may produce cognitive, affective, and motor responses and thus may result in neural firing in portions of the nervous system corresponding to each of these. Connections between the three types of neural responses may be either required (by the way the organism is originally "wired") or acquired through learning. We thus derive the possibility that there may be (in fact probably are) cognitive mediating mechanisms, and motor mediating mechanisms as well as affective mediating mechanisms. These may all be conceived as sets, e.g., stimuli may come to elicit a cognitive expectation, a motor preparation, an affective anticipation, or *all three* simultaneously or in any combination.

In almost all (if not all) responses to stimulation, all three aspects are involved; and thus the mature organism responds to incoming stimuli with cognitive, affective, and motor components. Differentiating the affective component for detailed analysis must not lead us to consider it a separate entity. On the other hand, the utility of conceptualizing the three components lies in the fact that various orientations to the environment can be conceived of as reactions that involve more of one component than of another. For instance, a simple motor task involves a series of preparatory motor components that, once acquired, may proceed with very little assistance from cognitive or affective components. Yet the chaining in a motor task such as tying a shoe is based on components described by Hull as pure-stimulus acts, involving mediation and possibly subsumable under the concept of motor mediating mechanisms.

Cognitive processes may proceed with minimally apparent motor or affective components, as in unobstructed thinking. A predominantly cognitive situation with minimal affective or motor components is illustrated by certain types of "set." The predisposition developed by subjects in the Luchins (1942) water-jar demonstration is an example. Subjects are required to solve problems cognitively based on the supposed situation of having an unlimited supply of water and three water jars (A, B, and C) which hold specified quantities. The task is to obtain an amount of water that can be done only by various combinations of the three jars. The subject may be presented with six problems that are solvable only by the formula $B - A - C$. The problems following these set-inducing problems may be solved by the above formula or by the simpler procedure $A - C$, or in other problems $A + C$. Subjects who have solved problems 1 through 6 use the more cumbersome procedure in subsequent problems more often than subjects who start with problem 7, which may be done either way. The set or *Einstellung* established in this way may be conceived of as the result of a predominantly cognitive mediating mechanism (possibly the cognitive correlate of the formula in whatever terms the subject conceptualizes it). The point for us is that this predisposition is primarily cognitive, although, of course, it may have minimal motor and affective components.

To think of concrete examples of mechanisms that are primarily affective and practically devoid of cognitive and motor components is difficult. This may indicate one of two things: they do not exist in isolation, and therefore affective mediating mechanisms are always accompanied by large components of cognitive and motor aspects. More probably it reflects the facts (1) that we are forced to communicate in the cognitive realm and hence find it hard to think (cognitively) of a noncognitive example; and (2) that the affective mediating mechanisms that we can describe resulted originally from the association of a primary affect with a stimulus to which we could attach a verbal (cognitive) label, and therefore a cognitive component is present. Put another way, a predominantly affective mediating mechanism is a "feeling," and it is one of those feelings that is hard to describe, since we have no culturally accepted and cognitively learned symbol which communicates it. It is a very private thing.

It is entirely possible, however, that affective mediating mechanisms in their purest form (with minimal although probably not nonexistent cognitive and motor components) may have been acquired very early in life, before the baby learned the primary cognitive tool, language, and when the child was mainly a passive recipient with few active motor responses available to him. It is entirely possible that the most distinctly loaded affective responses to stimulation may be residues from the earliest learning experiences, and that they may have a very distinctive character. This is especially probable in view of the fact that affective experiences are often thought to be most intense at this time of life, due to the inability of the child to cope with them, and due also to the lack of the comforting sense of time, which makes a present state of affect (especially negative affect) intolerable since there is no knowledge of the possibility of change in the future — no anticipation that "this too will pass."

It is obvious that the previous discussion raises the possibility of considering mechanisms with very low cognitive components the seat of the "unconscious." If unconscious is defined as unverbalized (McClelland, 1951), this connection follows. Unconscious as used by Freud has much surplus meaning beyond McClelland's definition, the primary distinction lying in the Freudian implication that much of the unconscious is the result of repression. This conception, too, might fit the notions of the three mediating mechanisms if some process of severing the connections between the affective and cognitive mechanisms could be postulated. Although it is wild speculation, it is possible that when the original situation involves intense (traumatic) affect, the connection between the affective and cognitive components may be severed by a sort of fuse-blowing phenomenon. (If intense affect is an electrical phenomenon, shock therapy may produce something like fuse blowing.) This analogy, however, leaves us with the typical problem of distinguishing between strong affect that tends to strengthen, and strong affect that tends to sever, the connections between itself and cognitive elements.

This digression into reasons why reactions that are primarily affective are difficult to specify leads us to suggest that we do have a general word for such a reaction, namely, anxiety. The phrase "free-floating anxiety" is meant to connote a cognitively unspecifiable "feeling." As such it could be seen as a reaction with maximal affect and minimal cognitive components. Freudian theory would suggest that the cognitive components have been repressed, but repression is not necessarily the only source of reactions that are primarily affective. We shall therefore suggest anxiety as a possible example, but leave the question open as to whether all anxiety involves repression. We would certainly not wish to imply that all reactions that are primarily affective are the result of the repression of cognitive components.

In attempting to think of examples of reactions that involve mainly affective mediating mechanisms, we are struck by the fact that one tends to look for reactions involving negative affect. We cannot suggest a good candidate involving positive affect. The term "ecstasy" comes to mind, but there is no clear definition for this. It does seem reasonable to assume that a generalized feeling of well-being apparently unconnected with cognitive content is a common experience. Finally, the phenomenon of *déjà vu* may give an example of a chiefly affective mediating mechanism. The feeling of having had this experience before is clearly primarily a "feeling." Most often the specific cognitive content is vague, and the affective component is predominant.

We have tried to suggest examples of reactions involving primarily one aspect, such as a motor preparatory reaction, a cognitive expectation, or an affective anticipation. More often experience involves mixed modes of two or of all three.

Because we are dealing with motivational phenomena, we have stressed the affective mediating mechanisms. Can we say then that in general they are more important than the cognitive or motor mediating mechanisms? In directing behavior we would say the affective mediating mechanisms are more important. The cognitive and motor aspects present the *possible* action alternatives in any situation, but the affective mediating mechanisms essentially determine the *choice* among the alternatives.

The general question of the importance of affective mediating mechanisms raises a final point that deals primarily with acquisition. We have taken a contiguity position with regard to acquisition of the relationship between stimuli and affective responses. We have not taken the position (although it is tenable) that an affective component is a necessary component to "weld" an association. We can conceive of the acquisition of connections between stimuli and any of the three types of mediating mechanisms, such as the association between a sign and an object, without any affective component. This would seem to be cognitive learning. But we are not attempting to account for all types of learning, and thus we confine ourselves to the statement that when an affective component is present it tends to become connected with any stimulus components present by contiguity. This means that when one of the relevant stimulus components occurs again it will tend to elicit an affective mediating mechanism, that is, an anticipation of affect.

Thus we are not assuming anything as broad as the statement that affect is necessary for learning, a position that is similar to the statement, reinforcement is necessary for learning. Since we have confined ourselves to the acquisition of affective assocations we cannot make such extrapolations. Although affective mediating mechanisms may be seen as similar to Miller's (1963) "go mechanisms" and to Mowrer's incremental or decremental stimulation, we are not constrained to postulate affect in all learning situations. Obviously, affect *is* a necessary condition for the specific thing that we are examining, namely, the acquisition of affective relationships.

In summarizing the present section, it may be said that we are attempting to emphasize the following points as important in the acquisition of affective orientations toward the environment:

1. Affect is elicited innately by certain stimuli in the environment. It may be positive or negative.

2. When a stimulus that innately elicits affect is consistently associated with a formerly neutral stimulus, this stimulus will acquire the capacity to elicit affect.

3. This acquisition process results in an affective mediating mechanism whose phenomenological correlate is a fractional portion of the innately elicited affect, and which takes the form of anticipation or arousal with all their physiological correlates.

4. The basic principle for the development of an affective mediating mechanism is that of contiguity between aroused affect and stimuli.

5. The stimuli that acquire the capacity to elicit affect through affective mediating mechanisms may be internal or external to the organism. Thus responses may come to elicit affect through response-produced affect. Through the affective mediating mechanism the organism may acquire anticipations of engaging in affect-producing behavior.

6. The question of the extinction of acquired affective mediating mechanisms may reduce to a statement that whenever the formerly neutral stimulus occurs in the absence of the affect aroused innately by another stimulus, the tendency for the neutral stimulus to arouse affect is weakened. This seems reasonable. However, we wish to explore the problem of the extreme resistance of some affective associations to extinction. For the time being we will leave this as a statement that is even more tentative than those above.

AFFECTIVE MEDIATING MECHANISMS AND MOTIVATION

If motivation is conceived of as the directing and organizing of behavior along affective lines, then a motive to act in a specific way in a specific situation is the anticipation that such an act will lead to a change in affect. More concisely, *a motive is the anticipation of a change in affect that is associated with a behavioral sequence under certain stimulating conditions.* Since the anticipation of a change in affect is an affective mediating mechanism, the crux of motivation is mediation.

As we have seen, affect and the mediation of affect are difficult things to conceptualize cognitively. For this reason the layman and the psychologist tend to talk about motives in terms of material things that are apparently associated with affective states. These things are considered goals or rewards and may be anything from a piece of candy to "fame and fortune." Sometimes the inference that the consequent or resulting state of the organism (the goal state) produces affect is correct. But sometimes this conceptualization leads to a faulty inference, especially in situations in which the behavior itself produces the affect and is not necessarily "instrumental" in attaining a goal. The person may appear to be striving to attain some end-state, but the end-state may not be what produces satisfaction (positive affect). Thus, apparently, the goal in a game of chess is to win. However, upon careful consideration, it is obvious that any fairly accomplished chess player could assure attainment of that goal by selecting carefully an inferior opponent. This is exactly what they do not do. Winning in itself is not important, but engaging in a challenging game appears to be what produces affect. Losing a well-played game is more satisfying than winning a poorly played one.

The concept involved here is intrinsic satisfaction, but the intrinsic-extrinsic distinction is oversimplified,[5] and classification of motives according to apparent consequent goal states is often superficial. How then can we move from the statement that in a specific situation a motive is the anticipation of affect, to a classification of types of motives that will help us predict behavior? So far we really have little more than a psychological hedonism. The observation of behavior to determine what the organism does with the inference that that is what it likes, and then the prediction of how it will behave in the future from those observations, involves a circularity. The circle can be broken either by *(a)* independent measurement of affect or *(b)* prediction by some notion of generalization [e.g. Meehl's (1950) idea that a reinforcer must be assumed to be trans-situational].

---

[5] Intrinsic motivation will be discussed in more detail in Chapter 6.

The independent measurement of affect would be a very valuable thing in predicting motivated behavior if the affective arousal model is an accurate description. Such measurement would tap anticipatory responses that, according to the model, precede more overt behavior. A measurement of antecedent affect would, therefore, help predict and explain motivated behavior. The measures available to psychology at present that might serve this function are physiological measures of emotions or arousal, such things as the galvanic skin response (GSR, the electrical conductance of the skin that is a function of sweat gland activity and influenced by the autonomic nervous system), or the electroencephalogram (EEG, a measure of electrical activity in the brain). The relationship of such measures to motivation, however, is very poorly understood and like most physiological measures of emotional arousal they do not distinguish between positive and negative arousal.

Recently Hess and Polt (1960, 1964) have found that the size of the pupils of the eye varies as a function of the interest the subject has in the stimulus he is looking at as well as other variables that may be related to motivation. This fascinating series of studies might result in a measure of affect that could even distinguish between positive (dilated pupils) and negative (eyes that are pin-points of hate) affect.

Even if we now possessed an adequate measure of affect, however, we still would be faced with the problem of deriving generalized response dispositions (motives) from it. Types of motives might be conceived of as affective generalization gradients[6] of mediation or the organization of dimensions of situations and behaviors that lead to affect. Motives then would be acquired affective generalization gradients, and they would have associated with them hierarchies of behaviors elicited by associated motor-mediating mechanisms. But we are still confronted with the problem of how specific motives (organizations) develop. Can we expect to find something, for instance, that looks like "the achievement motive"? In answering this question we move to the more general question of the acquisition of motives and leave the molecular level of internal hypothetical mechanisms.

The Acquisition of Motives — Learning or Imprinting?

Any attempt to derive an explanation for the acquisition of motives

---

[6] The notion of an affective generalization gradient is similar to Miller's drive generalization (Miller, 1948b; Webb, 1949). We conceive of something more than a gradient, however. Since affect is elicited by signs and symbols in adult humans, the stimuli which will cue off affect are probably organized or patterned according to the way the adult has learned to construe his world.

from reinforcement theory is hindered by two critical problems. First, the term "redintegration" hails from an earlier period in the history of psychology (Hamilton, 1859) and connotes a residue from a past association, but does not demand that the association be formed in the presence of reinforcement. This problem can be overcome by assuming that the affective party to the association is all that is necessary as Mowrer (1960a) does. A second problem from the point of view of affective arousal theorists such as Young (1961) or McClelland *et al.* (1953), is that an increase in stimulation (incremental stimulation for Mowrer) cannot lead to the learning of an approach response. Citing the discrepancy hypothesis, McClelland *et al.* (1953) would argue that incremental stimulation can lead to approach motivation.

It is probably possible to develop a consistent theory of the learning of motives that includes approach to increased stimulation and still remain quite close to the tenets of reinforcement theory. J. S. Brown (1953) has suggested that a motive, as defined by McClelland *et al.* (1953), is merely a very generalized constellation of more specific habits, learned very early and in a rather vague and generalized way, by the principles of reinforcement. If this line of thinking is followed, Brown suggests that McClelland's measures of a motive using fantasy productions is tapping a habit (possibly verbal) that is elicited by a stimulus (a Thematic Apperception Test picture) that is far out on some (similarity?) continuum from the stimulus under which achieving responses were learned. If the achieving response occurs in fantasy, i.e., generalizes this far on the continuum, then it can be predicted that under circumstances in which stimulus conditions are more similar to the learned stimulus, namely, in actual achieving situations, the subject will show achievement type behavior (see also Goss & Brownell, 1957; Brownell & Goss, 1957; Miller, 1959). If this analysis is accepted, McClelland has not achieved a measurement of motivation that is independent of the responses produced by it. One might ask if this is ever possible; but, at any rate, such an analysis places the McClelland technique in the category of a response-response theory, i.e., of predicting one set of responses from another. Ideally, a motivation theory would have more power if it could predict responses from antecedent events or internal states. A detailed discussion of this problem appears in Chapter 6.

Be this as it may, if one follows this rather plausible analysis by Brown, one is bound to end up feeling that the basic questions of motivation theory will be solved only when we learn much more about learning that occurs in a very general way, under varied conditions, and probably early in life. Such a conclusion fits with McClelland's careful discussion of the conditions of learning in early childhood (McClelland, 1951).

THE IMPORTANCE OF EARLY CHILDHOOD EXPERIENCE

McClelland has attempted to demonstrate that the Freudian hypothesis that the first few years of life are most important in the formation of personality, and by inference in the formation of motivation, is directly supported by principles from learning theory. On the face of it, when one thinks merely of conscious memory, the hypothesis seems to have little to recommend it, since it is obvious that the memory of the first few years of life is very poor. However, the effects of learning on behavior extend far beyond the realm of mere reportable memory. McClelland argues that early childhood experiences are important *(a)* because of the principle of primacy, *(b)* because they occur before the development of symbolic processes, *(c)* because many such experiences occur repeatedly and repetition leads to overlearning, and *(d)* because the conditions for forgetting are unique in early childhood.

From evidence supporting the principle of primacy McClelland concludes: ". . . it seems safe to infer that *part* of the relatively greater importance of childhood events lies in the mere fact that they occur first and therefore can shape rather than be shaped by other conceptions and later experiences" (McClelland, 1951, p. 342). With regard to undeveloped symbolic processes, McClelland says, "early experiences may assume such great importance in personality because they are not represented by the kinds of symbols, particularly verbal, which facilitate subsequent discrimination, assimilation, extinction, and control" (p. 343). From the fact that problems of early childhood dealing with feeding and bowel control occur thousands of times in the first two years of an infant's life, McClelland deduces, "there are few situations as important to the organism, outside early child training, that give such extensive opportunity through pure repetition for the learning of attitudes, expectations, and modes of adapting to problem situations" (p. 344). The primary conditions for forgetting are cited from McGeoch (1942) as interference by intervening activities, and altered stimulating conditions. McClelland says, "Actual unlearning is apparently most likely to occur when the same situation gives rise to incompatible responses, one of which may then be extinguished by lack of reinforcement. But such an opportunity for unlearning is not so likely to occur in the rapidly growing infant *(a)* when stimulus situations change quickly *(b)* when similarities among situations are not as great as they are when they can be grouped under a common symbol" (p. 345).

In a later section, McClelland combines these and some other principles under conditions that influence either the strength or the generality of affective associations. Under conditions that influence primarily the strength of the affective associations, McClelland sees the notion of primacy. In discussing Hunt's (1941) study of feeding frustration in young rats, he suggests that the finding that rats frustrated in infancy were found to hoard more as adults may, among other things, be a result of the fact that *"the affective arousal is more intense in infancy than later"* (McClelland, 1951, p. 445). He says further, "While the results of this experiment cannot be interpreted with any great certainty, they can be understood in terms of a hypothesis which states that the early-deprived rats had formed a strong association between frustration and dependence responses involved in nursing which was reinstated when frustration occurred in later life. Again the evidence is that the early association has a stronger or more permanent effect" (p. 445).

In support of the notion that affective arousal is more intense in childhood, McClelland says "Prior to the development of cortical control, nearly any stimulus will involve some autonomic discharge. As the child matures, the affective component apparently gets less and less and more and more specifically attached to certain cues or responses" (McClelland, 1951, p. 447). In terms we have used above, this might be restated to say that early childhood learning involves primarily affective mediating mechanisms, and as the child matures these are joined more and more by cognitive mediating mechanisms.[7] As we suggested in discussing the mediating mechanisms, the intensity of early affective responses may also be a result of the lack of time discrimination in the child. Thus McClelland points out, "the intensity of pleasure and pain is greater because the infant has not as yet learned to discriminate time, to anticipate in particular that certain experiences will come to an end. Affective states for the infant should have in consequence a certain 'timeless' quality which is difficult for adults to comprehend and which psychoanalysts have tried to get them to comprehend by stepping up the vividness of the language they use to describe the infant's phenomenal world" (p. 448).

Under conditions affecting primarily the generality of affective associations, McClelland says "affective associations laid down in childhood are often so exceedingly general because of the child's undeveloped powers of discrimination that they persist because it is difficult to produce the conditions that would make it possible to extinguish them" (McClelland, 1951, p. 452). One of the conditions that makes it difficult to extinguish affective association is the lack of symbolic control. "The use of symbols, especially language, favors specificity of learning largely because it enables the child to make the discrimination much more easily

---

[7] It is also possible that as cognitive control develops it tends to inhibit arousal from discharges in the reticular arousal system (see Berlyne, 1960, pp. 179–182).

between when it is appropriate to make a response and when it is not. He can group together what would otherwise be a large number of complex experiences, often separated by varying time intervals, under a single heading . . ." (p. 452).[8] The generalized threats and promises of childhood, according to McClelland, produce "a type of learning situation which may prevent unlearning because the responses are instrumental to goals which are so high, vague, or indeterminate that *it is impossible for the person to evaluate how well he is doing*" (p. 453). This type of generalized learning is also seen by McClelland to be produced under conditions of partial reinforcement. "Stated in its most general form, our proposition is that *any method of increasing the similarity between acquisition and extinction will delay extinction*" (p. 454).

Finally, McClelland suggests that in early childhood the stimulus conditions may be quite different from stimulus conditions in later life. Not only is the child smaller and dependent, and probably seeing the world from a different perspective, but he is also just beginning to learn the distinction between self and the world out there. "It may be hard to unlearn some early affective associations because they were learned *under cue conditions which cannot be reinstated and attached to new responses*" (McClelland, 1951, p. 457). In summary, McClelland says "For all these reasons and for others which are closely related, affective associations formed in early childhood are apt to be strong and very resistant to unlearning or forgetting. From the theoretical viewpoint there is no reason why such associations could not be formed *at any time in life* but more of the conditions we have laid down are apt to occur in childhood, particularly at the preverbal level" (p. 457).

Despite this excellent derivation of the importance of early learning experiences, one is left with the feeling that most of what is known about learning by reinforcement deals with very specific types of habits. One cannot escape the impression that we must discover many new things before we understand the learning of such generalized habits, motives, or affective associations.

Three things stand out that seem important in the learning of strong dispositional properties that may be called motives. First, they seem to defy extinction. Second, primacy is apparently more important than recency. Third, incremental stimulation may lead to approach rather than avoidance learning (Martin, 1963). One cannot help but be struck by the fact that these same three conditions are found in the phenomenon known as imprinting.

---

[8] Before symbolic control is attained, one might assume something more like an affective generalization gradient. After the learning of language, affect may "generalize" according to cognitive categories.

IMPRINTING AS THE ORIGIN OF MOTIVES

The fact that the three aspects just mentioned were so ably derived from reinforcement theory by McClelland must put us on our guard against assuming that learning and imprinting are completely distinct phenomena. As a matter of fact, strictly speaking the term "imprinting" was coined by Lorenz (1935) to account for a phenomenon noticed by himself and also by Heimroth in 1910 (cf. Hunt, 1963) in the grey-leg gosling. The term is most properly applicable to the phenomenon discussed by Lorenz and studied in detail by Hess (1959) and found most obviously in wild fowl. Hess has demonstrated in wild mallard ducks, among other organisms, that shortly after hatching and only during a short critical period, the duck will follow any moving object within its visual field and form a strange and apparently permanent affective attachment to this object. The imprinting of these ducks on duck decoys apparently has all the characteristics noted above and stressed by McClelland as important in the development of motives, namely, acquisition at a specific early period in life, extreme resistance to extinction, and acquisition under punishing conditions of incremental stimulation. If the term "imprinting" is to be reserved for this type of phenomenon in wild fowl, then it is obviously not the origin of human motivation.

However, the research on imprinting in birds has led to new interest in infantile experiences that has generated considerable data involving mammals, including human infants, that are relevant to the development of motivation. These data deal with very early development of affective relationships with other organisms either of the same or of different species. They stress the importance of affective arousal and demonstrate quite clearly that varying conditions of affective arousal in early infancy can have strong effects on the behavior of the organism even in his adult associations with other organisms. Knowledge is still very meager in this new area of research, and no one has explicitly attempted to demonstrate experimentally a relationship between these early experiences and what might be called a motive [with the possible exception of Harlow (1962), Harlow & Harlow (1962)]. It would be foolhardy at present to claim that the origin of all motives lies in imprinting; on the other hand, it is extremely probable that the very first affective relationships that an organism has with other organisms will be found to be related to the arousal of secondary affect (affective mediating mechanism) in the later life of the organism.

Scott (1962, 1963) has discussed the notions of critical periods and the process of primary socialization. Primary socialization is defined "as the process of formation of primary social relationships" (Scott, 1963, p. 2).

The period of primary socialization begins in the human infant at about five to six weeks of age and ends at about seven and a half months. "During this period the infant first becomes capable of visual perception, can make associations with visual stimuli, and shows a high development of the smiling response to any human face. Its beginning may be set at the time of the first smiling response to the mother, at about five weeks. This is a period in which anyone can approach and easily develop social relationships with a baby. As Bayley's (1932) data on the crying response show, the fear response to strangers slowly increases in this period but does not become serious until its end" (Scott, 1963, p. 28). The period of primary socialization is ended by the development of fear and the period in which the child no longer establishes relationships with strangers. The development of fear is the same phenomenon that Hess (1959) has demonstrated as producing the end of the critical period of imprinting in ducks. We thus have a period in which social relationships are easily formed in the human infant, probably more easily formed than at any other period of life. A possible index of positive affect, the smiling response, is highly developed during this period. It becomes inhibited by the fear response, which develops later, but smiling continues to familiar faces, even during the period when fear is strong.

The smiling response is of particular interest here as a possible indication of positive affect. Scott cites Spitz and Wolf (1946) as demonstrating that the human face is the primary stimulus or releaser for smiling in the human infant, and that nearly all babies from three to five months of age will respond to the adult face with a smile. Before the age of two months this smile is rare, and by six months smiling to the faces of strangers has dropped almost to zero.

Scott has studied another response commonly thought to be an indicator of positive affect in dogs, namely, tail-wagging. "In a sample of 160 pure-bred puppies, the first case of tail wagging was observed at 17 days of age, and 50% of all puppies had been seen wagging their tails by 30 days of age. These figures were based on ten minute observations, and the median age would undoubtedly have been much earlier if longer observations had been made. Two of the breeds showed marked differences from the rest, cocker spaniels showing early and basenjis late development of tail wagging. Thus the onset of the tail wagging response is associated with the early part of the period of socialization. In older puppies it appears in almost 100% of animals in reaction to human contact" (Scott, 1963, p. 23).

Apparently the human face is the innate releaser of a response associated with positive affect, the smile, and some aspect of the human comes to be a releaser of a similar response, tail wagging, in the dog. These re-leasers apparently are stimuli that produce affect in the sense that it was discussed in Chapter 3. Unfortunately, careful specification of the exact stimulus qualities associated with these affective responses awaits further research. We would like to know, for instance, exactly what stimulus elicits the first instance of tail-wagging in the puppy and what are the critical aspects of the stimulus that elicit this response early.

Another response commonly considered to be an indication of positive affect that has been apparently neglected in research is the purring of the cat. It would seem that research investigating the stimulus conditions that elicit tail-wagging in dogs and purring in cats might shed light on the re-lationship between stimuli and the production of affect. The only study of purring to be found was a charming study of all of the vocalizations of the house-cat (Moelk, 1944). Moelk found that if she spoke to cats, even strange cats, they would usually "speak" back. Apparently for the house-cat the human being is an important stimulus even when a very young kitten. Moelk notes that a litter of kittens that she observed very early chose human contact and stroking to nursing even when quite hungry, and stroking elicited purring. Such a finding is hard to reconcile with re-inforcement theory.

A reinforcement theory explanation of the development of tail-wagging, purring, smiling, or generalized affective social responses would stress their early association with some form of primary reinforcement such as feeding. The evidence, however, seems to indicate that this hypothesis is oversimplified. Scott says:

"One of the earliest hypotheses was that of the acquired social drive starting with the hunger drive and the process of feeding. Feeding re-wards the approach of the young animals to their parents and causes the young to associate pleasure with them. In time the parents themselves produce rewarding sensations, without actually having to feed their young. This hypothesis is a plausible one and has the advantage of simplicity.

"However, this hypothesis will not explain imprinting in ducks and chickens, where the attachment is normally formed before feeding takes place and where attachments can be formed to models which are in no way associated with feeding. The acquired drive hypothesis is more plausible in mammals, where every young mammal begins his life by suckling from the mother . . ." (p. 35). However, Scott cites studies by Brodbeck (1954), Fisher (1955), and Elliot and King (1960), all of which demonstrate "that a strong social bond between human handler and puppy can be formed in the absence of food reward and, in fact, will be formed in spite of punishment if the punishing person is the only social object available during the critical period. However, hunger has the effect of producing a stronger attraction between a puppy and the person feeding it" (p. 37).

Harlow (1958) has shown that the acquired-drive theory does not account for the acquisition of an affective relationship between a rhesus monkey and a dummy mother. The monkeys supplied with a comfortable terrycloth mother with no food source and an uncomfortable wire mother with a food source, formed a strong relationship with the terrycloth mother and went to the wire mother only for purposes of eating. Igel and Calvin (1960) have demonstrated a similar phenomenon with young puppies. They have also demonstrated that when given a choice between two comfortable mothers, only one of which produces milk, the puppies will choose the milk-producing model. Scott concludes that "While behavior of young animals can be influenced by reward and punishment . . . the process of forming a social bond or attachment is independent of these influences. We can state as the best hypothesis to explain the observed facts that a young animal during the critical period will become attached to any animal or object with which it comes into long contact, irrespective of the nature of the experience with it. However, we also have evidence that an intense emotional experience, whether rewarding or punishing, will increase the speed of forming the primary attachment" (p. 37).

The last sentence of this quote stresses the final point to be made here, namely, the importance of affective or emotional arousal. Evidence from Hess (1959) with ducks, Elliot and King (1960) with puppies, and Harlow and Harlow (1962) with monkeys indicates that strong affective social relationships occur even in the face of aversive punishing incremental stimulation. Apparently then, as Scott says, "We may also conclude that the speed of formation of a social bond is dependent upon the degree of emotional arousal, irrespective of the nature of the arousal" (Scott, 1962, p. 5).

THE JAMES-LANGE THEORY AND SOME RECENT EVIDENCE

So far we have discussed the problem of the acquisition of affective relationships without mention of theories of emotion. We have stressed the phenomenological aspects of affect and have slighted the physiological aspects, whereas much research on emotions reverses this emphasis. Inevitably, however, we must confront the well-known James-Lange Theory of emotion with its implication that emotional reactions are not the *result* of emotional arousal but *are,* in fact, the emotion. Such a position calls into question the stimulus-affect-response analysis, but is a step in the direction suggested by Ryle's notion of category mistakes (Chapter 2) of avoiding arbitrary distinctions between affect and other responses. It is uniquely appropriate to consider the Jamesian position here for three reasons. First, it helps us to break out of and call into question the affective-arousal model and emphasizes the artificiality of considering affective mediating mechanisms as separate entities. Second, there exists some very recent evidence concerning emotional reactions and more overt behavior that should be aired. Third, the James theory and the recent data bear on a conceptualization of the relationship between thought and action to be presented in the next section of the book as well as being related to the problem of self- or personal knowledge and the attribution process to be discussed in Chapters 9 and 10.

In 1890, James launched the theory of emotion that is contained in the oft-quoted statement *"that the bodily changes follow directly the perception of the exciting fact, and that our feelings of the same changes as they occur* IS *the emotion"* (James, 1890, p. 449). James presented this theory in opposition to the more common approach that "our natural way of thinking about these coarser emotions is that the mental perception of some fact excites the mental affection called the emotion, and that this latter state of mind gives rise to the bodily expression" (p. 449). This quote could be seen as a description of the affective arousal model and clearly it is rejected by James. Under the influence of Behaviorism, twentieth century psychologists have seized on some of the examples cited by James and conceived of the theory in purely behavioristic terms. I know that I am afraid because I observe myself running; I know that I am sad because I observe myself crying; I know that I am angry because I observe myself striking someone; in general, I learn about my own internal states by observing my own behavior in the same way that I learn about someone else's states by observing his behavior.

Here again we encounter the ambiguity noted in Chapters 1 and 2 between observing another's behavior and experiencing what goes along with our own behavior. Here again we shall stress the difference — we experience much more when we ourselves are afraid and running than we do when we merely observe running behavior in another. And the "more" is what we have called personal knowledge and it may be experienced without any reportable "observation."

It may be that James would today defend the behavioristic interpretation of his thesis; but, except for the previous examples involving running, crying, and striking, his argument is couched in terms of "feeling" and "bodily changes . . . so indefinitely numerous and subtle that the entire organism may be called a sounding board" (p. 450) rather than entirely in terms of observable behavior. The behavioral correlates of emotion mentioned by James are reflex acts (respondents) not voluntary acts (operants). It should be noted that James discusses voluntary movements in a separate chapter under the concept of "Will" and explicitly states in the chapter on emotion, "Without the bodily states following on the perception, the latter would be purely cognitive in form, pale, colorless, destitute of emotional warmth. We might then see the bear, and judge it best to run, receive the insult and deem it right to strike, but we should not actually *feel* afraid or angry" (p. 450). Apparently, then, it is an oversimplification to conceive of emotion in purely behavioral terms as nothing more than the sum of overt observable behaviors in the arousing situation. On the other hand, it is a mistake to conceive of emotion as some nonobservable entity that occurs prior to and causes behavior.

James' presentation initiated a host of studies of "cold" emotion by suggesting that *"If we fancy some strong emotion, and then try to abstract from our consciousness of it all the feelings of its bodily symptoms, we find we have nothing left behind,* no 'mind-stuff' out of which the emotion can be constituted, and that a cold and neutral state of intellectual perception is all that remains" (p. 451). Here we have an excellent example of Ryle's category mistake, of trying to abstract out of our concept of emotion some "mind-stuff" that is entirely devoid of any bodily correlate. To assume, however, that this means that the concept of emotion completely reduces to overt responses, does not contain a distinct feeling for the person experiencing it, does not embody a large component of personal and ultimately private experience, is only defensible as an extreme behavioristic posture based on the programmatic decision not to consider private aspects. Data that demonstrate that people do learn something about their own emotional states and become more self-aware thereby, do not demonstrate that observation of own behavior is the only way to become self aware. It is only within the context of the programmatic aspects of Behaviorism that such a mistake can be made. Behaviorism *assumes* that all knowledge about self and others comes from the observation of behavior. To demonstrate that *some* such knowledge is based in observation is *not* to demonstrate the *assumption* that *all* self-knowledge is based on observations of behavior.

The crux of the problem comes down to accepting or rejecting the private aspects of personal knowledge to the scrutiny of science. This is not an empirical question, it is a theoretical one. It is decided for you by the theoretical camp you choose, not by an *experimentum crucis*. To argue about it from different theoretical premises is fruitless, but to try to test it experimentally is not only fruitless but also expensive.

A series of recent studies, however, does shed new light on the problem by clearly demonstrating that subjects who experience emotional reactions within themselves in the absence of any obvious reason for the reaction apparently seek for a cognitive interpretation of their arousal and learn to label their arousal in terms of situational aspects and their own behavior.

Schachter and Singer (1962) demonstrated the importance of labeling emotional states by artificially inducing physiological arousal through injection of the drug epinephrine (adrenalin). Against a control of subjects given a placebo, those given epinephrine were either *informed* that they would experience side effects similar to emotional arousal or were *uninformed,* i.e., told that there would be no side effects. All subjects thought that the experiment had to do with the effects of a vitamin on their vision. During the experimental session they were suddenly confronted with a situation that could be seen as an explanation of an emotional state (euphoria or anger) in themselves. It was predicted and the data confirmed that "given a state of physiological arousal for which an individual has no explanation [uninformed group], he will label this state in terms of the cognition available to him . . . given a state of physiological arousal for which the individual has a completely satisfactory explanation [informed group], he will not label this state in terms of the alternative cognitions available" (Schachter & Singer, 1962, p. 397).

These results emphasize the cognitive aspects of emotion and make it clear that the interpretation of emotional arousal under these artificial conditions may not be immediately given to the person experiencing the arousal and strongly imply that a person learns through experience to label his subjectively felt emotional states.

Valins (1966, 1967a,b) has gone further to demonstrate that experiencing feedback from one's own body indicative of emotional arousal may influence his behavior toward the stimuli present at the time when he experienced the feedback. Male subjects viewed 10 pictures of semi-nude females and heard what they thought to be the amplified sound of their own heart beating. Actually, what they heard was a recording that was arranged so that for 5 pictures the heart rate remained constant whereas for 5 others it either increased or decreased markedly. In the first experiment, it was demonstrated that pictures accompanied by apparent change in heart-rate were subsequently preferred to the other pictures. In the second experiment, this effect was shown to be more marked for high emotional subjects than for low emotional subjects.

Bem (1965) has taken a behaviorist position concerning self-knowledge and argues that "an individual's belief and attitude statements and the beliefs and attitudes that an outside observer would attribute to him are 'inferences' from the same evidence: the public events that the socializing community originally employed in training the individual to make such self-descriptive statements" (Bem, 1965, p. 200). Put in the extreme, the answer to the question "Do you like brown bread?" is that I know I do because I observe myself eating it all the time. Bem says that this reply is "functionally equivalent" to the reply an observer might give for the man who always eats brown bread. "It seems unnecessary to invoke a fount of privileged self-knowledge to account for the reply" (p. 200). Bem is using behavioristic assumptions of objectivity to explain self-awareness and his major point is an alternative explanation of some results explained by others in terms of cognitive dissonance. What he has done very ingeniously is to demonstrate that the observation of our overt behaviors *often* helps us to understand ourselves better. To say that these are the only cues to self-understanding is only defensible within the confines of the behavioristic model that assumes (but can never demonstrate empirically) that overt behavior is the only reliable source of inferences. By the rules of the game, then, any "fount of privileged self-knowledge" is considered nonobjective, and unreliable, and is forthwith discarded.

Bem's studies should not mislead the reader into the belief that he has shown empirically that *all* self-knowledge comes from the observation of own behavior, just because *some* of it does. Working under the presupposition that only objective observations of behavior are reliable, he has shown that some self-knowledge is affected by such observations. He has not, however, proved empirically what is essentially a programmatic presupposition and hence not subject to absolute empirical demonstration.

What Bem *has* done, and quite dramatically, is to demonstrate the fact that a person may be influenced in his inferences about himself and others by observing his own or their behavior. He showed, for instance, that observers, told about a previous experiment (Brehm & Cohen, 1962) in which the subjects' behavior was influenced by reward conditions, could take the same conditions into account in inferring the subject's internal states. This shows that external conditions may be used to infer internal states, but not that they are the only information used when the internal state is that of the subject himself. Similarly, Bem has shown that an external condition (a colored light) previously associated with telling the truth, can influence a subject subsequently to justify a self-made statement that is discrepant from his true original belief by actually changing his reported belief toward the discrepant statement. Bem's major point is to indicate that such data as his provide an alternative explanation to certain results more often explained in terms of cognitive dissonance.

These studies by Schachter, Valins and Bem make it quite apparent that personal knowledge is a complex thing and that labeling of emotional states may be an important aspect of the acquisition of affective relationships. The assumption of a simple stimulus-affect-response model appears, in light of the James-Lange theory, to lead to an arbitrary distinction between affective responses and other responses. On the other hand, it seems too extreme to make the Behaviorist's assumption that all personal knowledge comes from observation of overt behavior. Personal knowledge is not given full-blown the first time a person experiences emotional arousal. From the subjective point of view, however, it may appear to be immediate and private despite its dependence on previously learned labels. Although some of its content may derive from observations of behavior, a large component of personal knowledge derives from a person's own private access to his affective states.

Conclusions

As should be obvious, as yet we know very little about the acquisition of affective relationships. What we do know seems to indicate that early learning experiences are very important but that a simple reinforcement theory that postulates the origin of all such relationships in primary reinforcement is inadequate unless the definition of primary reinforcement is stretched beyond recognition. Either positive or negative affective arousal may result in a strong affectional bond.

The problem of the general nature of affect and its relationship to motives and behavior still remains. Throughout this section of the book (Chapters 3, 4, and 5) we have pursued a course resulting in the postulation of affective mediating mechanisms supported by an underlying concept of affect and motivation that is based on a mechanical analogue. In terms of our earlier discussion (Part I), the affect we have been discussing is a "twinge" and the model is "para-mechanical." As long as this is kept firmly in mind, the analogy may be useful as in explaining fear instigated behavior; but attempting to stretch the analogy too far may lead to faulty inferences. The total picture of human motivation with its complex problems of the "self" and ego-orientation will probably never be completely reduced to this molecular level. It demands a broader conceptualization.

PART III

THOUGHT SAMPLING AND ACHIEVEMENT MOTIVATION

Chapter 6

THOUGHTS, ACTION, AND ACHIEVEMENT MOTIVATION

As a first step in moving beyond the molecular model of affect we shall consider the uniquely human motive called achievement motivation. As originally developed by McClelland *et al.* (1953), this motive was conceptualized as a result of learning based on just such a model as presented in Part II. However, recent developments have indicated that such a model may be inadequate, and have raised the more general problems of the relationship between thoughts used in measuring the motive and action (what we called the twentieth century mind-body problem in Chapter 2), and of the origin of achievement motivation in personal causation.

We shall postpone a more detailed discussion of the relationship between the McClelland-Atkinson conception of achievement motivation and our conception of personal causation until we have become more familiar with some of the theoretical aspects of and research findings resulting from the McClelland-Atkinson formulation. For the present we shall stress that in this formulation we begin to find some empirical evidence for the relationship between thought and action that is relevant to our concept of the importance of personal knowledge.

The Achievement Motive

Since about 1950 when a group of researchers at Wesleyan University (McClelland *et al.,* 1953) devised a technique for measuring the achievement motive (*n* Achievement), a tremendous amount of research has been reported by McClelland and Atkinson, their colleagues, critics, and students. The two major protagonists who collaborated in devising the concept of achievement motivation have subsequently moved, both geographically and theoretically, in different directions. McClelland moved north from Wesleyan to Harvard University and followed a research strategy based on the assumption that careful specification of what the achievement motive really is cannot be achieved *a priori* but must be the result of extensive empirical investigation (McClelland, 1958). This approach is roughly akin to a sculptor who continuously finds the form of his statue in the stone rather than imposing the form on the stone from the beginning. Thus McClelland continuously forms and refines his conception of the achievement motive from the incoming empirical data. His current concept has surprising new aspects not envisaged in the early sketch (compare McClelland *et al.,* 1953; McClelland, 1961).

Atkinson moved west from Wesleyan to the University of Michigan and has devoted a considerable amount of his energy to developing a theoretical model to guide his empirical research in the area of achievement motivation (Atkinson, 1957, 1958). This approach is more like that of the mathematician who attempts to define his area of interest, devise constraints in the form of axioms and postulates, and then deduce testable hypotheses. As in any area of empirical science the mathematical deductions can be tested and made more precise by confrontation with empirical evidence.

Atkinson has not spent all of his time devising a model nor has McClelland spent all of his time collecting data. The difference between them is a matter of relative emphasis, and the result has probably been more productive than if they had both followed the same research strategy. McClelland has often supplied empirical evidence that fit the deductions of Atkinson's model as in the case of McClelland's early study of risk-taking behavior in children (McClelland, 1958). Conversely, Atkinson's model has supplied a structure to clarify data, for example in the area of occupational preferences of people with high *n* Achievement (see McClelland, 1961, pp. 246ff). Clearly, Atkinson's model did not spring full-blown out of the blue, nor does McClelland collect data with no theoretical structure in mind. The two approaches complement each other, and in fact there is much overlap between them.

The cornerstone of this research is the measurement technique, but even more basic is the concept that lies behind the technique. The two different theoretical emphases lead to slightly different conceptions of the achievement motive although both McClelland and Atkinson use the same measurement technique. In mathematical model building, the motive concept becomes a variable in an equation designed to predict action. For instance, Atkinson (1958) proposes the equation in the following form. "The strength of motivation to perform some act is assumed to be a multiplicative function of the strength of the motive, the expectancy (subjective probability) that the act will have as a consequence the attainment of an incentive, and the value of the incentive: Motivation = f (Motive × Expectancy × Incentive). . . . A motive is conceived as a disposition to strive for a certain kind of satisfaction, as a capacity for satisfaction in the attainment of a certain class of incentives. The names given motives — such as achievement, affiliation, power — are really names of classes of incentives which produce essentially the same kind of experience of satisfaction: pride in accomplishment, or the sense of belonging and being warmly received by others, or the feeling of being in control and influential" (p. 324). A motive is the disposition to strive for something; a particular motive is the disposition to strive for a particular type of satisfaction; the achievement motive is the disposition to strive for satisfaction derived from *success in competition with some standard of excellence*.

The achievement motive is assessed by taking *thought samples* in the form of short stories written by the subjects. Subjects who demonstrate particular types of associative networks involving achievement themes and defined as achievement imagery are prone to certain types of action such as moderate risk-taking, energetic innovating activity, taking personal responsibility for results of action, attempting to get and use knowledge of results of action. These characteristics form the Achievement Syndrome discovered by McClelland (1961) to be the empirical concomitants of high achievement motivation.

It is eminently reasonable to assume that there is a connection between the thoughts and actions of a person but psychologists are the first to point out that the connection is not a simple one. For instance, why are thoughts produced in writing a story but not self-reports of achievement motivation related to achievement behavior (de Charms, Morrison, Reitman, & McClelland, 1955)? The actual connection between the measuring technique used to tap the achievement motive and the behavior it predicts is still shrouded in mystery despite the millions of words that have been written about projective techniques, unconscious motives, etc.

THE MCCLELLAND-ATKINSON MEASUREMENT TECHNIQUE

Before we can confront the more basic questions of the relationship between a motive (measured by thought sampling) and behavior and ultimately the relationship between thought and action, we must look in detail at the measurement technique. The technique of thought sampling used to measure the achievement, affiliation, and power motives is carefully presented in Atkinson (1958). A briefer and more discursive description may be found in Brown (1965). Our main concern is to sketch the technique for the reader so that we may proceed to the technical question of how it was developed and ultimately to more theoretical questions.

Thought samples are collected in a standardized situation as follows. Subjects seated in a classroom are told that they are to participate in a study of creative imagination. They will see several pictures projected one at a time on a screen. After they have observed the picture for a short time, it will be turned off and they are to create and write an interesting story about the character(s) in the picture. They are told that the protocol placed before them has a separate page for each story containing questions that will help them to finish a complete story-plot in the short time allowed.

After any questions are answered, the lights are dimmed and the first picture is shown for approximately 20 seconds. With light restored the subjects write their story for 4 minutes, having been encouraged to spend approximately 1 minute on each of the following groups of questions: 1. What is happening? Who are the persons? 2. What has led up to this situation? That is, what has happened in the past? 3. What is being thought? What is being wanted? By whom? 4. What will happen? What will be done? After 4 minutes have elapsed, the subjects are told to turn to the next page; the lights are dimmed for the second picture and the same procedure is followed. Typically, four to six pictures are used, the best known of which depicts a boy sitting at a desk resting his forehead on one hand. A large selection of pictures have been tested and are described by Atkinson (1958) along with recommendations for a standardized set.

These few short stories constitute a sample of the thoughts of each subject collected under standardized conditions. The subject is essentially free to express any thought that he sees as relevant to the picture, although the picture obviously reduces the number of thoughts from which he selects. The picture cues have a clear effect on the content of the stories (McClelland *et al.*, 1953).

Thought samples of this type may be content analyzed for many things. The technique was first devised to elicit stories whose content indicated achievement motivation and the pictures were selected with this in mind. Although techniques for measuring other motives have since been devised (Atkinson, 1958), we shall confine our discussion to the achievement motive.

The definition of achievement motivation upon which the content analysis is based is *"success in competition with some standard of excellence.* That is, the goal of some individual in the story is to be successful in terms of competition with some standard of excellence" (McClelland *et al.,* 1953, pp. 110–111). Any indication of this theme in a story qualifies the story to be scored for *achievement imagery*. In addition to definite statements about competition, the inference that competition is involved in the story may be derived from indications of *unique accomplishment* or *long term involvement*. When "one of the characters is involved in accomplishing other than a run-of-the-mill daily task which will mark him as a personal success" (p. 113), the story is considered to contain achievement imagery. Similarly when "one of the characters is involved in attainment of a long-term achievement goal" (p. 113) such as "being a success in life, becoming a machinist, doctor, lawyer, successful businessman, and so forth. . ." (p. 113), achievement imagery is scored.

If a story qualifies under one of these headings, it may then be examined for ten subcategories that derive from a behavioral analysis of a striving situation. A person who is striving for an achievement goal may actually be described in the story as wanting it. If so, the subcategory *"Need"* is scored. The striving person may indicate anticipation of success or apprehension about failure. These form the subcategories of *Positive* or *Negative Goal Anticipation*. The person may indicate positive or negative feelings associated with the attainment of the goal from which *Positive* and *Negative Affect* may be scored. The person may engage in actual striving behavior in which case *Instrumental Activity* is scored. Another person in the story may help the hero attain his goal. This category is called *Nurturant Press*. The person may encounter obstacles along the way to the achievement goal and they may be either physical or personal. These form the categories *World and Personal Blocks*. Finally, if achievement orientation constitutes the central plot of the story *Achievement Thema* is scored. These ten subcategories are only scored if the story was originally judged to have achievement imagery. Other stories are consigned to the *Unrelated Imagery* category or, if they describe specific task situations but do not qualify for achievement imagery, they are categorized as containing

Task Imagery. An unrelated imagery story is assigned a score of negative one; a task imagery story is assigned a score of zero; and an achievement imagery story is assigned a score of positive one plus one for every subcategory that appears. No subcategory is scored twice within the same story.

This rather elaborate system of content analysis can be learned to a criterion of greater than 90% interscorer reliability, but it takes intensive effort to acquire the skill. We will not concern ourselves with reliability of scorers or of the test as they have been treated elsewhere (McClelland *et al.*, 1953; Atkinson, 1958; Brown, 1965). Suffice it to say that high scorer reliability is usually meticulously adhered to, whereas test-retest reliability is disappointingly low, some reasons for which McClelland (1958) has discussed in detail.

Our major concern at this point is to present the original research that was used to develop scoring categories and to validate the measure. Although this research is presented in complete detail in McClelland *et al.* (1953), it is sometimes difficult to see the overall strategy in the welter of research findings. We shall concentrate on the strategy with the dual purpose of highlighting its strength and at the same time of finding cues to the present status of the measurement technique and its theoretical relevance to the problem of motive measurement and more broadly to the relationship between thought and action.

The categories presented above resulted from an empirical examination of stories written under conditions of achievement stress as compared to non-stress conditions, but this is only part of the story. Conceptually, the search for the scoring categories and for their relationship to other behaviors took at least four distinct steps.

Step 1. Demonstration That Relevant Changes Occur in Thought Samples Collected Under Various Levels of Drive

Before approaching the more complex problems of achievement motivation, Atkinson and McClelland (1948) selected the easily manipulable hunger drive to demonstrate that thought samples collected under high drive differed in characteristic ways from samples collected under low drive. This study was in the tradition of the studies of the effects of needs and drives on perception and cognition (Postman, 1953) and the concept of measuring motives in thought samples derives originally from the concept of apperception (Murray, 1943) and projection (Freud, 1900; see also Anna Freud, 1936) as found in stories.

Atkinson and McClelland (1948) arranged to test Navy men who had not eaten for 1, 4, and 16 hours. This formed the manipulation of different intensities of need or drive. All of the men wrote eight creative stories under similar instructions as were described above for measuring achievement motivation. In this case, however, the pictures were specifically selected to suggest themes relating to hunger, food, and related activities. The stories were coded for food-related imagery, food deprivation themes, and several other categories. Careful analysis of the individual categories led to the development of a general index of the need for food that increased significantly as the hours of food deprivation increased in the three groups of subjects. This result confirms the effects of varying intensities of drive on the content of thought samples.

An interesting result of the analysis of separate content categories indicated that "As hunger increased, there was no overall increase in the percentage of Ss showing food imagery or food themas, but there was a decided increase in the percentage showing food deprivation themas, characters expressing a need for food, and activity successful in overcoming deprivation, but not always instrumental in getting food. On the other hand, as hunger increased, there was a decided decrease in the amount of goal activity (eating) and in friendly press favorable to eating" (Atkinson, 1958, p. 62).

These results were seen as similar to the results of an earlier study (McClelland & Atkinson, 1948) of the effects of hunger on the perception of objects. This study found an increase in the perception of objects instrumental to eating but not of food objects with increased hunger. The authors argue that stories showing need deprivation and instrumental activities meant to reduce the need are more indicative of strength of need than are the stories containing discussions of goal activity such as descriptions of food and eating. When a person is hungry, thoughts about how to get food (instrumental activity) are more adaptive than dreams of large banquets and feasts. Apparently, the thought samples are tapping some kind of adaptive orientation rather than a more Freudian type of wish fulfillment in fantasy.

This study takes the first step in demonstrating the effects of motivational states on thought samples. The use of hunger has the advantage of showing this effect with the need most often used in learning studies based on drive- or tension-reduction theory (Hull, 1943).

Step 2. Demonstration and Selection of Specific Indicators of Achievement Motivation That Vary with Induced Changes in the Achievement Motive

The basic concept here is arousal as discussed in McClelland's affective-arousal model (McClelland *et al.,* 1953, pp. 27ff). The technique is to arouse the achievement motive in some subjects and not in others and look for differences in content of thought samples written under the two conditions.

McClelland *et al.* (1953) describe in detail an experiment in which they tried different types of arousal. Following the lead of the importance of deprivation in the hunger studies, they tried to create various conditions of achievement deprivation by inducing a failure orientation in some subjects and a success orientation in others. Immediately preceding the writing of creative stories, subjects experienced either failure or success in some experimental tasks such as solving anagrams. This technique resulted in some interesting findings to which we shall return later. However, a technique of arousing achievement motivation by verbal instructions similar to ego-involving instructions was apparently more successful than attempts to induce feelings of achievement deprivation. "The analogy with hunger proved misleading, . . . since it led us to expect that the degree of arousal would be a direct function of *deprivation* (e.g., failure) and an inverse function of *satiation* (e.g., success) . . . In the beginning our focus of attention was on manipulation of success and failure with the expectation that a 'Success' group would show the lowest *n* Achievement, a 'Neutral' group a moderate amount, and a 'Failure' group the highest amount. Later it became apparent that the motive had to be aroused by instructional cues and the like before its course could be affected by success and failure. . ." (pp. 99–100).

The instructional cues used in the achievement-oriented condition stress that the procedures in which the subjects are about to participate are used to select leaders, predict generalized success in career and a high general level of intelligence. After mentioning that the tests to be taken were used to select officer candidates; the arousal instructions conclude: "In short, these tests demonstrate whether or not a person is suited to be a leader. The present research is being conducted under the auspices of the Office of Naval Research to determine just which individuals possess the leadership qualifications shown by superior performance on these tests" (McClelland *et al.,* 1953, p. 103). The subjects were mostly ex-servicemen for whom this type of arousal would be peculiarly appropriate.

By contrast, in the relaxed condition every effort was made to de-emphasize the importance of the tests by having them presented as of as yet unknown value that the experimenter, a graduate student, was trying out. He avoided any indication of involvement in the outcome and did not even require the subjects to sign their names to the protocol.

Between the relaxed and the achievement-oriented condition along the dimension of arousal the experimenters created a neutral condition that stressed that the subjects had a task to perform but gave no indication of its purpose. The experimenter was serious and business-like, but did nothing to either emphasize or de-emphasize achievement orientation.

One hundred and seventeen men participated in the experiment, thirty-nine under each condition of arousal. All of the categories described above were scored in the four stories from each subject and the frequency of all categories increased with increasing arousal. Highly significant increases were found for Achievement Imagery, Need, Instrumental Activity, Positive Anticipatory Goal state, Negative Anticipatory Goal state, Positive Affective state, and Achievement Thema. Nurturant Press, Personal and World Blocks, and Negative Affective states did not reach the criterion set for significance that was high ($p < .004$) to take into account the fact that the categories could not be considered independent of each other.

This step in the procedures for developing the measure of achievement motivation clearly shows that relevant indicators derived from a behavioral analysis of the instrumental sequence are affected by arousal techniques that stress intelligence, careers, and leadership. This type of arousal is quite different from the technique used in the hunger studies or in inducing success or failure, i.e., varying relative deprivation of the goal of the motive to be measured. In the manipulation of deprivation through induced success or failure on laboratory tasks prior to writing the creative stories, the categories that did not increase significantly with achievement arousal (Personal and World Blocks, Negative Affective states, and Nurturant Press) were found to change. The Blocks and Nurturant Press were found more under both success and failure conditions than in the relaxed condition and the highest incidence was after failure. Negative Affective states were most evident also after failure although this finding was not significant. In the end, all ten subcategories were used in forming an overall index of achievement motivation.

In the above experiment, different subjects participated in the different arousal groups. Lowell (1950) has also demonstrated increases in all categories when the same male college subjects were first tested under neutral conditions and then a week later under achievement arousal conditions. A similar technique administered to 21 ninth-grade Navaho boys produced essentially similar results.

Step 3. Demonstration That Other "Achievement Related" Responses Vary with Induced Changes in the Achievement Motive

Step 2 above showed a relationship between thought content and arousal instructions. The logical next question to ask is whether arousal instructions increase other motivated behavior such as productivity in laboratory tasks? In a study designed to test the relationship between the recall of completed and incompleted tasks and achievement motivation, Atkinson (1950) obtained such a measure of productivity, i.e., the number of simple paper and pencil tasks that the subjects completed in a given amount of time. The tasks were given to different groups under Relaxed, Task (Neutral), and Achievement-oriented conditions and the number of tasks completed increased as the achievement orientation of the instructions increased.

Step 4. Demonstration That Subjects Who Score High on the Number of Achievement Categories in Their Thought Samples Have Different Motivational Characteristics from Subjects Who Score Low

This, of course, is the most important step in demonstrating the construct validity of the measure. The early validation studies concentrated mainly on showing that the "high need achiever" had significantly higher productivity on laboratory type tasks than the "low need achiever." Thus McClelland *et al.* (1953) report high *n* Achievement subjects surpass the lows on *(a)* paper and pencil tasks completed in the Zeigarnik type experiment (Atkinson, 1950), *(b)* addition problems solved in a given amount of time, *(c)* scrambled words solved in a given amount of time, *(d)* gain in number of scrambled words solved over a period of time indicating greater learning. Achievement motivation was also shown to be related to recognition thresholds for achievement related words and moderate relationships were found between college grades and achievement motivation although the relationship between achievement motivation and school behavior has subsequently turned out to be rather complicated (Morgan, 1952; Ricciuti, 1955; Ricciuti and Sadacca, 1955; Lazarus, Baker, & Mayer, 1957; Vogel, Baker, & Lazarus, 1958; Jordan & de Charms, 1959).

Since the original validation studies, an enormous amount of research has attempted to relate achievement motivation to many other aspects of the individual. Probably the most outstanding and well-replicated finding is the relationship between achievement motivation and moderate risk-taking (Atkinson & Litwin, 1960). People with high achievement motivation tend to take calculated, moderate risks rather than speculative ventures or a "sure thing" when their skill is involved. Around this finding McClelland (1961) has built his concept of the Achievement Syndrome with stress on the entrepreneurial behavior of people with high *n* Achievement. As we saw earlier, the research reported by McClelland (1961) indicated that the person with high achievement motivation is characterized by *(a)* moderate risk-taking strategies, *(b)* energetic and novel instrumental activity to attain his goals, *(c)* willingness to take individual responsibility for his actions, *(d)* desire for knowledge of results of his actions, and *(e)* long-range planning and organizational abilities. All of these findings add to the stature and construct validity of the achievement motive concept.

We have merely sketched the highlights of the research that has been carried out to validate the measure, arbitrarily dividing it into four steps for the sake of clarity. One more minor step should be mentioned, namely that McClelland *et al.* (1953) even asked one group of subjects to try to "fake" high scores of achievement motivation in their thought samples and their scores turned out to be no higher than scores for "non-fakers."

There is no other measure of human motivation that has been subjected to such rigorous tests of validity. But so far we have looked at the area with rose-colored glasses and have not mentioned the great difficulties that a researcher inevitably encounters when he chooses to use the measure of achievement motivation in his research.

Critique of Achievement Motivation

A critique of an area of research such as the measurement of achievement motivation is the kind of thankless job relished by psychologists. A few negative results are enough to put together a paper that casts doubt on years of work. Strangely enough little critical comment has appeared in print concerning the achievement motive,[1] although much informal criticism can be heard in discussions.

What criticism does exist usually takes the form of carping over specific findings that do not replicate or behaviors that "should" be predicted by a measure of achievement motivation, such as group leadership or academic success, but are not. Such criticisms are easily handled by McClelland's (1958) empirical approach that says, in essence, we find out what the achievement motive really is by research and apparently it is not related to group leadership or to most conventional measures of academic success.

There is a dearth of discussions of more basic issues such as why a 30-minute measure of the thought processes of an individual *should* predict a wide variety of behaviors. A critique at this level is hard to

---

[1]Exceptions to this are McArthur (1953), Reitman (1960), Vogel *et al.* (1958), and Klinger (1966).

substantiate because again the empirical answer is that scores derived from the thought samples are related to some types of behavior and are not related to other types. It is important to ask the question in its baldest form — how can thoughts predict action? — in order to bring out some hidden assumptions that lie behind such a question.

Once the air is cleared of unwarranted assumptions at the most basic level, it may be possible to proceed to the more practical level and gain some insight into the fact that the measure of achievement motivation, despite several attempts to refine it, remains almost two decades after its conception the same crude instrument with a discouraging penchant for quixotic fluctuations in any single experiment attributable to extreme sensitivity of measurement (McClelland, 1958) or to unreliability.

How Can a Measure Derived from Thought Samples Predict Action?

There are two different answers to this question that depend on the way the word "predict" is interpreted. Thoughts do not cause actions in the simple mechanical sense of causation. If we are looking for a simple "causal" relationship between antecedent thoughts and consequent actions, we will be disappointed. This is primarily a conceptual not an empirical matter, but there is certainly plenty of evidence that there is no one to one relationship between specific thoughts and particular action sequences. The rationalistic psychologies of the eighteenth and nineteenth centuries have been laid to rest in any such extreme form.

On the other hand, the extreme Behavioristic psychology that rejects thought as having any place in psychology is also passé. Even a position that thoughts are merely epiphenomena is incapable of explaining the evidence for relationship between measures derived from thought samples and action sequences observed in the same subject. No one would claim that thoughts about competition with a standard of excellence impel a person to choose a moderate risk-taking strategy in the sense that a cue ball impels the eight ball to roll in a certain direction. On the other hand, it is impossible to deny that an empirical probabilistic relationship exists between the occurrence of competitive thoughts and moderate risk-taking strategies in subjects.

We have put the question of the relationship between thoughts and actions in a way that hurls us headlong into at least three unwarranted presuppositions. First, that thoughts precede action, second that some quasi-mechanical causal sequence exists between them, and third that thoughts are somehow different from action. Laid end to end these are obviously unacceptable. As we saw in Chapter 2, the categorical distinction between thoughts and actions is a result of the philosophical legacy of eighteenth and nineteenth century philosophical acceptance of psychophysical dualism, i.e., the position that the Mind (and its thoughts) is different from the body and obeys different laws. In the twentieth century, this notion has inadvertently been fostered by Behaviorism in those psychologists who accept the primacy of action in the study of psychology but are still interested in thought processes. Interestingly enough, Behaviorism gives us the category that includes both thoughts and actions and thus helps us to avoid a category mistake. If both thoughts and actions are conceived of as behavior some of the verbal haze created by trying to make thoughts a special category is cleared. One behavior may be correlated with another, one behavior may even appear to impel another in some causal way although the empirical evidence for this always reduces to probability statements.

Let us turn now from these philosophical aspects to the actual explanations given for the relationship between the index of achievement motivation derived from thought samples and what we will now call *other* types of behavior.

Projection

We have carefully and consistently referred to the achievement motive as thought sampling, but in the original conception (McClelland, 1951) the measure was considered as a projective technique. The technique of collecting thought samples is a modification of Murray's (1943) Thematic Apperception Test (TAT) which is commonly referred to as a "projective test." It is our contention that the concept of projection serves to complicate rather than clarify the explication of the relationship between the achievement motive measure and other manifestations. For this reason we have taken pains thus far not to refer to the measure in the common way as the TAT or as a projective measure of motivation. Be that as it may, let us look at the earliest conception of the measure as a projective technique.

Prior to the development of the measure of achievement motivation, experimental research on the Freudian concept of projection (as well as other defense mechanisms) was beginning to appear (Bellak, 1944; Sears, 1936; Sanford, 1937) spurred by Murray's work (1938, 1943) with the TAT. As Bellak (1944) points out, the concept first appeared in Freud's writings in 1894. In an authoritative source of psychoanalysis (Healy, Bronner, & Bowers, 1930) it is defined as "A defensive process under the sway of the pleasure principle whereby the ego thrusts forth on the external world unconscious wishes and ideas which, if allowed to penetrate into consciousness, would be painful to the ego" (quoted in Bellak, 1944, p. 354).

Taking the psychoanalytic concept as is, involves other concepts such as the ego, the unconscious and repression, and leaves us with the restriction that what is projected must be painful and outside the awareness of the subject. We shall avoid a long discussion of the relationship between awareness and the unconscious as well as pain and repression by noting that Murray's concept of projection as applied to the TAT is less restrained than this, albeit less specific conceptually. In the Murray conception of the TAT, the needs or motives of the story writer are "projected" onto the heroes of the stories. McClelland (1951, pp. 549ff) discusses the difficulty of knowing what aspects of the hero in a story may be assumed to apply to the writer and what may not (cf. Lindzey & Kalnis, 1958). The conclusion of the discussion quoted from Murray and accepted by McClelland is that evidence about the storywriter's personality drawn from his stories are to be regarded as "leads" that need to be checked in other realms of his behavior.

A particularly confusing element is introduced by assuming that some of the needs projected onto the heroes are unconsciously present in the writer. Murray does not assume that all the "leads" derived from the stories represent repressed and hence rejected needs. This places the story analyzer in a typically psychoanalytic-theory-induced quandary: Is the manifest content of a story to be taken as a straightforward conscious expression of the personality or a defense against some other rejected characteristic? To be a little clearer, we may assume that most subjects who are telling a story to a psychologist will more or less consciously try to inhibit certain responses and stress others in order to present a good picture of themselves. How do we know whether a strong theme in a protocol is actually very important to the subject or represents a defense against talking about another theme that is really the important one? The answer is that we need more information from other sources and ultimately we may need a complete clinical study of the individual. Murray's TAT was developed as one measure in this type of analysis in depth, but McClelland et al. (1953) are using it as an experimental tool to tell us one thing about many subjects. The subtle, intense analysis of each individual is given up for a more superficial indication, but the measure is still fraught with these difficulties.

Bellak (1944) has pointed out that the actual story content of the TAT may result from at least three sources. The stimulus picture sets limits and some of the content is determined by the picture. Within these limits, the storyteller may exhibit stylistic or expressive habits in the way he treats the content. Finally, he may project his needs into the story. The distinction between projection and expressive behavior is primarily made by distinguishing between what the story character does and how he does it. The expressive behavior elaborates how the hero behaves after the need projection has determined what he will do.

All of these distinctions are vague but basically they come down to a general statement that what a person tells about in a story should be related to the ways he goes about doing other things in his life. The major argument for the TAT as a measuring instrument is that it reduces inhibitions and defenses and may tap unconscious motives.

Although we have probably done little to clarify the argument for thought sampling as a "projective technique," it should be clear that use of the projection concept raises more problems than it solves in the concrete instance of achievement motivation. There is little reason to assume that people in an "achieving society" such as the United States typically repress and therefore project the achievement motive. Quite the contrary, given half a chance they will probably try to stress their achievement qualities and may repress the anti-achievement aspects of their personalities. We must look further, then, for the answer to our question about the relationship between the achievement motive index and other instances of behavior.

The Stimulus-Response Approach

McClelland and his associates have never stressed the concept of projection in the Freudian sense, although in the early studies they referred to their measure as indicating the projective expression of needs (Clark, 1952; McClelland, Clark, Roby, & Atkinson, 1949; Atkinson & McClelland, 1948; McClelland & Atkinson, 1948). This early use of the concept soon gave way to a more behavioral analysis. In an early statement, McClelland (1951) presented the Bergman and Spence (1944) distinction between Stimulus-Response (SR) relationships or laws $[R = f(S)]$ and Response-Response relationships $[R_1 = f(R_2)]$. Much of the methodological literature of psychology assumes that the prototype for experimental research is the SR type relationship which is often assumed to result in causal laws (Selltiz *et al.,* 1959). Research based on RR relationships is relegated to the lower status position of "correlational research."[2]

---

[2]It need hardly be said, that the present author is suspicious of a distinction that draws its prestige from the assumption that one relationship is more "causal" than another unless careful consideration is given to the meaning implied by the "cause." McClelland (1951, pp. 77–81) presents a useful discussion of the relationship between SR and RR type laws.

With respect to the achievement motivation index (called the TAT score), McClelland starts with the empirical finding that the score is a function of arousal.

$$\text{TAT score} = f \text{ ("ego-involving" instructions)} \tag{1}$$

This is an SR relationship because the TAT score is a measure of the response and the instructions form the stimulus.

Arousal is only a temporary thing but if a person can be consistently aroused by ego-involving instructions time and time again, this indicates a potentiality for achievement arousal. This individual potentiality is a dispositional property of the personality that is not directly observed but is inferred. An inferred dispositional property calls for the use of an intervening variable (a type of X variable) in the theory at the very least. If the X variable is allowed to take on surplus meaning (over and above that derived from the empirical equation relating S's with R's where X forms a mathematical intervening variable), that is if we are willing to speculate about other aspects of the dispositional property assumed to account for X, then X can be given a name like the achievement motive (n Achievement) and becomes a hypothetical construct.[3]

McClelland postulates n Achievement as a hypothetical motivational construct that is a function of the summation of past experiences of "ego-involving" situations.

$$n \text{ Achievement} = f \text{ (past "ego-involving" situations)} \tag{2}$$

If responses (the TAT score) elicited by situational arousal ("ego-involving" instructions) are derived from learning that is the result of the sum of past "ego-involving" instructions, and the hypothetical construct n Achievement is a function of this same sum of past experiences, then:

$$\text{TAT score} = f \text{ (past "ego-involving" experiences)} \tag{3}$$
$$\text{and}$$
$$\text{TAT score} = f \text{ (}n \text{ Achievement)} \tag{4}$$

The TAT score is thus derived from an SR relationship but the hypothetical construct n Achievement allows the assumption that the stimuli

---

[3]Our distinction between "intervening variable" and "hypothetical construct" is roughly analogous to the more carefully drawn distinction proposed by MacCorquodale and Meehl (1948).

eliciting achievement responses need not be external experimental arousal stimuli (the "ego-involving" instructions) but may be a potential for arousal (a dispositional property) carried around within the individual that has resulted from learning in past instances of arousal.

If we now assume that the TAT score is a reliable measure of that internal stimulus, we can then formulate another SR relationship that predicts that other types of achieving behavior, for instance striving, will be a function of the strength of the internal stimulus or personal arousal that is inferred from the TAT score. The SR relationship now takes on the form

$$\text{Striving, etc. (achieving responses)} = f \text{ (internal stimulus)} \qquad (5)$$

and since the TAT score is also a function of the internal stimulus we have

$$\text{Striving, etc. (achieving responses)} = f \text{ (TAT score)} \qquad (6)$$

We have thus derived an answer to our question — How can a measure from thought sampling (TAT score) be used to predict other types of responses? — using strong SR relationships and the hypothetical construct n Achievement. What's more, there are empirical data to support most of the steps since the validation procedures have shown that the TAT score is a function of arousal (Equation 1) and that achieving responses are related to the TAT score (Equation 6). A study by Winterbottom (1958) may be used to support Equation 3 since she found a relationship between the TAT score and childhood independence training (past "ego-involving" experiences). Equations 2 and 4 contain the hypothetical construct "n Achievement" which is by definition unmeasurable, and therefore the equations are theoretical and not empirically verifiable. Equation 5 containing the new component (internal stimulus) remains to be justified.

Actually some of the basic assumptions of McClelland's underlying theory of motivation have slipped in here, and these must be presented to account for the "internal stimulus." Two postulates in that underlying theory are: (a) all motives (such as n Achievement) are learned, and (b) a motive is the redintegration by a cue (stimulus) of a state of affect (McClelland et al., 1953).

Basing these postulates on the conception of the arousal of affect by the discrepancy between stimulation and adaptation or expectation (the discrepancy hypothesis as discussed in detail in Chapters 3 and 4), the theory assumes that the internal stimulus referred to in Equation 5 is a state of affect. Affect, it will be remembered, is one of those convenient concepts like Hull's fractional-anticipatory-goal-responses ($r_g s_g$) that is both an emotional response and the resulting internal feeling or stimulus. Any external stimulus may acquire the capacity to arouse affect through a process of learning that involves past experiences of the association by contiguity of the stimulus and affect aroused by some discrepancy between adaptation or expectation and stimulation. In the instance under discussion, it may be assumed that "ego-involving" instructions have in the past been associated with affective arousal and, to the extent that they have, will serve as the cue (stimulus) for the redintegration of affect in the present situation. This affect, which if redintegrated by an achievement stimulus may be assumed to be the core of the achievement motive, forms the stimulus that then elicits achievement behavior. For the person with high achievement motivation, many stimuli including ego-involving instructions and certain types of TAT pictures will redintegrate affective arousal with a resulting push toward achieving behavior. For the person with low achievement motivation, few if any relevant stimuli will arouse affect and therefore achieving behavior will not result.

Using this reasoning, it can be argued that the TAT score is a measure of affect aroused by relevant achievement cues (in instructions or TAT pictures) and since affect is what energizes and directs behavior the measure derived from thought samples may be used to predict other types of achievement responses. Thus we have derived an answer to our original question using entirely behavioristic stimulus-response relationships, the hypothetical construct *n* Achievement, and the semi-empirical concept of affect. We say semi-empirical because we must assume that the TAT score is a measure of aroused affect. TAT stories do include actual statements of affect over achievement goals and these enter into the measure, but the measure itself is a composite that includes more than expressions of affect and can at best only be considered a rough index of affect. If we accept the foregoing derivation completely, the ultimate in measures of motivation reduces to a sensitive measure of affect.

Our original statement of the question in terms of the relationship between thoughts and action makes little sense in the behavioristic analysis where thoughts are ruled out of consideration. On this interpretation, thought sampling is no more than a technique of arousal of internal stimuli and of recording responses.

The Response-Response Approach

But what have we done? On the face of it Equation 6 [striving, etc. = f (TAT score)] involves no stimulus at all, both parties to the equation are responses. Are we left with the lower class R-R or correlational type relationship despite this valiant attempt to derive it from SR laws? Not if we can assume that affect is a concept with special significance, that it is a stimulus although it is also a response, that it has dynamic qualities that energize and direct other less fortunate responses, and finally that we can measure it.

J. S. Brown (1953), for one, is unable to swallow all of these assumptions despite the fact that they stem directly from Hullian theory as we saw in Chapter 3. He has stated the case, supported by some data from Goss and Brownell (1957) that the TAT measure is really tapping responses to stimuli that are elicited by stimuli far out on a generalization continuum from the stimuli originally present when the response was learned. If achieving responses are found under such conditions, it is reasonable to assume that they are strongly learned and to predict that, when other stimulus conditions prevail in the future that are more like those under which original learning occurred, similar responses will occur. This is basically an R-R relationship.

Let us try to make this explanation clearer by example. Suppose we know that one group of rats has been trained to press a bar whenever they saw a face through the clear plastic end of their cage, but that another group had no such training. To make it more like learning in life, we may even say that the faces used in training varied considerably (the experimenter, his assistant, the custodian, visitors to the lab, etc.) but they were always male. We do not know which group of rats has learned the habit but wish to find out empirically, although we cannot present a real male face to the rats. We set up a test using a picture of the face of a female. Assuming that the pictured female face is somewhere along a stimulus similarity continuum with the original learning stimuli (real male face), we ought to be able to pick out the group of rats originally trained, by observing more bar pressing in response to the picture than among the nontrained rats. From this response evidence, we could predict a future response in one group of rats when a real male face is again presented. Similarly, one can argue that responses to TAT pictures are generalized from earlier learned responses and are predictive of future responses to stimuli on the same generalization continuum. Any such relationships thus found are R-R type relationships.

Obviously this explanation has some things in common with the previous SR explanation. Both assume that the TAT scores are the result of past learning. The SR explanation is more powerful in that it assumes that the TAT actually measures an energizing and directing stimulus (affect) that can be assumed to be aroused by other relevant stimuli and that takes a direct hand in the resulting behavior.

There is much to recommend the SR over the RR analysis according to Bergman and Spence (1944), but the SR analysis rests primarily on the conceptual device of assuming that an affective response is also a stimulus. Several theorists have cogently argued this point since Hull, and Mowrer (1960a,b) has made it clear that this may be the behavioral explanation of feedback. Feather (1963) has discussed Mowrer's (1960a,b) concepts of hope, fear, relief, and disappointment as aspects of expectancy-value theory. There is, therefore, considerable evidence that both the response and the stimulus (feedback from the response) aspects of any action must be taken into account.

The trouble with the SR formulation is not that it has come to derive RR relationships from SR laws in the more or less slick manner demonstrated. The trouble lies in the assumption of some temporal sequence between the S and the R, namely, that the S always precedes the R. Having swallowed that assumption, which is necessary to make the SR law more basic than RR relationships, it is easy to fall into an oversimplified notion that the S somehow impels, energizes, and directs the R, i.e., to fall into the interpretation that the S causes the R in some para-mechanical way. Such an explanation has carried us far and may be accurate in cases in which some affective stimulus precedes action. It seems most useful, for instance, in the case in which conditioned fear or anxiety is actually felt before anxiety reducing behavior is initiated. It may even apply when positive affect precedes behavior, as when a person eagerly awaits an event and prepares for it. In short, when the hedonic dimension of pain and pleasure is exaggerated in the learning of affective responses, the stab of fear and the thrill of anticipated pleasure may seem to impel the immediately following behavior. In such cases, behavior seems regulated by the pleasure principle. Most behavior, however, occurs in a far more subtle setting where it would be extremely difficult to isolate a specific antecedent affective stimulus that energized and directed the behavior.

Recalling Ryle's (1949) arguments, it is a mistake to assume that "thrills, twinges, pangs, throbs, wrenches, itches, prickings, chills, glows, loads, qualms, hankerings, curdlings, sinkings, tensions, gnawings and shocks" (pp. 83–84) precede and somehow energize all behavior. The mistake involves the "Bogy of Mechanism" and a category mistake of assuming that affective responses are somehow in a different category from other responses. In terms of the measurement of motives, it is a mistake to attempt to convert what is essentially an RR relationship [Achievement behavior = f (TAT score)] into an SR relationship by constructing the concept of affect produced by the antecedent response that can then be said to cause the consequent action.

Actually, McClelland never spelled out the chain of hypothesized events in as much detail as we have. He has never stressed the concept of affect as a type of thrill or pang and he has always been very wary of the notion of causation. "Somehow the whole concept of causality seems quite irrelevant when applied to a construct like n Achievement which was invented for theoretical purposes. We can say that n Achievement accounts for the observed phenomenon or correlation, but it seems incorrect to say that n Achievement causes the correlation, at least in any 'forceful' sense" (McClelland, 1951, p. 96). Seductive as the behavioristic analysis appears, we seem forced to delve deeper in order to increase our understanding of the relationship between analysis of thought samples and action samples.

Agitations (Needs and Drives) vs. Inclinations (Motives)

Ryle (1949) makes a distinction between agitations and inclinations that we shall adopt and relate to behavior instigated by needs and drives of the physiological organism and behavior associated with social motives such as n Achievement. Our main point is that the behavioral analysis that assumes the presence of an instigating affective stimulus may be adequate in dealing with hunger, thirst, and even fear and anxiety, but that it is not adequate in dealing with a motive such as n Achievement. The behavioral analysis assumes a "twinge" of affect that impels the consequent behavior. This "twinge" of affect is what Ryle means by *agitation*. The *inclination* to strive for personal accomplishment as found in n Achievement cannot be reduced to such a "twinge."

To say that a man searches for food because he is hungry may be construed as saying that his searching was caused by the occurrence within him of a particular feeling (hunger pangs, weakness, etc.) that impelled action (recall Neal Miller's definition of a drive as a strong stimulus that impels action). It is far less clear that the statement "he strives for personal accomplishment because of his achievement motive" should be construed as saying that "his striving was caused by the occurrence within him of a particular feeling or impulse for achievement." It may better be construed as saying "he strives on being confronted with a challenging task and his doing so satisfies the law-like proposition that whenever he finds a chance of securing successful completion of a challenging task, he does whatever he thinks will produce success."[4] The first interpretation is what Ryle calls behavior resulting from agitation, and we would see it as appropriate to needs and drives such as hunger, thirst, fear, and anxiety. The second interpretation involves "inclinations" of the sort found possibly in "appetites" or food *preferences,* or in social motives not primarily driven by fear or anxiety.

The motive concept describes a dispositional property of an individual that leads to "whenever" statements but not to para-mechanical causal chains. "Impulses, described as feelings which impel actions, are para-mechanical myths" (Ryle, 1949, p. 114). "To explain an act as done from a certain motive is not analogous to saying that the glass broke, because a stone hit it, but to the quite different type of statement that the glass broke, when the stone hit it, because the glass was brittle. Just as there are no other momentary actualizations of brittleness than, for example, flying into fragments when struck, so no other momentary actualizations of chronic vanity need to be postulated than such things as boasting, daydreaming about triumphs and avoiding conversations about the merit of others" (pp. 86–87). To paraphrase "no other momentary actualizations of chronic achievement motivation need be postulated than such things as striving, moderate risk-taking, writing stories about competition, taking personal responsibility, etc."

> How does the law-like general hypothetical proposition work? It says, roughly, that the glass, *if* sharply struck or twisted, etc. *would* not dissolve or stretch or evaporate but fly into fragments. The matter of fact that the glass did at a particular moment fly into fragments, when struck by a particular stone, is explained, in this sense of "explain," when the first happening, namely the impact of the stone, satisfies the protasis of the general hypothetical proposition, and when the second happening, namely the fragmentation of the glass, satisfies its apodosis.
>
> This cannot be applied to the explanation of actions as issuing from specified motives. When we ask "Why did someone act in a certain way?" this question might, so far as its language goes, either be an inquiry into the cause of his acting in that way, or be an inquiry into the character of the agent which accounts for his having acted in that way on that occasion. I suggest, . . . that explanations by motives are explanations of the second type and not of the first type (Ryle, 1949, p. 89).

This conception of motive as a dispositional property suggests that the

---

[4]The above is paraphrased from a section of Ryle (1949, p. 89) where his example is of a vain man.

achievement motive "explains" behavior when certain other conditions exist. The other conditions may be ego-involving instructions, but the motive concept satisfies the condition that whenever ego-involving instructions are given this man will strive because of the motive. The motive concept supplies a "reason" for behavior that is not part of the causal chain of physical or objective facts that obtain in the specific instance.

> . . . to explain an action as done from a specified motive or inclination is not to describe the action as the effect of a specified cause. Motives are not happenings and are not therefore of the right type to be causes. The expansion of a motive-expression is a law-like sentence and not a report of an event (Ryle, 1949, p. 113).
>
> To say, then, that a certain motive is a trait in someone's character is to say that he is inclined to do certain sorts of things, make certain sorts of plans, indulge in certain sorts of daydreams and also, of course, in certain situations to feel certain sorts of feelings. To say that he did something from that motive is to say that this action, done in its particular circumstances, was just the sort of thing that that was an inclination to do. It is to say "he *would* do that" (Ryle, 1949, pp. 92–93).

Ryle has helped us to cut through some of the verbal and logical muddle and clarified the distinction between an explanation in terms of antecedent events that we may see now as an SR relationship, and an explanation based on a dispositional property such as a motive. As a result, our original question about the relationship between thought samples and action becomes even less tenable in any sense of a chain leading from thought to action. Writing characteristic stories illustrating certain types of thought sequences can only be seen as another example of just what "the person with high achievement motivation *would* do"; that is, such behavior is merely one type that occurs "whenever the person is asked to create stories in response to certain pictures." And it is correlated with other behaviors such as striving, that occur whenever this person meets a challenge. More and more it appears that we must reject any notion of the TAT as a measure of thoughts that precede and somehow impel achievement behavior, and accept some form of correlational analysis, although not necessarily the strictest form of RR that rules out thought and sees the story as only a series of specific responses. Thoughts need not be relegated to a category entirely separate from actions and essentially ghostlike. But neither must we reduce both thoughts and actions to specific muscle twitches.

We are no longer concerned with the "prediction" of actions from indications in the TAT of logically prior states. We must now turn to the questions: Why are the thoughts that are produced in the stories correlated with more overt actions? Why are thought samples a good measure from which to infer the dispositional property n Achievement? Why are they any better than some measure of more overt achievement behavior?

The spectrum of behavior analysis may be said to run along a continuum of generality-specificity. The motive concept was devised to help give a generalizable explanation of specific behaviors, and it is always in danger of being pushed to one extreme or the other. A single sovereign concept that attempts to explain all behavior such as "the pleasure-principle" with its hedonistic connotation, or Freud's libido, or drive-reduction theory, tends toward the overly general. On the other hand, instinct or motive "catalogues" tend in the direction of too great specificity and may result in naming a motive or instinct for every behavior we wish to explain.

To be useful, the motive concept must lie somewhere between these two extremes although, if it does, it will suffer on the one hand from failure to predict some specific responses and on the other from not encompassing all behavior under one explanatory principle. It seems to be an axiom in science that the more global the concept the greater its utility in simplifying the data, but the less is its ability to cope with any specific datum.

In his definition of the achievement motive, McClelland has attempted to remain at a general level and yet deal with more or less specific behavior patterns such as risk-taking, etc., that make up the general syndrome involving entrepreneurial behavior. This attempt to stay in the middle of the generality-specificity continuum is the key to understanding the concept of achievement motivation and is responsible for both the strengths and the weaknesses of the system.

The choice of the technique of thought sampling can be seen in the light of this discussion as a choice of a more general and generalizable indication of achievement orientation than any specific achieving response. The argument runs, if a person's thoughts are saturated with achievement themes, especially if they indicate affective involvement, this should be indicative of a generalized achievement orientation that should affect the person's behavior under many and varied circumstances. If this is true the thought sample measure should give a more general and hence more useful measure than measures of more specific achieving responses. There is evidence for the relationship between the n Achievement measure and a broad gamut of more specific behavior patterns, and even evidence that the measure is more useful than other measures such as a questionnaire (de Charms et al., 1955; Atkinson & O'Connor, 1966; Marlowe, 1959). Accepting the data, let us try to be more specific than the statement "achievement thoughts are related to achievement behavior."

We have argued against any para-mechanical notion that the affect contained in the stories is indicative of an internal stimulus that impels actions; we would certainly reject any assumption that the thoughts themselves impel action; but we are perfectly willing to assume, as McClelland (1955a) does, that thoughts, or mental content in general, are fair game for psychological study. If we want to assume a behavioristic posture, we may even call thoughts "responses." The advantage of this is to emphasize that they are not to be placed in a different category (Ryle's category mistake) from more active and observable action sequences. If thoughts are conceived of as psychological phenomena that are subject to similar exigencies as action sequences, we have given a rationale for their being correlated with action sequences; but we may have also demolished any argument that they should be uniquely suited to give a more generalized indication of a person's dispositional properties.

We must, therefore, admit some distinction between thought and action (it seems almost ridiculous to be brought to this extreme) without relegating thoughts to limbo again.

WHY MEASURE MOTIVES THROUGH THOUGHTS?

Thoughts are freer from inhibitions than overt actions. Thoughts are more general than action sequences. Thoughts may be related to many different action sequences. Characteristic thought patterns may be associated with different action sequences under different circumstances and may form the basis for categorizing the actions into a syndrome. Categories may be used to develop law-like statements of the type, "whenever X occurs the person whose stories are saturated with these thoughts will be disposed to respond with Y," i.e., the dispositional properties of the individual that are indicated by his thought processes.

We need to assume a Jamesian type relation between thought and action and then we may see why thoughts are a good indicator of motives and also why thoughts may be related to action sequences, but that the relationship is imperfect especially under conditions of behavioral compulsion and inhibition.

The basic notion comes from William James' concept of ideomotor action and is stated as follows: *"Every representation of a movement awakens in some degree the actual movement which is its object; and awakens it in a maximum degree whenever it is not kept from so doing by an antagonistic representation present simultaneously to the mind"* (James, 1890, p. 526). By the principle of feedback, we may assume that the reverse is true also, i.e., the actual movement awakens a representation of it in thought.

The "representation of a movement" is a thought that occasions the movement unless another thought interferes to inhibit it. In the young child, the thought and the action occur simultaneously through lack of inhibition. In the adult, inhibition is so strong that many thoughts appear to precede action in a decision-making sequence. The thought that wins out appears to precede the action and hence impel or motivate it; but again we are falling into the trap of assuming that the organism is basically inert and that some specific thought, charged perhaps with anticipatory affect or accompanied by a Wundtian feeling of innervation, breaks through the inertia and leads to action. Such an inert theory asks in a para-mechanical way — What is the energy force that makes some thoughts occasion action?

If we assume that all thoughts occasion actions, we are then left with the converse problem of explaining why we do not see the action results of some of the thoughts. Diagrammatically this may be presented as follows:

$$T_1, T_2, T_3, T_4, T_5, T_6, \ldots T_n$$
$$\searrow \qquad\quad \searrow$$
$$A_3 \qquad\quad A_6$$

$T_1, T_2 \ldots T_n$ represent a sequence of thoughts; A_3 and A_6 represent observed actions. A para-mechanical inert theory picks out T_3 and T_6 as the unusual events and tries to determine something about them that impels A_3 and A_6 such as a feeling of innervation or an anticipatory twinge of affect. James would no doubt assume that $T_3 \rightarrow A_3$ and $T_6 \rightarrow A_6$ represent the normal state of affairs. What needs explaining is why T_1, T_2, T_4, T_5 did not lead to $A_1, A_2, A_4,$ and A_5. The answer is that T_1 and T_2 occasion antagonistic or conflicting actions that cancel each other. Similarly for T_4 and T_5.[5]

As an example of the relationship between thoughts and action let us take the phenomenon of reading. When a person reads he is usually silent although presumably thoughts are passing through his head. We may ask him to read aloud and assume that it takes extra effort to do so,

---

[5]It is interesting to note that if the above diagram were made up of Ss and Rs (stimuli and responses) and the problem involved learning, i.e., why certain Rs appear connected with certain Ss, the difference in approach noted between the para-mechanical inert theory and the Jamesian approach turns out to be identical to the difference in approach of reinforcement and contiguity theories of learning. Reinforcement theory looks for a principle to explain the connection of an S with an R; contiguity theory looks for interference that can explain why an S does not produce an R that has occurred in the past (see Chapter 5 above).

and we may be led to ask the question: What is the nature of the extra energy (or act of volition in James' terms) that results in reading aloud? However, if we examine the history of the thought-action sequence involved in learning to read, it is clear that the person learned to read aloud first and later developed the facility to inhibit the overt response and hence read silently. In fact, silent reading is often accompanied by quite discernible movements the extent of which depends on the reader's ability to inhibit overt responses. The notion that thought and actions are essentially two aspects of one psychological phenomena, that $T_3 \rightarrow A_3$ is the normal state of affairs, and that silent reading is the result of successfully suppressing the overt action component is only novel in the context of the post-Cartesian era described by Ryle (1949) where the category mistake of separating thought and action is rampant. "Keeping our thoughts to ourselves is a sophisticated accomplishment. It was not until the Middle Ages that people learned to read without reading aloud. Similarly a boy has to learn to read aloud before he learns to read under his breath, and to prattle aloud before he prattles to himself. Yet many theorists have supposed that the silence in which most of us have learned to think is a defining property of thought . . . .

> The combination of the two assumptions that theorising is the primary activity of minds and that theorising is intrinsically a private, silent or internal operation remains one of the main supports of the dogma of the ghost in the machine. People . . . even come to suppose that there is a special mystery about how we publish our thoughts instead of realising that we employ a special artifice to keep them to ourselves (Ryle, 1949, p. 27).

We can now see several implications of assuming that thoughts and actions are under ordinary circumstances found together. A sample of a person's thoughts should give a broader indication of his inclinations or action tendencies than should a catalogue of his actions. For one thing, it is harder for a person to control his thoughts voluntarily than to control his actions.[6] As a result we should be able to explain certain actions from thoughts that are uninhibited by other thoughts, and we might even find two conflicting thought patterns that would explain the omission of certain acts. There are also several specific implications for the measurement of motives through thought samples.

It must be remembered that the thought sampling technique used to

---

[6]McClelland (1965a) emphasizes this point as follows: "Isak Dinesen tells the story of the oracle who told the king he would get his wish so long as he never thought of the left eye of a camel. Needless to say, the king did not get his wish, but he could easily have obeyed her prohibition if it had been avoid *looking* at the left eye of a camel" (p. 326).

measure *n* Achievement is not a pure sample of thoughts. The thoughts must be translated into action in the form of writing the story in order to appear in the sample. There are at least two consequences of this. To the extent that the stories are written under constraining conditions, the content of the stories and the thought sample should be *(a)* less representative of the total population of thoughts being sampled but *(b)* more representative of thoughts that actually lead to action under these constraining conditions. In the particular case of achievement motivation this means that thought samples taken under ego-involving conditions will be representative of the types of thoughts that lead to action under pressure and constraint. When strongly pressured to do so almost everyone will produce achievement thoughts and actions, especially in the achieving culture of the United States. But the achievement pressure raises strong conflicts. Many conflicting achievement thoughts may cancel each other and not reach the level of achievement action so that many but conflicting thoughts in samples collected under ego-involvement may fail to explain other achievement behavior even under similar arousal conditions.

The ego-involving or achievement arousal instructions are often considered to induce debilitating anxiety in subjects (Mahone, 1960). For this reason, Atkinson and his students (Atkinson, 1958; Atkinson & Feather, 1966) have used a questionnaire measure of test anxiety in conjunction with the thought sample measure of *n* Achievement to increase the power of the instrument. According to our previous analysis, the *n* Achievement instrument should be least valuable when pressure is on, as in a school testing situation. On the other hand, a straightforward questionnaire measure of test-anxiety such as the Mandler-Sarason (see Mandler & Cowen, 1958) asks subjects how anxious they feel when taking tests and would be expected to correlate with results of pressure tests.

Our analysis conforms with data that show that questionnaire measures are more highly correlated with results of tests taken under pressure than are thought sample measures of achievement motivation. The results of studies relating *n* Achievement alone to school grades and achievement tests are not very encouraging (McClelland *et al.*, 1953; Morgan, 1952; Ricciuti, 1955; Ricciuti & Sadacca, 1955; Jordan & de Charms, 1959) although McClelland *et al.* (1953) report that the relationship with grades increases if the *n* Achievement score is based on the difference between a score derived under neutral and one derived under aroused conditions. This could be the result of selecting subjects who perform best under pressure both on the TAT and on school tests.

Alpert and Haber (1960) have found quite consistent results correlating questionnaire measures of test-anxiety with grade-point average and examination grades. When a questionnaire measure of anxiety is combined with *n* Achievement, a strong relationship is found between this composite measure and reading and arithmetic scores on a standardized achievement test (O'Connor, Atkinson, & Horner, 1966). These results seem to indicate that the greater the similarity between the testing conditions the higher the relationships found. To relate to achieving behavior under pressure, the thought samples should be collected under pressure; but even this does not make them as valuable as straightforward questionnaires concerning anxiety aroused by pressure. One may question whether the measure of achievement motivation derived from the aroused condition does not lose much of its general applicability and approach the specificity end of the generality-specificity dimension and thereby lose much of its value as compared to questionnaires or other trait measures. It has generally been found that *n* Achievement (measured under neutral conditions) relates to different, and we might say, more general behavior than questionnaire measures (de Charms *et al.,* 1955; Marlowe, 1959; Atkinson & O'Connor, 1966) and *n* Achievement scores measured under neutral conditions show only a slight positive relationship with the questionnaire measure.[7]

Aroused ego-involving as well as neutral and relaxed conditions were used to validate the *n* Achievement measure but experience indicated that scores derived under neutral or task conditions were more often a better indicator of other types of achievement behavior. This was assumed to be the result of debilitating anxiety that affected scores derived from the aroused condition. Neutral or task conditions should decrease the number of conflicting thoughts that cancel each other out and give a less restricted and more representative sample of the ongoing thought processes than aroused conditions. By the same argument, however, relaxed conditions might be expected to be most useful since they should produce the least restricted and most representative sample of thoughts. Why then does the task condition turn out in practice to be the most useful?

The answer to this question involves the generality-specificity dimen-

---

[7]Recently Sherwood (1966) demonstrated that these relationships between *n* Achievement and self-report questionnaire measures and even other behavioral measures can be made quite substantial if subjects study the theory of achievement motivation for two weeks before filling out the self-report. This is not surprising but merely indicates that lack of validity in questionnaire measures may be reduced by training the subject to understand what the psychologist means by achievement motivation.

sion as well as an understanding of the conditions under which most achievement behavior occurs in life. As we said above if the behavior that we want to relate to *n* Achievement is measured under pressure then it might be best to measure *n* Achievement under aroused conditions. In fact, the exact conditions under which the other behavior is measured should be used in giving the TAT if possible. This gives a measure of thoughts under very specific conditions but should decrease the general applicability of the *n* Achievement measure. If a more general measure is desired, arousal for the TAT should be less specific. At the other extreme, that is in the relaxed condition, a very generalized sample of thoughts should be obtained. This might give a more representative sample of thoughts of the subject, but the relaxed condition is not similar to conditions in life when a person is met by an achievement challenge. This line of reasoning clarifies why the "Task" or "Neutral" measurement condition is most often chosen in measuring *n* Achievement. This condition lies somewhere between the extremes of specific arousal and generalized lack of arousal, and is, therefore, more consistent with the notion of a motive as a moderately general dispositional property rather than a specific trait or an all-inclusive behavioral mainspring. We have succeeded in placing the general-specific dimension parallel to the freedom-constraint dimension and can now see that measurement under extreme constraint gives extremely specific prediction. Analogously other points on the two dimensions are related.

The general conclusion from this discussion is that the testing conditions for the measurement of *n* Achievement should be made as similar as possible to the conditions under which other behavior is observed if we wish to obtain high correlations with that behavior. For example, if we wish to relate examination grades to results from thought samples, the samples could be collected in an examination setting and the pictures used could depict students taking exams and other school situations. The practical utility of such measurement may be great, but a measure derived under such conditions would hardly qualify as a measure of generalized achievement motivation as defined by McClelland *et al.* (1953).

THE PROBLEM OF INTENSITY *vs.* EXTENSITY

Another way to approach the problem of specificity *vs.* generality of the achievement motive is by making a distinction between the measurement of the *intensity* or the *extensity* of the motive. Following the Jamesian conception of the coordination of thought and action, it makes sense to say that the more often achievement thoughts occur in thought samples the more often the corresponding achievement behavior should be found. This is our basic explanation of the value of measuring motives in thought samples. But we do not obtain a representative sample of all the thoughts that occur to the person under all conditions. As a matter of fact we obtain a rather restricted sample—restricted first by the testing conditions as explained above and second by the pictures used to elicit the stories. The suggestion that school pictures might be used to measure achievement motivation in the school setting is an example of one way the stimuli might be even more restricted than in the present form of the test. A sample of thoughts from such a restricted set might be assumed to measure the *intensity* of the specific motive to achieve in school.

The measure of achievement motivation as presently constituted, however, may be said to measure the *extensity* of achievement thoughts in several areas of endeavor including school, business, etc., not the intensity in one specific area. The fact that the measure is designed to measure extensity rather than intensity should be kept in mind in using the measure because it has some very specific implications. Ideally, a measure of extensity would sample from a population of all areas in which achievement thoughts might occur. If areas are defined by picture content then ideally the first step in measuring extensity would be to sample a broad array of pictures. If the goal is to ferret out achievement imagery in any possible area of a person's thoughts then the sample of pictures to be used should be much larger than 4 or 6 and much more representative of all possible situations in a person's life. In short, the logic of a pure notion of extensity dictates measurement through two sampling procedures—a sampling of pictures and a sampling of responses to the pictures that indicate the population of thoughts being tapped.

There are several reasons why such an approach is impractical and unrealistic, the most compelling of which is that subjects would soon begin to tire of writing stories to a large number of pictures, and Atkinson (1954) has shown that the value of n Achievement scores derived from stories written after ordinal position 4 drops drastically.

It cannot be claimed that in devising the measure McClelland *et al.* (1953) rigorously sampled randomly all possible pictures. On the other hand, it should be remembered that many pictures have been used and sifted down to the standard set suggested by Atkinson (1958). One hundred and three pictures are listed in Atkinson, and these are only some of those that have been used.

Although no rigorous procedure was used to select the most often used pictures, the rough criterion for selection of pictures may be assumed to have been that they seemed to work. More concretely, this probably means that subjects typically produced achievement imagery in the stories. A second aspect that led to selection of a picture was that the imagery produced was reliably scorable, i.e., it was easy to identify and not clouded with other types of imagery. The result is a set of pictures dealing primarily with task situations that are most often seen as involving professional occupations or schoolwork. The type of subject used and the validation sample (college men from New England schools) may have had a strong determining effect on the fact that the resultant measure is most clearly related to entrepreneurial behavior. This sifting process that resulted in the oft used pictures and in the scoring categories, obviously led to the scoring of strong cultural values concerning the man of action rather than thought. Much as academics like to eulogize scholars and scientists, they are not very highly represented in cultural heroes and they are often too unique to lead to a stereotyped image that would appear over and over again in brief stories of college sophomores.

But let us return to another implication of assuming that n Achievement is a measure of the extensity of the motive. A group of men selected from thought samples that contain indications of competition with a standard of excellence in several areas may be expected to show a generalized orientation toward competition. They may be expected to show a cluster of traits in several different areas that they apparently see as achievement related. In short, the achievement syndrome, defined as a cluster of traits appearing in several areas of endeavor, is just what the thought sample seems to measure.

When we attempt to push the measure beyond explanation into prediction for the individual, a measure of extensity may be disappointing. Although, generally, men who have many achievement thoughts may tend to be moderate risk-takers, one particular man may have many of the other characteristics but not show moderate risk-taking in the setting in which we observe him. A syndrome is made up of several traits. Persons A and B may both be said to have the syndrome when A has traits 1, 2, 3, 4 and 5, and B has traits 2, 3, 4, 5 and 6. If, however, we measure only traits 1 and 6, persons A and B may be seen as quite different.

The same logic applies if we assume that the pictures used to elicit thoughts sample areas of the person's conceptual map. If person A writes achievement stories to pictures depicting school and business situations and person B writes achievement stories to pictures depicting an operation scene and inventors, they may both have identical scores for n Achievement, but they may behave quite differently in school and business, or in creative and professional settings.

In measurement terms, we can make this point more clearly and emphasize the possible misuse of n Achievement scores. Most psychophysical scales are intended to measure intensity. For instance, in sensory psychology the wave amplitude of a sound producing device may be varied and the subject asked to indicate on a scale how loud the sound is. It is assumed that if the subject can really discriminate between all stimuli presented along a dimension of loudness that is correlated with wave amplitude, then one stimulus in the middle of the range will be reported as louder than all stimuli of smaller wave amplitude, and less loud than all stimuli of larger wave amplitude. By comparing all stimuli with all others along the loudness dimension scale, values may be determined for each stimulus and a psychological scale of intensity of perceived sound developed.

This logic has been applied to the measurement of attitudes, which are psychological variables without a physical correlate. The intensity of attitudes may be scaled by what is known as the Guttman technique. The logic behind the measurement of intensity of attitudes allows the experimenter to order subjects with regard to each other and to predict rather specific behaviors from the ordering depending on the reliability of measurement.

Often this same logic is erroneously assumed to apply to the measurement of n Achievement. In what sense can a person (A) who writes achievement stories about inventors, doctors, and businessmen and attains a high score be said to be higher in n Achievement than one (B) who writes an achievement story about schoolwork but not about inventors, doctors, and businessmen and receives a relatively low score? If we observe many types of behavior in many situations, we may assume that person A will show more general achievement behavior than person B; but if we measure only school behavior the reverse may be true. To devise a measure that would discriminate on school achievement alone, we might obtain six pictures of school situations ranging from one that elicits an achievement story from almost everyone (say a test situation) to one that elicits an achievement story from very few. If school achievement is a unidimensional concept, we should find that a person with strong school achievement motivation would write an achievement story to even the weakest picture in addition to all the others. A person with only moderate motivation would give achievement stories to only the fairly strong and strong cue pictures, and a person with very weak motivation would give achievement stories to only the strongest cue picture or none at all. With such an instrument, responses and hence subjects would be scalable by the Guttman technique and the rather specific behavior of school achievement should be highly correlated with this measure of intensity of the specific type of achievement motivation.

The more general measure of extensity of the motive as measured by the McClelland-Atkinson technique should not be scalable by the Guttman technique for the simple reason that in a six picture measure two subjects could obtain the same score from entirely different pictures and hence have entirely different types of achievement motivation.[8]

We have discussed scaling in some detail to make a specific point that is often overlooked by researchers who use the measure developed by McClelland *et al.* (1953). Intensity of motivation in a specific setting is not what is measured. From the point of view of specific prediction, this is a great disadvantage. From the point of view of measurement theory and scalability, it may be said that the *n* Achievement measure is not very respectable. But measurement and scaling theory are based on the concept of measurement of intensity with the goal of prediction of specific responses. Apparently it is a mistake to use the achievement motive measure as a measure of intensity with the goal of relating it to some specific other measure. The measure does not partake of the virtues of unidimensionality and scalability as prescribed by measurement theory. Does this mean that the measure should be abandoned in favor of attempts to develop a more scalable measure of intensity? The answer to the question depends on what you intend to do with the measure. If you wish to predict quite specific things like school achievement, as assessed by examinations or standardized achievement tests, and to predict for individuals, then the development of a test of intensity is called for and the use of the present technique of assessing *n* Achievement is inappropriate or at least sure to account for only a small portion of the variance of standardized achievement tests. However, if a much more general response pattern is to be investigated, the measure of extensity may be more useful. The logic is simple. The measure taps thoughts about achievement in several areas of endeavor with specific emphasis on entrepreneurial behavior. If a person who has many such thoughts under several different situations is observed *over a period of time* in which he may be confronted with some of these situations, we should assume that he will react in achievement ways more often than not. The difference between this and prediction from an intensity measure is that a good specific intensity measure will predict rather specific behavior in a single testing situation, or situations that are specifically similar to each other. The extensity measure will relate to the general trend of behaviors over a period

---

[8]In an unpublished study, the author and Mrs. Virginia Carpenter have demonstrated that a six-picture measure of *n* Achievement derived from a standard set does not, in fact, meet the criterion set by the Guttman technique for unidimensional scalability (Stouffer, Guttman, Suchman, Lazarsfeld, Starr, & Clausen, 1950). Using pictures in the school setting alone, there was preliminary evidence that one might devise a set of pictures that would result in scalable scores along a dimension of intensity of school achievement motivation.

of time that are less specifically similar to each other but may all fall under the general heading of competitive, or challenging situations.

In answer to the question what advantages does extensity measurement of achievement motivation have over a possible intensity measure we could say, "An extensity measure relates to success in life; an intensity measure relates only to success on a particular test at a particular time." We have stated it in this way to emphasize the possible role that extensity measurement might play. It is hard to defend it against the onslaughts of scaling theory based on the notion of intensity. It must be seen in light of its own purpose not as a measure of intensity.

This is not to say that improvements in the measure cannot be made, indeed they are badly needed. But the person who sets out to improve the measure should decide whether he wishes to improve it by converting it into a more conventional measure of intensity of a specific individual characteristic or improve it as a measure of extensity. The two are quite different and in this realm it is probably impossible to have one instrument to measure both well.

There are at least two kinds of evidence that support this analysis of n Achievement as a measure of extensity. Some of the recent data deriving from McClelland's theorizing indicate that n Achievement does relate to career patterns; and, at the most general level, the amount of achievement imagery in the literary productions of various cultures is related to the amount of "success" the culture has in economic competition with other cultures (McClelland, 1961). In general, it may be said that the extensity measure of n Achievement is proving to be more valuable in relation to cultural orientations and long-term career patterns of individuals than in predicting specific responses such as school achievement or exam-taking behavior. Incidentally, this may explain why Atkinson has had to adopt the anxiety questionnaire as an adjunct to n Achievement in order to be able to predict the more specific responses that he is studying.[9]

ACHIEVEMENT MOTIVATION AND GENERAL BEHAVIOR PATTERNS

McClelland (1965b) reports that the original sample of subjects tested at Wesleyan in the validation procedures for n Achievement have gravitated in large numbers toward entrepreneurial business occupations subsequent to graduation from college. A check of the alumni directory indicated that 83% of the men who could be classified as entrepreneurs had high n Achievement scores as sophomores in college while only 21% of those classified as non-entrepreneurs had high n Achievement. These

---

[9] For more on this see Chapter 7.

results indicate the ability of the *n* Achievement measure to explain career patterns over a crucial period when career choices are being made.

The data that relate *n* Achievement to cultural "success in competition" with other cultures are presented in detail by McClelland (1961). As examples of two types of relationships, we can see that cultures whose literature contains many thoughts about achievement are predominantly more advanced economically and that over time economic development within a culture is related to the level of *n* Achievement found in the literature of the culture.

McClelland (1961) collected a large sample of children's readers dated around 1925 and intended primarily for 4th graders from 30 countries throughout the world. These readers were content analyzed for *n* Achievement, resulting in an *n* Achievement score for each country. In addition, data on national income per capita and electricity produced in kilowatt-hours per capita were collected for each country in the period subsequent to 1925 up to about 1950. The results show a striking relationship between these measures which may be interpreted as a relationship between culture-wide thoughts about achievement, as found in the material taught to children, and cultural entrepreneurial behavior or technological advance, as measured by the economic indices. As in the case of the Wesleyan students, the measure of *n* Achievement was related to entrepreneurial behavior measured over a subsequent period of time.

Within one culture de Charms and Moeller (1962) measured *n* Achievement at 20-year intervals in children's readers from the United States beginning in 1800 and continuing through 1950. During this period the amount of *n* Achievement increased steadily until 1900 corresponding with a tremendous increase in economic activity in the United States. Since 1900, the amount of *n* Achievement has begun to decline. This curve was found to reflect very closely an economic index derived from the number of patents issued each 20-year period.

Apparently, achievement motivation of an individual or a culture is related to the direction taken by the individual or culture in a subsequent period. This should not be interpreted as indicating, however, that thoughts necessarily precede action. The studies that deal with the span of several years cannot give us any notion of the temporal relationship between thoughts and action. True, McClelland has argued that a rise in achievement thoughts in the literature of a culture typically precedes a spurt in economic development, but the links in the chain between these two points involve much individual behavior. Such data will never tell us which came first in an individual, the thought or the action.

As an antidote to the sequential thinking to which we are so prone when confronting the relationship between thought and action, we may cite an instance in which the sequence is apparently reversed. In reanalyzing the extensive data of a longitudinal study, McClelland (1966) found that the actions of an adolescent are related to the thoughts he will have when he becomes an adult, whereas his adolescent thoughts do not predict very well his adult behavior. In relating imagery found in thought samples to activities, "adolescent activities predict adult imagery scores much better than adolescent imagery predicts adult activities, suggesting imagery may be more the result than the cause of action" (McClelland, 1966, p. 479).

Personal Knowledge and Intrinsic Aspects of Achievement Motivation

There is a basic ambiguity in the concept of achievement motivation as measured in thought samples. The theoretical goal of the motive is success in competition with a standard of excellence but not the objective concomitants that may result from success, such as money, praise or prestige. "Success" is an intrinsic factor; money and prestige are extrinsic. A feeling of success can only come from within, whereas rewards come from external sources and are extrinsically related to the activity involved. Conceptually, n Achievement is defined in terms of the intrinsic goal of success. Operationally, this intrinsic goal often must be inferred from extrinsic goals mentioned in the story. The extrinsic-intrinsic distinction is difficult to maintain (Smith, 1966) when attempting to assess whether a person is acting from a strong achievement motive or from a motive to accumulate fame and riches. He may merely be striving for his own satisfaction and incidentally have riches and fame showered on him (as many of our cultural heroes are supposed to have done) or he may start out to make a million dollars and find that the game is more satisfying than the prize. More realistically, he may want fame and riches and at the same time want to attain them in a way that is personally satisfying. In short, the achievement motive is not precisely defined nor can it be in terms of physical operations.

Basically the trouble arises in the uncharted area of the surplus meaning of the word "achievement." Each of us has his own private concept of achievement and this concept may be partially related to objective phenomena in the physical world but ultimately a crucial aspect of the concept comes from personal knowledge — the immediate knowledge that I am motivated. As we saw in Chapter 1, any motivational concept has this first person aspect and involves what Bridgman (1959) called "introspectional words in the private mode." It is this aspect of the achievement concept that can never be objectively specified exactly. The general definition presented in the scoring manual derives from a type of operational analysis of the personal aspect that resulted in the manual for content analysis. The directions in the manual are not entirely concrete and objective and allow the scorer to consult his own personal knowledge about achievement in arriving at scoring decisions. It is precisely this personal knowledge element of the technique that makes it unique as a first attempt to come to grips with the problem of approaching the scientifically communicable meaning of a concept that derives primarily from personal knowledge.[10]

In light of this discussion, it seems reasonable to assume that the intrinsic aspects of achievement motivation are those most closely associated with personal knowledge and the knowledge of personal causation. The fact that our approach to the specification of the achievement concept is far from perfect can be seen in the difficulty of differentiating between the intrinsic goal of success and the extrinsic concomitants that may accompany success. It is even further compounded by the fact that the man with high *n* Achievement may desire extrinsic concomitants not so much for their material value but for their symbolic value in demonstrating his success.

Achievement Incentives

Atkinson (1958) has tried to deal with this problem by introducing the concept of incentives into his equation for motivation: [Motivation = f (Motive × Expectancy × Incentive)]. The specific motive is defined in terms of the class of incentives that satisfy the motive. Unfortunately, the extrinsic aspects of specific incentives and the intrinsic aspect of satisfaction of the motive are not adequately separated conceptually or operationally. "The incentive variable . . . represents the relative attractiveness of a specific goal that is offered in a situation, or the relative unattractiveness of an event that might occur as a consequence of some act. Incentives may be manipulated experimentally as, for example, when amount of food (reward) or amount of shock (punishment) is varied in research with animals" (Atkinson, 1957, p. 360).

This passage makes the incentive appear to be extrinsic, "a specific goal" that is "a consequence of some act" that "may be manipulated ex-

---

[10]This paragraph completes the argument started in Chapter 2, under Operational Analysis of Personal Knowledge and the Scientific Use of the Operation of Projection, that the technique (described in detail earlier in this chapter) of content analysis of thought samples is basically a first step in the direction of attaining scientific evidence concerning personal knowledge. A more complete discussion of personal knowledge will be presented in Chapter 8.

perimentally;" it is, hence, under the control of the experimenter, not the subject.

However, "A motive is conceived as a disposition to strive for a certain kind of satisfaction, as a capacity for satisfaction in the attainment of a certain class of incentives. The names given motives—such as achievement, affiliation, power—are really names of classes of incentives which produce essentially the same kind of experience of satisfaction: pride in accomplishment, or the sense of belonging and being warmly received by others, or the feeling of being in control and influential" (p. 360).

This passage makes the name of the motive contingent upon a class of incentives that produce *satisfaction*. If incentives are "specific goals," then they are extrinsic to the acts performed in attaining them. The satisfaction derives entirely from the attainment of the goals and is independent of the activity. The use of the phrase "capacity for satisfaction," however, lends an intrinsic flavor as does "pride in accomplishment."

That Atkinson conceives of incentives intrinsically becomes clearer when he applies the motive-expectancy-incentive formula to choice situations involving risk, the so-called risk-taking experiments that have their roots in level of aspiration studies (Escalona, 1940; Festinger, 1942; Lewin, Dembo, Festinger, & Sears, 1944). Atkinson ties the determination of intrinsic incentive value directly to expectancy in the following way.

> Elaboration of the implications of the multiplicative combination of motive, expectancy, and incentive, as proposed to account for strength of motivation, will be instructive if we can find some reasonable bases for assigning numbers to the different variables. The strength of expectancy can be represented as a subjective probability ranging from 0 to 1.00. But the problem of defining the positive incentive value of a particular accomplishment and the negative incentive value of a particular failure is a real stickler. . . .
>
> The author will . . . assume that degree of difficulty can be inferred from the subjective probability of success P_s. The task an individual finds difficult is one for which his subjective probability of success P_s is very low. The task an individual finds easy is one for which his subjective probability of success P_s is very high. Now we are in a position to make simple assumptions about the incentive values of success and failure at a particular task. Let us assume that the incentive value of success I_s is a positive linear function of difficulty. If so, the value $1 - P_s$ can represent I_s, the incentive value of success. When P_s is high (e.g., .90), an easy task, I_s is low (e.g., .10). When P_s is low (e.g., .10), a difficult task I_s is high (e.g., .90). The negative incentive value of failure I_f can be taken as $-P_s$. When P_s is high (e.g., .90), as in confronting a very easy task, the sense of humiliation accompanying failure is also very great (e.g., −.90). However, when P_s is low (e.g., .10), as in confronting a very difficult task, there is little embarrassment in failing (e.g., −.10). We assume, in other words, that the (negative) incentive value of failure I_f is a negative linear function of difficulty.

> It is of some importance to recognize the dependence of incentive values intrinsic to achievement and failure upon the subjective probability of success. One cannot anticipate the thrill of a great accomplishment if, as a matter of fact, one faces what seems a very easy task. Nor does an individual experience only a minor sense of pride after some extraordinary feat against what seemed to him overwhelming odds (Atkinson, 1957, pp. 361–362).

It is clear from this that Atkinson is concerned with *intrinsic* incentives such as a "thrill of accomplishment." He developed a model based on this assumption that intrinsic incentive value can be *inferred* from subjective probability of success. The model *predicts that subjects with a strong motive to approach success (feel the thrill of success) and a weak motive to avoid failure will choose moderate-risk situations. Subjects with a weak motive to approach success and a strong motive to avoid failure will shun moderate-risk situations.*

RISK-TAKING EXPERIMENTS

Several empirical studies have been presented to confirm these predictions and hence support the model. Many of these studies have confined themselves to investigating only subjects with high *n* Achievement and low anxiety or with low *n* Achievement and high anxiety and have not reported results from nearly half of the subjects tested (Littig, 1963; Litwin, 1966; Feather, 1961, 1963; Moulton, 1965) or have used a composite measure subtracting standardized anxiety scores from *n* Achievement scores (O'Connor *et al.,* 1966; Atkinson & O'Connor, 1966). Although the latter technique is more defensible, either technique is warranted only if derivations from the original model are assumed. The emergence of other relationships involving groups of high *n* Achievement-high anxiety or low-*n*-Achievement–low-anxiety subjects are arbitrarily precluded.

Fortunately, Atkinson and Litwin (1960) have tested the relationship between *n* Achievement, test anxiety, and risk-taking using all subjects. They measured *n* Achievement (the tendency to approach success) and test anxiety (the tendency to avoid failure) in 49 college males. There was no correlation between the two measures so the subjects could be classified as high on both, low on both, or high on one and low on the other. The groups of most interest were the high-*n*-Achievement–low-anxiety group and the low-*n*-Achievement–high-anxiety group.

All subjects played a ring-toss game in which they could choose to shoot a ring at a peg from any distance ranging from 1 foot to 15 feet. The dependent variable was the distance from which they chose to shoot on each of their 10 shots whether they were successful or not.

The ring-toss game was designed to be analogous to Atkinson's theoretical model. The subjective probability of success was assumed to range from very high at the 1-foot distance to very low at the 15-foot distance. The positive incentive value of success was assumed to increase and the negative incentive value of failure to decrease as the subject stood further from the peg. Success from a large distance should be a thrill, failure of little consequence; failure from a close distance should be very disappointing, success of little consequence.

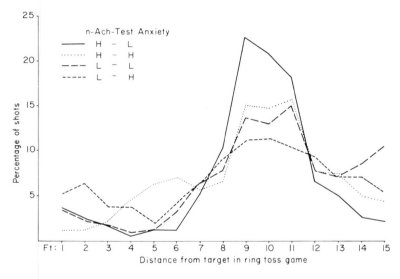

FIG. 6.1 Percentage of shots taken from each line (Atkinson & Litwin, 1960, p. 55).

Figure 6.1 shows the results of the study. As predicted, subjects with high *n* Achievement and low anxiety (H-L) take more shots from the intermediate, moderate-risk distances of 9, 10, and 11 feet. Subjects with low *n* Achievement and low anxiety spread their shots over the entire range from 1–15 feet, and avoid the range 9–11 more than any other group. The high–high and low–low groups fall between the two extremes. Separate analyses in terms of *n* Achievement alone and anxiety scores alone show that both measures, although independent of each other, predict moderate risk-taking; that is, subjects with high *n* Achievement take more moderate risks than subjects with low *n* Achievement and subjects with low anxiety scores take more moderate risks than subjects with high anxiety scores.

To return to our discussion of intrinsic *vs.* extrinsic incentives, it seems reasonable to assume that the incentives for shooting from different distances were a function of the perceived difficulty. The incentive for shooting from any distance was not specified by objective points awarded by the experimenter or any other obvious extrinsic device. On the face of it, the ring-toss game seems to operationalize Atkinson's concepts of subjective probabilities and incentives.

The actual incentives for the ring-toss game were purposely not carefully established. The aim of the experiment was to emphasize friendly competition in a situation as close to a real game as possible. Many subjects apparently gathered around while one took his turn. "There was a good deal of informal banter during the session. No attempt was made to interfere with or to control the lifelike situation" (Atkinson & Litwin, 1960, p. 54). Under these conditions the watching group may have had a strong effect on the behavior of the subjects and the incentives for doing well may have been strongly affected by desire for group approval. The situation raises the question: Is the primary incentive to do well or is it to receive the acclaim of the crowd?

This question is more than a problem of the specific experimental operations of this study; it is a basic question about the goal of achievement motivation in general. Atkinson and Reitman (1956) and Smith (1966) present some evidence that n Achievement is most highly related to performance only when excellence is stressed through achievement arousal and when the subject is left alone during his performance. They compared this relatively pure achievement arousal with what they called multi-incentive arousal in which, in addition to achievement arousal, attempts were made to arouse other motives including the affiliation motive that may have been aroused by the presence of observers in the Atkinson and Litwin ring-toss situation.

De Charms and Davé (1965) attempted to heighten the relationship between achievement motivation and risk-taking behavior by conducting an experiment quite similar to the Atkinson and Litwin experiment except that (a) actual probabilities of success were determined for each subject from each distance so that he himself would know his probabilities and (b) each subject played the game in the presence of the experimenter alone with no group to cheer him on.

Seventy-one fourth, fifth, and sixth grade boys attempted to shoot a volleyball into a basket placed on the floor. They could choose distances ranging from 4 to 22 feet, and before taking 20 shots from any distance they chose each had taken 10 shots from each distance and was aware of his own probabilities of success from each distance. Test anxiety and n Achievement were measured as in the Atkinson and Litwin study.

The results were surprising in that under these conditions, designed to operationalize more exactly the Atkinson model by determining in advance subjective probabilities, neither n Achievement nor anxiety was significantly related to risk-taking strategies as in the earlier experiment. A measure of hope of success and fear of failure derived from the thought samples did relate to risk-taking, however. Subjects who had both positive and negative aspects in their stories, i.e., who were both hopeful of success but aware of obstacles and the possibility of failure, stood out as those who achieved more success in shooting and also confined their choices of shooting distances primarily to the range where they had between 30 and 50% probability of success.

De Charms and Davé (1965) feel that these results indicate the necessity of differentiating hope of success and fear of failure as measured in the thought samples from n Achievement and anxiety. The major innovation in the experiment, however, is that actual subjective probabilities of success were obtained for, and reported to, each subject. Such a procedure may not, in fact, give a more precise knowledge of the person's *subjective* probabilities of success as it was intended to do. It may actually demonstrate to the person with high n Achievement that there is more risk involved than he normally tends to think. McClelland[11] has pointed out that it is possible "that the person with high n Achievement chooses moderate risks (as objectively defined) because he really believes subjectively that for *him* there is *no* risk. If you show him there *really* is a risk, he may lose his famed self-confidence!" If we accept this explanation, we are left with the problem of explaining the fact that subjects with high fear of failure and high hope of success still prefer moderate risks even when they know their own capacities. These subjects may have a more realistic outlook than subjects who continually produce either success or failure imagery (but not both) in their stories. As a result this group (the high-highs) may be least vulnerable to having their confidence undermined.

Whatever the reason for the de Charms and Davé (1965) results, they do make it clear that a person's subjective probability of success is a fragile variable that has probably never been adequately operationalized. Conceivably it is one component in Atkinson's theoretical model that is highly contingent on personal knowledge of past success and failure in situations involving personal causation. Since intrinsic incentives are intricately linked to subjective probabilities, incentives are also tied to personal knowledge. In summary, it seems that Atkinson may have tried

---

[11]Personal communication.

to operationalize intrinsic incentives, which are clearly a first-person subjective phenomena, through the apparently more objectifiable concept of probability of success. But this, in turn, appears also to be a concept deriving primarily from personal knowledge and therefore difficult to objectify.

Skill vs. Chance

In addition to situations like the ring-toss game where skill is involved and the subject has control over the outcome and can feel pride that *he* did something to succeed, Atkinson and his colleagues present some data that indicate that *n* Achievement may be related to risk-taking in a pure gambling situation where no skill is involved, where the subject has no control over the outcome, and where he can only feel pride in having been lucky or having accumulated the extrinsic rewards offered in the game.

Littig (1963) tested the following hypotheses derived from Atkinson's theory. ". . . (1) when motive to achieve success (M_s) is stronger than motive to avoid failure (M_{AF}), intermediate probabilities of success will be preferred; (2) when $M_{AF} > M_s$, intermediate probabilities of success will be avoided.

"M_s was inferred from content analysis of TAT stories for *n* Achievement, and M_{AF} from the Mandler and Sarason Test Anxiety Questionnaire. Probability preferences were assessed in a game of poker dice in which points were bid to play against poker dice hands having, respectively, .10, .30, .50, .70, and .90 probabilities of being beaten. . . .

"The results supported Hypothesis 2 but did not support Hypothesis 1" (Littig, 1963, pp. 426–427).

These results plus others from Atkinson, Bastian, Earl, and Litwin (1960) indicate that Atkinson expects *n* Achievement to predict in chance situations. In a chance situation, the result is completely externally determined, the reward extrinsically associated with certain chance events, and the subject has no opportunity to feel any personal causation. If *n* Achievement is related to behavior in purely chance, i.e., extrinsic incentive situations, then it has more of the extrinsic component than is apparent in most of the theoretical discussions.

Unfortunately, whether *n* Achievement is actually related to risk-taking in chance situations is still open to question. The Littig experiment suffers from the defect, mentioned above, that subjects with high *n* Achievement and low anxiety were compared with subjects with low *n* Achievement and high anxiety. Of 50 subjects originally tested for *n* Achievement and anxiety, only 16 were selected for the experiment and those high-high or low-low on the two measures were specifically excluded. This procedure makes it impossible to determine whether the relationship found was a function of n Achievement at all; for the results could have been simply attributable to a relationship between risk-taking and test anxiety. Apparently high n Achievement subjects ($M_s > M_{AF}$) tended to prefer high probabilities rather than moderate risks, and Littig interprets this as an attempt "to exert some control over the outcome of the game. . . ." (Littig, 1963, p. 426).[12]

Reversed Incentive Studies

In some risk-taking studies, subjects are awarded points that are scaled to conform with the inferred achievement incentive values, i.e., more points for success from distances of lower probabilities. Under such conditions, the subject may seek to test his skill (an intrinsic factor derived from the desire for personal causation) and at the same time to accrue a maximum number of points (the extrinsic factor). In other words, both extrinsic (points) and intrinsic (personal causation) factors work in the same direction and complement each other. In such a situation, it is impossible to know whether the subject is primarily intrinsically motivated to test his skill or is extrinsically motivated to accrue points.

A crude way to separate these factors has been devised in two unpublished studies. In both studies a risk-taking task involving a shuffleboard game was used. [13] The device used to attempt to separate the effects of intrinsic factors from extrinsic incentives was to reverse the extrinsic incentives in one-half of the trials for each subject. Thus, on all of his trials the subject was confronted with a choice of several distances from which to make his shots; however, on one-half of the trials, he received more points for success the farther away from the goal he chose, and, on the other half of the trials, he received more points the closer to the goal he chose. In one-half of the trials the extrinsic incentives were scaled as in previous risk-taking studies; in one-half of the trials the extrinsic incentives were reversed. The reversed incentive situation con-

---

[12]Some other data from Atkinson, Bastian, Earl, and Litwin (1960) seem to indicate a relationship between n Achievement and betting preferences, but Heckhausen (1967) has pointed out that this result may be due to a transfer effect from the other games of skill that were included in the experiment. The same problem plus the use of only selected achievement- and failure-oriented subjects (40 of the original 78) is involved in Litwin's (1966) study of both skill and chance games.

[13]David Mahan, Virginia Carpenter, James Walker, and Rob Schaub helped conduct the experiments.

fronts the subject with a conflict between accruing many points (the extrinsic incentives) by standing close to the target, which takes very little skill, and standing farther back from the target where fewer points are awarded for success but the intrinsic demonstration of skill comes into play. Comparing the reversed and the normal incentive conditions for each subject indicates the importance to him of the extrinsic incentives. If reversing the incentives has a large effect on his behavior, we assume that the extrinsic motivation to accrue points is dominant. If reversing the incentives has little effect, we assume that intrinsic motivation to test his skill is dominant in the subject.

This technique was administered to 34 eighth grade students in one experiment and to 151 college students in another. N Achievement was measured on all subjects and the thought samples were also coded for hope of success and fear of failure in the same way as in the de Charms and Davé (1965) experiment.

The data from both experiments were converted into means representing the mean distances from the goal that each subject stood (1) under the normal and (2) under the reversed incentive conditions. The dependent variable was the difference between the mean distance of shots taken under normal incentive conditions, and the mean distance of shots taken under reversed incentive conditions.

The results of both studies indicated that boys with low hope of success and high fear of failure failed to be affected by the change in extrinsic incentives while all other subjects were. Apparently, the behavior of this one group of boys was more strongly attuned to the intrinsic incentive of testing their skill than to the extrinsic incentive of accumulating points.

Why should this group resist extrinsic incentives and continue shooting when the incentives were reversed from positions where they could feel personal accomplishment? One might speculate that "fear of failure" was coded in the thought samples when the characters encountered difficulties, were concerned that they might fail, or when the outcome of the story was failure or, more often, questionable. "Hope of success" was scored when the characters encountered no difficulties, were primarily expecting success, and when the outcome of the story was clearly success. The positively oriented stories (coded hope of success) were primarily concerned with positive goals and outcomes with little mention of the grubby work and discouragement that may precede the attainment of the goal. These stories could represent flights of fancy about "pie in the sky" goals with no realistic appraisal of the means of attaining them. The stories that contained discussions of difficulties, concern over failure, and questionable outcomes, may have in fact been more realistic with regard to the means of attaining achievement goals. In short, one could see the optimism of the first stories as unwarranted and leading to a tendency to concentrate on extrinsic goals and to grasp them by the easiest means; whereas the more pessimistic stories indicate a willingness to confront difficulties and to concentrate on the means of accomplishment rather than on extrinsic rewards.[14]

Unfortunately, the reversed incentive procedure that offers high scores for success in easy and low scores for success in difficult tasks is quite unusual to the subjects. As a result they may have been skeptical although they went along with the game. If this effect were strong (and we have no objective way of knowing whether it was), the results may indicate more about whether the subjects believed the experimenter than about the effects of intrinsic *vs.* extrinsic incentives. Since the technique is open to alternative interpretation, these studies do more to indicate the difficulties of distinguishing between types of incentives than they do to clarify the ambiguity noted in the definition of *n* Achievement. Nevertheless, the reversed incentive studies present a paradigm that is worth pursuing in which the subject may attain an extrinsic reward without much effort but thereby renounces a feeling of intrinsic satisfaction. Or he may choose the intrinsic goal of satisfaction in his own skill and thereby renounce the extrinsic rewards. If a less contrived situation containing these elements can be devised, it may help in unraveling the extrinsic-intrinsic aspects of *n* Achievement.

Summary

In this chapter we have tried to do two things: *(a)* confront the problem of the relationship between thought and action *(b)* review and criticize the theory and research concerned with the measurement of motivation by sampling people's thoughts with specific emphasis on the achievement motive. The relationship between thought and action is a basic problem that has stimulated endless philosophical debate. The measurement of achievement motivation is, comparatively, a small area of psychological research that gives us an empirical base upon which to build a conceptual structure of the relationship between thought and action.

To the less philosophically oriented person the more important prob-

---

[14]This distinction may be similar to one found by Lasker (1966) in a study of businessmen given a course intended to increase their *n* Achievement (see Chapter 7). The men who were unusually active after the achievement motivation training course had previously written stories with specific references about the means of attaining goals. The inactive men had written stories characterized by vagueness as to means and lack of realism as to goals.

lem may be seen as the critique of the validity of the measurement of achievement motivation. From this point of view speculation about thoughts and actions may seem trivial — adding confusion to the discussion of *n* Achievement.

In this instance, we feel that two themes are better than one although we have constantly felt the urge to separate them. Now that we have reached the summary we shall do just that and try to summarize first the conclusions that we have come to concerning thought and action and then summarize the critique of the measurement of achievement motivation.

How Do Thoughts Cause Action?

Posing the question implies three things *(a)* thoughts precede actions, *(b)* there is some forceful deterministic connection between them, *(c)* thoughts are somehow different from actions. We cannot accept these implications. It would be impossible to verify that every action is preceded by a deterministic thought and it is certainly obvious that not all thoughts lead to action. Just as good a case may be made for actions leading to thoughts, and, when we try to differentiate between action and thought, we find that the distinction is crude and imprecise. If we look close enough, we can almost always find an implicit action component that accompanies almost any thought. Is thinking really nothing more than a series of minimal responses?

William James' conception of thought and action as two aspects of one thing helps us avoid the category mistake of making ghosts out of thoughts and conceiving of actions purely in mechanical terms. A behavioral act or sequence is the basic phenomenon. The outside observer sees overt manifestations of it; the actor may see the overt manifestations of his act, and he is also privy to his own mental and emotional experiences. The observer can share these only if the actor can translate them into some overt behavior that communicates to the observer. What the actor experiences forms his personal knowledge; and, since he is privileged to withhold some of this experience from being overtly expressed, he may experience thoughts and emotions that are not observed by the onlooker. On the one hand, it should be clear that a complete psychology should include the experience of acting or inhibiting an act as well as the observation of it; but, on the other hand, a direct line to the thoughts of a person would not give us a perfect instrument for the prediction of behavior. As things stand at present, prediction from one series of specific overt acts to another should be much more reliable than prediction from acts that communicate thoughts to other more specific overt acts. The value of attempting to gain samples of thoughts (through communicative acts such as writing) is not in increasing the predictability of specific other acts, but in arriving at a broader picture of the actor's predispositions to act over a period of time and under many different circumstances.

Achievement Motivation

The achievement motive is a general concept defined as the tendency to strive for success in competition with a standard of excellence. Such a definition gives the concept a measure of generality that has both good and bad consequences. The definition is intended to stress intrinsic satisfaction, but when the motive concept is used in conjunction with the concept of incentive, as in Atkinson's theoretical model, it is often difficult to distinguish the extrinsic from the intrinsic aspects. In this respect, the model may reflect the difficulty of making such a distinction in dealing with an actual case of competition. The goal of a story written by a subject may be used to infer a concern over competition when no competition is actually indicated. In practice, such stories occur very often but the scoring manual does little to help the scorer decide what kinds of concrete goals are achievement goals. There is involved here a semantic difficulty with the word "achievement." Any goal may be "achieved," but the achievement does not apply to the goal but to the attainment of it. Strictly speaking it is incorrect to talk about "achievement goals" but about goals from which achievement can be inferred. Much of the lack of clarity about, and unreliability of, scoring probably results from this semantic muddle. The only kind of achievement involved in n Achievement is achievement through competition. Goals that are "achieved" by other means should not be included, strictly speaking, in n Achievement. To score for n Achievement because a person is seeking a long-term goal is to make an inference that competition is involved and the scorer usually has to rely on his own personal knowledge of the culture in order to make the inference.

The measure of achievement motivation through thought sampling allows the subject to talk about whatever goals he himself chooses. He is only restricted by arousal conditions and picture content. To the extent that he is unrestrained, an unbiased sample of thoughts should be obtained. The underlying rationale for the technique is to sample the *extensity* of the thoughts about achievement rather than their *intensity*. Measurement based on the concept of extensity aims at *generality* rather than *specificity,* and results should relate to general predispositions and to behavioral trends over time rather than to specific behavioral patterns.

As a result, conventional indices of reliability and validity are not easily applied to the measure of achievement motivation. The basic qualities of scalability usually found in measures of intensity are not applicable to the *n* Achievement measure. Improvements in the measure, and they are badly needed, should be approached with an understanding of the rationale underlying the technique and either stay within this rationale involving extensity or attack the problem of developing a measure of intensity to relate to specific behaviors.

Although the early conception of *n* Achievement derived in part from concepts of need and drive to which the notion of intensity is applicable, it should be noted that the notion of intensity of *n* Achievement is now foreign to McClelland's concept of a motive as a broadly generalized associative network of ideas. The notion is not so much that an intense motive drives intense action, but that thoughts that extend into and pervade many spheres of behavior mold the direction in which the person's behavior will carry him over a period of time. It is hard to shift the emphasis from intensity when the common sense notion of motivation is so strongly prone to an intensive interpretation. McClelland has not discussed the intensity-extensity problem recently in print, and it is clear that he himself often uses terms that imply intensity of motivation and indeed it may not be entirely incorrect to infer intensity from extensity. In using the measure one should keep in mind that the *n* Achievement score is, to a large extent, a measure of the extensity of achievement thoughts.

Chapter 7

ACHIEVEMENT MOTIVATION
TRAINING COURSES

A recent trend in research on achievement motivation may be seen in attempts to increase the motivation of people through training. Under-developed countries have fewer people in them with high achievement motivation (McClelland, 1961) so McClelland reasoned that one way to help these countries advance economically and technologically was to try to increase the achievement motivation of some of the people in the country. Dealing with child-rearing practices is one way to affect the motivation of an individual (Winterbottom, 1958), but McClelland sought a way that would have more immediate results. Why not try to teach the businessmen of the culture to act like people with high *n* Achievement?

The answer to that question raises many others such as: Can you change motives? Should you change motives? How do you go about changing motives? What effects result from attempts to change motives? In this chapter, we shall look for answers to these questions.

Cultural Conflict over Achievement Values

There is probably no culture in the world more attuned to achievement values than the culture of the United States; there is no set of values that is more important and at the same time more subject to conflict in this culture. The self-made man is highly valued, but when he attains power through the accumulation of wealth or status that is higher than "the man in the street" he is immediately suspect. The culture reveres the Horatio Alger hero who is eager for financial success through a combination of "luck, pluck and virtue" (Fink, 1962, p. 17). At the same time it laughs in derision at the Sinclair Lewis portrait of the gauche but successful busi-nessmen in the character of Babbitt. Much of the economic prosperity of the United States is based on the energetic activity of its businessmen, yet "entrepreneur," "bureaucrat," and even "businessman" are often terms of opprobrium. A business career is not a high prestige career compared to a doctor, lawyer, or scientist (McClelland, 1961). A businessman pursues his own interests — money; a professional man is characterized by disinterestedness and pursues justice or knowledge or the health and good of mankind (Parsons, 1949). The businessman is suspect, the professional man is not. No elaboration is necessary to make the point that achievement values are of major importance in the United States, nor does it take much to demonstrate that the values often come into conflict with other strong values and attitudes, such as suspicion of wealth, power, and authority.

As conceptually defined in terms of intrinsic satisfaction deriving from success in competition, the achievement motive should result in the type of behavior that is strongly valued by our culture, such characteristics as self-reliance and the instinct of craftsmanship. Certainly the most revered men in our culture must be strong in achievement motivation — the scientists, the statesmen, the doctors. They are the disinterested men who are searching for "the truth" without regard for personal sacrifice; surely they are the men of "achievement."

It may come as a shock that the prototype "Mr. Achiever" is not the scientist whose achievements are world renowned, but the businessman, or to be more specific, the entrepreneur. McClelland's attempts to discover what the achievement motive is have led to investigations of the traits of a man with strong achievement motivation. The research all points in the direction of a rather specific cluster of traits that make up the Achievement Syndrome. For McClelland, the one word that epitomizes this syndrome is the entrepreneur. The entrepreneurial spirit of achievement emphasizes self-reliance and personal responsibility, the taking of calculated risks, careful planning and checking of progress with constant emphasis on the careful use of one's own skill and the conservation of time. A man with these traits is the restless innovator in business and must not be confused with the stolid, unimaginative bureaucrat who also inhabits the business world. Mr. Achiever is the innovating entrepreneur, not the bumbling bureaucratic Babbitt.

The evidence supports the interpretation that strongly valued and, at the same time, conflict-arousing characteristics go into the entrepreneur as McClelland describes him. The very fact that the negative connotation of entrepreneur must be denied indicates the main point that is to be emphasized. Any discussion of achievement motivation touches on strong cultural values and is subject to distortion unless a very clear conception of the motive is adhered to; but no clear definition is available. The theoretical conception of a motive as a variable in an equation tells us little about the specific motive that is defined in terms of incentives (Atkinson, 1958). The incentive defined as intrinsic satisfaction leaves the burden of careful specification of what leads to satisfaction to personal knowledge. And the personal knowledge derives from our cultural heritage and leads directly back to the conflicts in the area. The conflict becomes acute when intrinsic satisfaction is inferred from extrinsic rewards.

The Achievement Syndrome was derived from empirical studies that give an indication of the types of behavioral traits manifested by people with high achievement motivation. These traits are theoretically neutral; but, in considering the syndrome, one is naturally led to ask whether it is a good thing to have achievement motivation. This is especially true in considering attempts to train people to have higher achievement motivation. Before we look at these Achievement–Motivation–Change projects let us confront the question: Is it a good thing to try to change the motivation of a group of people?

Should Motives Be Changed?

If you mention to a school teacher that it may be possible to change the motivation of her pupils, she will invariably show great interest. In fact, one of the most ubiquitous questions among teachers is: How can I motivate my students? To motivate students is obviously a "good thing" and achievement motivation training ought to be just what is needed in the schools. Most teachers realize upon reflection that the problem is more complex than just motivating the students, however good that seems at first. Students are already motivated for something; the problem is that they are not motivated for the things that the teacher wants. At this point, doubts begin to be raised. What right does a teacher have to determine what the children should be motivated for? What right does she have to change them in such a basic realm as motivation? The cultural value of individual freedom and autonomy is as strong among teachers as among any other members of our society. Children originate their own behavior, and, theoretically, the teacher merely teaches them to attain a greater freedom. Has the teacher any right to attempt to change a basic personality trait of her pupils?

Initial acceptance of achievement motivation training projects may quickly turn to doubt when the problem of individual freedom is broached. The ethics of changing human beings is a very touchy subject, but clearly teaching is intended to have some effect — to induce some change in the student. When this is accepted, the much more critical question of what kinds of changes should be attempted can be confronted. When a teacher asks himself this question, he is really confronted with the problem of his own values. Conflict between the freedom of the individual and the job of teaching, i.e., changing students, is inevitable.

If this conflict is resolved by attempts to choose carefully the goals to be sought when teaching, the next question becomes: What are the effects of achievement motivation training? This is closely followed by the question: For whom is it appropriate? From the oversimplified notion that "achievement motivation" is good and all students should be trained in it, we have quickly arrived at the more sensible question about its appropriateness.

Research has given us a picture of the man with high achievement motivation. He is the man who takes moderate risks, attains his goals through energetic and novel instrumental activity, likes to take individual responsibility and to know the results of his actions, plans and organizes his life, and is concerned about the use of his time. Is he, in fact, a Babbitt who "As he approaches the office he walked faster and faster muttering, 'Guess better hustle.'"? Is he one of the "Men who had made five thousand, year before last, and ten thousand last year, were urging on nerve-yelping bodies and parched brains so that they might make twenty thousand this year; and the men who had broken down immediately after making their twenty thousand dollars were hustling to catch trains, to hustle through the vacation which the hustling doctors had ordered" (Lewis, 1922, p. 128)? Is he the man who plans and organizes his life around controlling political parties to further his business interests all in the name of aggrandizing his hometown in competition with other towns in his area? In short, is he the ultra-conforming, back-slapping glad-hander that is one of our pictures of the businessman as seen in the satirical portrait of Babbitt as portrayed by Sinclair Lewis?

Or is the high achievement motivated man the one who uses his risk-taking strategies, his energy, his planning and conserving of time for less egotistical goals, for culturally accepted altruistic ends such as promoting science or social welfare? Or did the Babbitts in fact promote the technological and economic prosperity of the United States while seeking their own materialistic gains?

Such questions cannot be answered scientifically at present but they invariably come up in discussions of achievement motivation training projects. It is right that they should for when a psychologist sets out to change someone the very least he should do is consider the consequences. It should be clear that the achievement syndrome is a cluster of traits that relate to the way a person goes about attaining his goals and has little to say about what the goals are. As we saw in the previous chapter, the way the achievement motive is measured emphasizes success in competition but attempts to leave the concrete goals of competition to the discretion of the story writer. One answer to the ethical question about achievement motivation training is to stress that the training is primarily aimed at giving the trainee techniques to attain success at any goal that he chooses, thereby leaving the responsibility squarely on the shoulders of the trainee.

This is inadequate, however, if we take seriously the evidence that Wesleyan students with high n Achievement choose entrepreneurial occupations in inordinate proportions (McClelland, 1965b). Better to face the fact that the training as it stands may have a prejudicial effect on the long-range goals of the trainee and use the present training techniques (that were developed for use with businessmen) only in appropriate settings. Another alternative to be discussed later is to try to broaden the training to include the more inclusive definition of "achievement of any goal."

Can Motives Be Changed?

The foregoing has attempted to bring out into the open some of the ethical problems inherent in motivation change projects and has assumed that with our present knowledge motivational change can be attained. We will present evidence later in this chapter that derives from the few studies that exist, but first it should be mentioned that a typical reaction to a proposal to change motives is that it cannot be done. Freudian psychology strongly implies that personality characteristics such as basic motivational patterns are instilled in early infancy. If motives are to be molded at all, the person must be captured as a very young child.

Whether motives can be changed, and, if so, at what age, is an empirical question, and we have very little scientific data to go on. McClelland (1965a) has set forth a series of propositions which at one and the same time provide a theoretical justification for the assumption that motives can be changed and a structure around which change projects may be developed.

McClelland's propositions follow:

> *Proposition 1. The more reasons an individual has in advance to believe that he can, will, or should develop a motive, the more educational attempts designed to develop that motive are likely to succeed. . . .*
> *Proposition 2. The more an individual perceives that developing a motive is consistent with the demands of reality (and reason), the more educational attempts designed to develop that motive are likely to succeed. . . .*
> *Proposition 3. The more thoroughly an individual develops and clearly concep-*

tualizes the associative network defining the motive, the more likely he is to develop the motive. . . .

Proposition 4. The more an individual can link the newly developed network to related actions, the more the change in both thought and action is likely to occur and endure. . . .

Proposition 5. The more an individual can link the newly conceptualized association-action complex (or motive) to events in his everyday life, the more likely the motive complex is to influence his thoughts and actions in situations outside the training experience. . . .

Proposition 6. The more an individual can perceive and experience the newly conceptualized motive as an improvement in the self-image, the more the motive is likely to influence his future thoughts and actions. . . .

Proposition 7. The more an individual can perceive and experience the newly conceptualized motive as an improvement on prevailing cultural values, the more his motive is likely to influence his future thoughts and actions. . . .

Proposition 8. The more an individual commits himself to achieving concrete goals in life related to the newly formed motive, the more the motive is likely to influence his future thoughts and actions. . . .

Proposition 9. The more an individual keeps a record of his progress toward achieving goals to which he is committed, the more the newly formed motive is likely to influence his future thoughts and actions. . . .

Proposition 10. Changes in motives are more likely to occur in an interpersonal atmosphere in which the individual feels warmly but honestly supported and respected by others as a person capable of guiding and directing his own future behavior. . . .

Proposition 11. Changes in motives are more likely to occur the more the setting dramatizes the importance of self-study and lifts it out of the routine of everyday life. . . .

Proposition 12. Changes in motives are more likely to occur and persist if the new motive is a sign of membership in a new reference group (pp. 324–330).

These propositions derive from McClelland's conception of motives as "'affectively toned associative networks' arranged in a hierarchy of strength or importance within a given individual" (McClelland, 1965a, p. 322). The salience of the motive, i.e., its position in the hierarchy, is indicated by the extensity of the associative network. If achievement thoughts are prevalent in thought samples then the associative network characteristic of achievement motivation is high in the hierarchy. Similarly, the associative network of a person with high achievement motivation can be characterized by the thoughts typically found in his thought samples. At the simplest level, if a motive is nothing more than the associative network, then to change a motive is merely to change a person's associative network. A simple theory that assumes that thoughts cause action might be satisfied with this alone, and an oversimplified view of an achievement motivation change project may encourage the assumption that all the project does is try to teach the person to think the way an achievement motivated person does.

Teaching the person to think achievement thoughts is one step and a rather crude one at that. Trainees write stories and then are taught the *n* Achievement scoring procedure so that they can content analyze their own stories. They are then taught to write stories with more achievement categories in them and encouraged to think in these categories whenever possible. If achievement thoughts cause achievement behavior this should be all that is necessary. If the achievement motive is nothing more than the thoughts and they constitute the entire associative network then training in the scoring is all that is required.

The stress on the associative network as constituting the motive in McClelland's paper may lead to this oversimplified view; but if the motive and hence the associative network is *only* the thoughts, then why is Proposition 3 alone not sufficient?

Simply training a person to write stories with many achievement categories in them is a little comparable to giving a student the answers to an I.Q. test and claiming that you have changed his native intelligence, or like asking a person to make hostile statements when he is not provoked in order to make him aggressive. To think of the associative network as *only* thoughts about achievement is a mistake.

In Chapter 4 of this book, we discussed what we called mediating mechanisms following Mowrer (1960a,b). We suggested that conceptually, at least, three types of mediating mechanisms may be postulated, namely, cognitive, affective, and motor mediating mechanisms. We further suggested that affective mediating mechanisms lie at the heart of motivation but that they never occur in isolation. In light of this and what we learned about thoughts and actions going together in the last chapter, we now suggest that a motive is actually a combination of all three types of mediating mechanisms, i.e., the associative network is composed of cognitive, affective, and motor aspects. Instilling primarily the cognitive aspect by training in the scoring categories is only one third of the story and should not result in a very effective way of changing the motive. Changes in the cognitive aspect, i.e., increasing the number of achievement thoughts and decreasing the number of interfering thoughts, must be accompanied by changes in the affective and motor or action components, that is a change of all the aspects of the associative network.

We have broadened the concept of associative network beyond the cognitive component, and, since the word "associative" has primarily cognitive connotations, we might do better to refer to that network as a neural or mediating network. McClelland's concept of associative network has its roots in Hebb's (1949) notion of a motive as an organized pattern of neural excitation that he calls the phase sequence. "The term motivation then refers (1) to the existence of an organized phase sequence,

(2) to its direction or content, and (3) to its persistence in a given direction, or stability of content [p. 181]. . . . (1) the phase sequence is independent of input from any specific sensory mode; (2) it has a central priming action that reinforces some sensory stimulations and not others; and (3) it evokes specific forms of behavior, since each phase in the phase sequence may have its specific motor facilitation" (p. 191). McClelland *et al.* (1953) use this "stimulus pattern model" in developing the theory underlying the achievement motive. Thought sampling may be seen as one way of tapping the predominant networks and assessing their content, but the cognitive aspects must be connected with the affective and behavioral aspects to result in a full-blown motive. The other propositions for the development of a motive presented by McClelland (1965a) are attempts to tie in the affective and behavioral components.

The core propositions appear to be 3 and 4 since they are directed toward instilling the cognitive component of the new associative network and relating it to action components. The other propositions attempt to prepare the recipient for this new or significantly more salient network (Propositions 1, 2, and 8) to make sure that it is related to other networks and receives its recognition in the recipient's life, self-image, and values (Propositions 5, 6, 7, and 11), to assure that he will check his progress (Proposition 9), and to assure that the training occurs in an atmosphere of positive affect and will be reinforced by the trainee's associates (Propositions 10 and 12).

What, concretely, is done in a training course to operationalize these propositions and make them into inputs? As we said previously, the cognitive associative network input (Proposition 4) consists largely of teaching the trainees to think the kinds of thoughts found in the thought samples of people with high *n* Achievement. To start with, they write stories, then they study the scoring categories and score their own stories. Then they try to write stories with as many achievement categories in them as possible. This procedure shows them that they can recognize achievement thoughts in their own and other people's productions. They learn that whenever a problem arises in their own life they can think of the behavioral sequence underlying the scoring categories and identify their goal and decide whether it is an achievement goal or not. They can decide whether they really want it *(Need)*[1] by investigating their feelings of affect about it *(Positive & Negative Affect);* they can ask themselves whether they anticipate success or failure *(Positive & Negative Goal Anticipation);* they can investigate what kinds of interference they may

---

[1]The words in parentheses refer to the scoring categories as discussed in Chapter 6.

encounter either due to their own inabilities *(Personal Block)* or from external sources *(World Block);* they can think about specifically what they need to do to attain the goal *(Instrumental Activity)* and if they can get any help from other sources *(Nurturant Press)*. Such careful self-analysis and planning moves the trainee beyond developing the cognitive associative network and begins to help him tie it in with affective and be-havioral components that are important to him.

But before he can apply the new technique to real problems he practices it in games where the outcome does not "really count" but where he can see how the strategy works. Numerous games have been developed to help tie the cognitive to the affective and behavioral aspects. The games are designed to demonstrate that careful analysis of risks, and careful checking of personal skill lead to success in competitive situations. Games using ring-toss, shuffleboard, darts, racing cars, and puzzles quickly show the advantages of taking moderate risks based on careful analysis of results indicating individual skill. Probably the most successful game is called "The Business Game." It was designed for the training of business-men and places each player in the position of managing a corporation and making contracts to build toy rockets or tractors for the government. The player buys parts and actually assembles models using tinker-toys or erector sets. The point of the game is that the production time is limited so that the manager-worker must carefully calculate how many models he can make according to his own skill in the time allotted. If he over-estimates, he buys too many pieces and sustains a loss; if he under-estimates, he fails to use all of the time in production and does not maximize his profits. The business game is a highly involving exercise that places the player in competition with all other players and with his own past performance, since several contracts are made and he can try to better his past record. The player obtains immediate feedback in terms of gains or losses concerning his decisions. For the businessman, the game often can be seen as applicable to the problems that he faces every day.

An attempt is made during the course of the training to insure that the lessons learned from applying achievement thoughts to games are trans-ferred to real life goals (Propositions 5 and 8) by having the participant analyze his goals in an inventory and select a specific goal that he may reasonably expect to achieve within the next two years of his life. He is encouraged to work out a plan for attaining his goal and attempts are made by means of follow-up questionnaires or interviews to help him check on his progress (Proposition 9).

These procedures deal more or less directly with achievement motivation and goals. In addition to these inputs, the entire training course is placed in the setting of self-analysis. Concretely, the trainees usually write a short essay in answer to the question "Who am I?" Extensive discussion ensues in which the participants introspect about themselves and their goals. The aim of this procedure is to increase their self-understanding (Propositions 6 and 11) and to encourage them to see themselves as achievers. Such a critical self-analysis is apparently best carried out in a warm, accepting atmosphere (Proposition 10) and often takes on the aura of group therapy sessions. Some of the techniques developed for training in group-dynamics (so-called T-groups) (see Bennis, Schein, Berlew, & Steele, 1964; Bradford, Gibb, & Benne, 1964) are used in an attempt to establish a reference group (Proposition 12) the members of which have gone through the same experiences. The group is encouraged "to keep in touch with each other" after the course is finished.

Propositions 1 and to some extent 2 are operationalized by attempts to insure that the trainees have chosen to participate rather than feel that they were pushed into the course. These inputs involve "selling" the course; with businessmen, this usually constitutes giving them results of studies that show that people with achievement motivation tend to be successful in business, and that achievement motivation in a culture promotes economic development.

It should be clear that many variables go into achievement motivation courses, and that the whole package is designed to have a practical impact resulting in increased entrepreneurial behavior of the trainees. Theoretically, the inputs may be classified in several different ways. The effects of the training may be the result of the emphasis on group phenomena in a therapeutic setting and may have little to do with the actual learning of the achievement thought-action complex. Within the thought-action complex, it may turn out that training in one aspect overshadows the other or that both are necessary in order for either to be effective. All of these questions may find answers in what McClelland (1965a) calls a subtractive design. "Our overall research strategy, therefore, is 'subtractive' rather than 'additive.' After we have demonstrated a substantial effect with some 10–12 factors working to produce it, our plan is to subtract that part of the program that deals with each of the factors to discover if there is a significant decline in the effect" (p. 323).

Such a design may take years to complete because of the host of practical problems involved. In addition to these, there is the problem of measuring the effects of the training. No measure derived during or immediately after the course would be adequate since the achievement motive is conceived of as a variable that should have long-term effects.

Nor will any single measure, such as amount of money earned, be adequate. The best measure of the effects of these training courses may only be obtained through follow-up interviews or questionnaires that may drag out for several years after the course and that are designed to uncover any types of behavior that might be considered entrepreneurial.

Achievement Motivation Training Courses

The courses that have been conducted have been essentially attempts to compare groups who have had more or less complete achievement training courses with other relevant nontrained groups, and to compare the behavior of trained groups prior to training with their subsequent behavior. The appropriateness of achievement motivation training for the trainees is apparent when dealing with businessmen, but it becomes more of a problem in dealing with other groups. In our previous discussions of appropriateness, we presented some of the problems encountered when it is decided to give achievement motivation training to school children. As we saw, this seems a natural thing to do at first, but soon the wisdom of it may be questioned. There is far more evidence to support the value of the training for businessmen than there is to support it for the public schools in general. In view of this, at least two criteria are usually considered in choosing a school population. Rather than choose any group of school children, attempts are made to select either recognized underachievers who may be considered undermotivated, or students who are preparing to enter the business world such as high school boys who are taking vocational or business training rather than college preparatory courses.

Underachieving High-School Boys

Some preliminary results reported by Burris (1958) indicated that n Achievement counseling of college underachievers significantly improved their grades. Subsequent to this study, Kolb (1965) initiated the first full scale attempt to give an achievement motivation training program. In the summer of 1961, fifty-seven underachieving high-school boys (I.Q. > 120, average grade $< D+$) attended a special six-week course at an Eastern University where they were given instruction in History, English, and Mathematics. Kolb randomly selected 20 of these boys, assigned them to one floor of the dormitory, acted as their counselor, and conducted an achievement motivation training course with them using the other boys as controls.

At the beginning of the six-week period, the achievement motivation trainees were required to meet with Kolb regularly; but as time progressed responsibility for attending sessions as well as for handling dormitory problems was gradually turned over to the boys. The procedures used in the course were essentially of three types; training in achievement thought patterns, games involving achievement behavior patterns (moderate risk-taking and use of feedback), and group discussion and individual counseling about life problems and conflict over achievement. The boys produced thought samples, learned to score them for n Achievement, and practiced using the categories. They played the "racing-car" game and were encouraged to consider their own behavior from the point of view of what kinds of risks they took, how much they wanted to win, and how well they judged their own ability. They also played the "business game" and assessed their own behavior in similar ways. The counselor spent hours leading group discussions and doing individual counseling and attempted to present himself as a role model of the person with high n Achievement.

Several personality and ability measures were available to demonstrate that the boys who were selected for achievement motivation training could be considered comparable to the group who attended only the content classes but did not receive achievement training. A measure of socioeconomic status of each boy was obtained from his father's occupation.

The major dependent variable was change in school grades. Average grades prior to the summer program were obtained for all the boys to form a baseline; and in two follow-up periods grades were assessed one and three school semesters after the summer training. The results indicated a small and insignificant difference favoring the achievement training (experimental) group as compared to the others (control group) on the first follow-up, one semester later. But after three semesters, the difference was significant indicating that the experimental group had improved more than the controls.

A more detailed look at the data indicated that the improvement in grades was confined primarily to the trained boys whose fathers' occupations were classified as high in socioeconomic status (High SES). There was no real difference between the low SES experimental boys and the controls, be they high or low SES. These results may be seen in Figure 7.1. In general, all boys improved their grades between the pretraining period and the first follow-up, but the high SES experimentals improved most. In the period between the first and second follow-ups, the high SES experimentals continued to improve while all other boys showed a decline in grades.

These results seem to indicate that the only lasting effect of the summer experience was for high SES achievement trained boys. The other boys, including low SES achievement trained and either high or low SES boys who just attended the content classes, appear to have improved their grades slightly for one semester and then to have declined to a level only slightly better than their pre-summer experience level. While the high SES achievement trained boys were improving from a D— average to a C+, the others moved from a D+ to a C— and then back to a point almost half-way between D+ and C—.

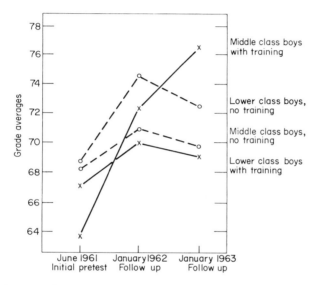

Fig. 7.1. Average change in grade of 14-year-old boys who received achievement motivation training (solid lines) and of boys who received no training (broken lines) (from Kolb, 1965).

There are at least three possible and related explanations for the superior performance of the high SES experimental group. (1) They come from a social class that is known to be more achievement oriented (Rosen, 1956), and therefore may have in their background more of the independence training that promotes high n Achievement (Winterbottom, 1958). (2) They may have gained more from the achievement training course. (3) They may have been able to maintain the learning from the course because they returned to a home environment in which achievement behavior was reinforced and encouraged, whereas the low SES boys returned to an environment in which achievement behavior may have been discouraged.

The third explanation is proposed by Kolb. Essentially the lower SES environment is seen as tending to extinguish the achievement behavior once learned whereas the higher SES environment reinforces it. Kolb rules out the explanation that high SES subjects gained more from the course on grounds that none of the measures of course participation obtained from counselor ratings and objective measures was related to SES.

An explanation based on the fact that the high SES boys came from a more achievement oriented culture than the low SES boys complements Kolb's explanation that they went back to a more achievement oriented culture, but it also bears directly on the problem of whether motives can be changed after they are established early in life. McClelland (1965a) argues that these training courses result in the acquisition of a new motive. If it turns out that only people who originally came from an achievement oriented culture maintain the benefits of the course, one could argue that the course is not implanting a new motive where none existed, but is merely rejuvenating one that was implanted early. Theoretically a strong case could be made, based on a venerable principle of learning, that a reactivation of traces laid down in childhood should have a more lasting effect than the introduction of new traces (Jost's Law; see McGeoch & Irion, 1952). Achievement training for boys who received independence training in childhood should be more enduring than for boys who have no such early training to which the present training can be related. There is evidence (McClelland, Rindlisbacher & de Charms, 1955) of a relationship between independence training and SES, and since independence training has been related to level of n Achievement, we can check the Kolb data for a relationship between SES and initial n Achievement. The correlation is $+.22$ for 18 boys, a result which leaves the issue up in the air. It is positive, as would be expected if the high SES boys had more achievement training prior to the course than the lows, but it is insignificant. A positive demonstration of the effects of past learning in interaction with achievement training on change in grades or other behavior would best be obtained by assessing the amount of independence training the boys received in childhood. If it turned out that boys who had little independence training at the optimum time in childhood showed meagre long-lasting effects of achievement motivation training, one would question whether training after childhood could actually lead to the acquisition of a new motive and one might conclude that such training merely results in the reactivation of a motive that may have lain dormant or been frustrated (in the case of achievement) by frequent failures.

Fortunately, the case is not as black and white as we have painted it since no child receives *no* independence training and the concept of absolute zero achievement motivation is meaningless. Other things being equal, a boy with low *n* Achievement to start with stands to gain more from training than one with high *n* Achievement. If inhibiting effects of past learning or the lack thereof and of the environment to which the trained boy returns can be discovered and techniques developed to overcome them, then the training should result in greater benefits for the low *n* Achievement person. Some indication that this effect is operative may be found in Kolb's finding of a —.30 relationship between initial *n* Achievement level and change in grades. Although not significant this finding shows a tendency for boys initially low in *n* Achievement to achieve greater increases in grades subsequent to *n* Achievement training than boys initially high in *n* Achievement.[2]

Business Executives in the United States

Aronoff and Litwin (1966) report the results of an achievement motivation training course given to a group of middle-level executives working for a corporation that is described as "one of the most dynamic and rapidly-growing in the world" (p. 4). The men who were trained were compared with a matched group of men who participated in a four-week management development course.

Sixteen men attended the achievement training course for 5 days in residence at an estate maintained by the corporation for its management courses. Only 11 of these remained in the company for two years so that the follow-up could be made. Training concentrated primarily on conceptualizing achievement motivation, relating it to the executives' problems, achievement behavior (the business game), and achievement goal setting.

Comparisons were made between rates of advancement of the 11 achievement trained men and their matched partners who attended the corporation course. Advancement was scaled as follows: a man who had been demoted was given a score of negative one (—1); a man who remained at the same level and obtained less than a 10% raise in salary was given a score of zero (0); a man who was given a significant promotion was given a score of positive one (+1); a man who had been promoted several levels or had received an unusual salary raise was given a score of positive two (+2). Each of the 22 men in the trained and untrained groups received an advancement score for the two-year period prior to the

---

[2] See data reported later in this chapter on businessmen from Kakinada, India, for a similar finding.

course and the two-year period after the course. Comparing rate of executive advancement between those who took the *n* Achievement training course and those who took the corporation course shows significantly greater advancement among the achievement trained executives.

This study indicates the effects of achievement training on executives in the United States. The men can be assumed to be of rather high *n* Achievement to start with, but apparently training can increase behavior that leads to unusual advancement within a corporation even in men of initially high *n* Achievement.

Indian Businessmen

That achievement motivation training of important businessmen might spur economic and technological advance in developing countries was a reasonable inference from McClelland's (1961) evidence of the relationship between *n* Achievement and economic development. Finding a setting for such training courses where the people can be convinced of the value of training, where there is some hope of a substantial effect, and where the effect can be measured is very difficult. McClelland has attempted to start training courses in several countries such as Mexico and India. So far, follow-up data are available from two different studies conducted in India.

In 1963, thirty-four businessmen from the Bombay area attended training courses similar to those described above except that they were not conducted in a retreat setting and did not emphasize warmth and group phenomena. A measure of business advancement similar to the one used by Aronoff and Litwin (1966) was developed using a scale from -1 to $+2$. Starting a new business venture was added as a criterion of unusual advancement. Data on 30 trained men and 11 untrained men were collected for the two-year period prior to and the two-year period following the course. "Of the 30 on whom information was available in 1965, 27% had been unusually active before the course, 67% after the course ($\chi^2 = 11.2, p < .01$). In a control group chosen at random from those who applied for the course in 1963, out of 11 on whom information has so far been obtained, 18% were active before 1963, 27% since 1963" (McClelland, 1965a, p. 332). The results of this first Indian study were obviously encouraging.

In 1964, McClelland in collaboration with an Indian Government Society, the Small Industries Extension Training Institute, selected two small cities as sites for intensive efforts to train as many of the principal businessmen as possible. The training sites were Kakinada, in Andhra Pradesh, and Vellore, in Madras Province. Results of an intensive follow-up of this research are reported by Lasker (1966) who attempted to visit and interview all of the trained men in the summer of 1965.

The four courses given in Kakinada to a total of 52 men were the most complete reported so far from the point of view of McClelland's 12 propositions. They were residential, stressing warmth, group phenomena, and individual self-analysis as well as training in the achievement thought-action associative network and future planning. A special attempt was made to confront Indian values that seemed to the trainers (who were Indian for the most part) to inhibit achievement and entrepreneurial behavior. The training in Vellore was discontinued after two groups and those who were trained were less powerful in the community, being younger, less wealthy, and less often managers of their businesses, than their counterparts in Kakinada. A third city, Rajahmundry, was chosen as a control for Kakinada, using economic indexes, and no training was given there.

A measure derived from interviews of unusual business activity similar to that used with the Bombay men was obtained for a period of two years prior to the course and at 3 six-month intervals after the course in Kakinada. In Vellore, the same was done except that the last follow-up interviews after 18 months could not be obtained. Nontrained businessmen were interviewed in 1966 by Rajahmundry in an attempt to obtain a base rate of unusual activity for nontrained men comparable to the trained men in Kakinada.

The basic results are presented in Table 7.1. In order to qualify as

TABLE 7.1

Percentage of Men Who Were Unusually Active
Before and After Achievement Motivation Training

	Percent unusually active			
	2 years before training	6 months after training	12 months after training	18 months after training
Experimental groups				
Kakinada (*N* = 52)	14	19	33	47
Vellore (*N* = 27)	0	11	22	—
Control				
Rajahmundry (*N* = 57)			21	

having engaged in unusual activity a man had to have received a score of positive two on the scale from −1 to +2. In other words, he had to receive either an unusual promotion or an unusual raise in salary, start a new business, or significantly improve procedures in his old business.

The results in Table 7.1 show statistically significant increases in unusual activity in both Kakinada and Vellore. The increase is striking in Kakinada, but much less so in Vellore. Actually in Vellore, only 6 of the 27 men became unusually active after 12 months, a statistically significant but not very impressive result. Another analysis (not shown in Table 7.1) indicated that the men of Kakinada were significantly more active after 12 months than the men of Vellore. Apparently the achievement training course was effective in both cases but only minimally so in Vellore. The difference may be attributable to the fact that the Vellore men were in a poorer position to innovate than the Kakinada men, being less wealthy, less powerful and younger. Clearly they were less active (0%) before the course than the Kakinada men (14%).

Comparing Kakinada with Rajahmundry (the control city) indicates that in the two years after the course in Kakinada significantly more of the trained men (47%) were active than the nontrained men of Rajahmundry (21%) in the same period. The Rajahmundry percentage can be seen as a base rate for business activity in the area in the years 1965–66. Kakinada achieved more than twice that base rate.

Since nearly half of the men from Kakinada (47%) became active after the course, it was possible to use activity-nonactivity as a criterion and look for indicators in the behavior of the men during the course that might predict their future activity. For instance, one can ask whether initial level of n Achievement is related to subsequent activity. The result is surprising at first glance. Of the subsequently active men, only 33% were above the median score on the initial measure of n Achievement, whereas 65% of the subsequently inactive men were above the median ($p < .05$). In other words initial n Achievement is *negatively* related ($r = -.24$) to subsequent activity. We may recall, however, that this is also what Kolb found with his underachieving boys where the correlation between initial n Achievement score and subsequent gain in grades was −.30.

Why should there be a negative relationship between initial n Achievement and achievement behavior subsequent to the course? Two possible reasons have been suggested. In discussing Kolb's results, we suggested that if factors that interfere with achieving behavior are overcome somehow, then participants who have low n Achievement initially stand to gain more from the course than participants who have high n Achievement initially. Another reason has been suggested for the men from

Kakinada. According to Atkinson's (1958) theory subjects with high n Achievement will be active primarily when they perceive a challenge in terms of a moderate probability of success. In Kakinada, success in business is generally considered to be of very low probability (high risk) and therefore it should not be as stimulating for subjects with high n Achievement. But why then is it more stimulating to subjects with initially low n Achievement who have received training intended to increase their motive? Would we not expect them now to shy away from business in Kakinada? The course was designed to encourage the participants to feel that the obstacles to business success were not insurmountable, i.e., to increase perceived probability of success in business in Kakinada. Possibly a change in perceived probability of success plus increased motivation were more successful with men of initially low n Achievement than with men who were initially high. Obviously there is no explanation that has been empirically substantiated, but it is interesting that both studies show greater gain for initially low subjects, indicating that working with this group of low subjects may be particularly rewarding rather than fruitless as was suggested from Kolb's finding that low SES boys did not benefit from the course. Data to be presented shortly indicate that environmental obstacles associated with a man's status in India may be the important thing blocking subsequent activity, a finding that tends to corroborate the explanation proposed by Kolb for the lack of gain in grades found in the low SES achievement trained boys a year and a half after their course.

One further finding was similar in Kolb's data and in Kakinada. Kolb reported a relationship between change in n Achievement score during the course and subsequent change in grades $(+.42, p < .10)$. After obtaining an initial n Achievement score, subjects were taught to write stories to obtain a high score. A high absolute change in n Achievement score means that a person starts low and changes greatly. Since training teaches subjects how to score high, they may all obtain similar high scores after training. If this is the case, a high change score merely indicates a low initial score and this correlation in Kolb's data may merely reflect the correlation reported earlier of change with initial n Achievement. Plus .42 is, however, slightly higher than $-.30$ (the reversal of signs is due to the change scores) and might indicate something more.

The Kakinada n Achievement data were analyzed by a regression technique that results in a change score that is uncorrelated with initial score and, in addition, indicates whether a subject changed more or less than would have been predicted from his original score. This technique gives a residualized change score based on the regression of the absolute gain score on the initial score. The resulting residual-gain scores can be conceptualized as indicating whether a person is an over-gainer or an under-gainer with respect to change in n Achievement. In Kakinada 75% of the men who subsequently became active were over-gainers on n Achievement score during the course, whereas only 35% of the men who were subsequently inactive were over-gainers. "To rephrase the result in more general terms, we now have the link which ties the course directly to the increased activity. It is not just those who went to the course who are more active: it is precisely those who learned most explicitly about n Achievement who are more active" (Lasker, 1966, p. 60).

There are some other findings from Kakinada of general interest, but they relate primarily to factors that inhibit achievement activity in India. We shall discuss them in the next section using them as a bridge between this discussion of achievement motivation training and a discussion of its implication for the broader concept of personal causation.

Summarizing the results of studies of achievement motivation training, we can say that it appears to have substantial effects (1) on the grades of underachieving high-school boys who come from middle and upper class homes, (2) on the income and professional standing of middle-level executives in a large United States corporation, and (3) on the business activities of small businessmen in India. These results are of great practical importance, and of considerable theoretical importance as a first step. Lest we be dazzled by research findings, however, we must say that scientifically we are a long way from knowing what "it" is that is effective in the course or what precise effects "it" has on behavior. The course was designed to increase achievement motivation, but consider for a moment the different results on subjects initially high *vs.* low on n Achievement. The result of the course should be that the lows come out acting more like the highs. But it looks like they come out acting more like the highs than the highs themselves. It is possible that the course is more effective in teaching n Achievement to the lows than to the highs. But it is just possible, in addition, that what a person learns in the course is not n Achievement at all but something else, or n Achievement plus something else, something more general such as increased feelings of personal causation. At present we really do not know.

Personal Causation and Achievement Motivation

We now know enough about one specific motive (n Achievement) to compare it with the concept of personal causation. In a sense we are taking up the discussion started in Chapter 1. In another sense we are returning to our critique of achievement motivation in Chapter 6; and finally we are rounding out our discussion of achievement motivation training courses. In our view all three are related.

In our critique of achievement motivation we stressed that the ambiguity of the concept derives from the fact that the definition in terms of success in competition must often be inferred from concrete goals (money, promotions, etc.) which may be indicative of other motives. A man may appear to be striving hard for success but actually be motivated by the need for security. Ideally, a motive should be defined in terms of a person's attitude toward, and affect over, certain types of instrumental activity. Competition with a standard of excellence is an example, but we cannot always obtain evidence for that so we try to infer it from certain goals. But if we had evidence that only the goal (money) was wanted and there was no joy in obtaining it through competition, we would hesitate to infer n Achievement. Our concept of motive is based primarily on intrinsic satisfaction rather than extrinsic rewards. If a person is assumed to derive intrinsic satisfaction from competition with a standard, we say he has n Achievement. Thus the specific motive, n Achievement, is defined by a specific type of activity that produces satisfaction.

If we broaden this concept and assume that satisfaction is derived from actively producing changes in the physical and interpersonal environment, we have the broader concept of personal causation. The person with n Achievement is the person who desires to demonstrate personal causation in competitive activity. The desire is apparently accompanied by a feeling that he can often succeed in competitive activities as shown by the data that indicate that high n Achievement subjects assign higher personal probabilities of success to certain tasks than do low n Achievement subjects (Litwin, 1966). In a competitive situation we might say then that the person with high n Achievement feels more personal causation than the person with low n Achievement. We may conclude that one component of n Achievement involves the broader concept of personal causation. To the extent that n Achievement is restricted to competitive activity it only deals with one aspect of personal causation.

Achievement motivation training contains a large component of competition. The business game, the ring-toss, and the racing-car game are all highly competitive games. But there is more to the training than competition. The stress on planning and realistic goals and the technique of thinking through a problem in terms of the achievement motivation scoring categories are techniques for encouraging the trainees to feel that they can actively do something to overcome obstacles, that they can actually be a causal force in their own environment. In other words, much of what happens in the training courses attempts to increase the subjects' feelings of personal causation. They are encouraged to feel more effective in handling their own problems than they did before, and everything is done during the course to treat them as responsible agents who are in control of their own destiny.

There is no necessary connection between increased feelings of personal causation and competition. Competitive activities constitute a realm in which a person can feel confident that he can originate effective changes to control his fate, but there are others. It may be that the training courses are having a broader effect than might be expected from the definition of achievement motivation in terms of competition. If this turns out to be the case, the training may be perfected to a point where it emphasizes more than the kind of competition found in entrepreneurial activities. The course may be tailored more to the needs of high-school boys who plan to become professionals or scientists.

Attempts in this direction are already underway but we must proceed with caution and not fall prey to the overly optimistic concept of achievement with its cultural halo that we saw at the beginning of this chapter. Training that increases a person's feelings that he can control his fate can have many consequences. The concept of personal causation helps us to see the goal of courses in a broader light, but ultimately more specific goals must be identified also. It is fine to increase feelings of personal causation in high-school boys, but what are we actually doing? Does the training actually help them in school and life?

We could speculate along these lines, but let us instead return to some data. We may ask the question: Are there any data to show (a) a relationship between n Achievement, personal responsibility, and our concept of personal causation, and (b) a relationship between achievement motivation, training, and personal causation?

The concept of personal responsibility is one of the major components of the Achievement Syndrome as presented by McClelland (1961), but it is not an explicit category used in scoring for n Achievement, i.e., it is not a major element in the measure of n Achievement. Nor is there much empirical evidence for it as a component of the Achievement Syndrome. McClelland (1961) cites data that subjects with high n Achievement will work just as hard for group goals as they will for individual goals (de Charms, 1956; French, 1958), but stresses that in both the group and the individual situation the high n Achievement subjects could derive individual satisfaction from success. The difference between the group and individual situations was more in terms of public recognition than individual responsibility. "The subjects with high n Achievement would probably have done less well if they had been told exactly what to do rather than who they were working for—themselves or the group, . . ." (McClelland, 1961, p. 230). In other words, McClelland predicts that high n Achievement subjects would prefer a condition that stressed personal responsibility to one that did not.

Horowitz (1961) has presented some evidence that subjects with high n Achievement choose to take personal responsibility when they can. Subjects played a game in which they assumed that they were salesmen traveling across the country contracting business for their firm. In each new town (12 in all) they were confronted with decisions that forced them to choose levels of risk, make use of feedback, and take personal responsibility. The only variable in this setting that correlated with n Achievement was personal responsibility ($r = +.29, p < .05$) and this was one of several correlations so it can only be seen as minimal evidence.

Apparently, the personal responsibility component of the Achievement Syndrome derives primarily from the theoretical conception of entrepreneurial behavior and has yet to be empirically related to n Achievement in a direct and unambiguous way.

As to achievement motivation training, Lasker (1966) devised a questionnaire that included what he called the Origin-scale to measure the degree to which the Kakinada businessmen felt that their behavior was determined by their own choosing or by external forces beyond their control. In fact, this scale was based on the strong values in Indian culture dealing with control of fathers over their children. Questions asked whether the businessman would prescribe behavior for his daughter, whether he would employ women, whether he would offer advice to an older relative, etc. The scale deals entirely with interpersonal relationships down the hierarchical ladder from the point of view of the businessman to his daughter or women in general, or up the ladder to an older male relative or his father. In this respect it is a very special case of a measure of personal responsibility tailored specifically to the Indian culture and measuring only how free they feel to break from conventional norms with respect to interpersonal family relationships.

The Origin-scale was not correlated with n Achievement score, nor was it related to the criterion variable of post-training entrepreneurial activity. There was a weak relationship between the Origin-scale and planning for activity. Lasker suggests that the scale is more related to talk about activity than to activity itself, a suggestion that fits with some earlier data that indicate that questionnaire indices of the Origin-Pawn variable (a short-hand term for a measure of personal causation to be discussed in detail in Chapters 8, 9, and 10) may be related to less behavioral measures such as the perception of other people (de Charms, Carpenter, & Kuperman, 1965) but are not related to actual measures of activity. A questionnaire measure was not related to behavioral measures in a study to be reported in Chapter 10 by de Charms, Dougherty, and Wurtz (1965, unpublished).

It is known that questionnaire measures devised to tap achievement motivation show only a slight relation to the standard measure derived from thought samples (de Charms *et al.,* 1955). One would expect, then, that analyses of the thought samples of the Indian businessmen for feelings of personal causation (the Origin-Pawn dimension) might be more fruitful than the questionnaire.

Lasker compared the thought samples of the post-training active men from Kakinada with the post-training inactives and found more indications of achievement conflict and defensiveness and less indications of specific planning and realistic confrontation with problems in the samples from the inactive men. These content categories, which he called (*a*) defensive set, (*b*) lack of specificity, and (*c*) conflict avoidance, are particularly interesting because they apparently tap aspects of the Origin-Pawn variable in thought samples. A careful look at Lasker's scoring manual indicates that "conflict-avoidance" is scored when a character in the story shows "(a) a desire to avoid interpersonal conflict by acquiescing to demands made by other figures in the story, (b) an attempt to avoid individual confrontation with problems by the use of the resources of a figure who assists the central character." The example given is "a worker does exactly what he is told to do by an authority figure, in order to receive a promotion" (p. 87). This is a clear example of a person avoiding individual responsibility and acting like a Pawn. The complete description of "conflict avoidance" stresses interpersonal conflict but many of the passages scored indicate a concern over authority relationships as would an Origin-Pawn scale.

"Defensive set" is again a category with elements of personal causation or the Origin-Pawn variable. "Many stories scored for defensive set are characterized by a concern on the part of figures in the story to maintain themselves in a state of subsistence, *without attempting any type of offensive acts*" (p. 89, italics added).

"Lack of specificity" is scored when stories "have a distinctly unrealistic flavor. The lack of realism is marked by a peculiar vagueness as to the nature of the problems, goals and actions in the story . . ." (p. 87). The stories show a desire for a vague goal but no indication that the hero has any realistic plan for attaining it or is engaged in realistic activity to attain it. We might infer that the hero has no strong conception that his own behavior can effect changes in the world to help him attain his goals.

These scales were empirically derived by comparing active and inactive men from Kakinada. They were not intended to measure the Origin-Pawn variable i.e., feelings of personal causation. They do, however, give some indication that thought-samples could be coded for this variable. Lasker's three subscales were cross-validated on the Vellore businessmen and predicted significantly those who were active after the training course. The scales are tenuous and the validation sample is small, but they do encourage the notion that the concept of personal causation and the derivative Origin-Pawn scale may be tapped in thought samples and that questionnaire measures may be of limited utility as they are in the measurement of achievement motivation.

The most pertinent data relating achievement motivation training to the concept of personal causation derive from a study that is at the time of this writing still incomplete. In the spring of 1966 a group of extreme underachieving high-school boys were selected and given an in-residence achievement motivation training course. Follow-up data collected for the trained group and a comparable untrained group during the fall of 1966 indicate that training (a) significantly increased grades, (b) significantly reduced school absenteeism, and (c) significantly reduced the drop-out rate. In addition, both trained and untrained boys were interviewed and the interviews were coded according to whether the statements made indicated predominantly Origin feelings (that the boy could control his fate) or Pawn feelings (that he was helpless to control his fate). The results show that more than half of the trained boys made predominantly Origin statements whereas all but one of the control boys made predominantly Pawn statements.[3] These findings, which are as yet highly tentative, nevertheless indicate that training may promote broader goals related to increased feelings of personal causation and may not be strictly limited to increasing n Achievement.

Summary

Data from several studies indicate that achievement motivation training courses that attempt to teach an associative network of thoughts, actions and feelings characteristic of people with high n Achievement result in (a) higher grades for high socioeconomic high-school boys, (b) promotions and raises for middle-level executives, and (c) increased entrepreneurial activity for Indian businessmen. Exactly what this means

---

[3] These preliminary data were reported to the author in a personal communication from Dr. Alfred Alschuler of the Achievement Motivation Training Project, Harvard University.

theoretically is still unclear. The courses seem to have practical importance for businessmen but more research needs to be done to make them more applicable to the school setting.

Individual responsibility is assumed to be a major component of the Achievement Syndrome as seen in entrepreneurial behavior but there is only scant evidence relating it to n Achievement. Nevertheless, training in taking responsibility is a major point of tangency between achievement motivation and personal causation. Achievement motivation training courses encourage the trainee to act and feel more like an Origin, that is, to feel he can originate desirable changes in his world, especially in competitive activities. To this extent, they deal with personal causation.

PART IV

PERSONAL CAUSATION

Chapter 8

MOTIVATION, OBJECTIVITY, AND PERSONAL CAUSATION

The concept of motivation useful for the psychology of human behavior can never be completely objectified. An enormous amount of confusion has been created by the failure to recognize and accept this fact. Psychology has been vigorously pursuing the goal of objectivity by defining in operational terms as many of its concepts as possible, but "motivation" has successfully resisted all attempts. When the operational trap is sprung the concept has vanished. In Parts II and III, we followed some of these attempts and emerged noting the inability of either the affect explanation or the thought-action paradigm to result in a comprehensive and completely objective explanation of motivated behavior. We continually felt the need to resort to the concept of personal knowledge. We have now arrived at the point at which we must return to some of the concepts presented in Part I and try to explain in more detail the problems inherent in objectivity and operational definitions, present the concept of personal knowledge, and state as succinctly as possible the concept of personal causation. In so doing we shall restate and elaborate what was implied in Part I.

Motivation, Objectivity, and Operational Definitions

The concept of motivation is meaningless for a completely objective study of behavior based entirely on operational definitions. The notions of motivation and motive are left over from the philosophic notions of will and volition which psychology has banned while retaining in emasculated form their essence under the heading of motivation. There simply is no objective phenomenal reality that can be identified as a motive. You cannot point to a physical object and say that is a motive, or point to a

257

sequence of behavior in a rat and say that is a motive. A motive is little different from many other useful entities in science, e.g., mass, energy, force, none of which can be objectified, and all such entities, including motive, are *concepts*. Concepts make their contribution to science at the theoretical level rather than at the empirical level.

In one very special way, however, the motive concept is different from most concepts in science. The motive concept has a personal or subjective flavor. Everyone learns as a child about his own motives. The child knows that *he* wants things and learns that he can do something to get them, that his wanting is the motive for his behavior. He is not taught this by others but learns it from his own experience. The basic reference point from which he judges all things is himself; and the judgment is based on a long history of purely personal experiences that result in knowledge about what he can and cannot do, what he does and does not want to do, and above all his feelings that *he* does things.

Knowledge derives originally from sense perception. First we learn by feeling and then, in addition, by doing. At first the baby must learn to distinguish himself from other things and other people. The very small baby does not know that his foot is *his,* and may treat it rather badly — he puts it in his mouth and bites it. He senses immediately that something is wrong, and it does not take many repetitions for him to stop biting.

Another object in the environment, mother's breast, does not produce discomfort when bitten. Somehow it is different. Slowly the child discovers that, although his foot and mother's breast can both be looked at, tasted, and felt with his lips, he does not experience the subjective sensation from mother's breast of being bitten while he is biting. He has one source of information from his foot that he does not have from the breast. The difference lies in the subjective source derived from his foot. Objects are differentiated as non-self because they produce no subjective feedback. The baby can see them and touch them, but he does not get the double feedback of touching and feeling the touch that he gets from his foot. The non-self objects are somehow less important.

At a later stage, the child learns that he can control the movements of the foot and ultimately that he can *do* things that change the objects in his environment. He discovers that to a certain extent he can control even those non-self objects, by contact with his body. The child learns that he can cause motion, noise, etc., in the objects around him. There is no doubt either to him or to his mother that he does cause motion and noise around him. If interfered with, he resists and persists in the activity. If he can talk, he responds to prohibitions with, "But I *want* to!" He has immediate subjective knowledge of wanting, desiring; and any observer will agree that he wants to—the implication being that he is motivated.

How does the observer *know* that the child wants to? No immediate knowledge is available to him through observation. How does he infer the motive? First, he observes persistence, resistance to inhibition, and the child's statement that, "I want to." He has observed similar behavior in himself and in others; but when observed in himself, he had additional knowledge to which he alone was privy, namely that *he* wanted to. This comparison with his own experience makes him sure that he is right in assuming a motive in the child. He is much surer because of this subjective knowledge than because of any objective data he may gather in watching the child. The subjective knowledge results in conviction.

When asked why he is sure, he will probably cite the behavioral symptoms of persistence, and maybe even the child's statement. Rarely will he give the real reason for his conviction, namely, that he has felt the motive when behaving that way, *because he may not even be aware that that is why he is so sure.* Besides, it is difficult to tell others how he felt, much less how he thinks the child feels. Anyone can look at the child's behavior, it seems to him, and tell that he is motivated. There is no need to go into a long explanation of how he feels.

Let us try to conceive of a purely thinking being similar to Condillac's (1754) sentient statue with no motives, a being that has never wanted anything, done anything, or caused anything; in short, a completely passive receptor of impressions. All this being knows is a series of sense impressions; he is powerless to do anything that will change them; he is, therefore, powerless to observe an action of his own followed by an external change, nor can he repeat the action to see if the external change will occur again. Will he ever differentiate himself from others? Will he ever learn to want anything? Will such a sensible but nonmotivated being ever arrive at the concept of motive? He may have all the data except the critical datum deriving from the subjective experience of *doing* something, without which the concept of motive is meaningless. In short, the concept of motive derives ultimately from subjective knowledge of actively causing things to happen in the world.

It should be clear that such knowledge is an intimate part of every human being. It is pointless to ask if it is innate or learned, as if that were critical. If the human being acquires it through learning, can we look for humans who have not learned it—some such being as discussed above? Clearly not, because any child without such a concept would not survive. We can therefore assume that all human beings, at least after a very early age, have the inchoate knowledge of volition that may be more or less cognitive but not entirely so.

Ultimately then, the concept of motive derives from experiences of self-induced changes in the environment. The concept in some form is characteristic of every member of the human species. When referred to self, the concept becomes so omnipresent that the on-going flow of behavior must be interrupted and inhibited for the individual to become consciously aware of something within him that is being resisted.

The behavior of others is most naturally assumed to be the result of internal factors similar to those that we feel in ourselves. Since we have knowledge of our own behavior and knowledge of theirs from observation, and since the knowledge of our own is always accompanied by feelings about volition, we easily assume that the behavior of others must be accompanied by such subjective knowledge. We further assume that such knowledge, available only to them, is the real explanation of the behavior, i.e., the motive behind it. In sum, the notion of motivation is conceived in subjective states, nurtured on personal experience, and finds its expression in individual behavior.

In Chapter 1 we suggested that the concept of physical causation has its roots in early learning of personal causation. A similar conception is implicit in Piaget's (1930) discussion of the origin of the child's conception of causation. Flavell (1963) supplies us with a concise statement of Piaget's argument.

> Just as with the other special developments, an understanding of the development of causality is furthered by first having some general notion as to where the infant begins and what he is developing towards. As to the former, Piaget finds it useful to define two kinds of precausality — like assimilation and accommodation, logically distinguishable but virtually indissociable in early cognitive functioning. . . . The first, *efficacy* (sometimes referred to as dynamism), refers to a dim sense that the inchoate feelings of effort, longing, etc., which saturate one's actions are somehow responsible for external happenings. Efficacy is therefore a causality of action-at-a-distance (since presence or absence of spatial connection between self as cause and event as effect is irrelevant to it) in which the cause is vaguely sensed as inhering in one's action without, however, the subject being sufficiently advanced to see self and actions as a separate causal agent in the universe. The second, *phenomenalism,* refers to the feeling that temporal (but not necessarily spatial) contiguity between any two events means that one caused the other. It leads to a kind of causal anarchy in which, as Piaget puts it, *"n'importe quoi produit n'importe quoi"* (1925, p. 33).
>
> Piaget's hypothesis is that the early stages of sensory-motor development are characterized by a causality best described as an undifferentiated mixture of efficacy and phenomenalism. As a knowledge of the evolution of space and objects would predict, this early causality knows nothing at all of objects as causal centers acting upon each other through spatial contact. With development, on the other hand, causality becomes both spatialized and objectified, and efficacy and phenomenalism, originally undifferentiated, break apart to undergo separate fates. . . .

Efficacy eventually becomes *psychological causality,* by which Piaget means the sense—now in a self aware of its thoughts and wishes—of causing one's own actions through volition, of willing to perform such and such action before performing it. And phenomenalism becomes *physical causality,* the causal action one object exercises on another through spatial contact (Flavell, 1963, p. 142).

The concept of physical causality, it seems, derives originally from personal knowledge, and it is not surprising that any attempt to base a discussion of motives on causes may lead to confusion as we saw in Chapters 1 and 2 above. This is especially true if it is assumed that causes can be completely objectified and therefore serve as a basis for the objectification of the concept of motive. In the developmental formation of the concepts the sequence is the other way round—physical causation develops out of personal causation.

The Primacy of Concepts

The position that motivation originates in subjective elements and that the notion of motive can never be reduced to operations and behaviors does not require of us complete rejection of empirical techniques and operational analysis. Such techniques help immeasurably in taking stock of where we stand at the present time and in communicating research findings. Empirical techniques do not tell us anything, however, about how to proceed on a course that will lead to discovery. Some other criterion is needed in the choice of what data to collect and what concepts to use. Discovery in science is crucially related to such decisions; and concepts derived from personal knowledge, such as the concept of motive, often provide the vague but indispensable guidelines for discovery.

Concepts are invaluable in that they guide thought and research into new areas, and it is precisely the surplus meaning, the meaning that cannot be reduced to operations as we saw with *n* Achievement in Chapter 6, that goads us into discovery. Concepts are primary; data and operations are secondary because discovery in science is primary and communication through objective operations is secondary.

The Value of Operational Definition

Once the priority of concepts over operations is established, the value of operational definitions may be assessed in terms of their contribution to the clarification of concepts and even of their role in promoting discovery. An operational definition never embodies an entire concept, but if judiciously selected it will communicate a major aspect of the concept precisely and concretely. This often seems to be the most important function of operational definitions, but prior to the reporting of research it has played a much more important role. In operationalizing his concept, the scientist has been forced to search his concept carefully for indications of its effects in physical phenomena. This is a giant step toward using the concept to understand data, i.e., toward making the concept usable and communicable scientifically as well as practically. This constitutes "operational analysis," similar to Bridgman's method as discussed in Chapter 2, as distinct from operational definition, which more often connotes a definition in objective terms than analysis of a concept. Operational definition may isolate the surplus meaning of the concept — the excess meaning that seems to be implied by the concept but that is not contained in the operational definition. It is precisely this excess that may be valuable in guiding future research leading to new discoveries, and it is in this role that operational definition can potentially make its greatest contribution to science.

In order of importance, operational definitions are valuable in that they *(a)* isolate unspecified elements of the concept for further study and thus promote discovery, *(b)* help relate the concept to physical phenomena, and *(c)* promote precise and concrete communication about certain aspects of the concept.

OPERATIONISM: A PROCRUSTEAN BED

Strict formal operationism, the position that all concepts must be defined in terms of physical operations, and that a concept has no meaning other than that contained in the operations, would reverse the order of importance of the aspects listed above. The goal of such operationism is to make concepts concrete and precise by the simple procedure of discarding any surplus meaning that is not contained in the operations used to define the concept. The word "surplus" deemphasizes the positive (plus) aspect and relegates it to the position of excess baggage. In this sense formal operationism makes a Procrustean bed[1] for concepts out of operational definitions, thereby discarding one of the major advantages of such definitions.

Operational definitions are often used to establish the validity of a concept. The generally accepted notion of validity is that the criterion for acceptance of a concept is the empirical support for it. This is what Cronbach and Meehl (1955) mean by construct validity. Attempts to validate concepts empirically help to make communication of concepts in

---

[1]There is a fable from ancient Greece that tells of a robber named Procrustes who had a famous bed that would fit any sojourner. A perfect fit was attained in the night when the robber stretched or mutilated his victims to make them conform to the bed.

conventionally accepted forms possible; and by isolating unsupported aspects of the concept, may point to areas for further study. Empirical validation does not tell us, however, what parts of the unsupported meaning are worth retaining for further study and what parts may be rejected. A criterion for distinguishing bonus aspects from excess aspects of surplus meaning would be extremely valuable. If we had such a yardstick for measuring ideas beyond their empirical support, we would have a way of distinguishing good from bad ideas.

Operationism and empiricism give us no help. In the extreme form, the dictum is to throw out *all* excess: what cannot be measured (reduced to operations) does not exist, which implies that existence depends upon present measurement techniques. If we change the dictum to read: if it cannot be measured it does not *yet* exist in communicable form, we have the enticing prospect that we may *learn* to measure it.

What part of the excess meaning should we start with? The logic of operationism gives us no formal guidelines; nevertheless, scientists are constantly facing this problem and making choices. These choices are not random but guided by concepts. Judgment of a concept is not suspended until empirical support has been obtained; a prior judgment supports the collection of data. In a sense the data are collected and presented to convince the scientist and his colleagues that the concept is useful.

Personal Knowledge

The scientist-philosopher Michael Polanyi (1958) has maintained that decisions and creative discovery in science are not based entirely on empirical evidence but to a large extent on personal knowledge. According to this position, the important decisions about accepting or rejecting a concept are made with regard to personal knowledge. Drawing heavily on Polanyi, our conclusions presented briefly in advance are as follows. Personal knowledge, the criterion upon which we base acceptance or rejection of concepts, derives from subjective as well as objective experience. The subjective-objective distinction actually becomes meaningless unless we wish to retain the terms and use them (somewhat inappropriately) *(a)* in the sense that subjective experience is uniquely derived by us from our own body — the feeling of being bitten while biting mentioned earlier; or *(b)* in the sense that objective knowledge is more easily communicated by conventional standards. The basic problem of obtaining knowledge from experience is (1) to arrive at universals, i.e., reliable generalizations, from our own experience, and (2) to find ways to communicate these universals to others.

In dealing with motives, the feeling of causal efficacy, of being the origin of a change in the environment, of *doing* something, is the basic universal. The fact that it cannot be measured reliably and hence communicated scientifically sets the problem rather than placing it out of bounds.

SUBJECTIVE AND OBJECTIVE DISTINCTION OVERSTRESSED

Subjective impressions are usually considered the antithesis of objective evidence. The subjective has an element of personal bias; the objective does not. Impersonalism is often proposed as the goal of objective science. In light of recent objectivist trends in psychology, it does not seem strange to say that we are attempting to arrive at impersonal knowledge about human beings. Such a statement might seem very strange, however, to a person who had had no contact with experimental psychology and thought that the goal of psychology was to help him understand himself and others. He might say, "How can you obtain *impersonal* knowledge about a *person?*"

The term "impersonal" is apparently misleading. The psychologists, especially clinical and social psychologists and even learning and motivation psychologists, are interested in knowledge about persons. They are attempting to formulate statements about universals that are true representations of personal states of the subject but are not contaminated by subjective states of the observer. The goal is to arrive at an understanding of the human being, including his personal states. In order to understand personal behavior, the observer will draw upon his own personal knowledge; but he must avoid contaminating his observations with his own momentary passions.

An observer, whether he is recording responses of an electronic wave analyzer, a rat in a maze, or a human subject in an experiment, ultimately depends on purely subjective sense impressions. Measuring devices, from rulers to Rorschach cards, are means of codifying the observer's subjective response so that it can be more reliably communicated to others. In the sense that all knowledge ultimately comes from sense impressions, all knowledge has its basis in the subjective. The crucial problem of measurement is not to attain objectivity, but to obtain a universally agreed upon technique of communication about subjective impressions so that other investigators may experience the same subjective impressions. These may be as simple as the impression derived from measurement of a physical object with a ruler.

Personal knowledge, like all knowledge, has elements of subjective states, and is often called subjective. The realization that some subjective aspects must be considered in psychology is creeping back after the objectivist revolt (cf. Bakan, 1956). These aspects are often cited as examples of introspection (see quote from Carnap, 1956, in Chapter 2). Our emphasis on the subjective aspects of measurement should not be interpreted, however, as a return to introspectionism. The psychology of introspectionism championed by Titchener at Cornell University at the beginning of the twentieth century (cf. Titchener, 1909–1910) stressed sense impressions. The trained introspectionist engaged in the "hard-labor of introspection" to avoid the "stimulus-error." The training allowed the observer to attend only to the perceptual process that a stimulus aroused in him rather than to the conscious content of the stimulus. A trained introspectionist looked at a chair, but avoided seeing a chair, by dint of hard labor, i.e., he avoided seeing a percept contaminated by his personal knowledge. He forced himself to attend to stimulus properties such as color, extensity, etc., that were immediately given. Introspectionism was the ultimate in attempts to attain objectivity and extreme objectivism was the basis for the foundering of the whole attempt.

There is an element of personal knowledge involved in perceiving a chair that makes it a chair and *not* a meaningless pattern of stimuli. The personal knowledge concerns "chairness" and can be distinguished from "that chair which is black and brown and has a school emblem on it and may have subjective associations for me." It should be clear that personal knowledge is *not* the report of a trained introspectionist avoiding the stimulus error, but the report of someone reacting to a stimulus with all faculties such as imagining and feeling, calling on his past experience, and seeing "a chair."

PERSONAL KNOWLEDGE AND BELIEF

The word "knowledge" is often used to connote something enduring, immutable, and unerring. Personal knowledge is not fixed, however, but is constantly changing. This is emphasized by philosophers who consider knowledge to be made up of a system of *beliefs*. For example, when I see the stimulus patterns reported by the trained introspectionist in the previous section, I say, "that is a chair." My reaction is based on previous experience and the accumulation of personal knowledge. What I am really saying is, "I believe that is a chair," but since my personal knowledge is so impelling, I feel no need to qualify by stating it as a belief. If the chair is odd, or dimly illuminated, I may actually say, "I believe I see a chair," but the uncertainty derives from comparison of the stimulus object with my personal knowledge about chairs. I do not doubt my knowledge of what a chair is; I am merely uncertain that the object that I see matches my knowledge.

In our earlier discussion of the observer who inferred from a child's persistent behavior that he was motivated, we noted that the observer would rarely say that he knew the child was motivated because he himself had felt the motive when behaving that way. The situation is similar to, but more complicated than, the dimly lit "chair." Just as in one case the observer does not bother to explain what a chair is but concentrates on telling you what he saw, so in the other case, he does not try to tell you what a motive is, but tells you what the child did, assuming that you have personal knowledge similar to his as to what motives are. It is fortunate that we can assume some communality of personal knowledge, for it would be difficult enough to communicate to someone in each instance what the essence of a chair is, much less what a motive is.

In stating, "I see a chair," I am completely committed to my concept of chair and I am stating a conviction that this object matches what I know as a chair. When I say, "He wants something," or more sophisticatedly, "He is motivated," I am stating a similar commitment to the notion of motivation which I hold. The main difference between the two is that all of my knowledge about chairs as objects is derived originally from an external source. Some (probably most) of my knowledge of motive is derived from internal sources. Not what *it* is and does, but what I *am* and *do*.

COMMITMENT

Commitment or conviction is inextricably enmeshed in belief and hence in personal knowledge. As William James says:

> Everyone knows the difference between imagining a thing and believing in its existence, between supposing a proposition and acquiescing in its truth. In the case of acquiescence or belief, the object is not only apprehended by the mind, but is held to have reality. Belief is thus the mental state or function of cognizing reality.... *In its inner nature, belief, or the sense of reality, is a sort of feeling more allied to the emotions than to anything else.* . . . . Consent is recognized by all to be a manifestation of our active nature. . . . What characterizes both consent and belief is the cessation of theoretic agitation, through the advent of an idea which is inwardly stable, and fills the mind solidly to the exclusion of contradictory ideas. When this is the case, motor effects are apt to follow (James, 1890, p. 283).

The commitment that grows out of personal knowledge gives a strong feeling of "truth" and "reality." In the end, science is founded on what we truly believe. The really basic things about science in general and the science of human behavior, in particular, do not come directly from crucial experiments, but from the accumulation of empirical evidence cast in the light of personal knowledge. Empirical and especially experimental evidence is invaluable in tempering knowledge, but concepts derived from personal knowledge in confrontation with evidence form beliefs. Empiricism that is divorced from organizing concepts is useless, bewildering, and, in the extreme, impossible.

Commitment to ideas is crucial in the guiding of scientific behavior and is paramount rather than secondary to empirical data. The scientist actively uses ideas to make sense of the data and to tell him what data to look at; he does not passively receive ideas that inhere in the data. That great ideas come from great experiments places the cart before the horse. More often it is the other way around.

Polanyi cites an example that he terms the "textbook story."

> . . . relativity was conceived by Einstein in 1905 in order to account for the negative result of the Michelson-Morley experiment, carried out in Cleveland eighteen years earlier, in 1887. Michelson and Morley are alleged to have found that the speed of light measured by a terrestrial observer was the same in whatever direction the signal was sent out. That was surprising, for one would have expected that the observer would catch up to some extent with signals sent out in the direction in which the earth was moving, so that the speed would appear slower in this direction, while the observer would move away from the signal sent out in the opposite direction, so that the speed would then appear faster. The situation is easily understood if we imagine the extreme case that we are moving in the direction of the signal exactly at the speed of light. Light would appear to remain in a fixed position, its speed being zero, while of course at the same time a signal sent out in the opposite direction would move away from us at twice the speed of light.
>
> The experiment is supposed to have shown no trace of such an effect due to terrestrial motion, and so — the textbook story goes on — Einstein undertook to account for this by a new conception of space and time, according to which we could expect invariably to observe the same value for the speed of light, whether we are at rest or in motion (Polanyi, 1958, pp. 9–10).

Polanyi cites a portion of Einstein's autobiography which in fact shows that he was concerned about the problem at the age of sixteen and came to an intuitive conclusion after a time. "There is no mention here of the Michelson-Morley experiment. Its findings were, on the basis of pure speculation, rationally intuited by Einstein before he had ever heard about it" (p. 10). Polanyi inquired of Einstein in 1953 and received assurance that, "the Michelson-Morley experiment had no role in the foundation of the theory" (p. 11). Einstein's intuition was vindicated by experiment, not the other way around. The intuition was a valid case of personal knowledge of a universal rather than an unreliable subjective impression.

The ultimate basis for any system of knowledge is personal knowledge of universals, but how can this valid kind of intuition be distinguished in advance from unreliable subjective impressions? Crucial to the attainment of personal knowledge of universals is commitment.

> In the theory of commitment the main division lies between experiences that are merely suffered or enjoyed and others that are actively entered upon (Polanyi, 1958, p. 312).
>
> On such grounds as these, I think we may distinguish between the personal in us, which actively enters into our commitments, and our subjective states, in which we merely endure our feelings. This distinction establishes the conception of the *personal*, which is neither subjective nor objective. Insofar as the personal submits to requirements acknowledged by itself as independent of itself, it is not subjective; but insofar as it is an action guided by individual passions, it is not objective either. It transcends the disjunction between subjective and objective (p. 300).

It is commitment that forces the individual to look beyond his individual passions and seek universals in personal experience. Subjective states result from passively enduring stimuli; personal knowledge is the result of actively interacting with the environment and forging knowledge from the active experience. Far from sinking into subjectivism on the one hand or encouraging disinterested observation on the other, this position argues for the active investigation of reality. Understanding is to be derived from actively inducing changes and observing results; a procedure that is the epitome of the experimental method. The emphasis on active intervention in the environment recalls early statements on the importance of experience by Dewey, and Kurt Lewin's dictum that if you think you understand a phenomenon you should try to change it. That understanding comes only with active participation, with the feeling of being able to change the phenomenon, is the general postulate of science for the attainment of universal knowledge. It is the same basic principle that is involved in the baby's development of the concepts of self and personal causation.

Commitment to the search for universals through personal knowledge may seem to be an uncertain foundation upon which to build the edifice of science. Nevertheless, it is Polanyi's proposal. The scientific study of motivation may be based on the concept of commitment to personal knowledge and at the same time have an obligation to investigate the effects of commitment and personal knowledge on behavior. To accept this position as the basis for a psychology of motivation constitutes a commitment (an act of faith) in itself. To accept the utility of studying phenomena related to commitment and personal knowledge and causation alone is merely to point out another area of potential interest. Acceptance of the former lends importance to the latter. The theory of commitment starts with an act of commitment. In this it is quite consistent.

THE OBJECTIVIST DILEMMA

Consistency of this type recommends Polanyi's position over objectivism. In fact, Polanyi rejects as inconsistent the popular position that the ultimate in science is objectivity. The inconsistency lies in what he calls the "objectivist dilemma." Although the basic posulate is that objectivity in everything is the goal and all statements are to be reduced to objective facts, the statement of the basic postulate itself cannot be so reduced. Put another way, the objectivist dilemma is as follows: to pursue objectivity is to start with a personal commitment that can never be objectified.[2] The choice made by Polanyi is to accept personal commitment as primary.

Logical arguments for the cogency of one epistemology as opposed to another are not very convincing to psychologists. But one need not accept Polanyi's entire argument concerning the basis of all scientific theorizing before examining the cogency of some of the concepts involved for the psychology of motivation. Polanyi's position has been used to set the stage for the presentation of a basic postulate.

Personal Causation: A Basic Postulate of Motivation

Man's primary motivational propensity is to be effective in producing changes in his environment. Man strives to be a causal agent, to be the primary locus of causation for, or the origin of, his behavior; he strives for personal causation. This propensity has its roots in his earliest encounters with his environment, forces him to actively engage his environment thereby testing and deriving valid personal knowledge from it, and is the basis for specific motives. His nature commits him to this path, and his very life depends on it. Personal causation of this sort is not to be taken as *the motive* for all behavior, however. It is an overarching or

---

[2]Polanyi cogently presents the logical argument that any scientific or logical system, when reduced to essentials, leaves "an irreducible residue of mental operations, on which the operations of the formalized system itself will continue to rely" (p. 258). He says further that this implies that, "It is nonsensical to aim at the total elimination of our personal participation" (p. 259). Gödel's theorems are cited as logical proof that the ultimate limits of formalization of logical thought depend on personal judgment. In essence, the argument (from Gödel) is that the complete consistency of any system of axioms can only be demonstrated by appeal to a wider system of axioms. But then the consistency of that wider system must be referred beyond it, and so on, *ad infinitum*.

guiding principle upon which specific motives are built. The environment sets different problems (obtaining food, achieving success, gaining friendship, etc.) that may help to define specific motives for individual behavior patterns. The dimension that underlies all of these is the attempt to overcome the problem through personal causation—the desire to be master of one's fate.

PERSONAL CAUSATION AND INDIVIDUAL MOTIVES DIFFERENTIATED

Personal causation is not a motive because it can apply to any motive as they are commonly defined. A person may strive for personal causation in interpersonal relationships thus gaining friendships and affiliation; he may strive for personal causation in overcoming problems in the physical world thus producing inventions and gaining fame for his achievement; he may strive for personal causation in influencing and manipulating other people and gain great power. In each case the general principle of striving for personal causation applies but the specific goals are different; the general orientation is toward being an Origin but the specific manifestation is toward goals generally classified under the heading of the affiliation, achievement, or power motives.

The defining characteristic of specific motives that differentiates them from the more general concept of personal causation is the goal of the motive. This is especially clear when the goal of a particular motive is a fairly carefully bounded class of objects such as food—the goal of hunger. A hungry person wants food, he may or may not feel that he is capable of obtaining it, he may or may not gain some extra satisfaction from getting it himself rather than having it given to him.

Our task in differentiating personal causation from motives would be tremendously simplified if motives were defined strictly in terms of the class of objects that satisfy them. The definition of most motives is, however, an attempt to bridge the gap between the objects and relationships in the physical world that form the goal of the motive and some internal feeling of satisfaction at reaching the goal. Attempts to objectify a concept that must contain both elements, the physical objects that are sought and the personal feeling of satisfaction attendant on obtaining them, are doomed to failure. That is why we have maintained that completely objective definition of the concept of motive is impossible.

The first step beyond defining motives in terms of physical objects that form goals is to realize that the goal is not just the object but the internal state of satisfaction that it gives. Having food is useless, one must eat it to reach the goal. This step can be taken by assuming an organismic component such as need and may carry us far.

Skipping over many intermediate steps that have formed the history of motivation and drive theory and were discussed in Part II, we come to the main point of this chapter. Having the objective goal or the feeling of satisfaction that comes along with its presence is insufficient to explain human behavior. The means of getting it may, in the long run, turn out to be more important to the understanding of human motivation than what the objective goal is. If I achieved the goal through my own efforts, my subsequent behavior will differ from my behavior if the goal was presented to me on a silver platter, so to speak. Attaining a goal through luck, chance, or through the benevolent agency of a helper is not the same as doing it myself. The feeling of personal causation can apply to any goal, to any class of goals that help to define a specific motive, and hence is a contributing factor to all motives.

In the simplest terms personal causation is not a specific motive because it involves no specific goal but can apply to the means of attaining any objective goal.[3]

The term causation in the phrase "personal causation" is definitely not meant to bring to mind Ryle's (1949) "unheard impacts of those little invisible billiard-balls." Such a reaction results from an overlearned attempt to objectify what the phrase, personal causation, *is* meant to bring to mind, namely, the personal knowledge of being an agent of change in the environment. The concept of personal causation should help us to avoid the pitfall of developing a motivation theory on a "para-mechanical myth" of a physical object (the human being) reacting to the physical impact of another physical object (a stimulus), the result being a causal sequence between stimulus and response.

The idea of personal causation that we are pursuing may be stated somewhat overdramatically as follows: A man is not a stone, for he is a direct source of energy; nor is he a machine, for the direction of the behavior resulting from his energy comes entirely from within him. Rather, *man is the origin of his behavior.* This forms the essence of the concept of personal causation.

A MAN IS NOT A STONE

A man acts as well as reacts. He is a source of energy with the capacity to direct the use of his energy. It is a very compelling fact phenom-

---

[3]One of the difficulties in differentiating personal causation from the motive concept is that the motive concept is ill-defined. We have assumed that most useful definitions involve some aspect of goals. With this in mind, it seems prudent to conceive of personal causation as something different. To consider it some kind of supermotive would only lead to terminological difficulties.

enologically that a man initiates his own behavior and has a hand in the course which it takes. A stone reacts but does not act. It has none of the attributes of an original source of energy and direction.

Nor Is He a Machine

A machine, be it a taut rubber band or an atomic plant, may have an internal source of energy that converts it from an inanimate object to a body with the potentiality for motion. The direction of the motion in a machine such as an automobile is left up to an external agent – the driver. But direction from within becomes more and more a reality in machines as science and technology move from mechanization, to automation, to cybernation. A machine needs to be directed constantly from without; an automaton is set originally to a predetermined course. Once set in motion it may appear to be internally directed, but there is no possibility for the robot to change its predetermined course. With the advent of cybernation, even this is possible. Feedback mechanisms allow a change in course at every state of the motion, but a restriction still remains – the changes in course are all determined by one or a very few criteria that are built into the "brain" that analyzes the feedback. The "brain" has little flexibility in changing the criteria. A guided missile may "home" on a heat source and may make little distinction between an "enemy" and a "friendly" heat source, but failure to discriminate may result in a misguided missile.

Human beings may also be misguided but basically their far greater capacity to distinguish and change criteria and direction of behavior – their far greater flexibility – sets them apart. The crux of the distinction may come down to our inability, as yet, to build into the electronic "brain" this increased flexibility. With technological advances a machine may some day simulate a man.

There is evidence, however, that some of man's fallibility may differentiate him from the machine. Theoretically, a computer can be programmed to investigate all possible moves in a chess game and finally to choose "the best move." It is already clear, however, that a human could not possibly do this and that chess masters do not go about their task in this way. A machine may simulate some of man's actions, but a man is not a machine.

A Man Is an Origin

The most basic postulate that we wish to present is that a man is the origin of his behavior. He is a unique locus of causality. Heider (1944,

1958) has developed the proposition that man is perceived as a locus of causality under certain conditions and it is a commonplace that men *feel* that their behavior is caused ultimately by them. Our postulate states more, i.e., that man *is* the locus of causality for his behavior. Without such a postulate behavior might be explained by external forces, but the psychological aspects of the term "motive" become superfluous.

This postulate is a direct result of assuming that the most basic human experience is that of effecting change in the environment — being a locus of causality. It is not meant to imply that a man *produces* his behavior *out of nothing,* for the concept of cause that implies production (out of nothing) is useless scientifically (cf. Chapter 2 above). Rather, the postulate implies that the behavior is *occasioned* or elicited by the unique combination of psychological and physical determinants within the human at a given time.

Stated in the occasioning rather than the production sense, this postulate is intended to stimulate investigation of determinants of behavior within the human (and lower organisms) rather than to imply that the locus, having been designated, is irreducible. The postulate merely states the problem that must be pursued if the concept of motive is to have any psychological foundation.

That man is the origin of his behavior means that he is constantly struggling against being confined and constrained by external forces — against being moved about like a pawn into situations not of his own choosing. Brehm (1966) has stressed the negative reaction to loss of freedom in his concept of psychological reactance. Looking at both sides of the coin, we may hypothesize that when a man perceives his behavior as stemming from his own choice he will cherish that behavior and its results; when he perceives his behavior as stemming from the dictates of external forces, that behavior and its results, although identical in other respects to behavior of his own choosing, will be devalued. Play that is forced becomes work; if one can choose his work without regard to external pressures and necessity, it takes on many of the aspects of play. In fact, one of the major components of the distinction between work and play is that work is something you do because you must; play is something you do because you want to.

ORIGINS AND PAWNS

We shall use the terms "Origin" and "Pawn" as shorthand terms to connote the distinction between forced and free. An Origin is a person who perceives his behavior as determined by his own choosing; a Pawn is a person who perceives his behavior as determined by external forces beyond his control. We hypothesize, and will try to present relevant data in later chapters, that feeling like an Origin has strong effects on behavior as compared to feeling like a Pawn. The distinction is continuous, not discrete—a person feels *more* like an Origin under some circumstances and *more* like a Pawn under others.

The personal aspect is more important motivationally than objective facts. If the person feels he is an Origin, that is more important in predicting his behavior than any objective indications of coercion. Conversely, if he considers himself a Pawn, his behavior will be strongly influenced, despite any objective evidence that he is free. An Origin has a strong feeling of personal causation, a feeling that the locus for causation of effects in his environment lies within himself. The feedback that reinforces this feeling comes from changes in his environment that are attributed to personal behavior. This is the crux of the concept of personal causation and it is a powerful motivational force directing future behavior. A Pawn has a feeling that causal forces beyond his control, or personal forces residing in others, or in the physical environment, determine his behavior. This constitutes a strong feeling of powerlessness or ineffectiveness.

Chapter 9

THE ATTRIBUTION PROCESS AND
INFERRED MOTIVATION

Perception and the Knowledge of Persons

A person can infer that another person is acting as an Origin, that the locus of causality for that person's behavior lies within himself; or he can infer that the other person is acting as a Pawn and, therefore, that the locus of causality for the person's behavior is really external to himself. In short, a person may use the Origin-Pawn variable as a category with which to order his perceptions of the behavior of people that he meets in social interaction. He may say to himself, "John is finally acting like himself (like an Origin) and doing what *he* wants in college, whereas before everything he did seemed to be dictated by his father's strong desire for him to become a doctor" (his behavior was seen as that of a Pawn).

When a person makes inferences about another person's motives he is acting like an amateur psychologist, i.e., he is doing something very similar in intent to what the motivational psychologist is trying to do in a more scientific way. As such, this behavior of attributing or inferring motives is doubly interesting to the psychologist. On the one hand, it is an interesting psychological phenomenon in itself, and on the other hand it is an attempt made by all people, most often without the aid of scientific training, to gain knowledge about other people in general and specifically about the motives, desires, and intentions that are related to behavior. It would be a mistake to assume that the layman's attempts at this are naive for all of us are human and engaged in social intercourse throughout our life and often psychologist and layman alike operate at a very sophisticated level in inferring characteristics of other people in the real world without consciously resorting to "scientific" techniques. At this level both parties are engaging in a quest for knowledge about other persons and both draw on empirical evidence of the observed behavior of the other person, and on personal knowledge of their own motives, desires, and intentions.

When the psychologist attempts to study the motives of others more scientifically, he may have great advantages over the layman in that he has techniques that allow him to remove himself from active participation in the situation so that his own predispositions will not be the primary determiners of his observations. Nowhere are the deficiencies of extreme objectivity more evident, however, than in the study of the acquisition of knowledge of the motives for other persons' behavior. Here, as in cases cited in Part II concerning the study of motives and learning, the objectivist dilemma has led psychologists to assume that motives like causes are inferred from the perception of physical characteristics and behavior manifested by the relevant objects in the world, namely, people. As a result psychology has attacked the problem of how people gain knowledge of other people as a problem of perception. The available data in this area are most often classified under the rubric of "person perception" or "social perception," and much of the research in this area starts with results deriving from studies of object perception and attempts to show that person perception may be subsumed under the more basic heading of object perception and that the relationships found to hold in the latter can be used to explain results in the former.

The area of research masquerading under the title "person perception" is not just an extension of the general study of the perception of objects, however; it is unique in that the "stimulus" studied and the subject "perceiving" it are similar creatures. This type of research is considering the *most important "stimulus" available* from the point of view of the psychology of human behavior, and is ultimately investigating the problem of how one human being learns about another. Such studies could form the central core of all human psychology, not just another area that curiosity has pricked us to investigate.

THE PROBLEM OF INFERENCES

Studies of object perception have often attempted to rule out conscious inferences as a determinant of responses. Controversy has raged over whether certain aspects attributed to a situation are immediately perceived or quickly arrived at through a process of inference so well learned as to be apparently immediate. Inferences made about other persons contain the unique element that one may infer from knowledge of his own feelings how another person may feel. It is probably easier and more immediate for a person to make inferences about another person than to make inferences about any other perceptual object because of the similarity between perceived and perceiver. The relevance of more immediate knowledge derived from personal experience seems to distinguish person perception from object perception and to demand a different view of the inference process in studies dealing with knowledge of other persons.

The problem of immediacy has always plagued the study of object perception because in perceiving an object a person has no direct source of knowledge about the object other than sense data, yet he often reacts as if he did. A person often reacts to a physical object as if it were another person, attributing, for instance, ominous motives to dark clouds and "menacing" waves. Attribution of human characteristics to physical objects is considered to be the result of primitive magical thinking. Such attribution to animals is anthropomorphism. Science has ruled that since the stimuli (clouds, waves, and animals) are not men it is an error to attribute man-like characteristics to them. This prohibition does not apply, of course, to the study of persons, but we are so accustomed to avoiding the "error" that we try to avoid it in this area also. We do this by failing to admit that we have a source of knowledge about ourselves that we do not have about other physical objects. We have private knowledge about our motives, for instance, which is often immediate as well as mediated by self observation, and such knowledge may well help in drawing inferences about other people. I surely would be wrong in attributing my motives to a stone, and I may be wrong in attributing them to a person. But I *may be right* when I attribute them to a *person*. In fact, I am probably in a better position to draw inferences about other people than I am to draw any other kind of inference.[1]

ATTRIBUTION NOT PERCEPTION

Persons are not merely "stimulus objects" and the process by which we get to know them is not perception but a *process of attribution*. What we are discussing is not person perception conceived narrowly in terms of perceptual processes, but the attribution process that occurs when-

---

[1] In contrast to the more accepted skepticism about the validity of inferences based on subjective knowledge, we shall stress their value. It should not be assumed, however, that we consider them to be infallible. For a discussion of biases and illusions that may appear in the attribution process, the reader is referred to Kelley (1967). He discusses the problem in much the same context as presented here and also ties it in with evidence concerning self-awareness of emotional states. Thus Kelley comments on studies by Bem (1965) and others that were presented in Chapter 5.

ever one person confronts another. We shall try to show that the really basic problems contained in this area demand a reconceptualization that accepts attribution and inferences as central, and the perceptual processes as only preliminary to this main event. Whereas much of the valuable research in the area of object perception has attempted to rule out the role of the perceiver, the great promise of the study of persons reacting to other persons lies precisely in capitalizing upon the truly psychological processes that occur within the subject between the time that he perceives another person and the time when he reacts to him.

We must consider at least four ways in which gaining knowledge of others is different from object perception. (1) A person is not a constant stimulus, but manifests dispositional properties that are more important in knowing him than are his perceptual characteristics. (2) Knowing a person is not like knowing a fact, nor is it even like knowing facts about him such as his perceptual characteristics. (3) Knowing a person involves knowing oneself, for self and other have similar characteristics. (4) To get to know a person is to change both the known and the knower.

A Person Is Not a Stimulus

It is impossible to assume that a person presents a constant stimulus to the observer. Certain physical characteristics are more or less unchanging, but these do not tell much about the person. The critical aspect for knowing a person is his behavior. When we say that person A knows person B well, we imply that A knows how B acts under certain conditions, how to deal with him, and what to expect of him. A is in a good position, because of his past experience, to predict B's behavior. Knowing one of the physical characteristics of B, such as that he has red hair, is little help in predicting his behavior. Knowing that B has a hot temper may be more useful, but a hot temper is not something that is perceived directly — it is something that is inferred from behavior. Every time A sees B he has red hair, and it does not matter whether it is a bright spring day or a dreary winter one, or whether B is talking to A or to his boss; but B is not in a temper or even showing angry behavior every time A sees him. To say that B is hot tempered is to say something about a dispositional property of B. (We even use the word colloquially, as in "sweet disposition.") Dispositional properties of persons are inferred from behavior. They are not perceived or immediately given. Evidence for a hot temper may be present in B's behavior today, but not tomorrow.

Another extremely important aspect used in evaluating the behavioral cues emitted by a person is the context. B may be hot tempered in dealing with his subordinates but "gentle as a lamb" in dealing with the boss; he may be domineering at work and subservient at home. In other words, a man's behavior varies depending on the situation in which he finds himself. The concept of role has been used by sociologists to account for differential behavior in different situations. In the extreme, one man may be seen as several different persons when he is playing different roles. The roles a man plays depend upon his knowledge of the people with whom he is interacting. In a job interview he tries to put his best foot forward; he may try to present himself as the type of person that he thinks the employer wants, and the employer may get a very different conception of him from that received by people with whom he works after he has taken the job. The sociologist, George Herbert Mead (1934), has stressed the different roles men play by showing their dependence on the audience for whom they are played. To the extent that men play many roles, wear many masks, they present quite different aspects to different perceivers. Erving Goffman has dramatized the varying character of cues presented by people in revealing themselves to others in *The Presentation of Self in Everyday Life* (1959). He sees behavior as a series of "performances" and discusses in some detail "the arts of impression management."

Sociologists such as Mead and Goffman have stressed the importance of the person's group or audience in determining his behavior. To a certain extent the person learns his part or his role from the group that makes up his audience. Thus the man may learn to play many roles in succession such as father and husband at home, business executive and big man with the secretaries at the office, and duffer on the golf course. When faced with the same audience on different occasions a person's behavior may show striking consistencies that are not evident when he is faced with another audience.

An individual may also show constancies of behavior in reacting to many or all of the people that he meets. Such constancies in behavior under widely different circumstances are called dispositional properties or personality characteristics. Psychologists look for dispositional aspects to explain behaviors under a broader conceptualization of personality characteristics that are carried from audience to audience. Knowledge of others is gained from assessing both role prescriptions and dispositional aspects.

The idea that a person can manipulate the impression he makes on others raises the question of authenticity. When is the authentic self being presented and when not? Authenticity implies some core characteristics that are part of the person being observed. To react to a person by saying, "He impresses me as a real phony," is to assume more than that the person is simply lying. Often such a reaction is the recognition of a dispositional aspect of a person who is constantly guarding against presenting himself as he really is. The fact that colloquial terms such as "phony" appear to have real meaning is simply indicative of the fact that people in general are quite sophisticated in their sensitivity to others and can deal meaningfully with a subtle judgment about an authentic self that might be presented by a person in playing various roles, and a self that does not ring true. Social psychology is far from understanding this level of sophisticated social interaction, although Halpin (1966) presents evidence of the far-reaching effect of the attribution of authenticity. We may suggest, however, that the inauthentic "phony" is seen most often as constrained to dissimulate, and hence as a Pawn to some external force. We might hypothesize that a person who is thought to be authentic would more often be seen as the Origin of his own behavior, unless he explicitly states that he is acting "under orders."

Knowing a Person Is More Than Knowing Facts About Him

If knowing a person were primarily a perceptual process, then once you knew a person you would always know him, just as once you can recognize a leopard by his spots you will always "know" a leopard when you see one. Such an over-simplified notion of knowing is inadequate. It assumes that knowing enough about a person to be able to recognize him is "to know" him. It further assumes that knowing, like perception, is an irreversible process. The "knowing" for which psychology is striving is not "knowing about"; it is not knowledge of certain perceptual characteristics that remain constant. Knowing another person is a process that is never complete as long as interaction with the person continues. One does not suddenly intuit once and for all what a person is like, nor does a rather complete and intimate knowledge of a person remain an accomplished fact. New information must constantly be available because people change.

Knowing Another Person Involves Knowing One's Self

Self knowledge has taken on the aura of a religious duty. The dictum, "know thyself," seems to have strong moral overtones. Regardless of the value of such overtones they have no place in our discussion. We are *not* saying that it is a "good thing" to know one's self. We *are* saying that both the knower and the known in human interaction are human beings and that for this reason the process of acquiring knowledge about another person may have special characteristics.

The known (another person) is more similar to the knower in this area than in any other area of knowledge. Personal knowledge may appropriately be used in assessing others, and the danger of anthropomorphism that we try to avoid in dealing with "things," i.e., the danger of assuming that the object of study has man-like characteristics, is no longer to be avoided. It is perfectly appropriate to attribute man-like characterisitics to another man. To the extent that I know about such characteristics from knowledge of myself, I may have knowledge about a man that is superior to that which I can obtain about an inanimate physical object. Men often assume that others are like themselves and this can be a source both of understanding and misunderstanding. Assuming that all others are like me can interfere with my knowledge of others, although it may give me an edge in learning to know other people who are really like me.

In order to understand one man's behavior in interacting with another and one man's knowledge of another, the psychologist needs to know about both men. One of the most interesting new aspects of research in this area is the mapping of the concepts used by the knower in reacting to another person. As we shall see, the understanding of the attribution process (a process whereby certain characteristics of a person are inferred from given knowledge) involves the study of the way trait constellations are formed and occur in cognition (Bruner, Shapiro, & Tagiuri, 1958), the study of correspondent inferences from behavior (Jones & Davis, 1965), and the study of personal constructs (Kelly, 1955) derived from knowledge of self and others.

Getting to Know Another Person Changes Both the Knower and the Known

Having pointed out that getting to know another person is a process over time, and that neither the knower nor the known can be considered constant during that time, the next step becomes obvious. An important source of change in both parties is obviously the interaction between them. This is the basic point of this section since in essence it implies the three preceding points.

Examples of interactive changes in behavior may be seen in games such as chess, where each move is contingent on the preceding move. Each person's behavior is to some extent a function of the behavior of the other. Jones and Thibaut (1958) refer to this as *reciprocally contingent behavior*. A more psychologically relevant example of such behavior may be found in strong interpersonal relationships that involve identification of a subordinate person with an idealized person as in some father-son, leader-follower, or teacher-student relationships. When the idealized leader behaves in a way that demonstrates that he has "feet of clay," i.e., is not so ideal after all, the follower's perception of the leader and his behavior toward him may change drastically. Even his feelings about himself may drastically change. As a consequence the leader's behavior toward him will change. For example, a study by de Charms and Bridgeman (1961), to be discussed later, shows that followers who assume that their leader is willing to try to comply with their wishes perceive him quite differently from followers who assume that their leader is unwilling to comply.

In this section we have stressed that to learn to know another person is not merely to react to constant perceptual aspects of that person but it is also to learn to predict the other's behavior from acquisition of knowledge of roles played by the person and dispositional properties such as motives and intentions of the person. To know another person is not to know once and for all, for knowledge of another person is a constantly changing, never ending process of getting to know. Aspects of both the perceiver and the knower are important. In short, neither the perceiver nor the perceived, neither the knower nor known, can be assumed to stand still. In fact, it is probably most important to assume that both parties are changed in the course of the interaction.

The Attribution Process

When a person attributes a personal characteristic to another person, he is using a general concept to explain specific instances of behavior. He is going beyond the realm of what he has observed into the realm of things that he knows about people in general (including himself) in an attempt to use concepts to "make sense" out of the other person's behavior. Some concepts make more sense than others, and some behaviors are easier to explain than others. To understand this attribution process more fully, it is necessary to seek the answers to the following questions: How does a person "know" whether his explanation of behavior is the "right" explanation? Where does a person acquire the storehouse of knowledge from which he derives the concepts used in the attribution process? What process does he go through in accepting one explanation and rejecting another?

Certain attributes are more appropriately related to specific behaviors than others. If a man consistently produces behavior that is in accord with stated intentions—if he arrives at meetings when he said he would, and does the work he said he would, etc.—it is more appropriate to say that he is "dependable" than to say that he is "friendly." One might, of course, make a case that these dependable-like behaviors actually resulted from his being "friendly," but it would take some explaining. A person who is surrounded by examples of his work that required intense effort is rarely accused of being lazy, yet he may think of himself as lazy. The hero of Thomas Wolfe's *You Can't Go Home Again,* standing amidst piles of manuscript in a Greenwich Village apartment, says to a friend, "Do you know what the reason is for all these words I've written? Well, I'll tell you. It's because I'm so damned lazy!" His friend, of course, is incredulous. The attribute "laziness" seems inappropriate on the evidence of extremely industrious behavior. Who is to say whether George Webber, Wolfe's hero, is lazy or industrious? Is his own attribution more valid than that of his friend?

These examples raise many questions. If we forego the temptation to look for some objective criterion and yet admit that implicit in the attribution process is some feeling of assent, some conviction that this interpretation is more "right" than that one, we may pose the most basic question: What leads to the conviction that a person is characterized by a certain attribute?

ATTRIBUTION: A MATCHING PROCEDURE

As a first approximation, the attribution process may be characterized as follows: During the course of interaction, person A observes specific behaviors performed by person B. At the same time person A has, from past experiences, a storehouse of knowledge about behavior of people in general as well as personal knowledge. In order to be able to comprehend all the discrete bits of data about behavior, A has some scheme of organization that allows him to chalk up many instances of behavior as similar in some sense and to store them all under one category. The category may take the form of a trait that he attributes to a person who performs these acts consistently. Getting work done on time, meeting appointments, etc., may fall into the category of dependability, and anyone who performs these behaviors with high probability is seen as dependable. The behaviors are attributed to a personal characteristic of the individual. The attribution process is essentially a matching between observed behaviors and categories or concepts supplied by the past experience of the observer.

There are several characteristics of the attribution process that may be illuminated by seeing it as a type of matching. First, we can ask what is being matched with what, i.e., what are the characteristics of the categories? Second, we can ask, what happens when a mismatch is encountered? Third, does the matching process affect the categories used by the person?

Conceptual categories are developed out of experience, and they may vary widely between individuals. The person is continuously using categories in perceiving the world (the simple process of recognition), and perceiving the world originally forms and continually molds and improves the categories.

In order to clarify the idea of categories as it applies to interpersonal relations, let us look at a technique developed by Kelly (1955) to determine what categories a person uses to distinguish between people he knows well. Kelly, in his Role Repertory Test, asks subjects to think of several people they know well, such as members of their own families and their friends. They are then asked to think of a specific triad of these people (e.g., brother, best male friend, and some other male acquaintance) and determine which two are alike and which one is different on an important personal quality. Subjects are then asked to identify the personal quality and to try to state its opposite. The personal quality and its opposite produced by the subject are assumed to be a dimension along which he characterizes people. The personal quality is a category in his head, an attribute that he finds appropriate to some people and not to others, a *personal construct* in Kelly's terminology. Some people use many personal constructs to help them understand and deal with their interpersonal world, whereas others use very few. Kelly proposes that the number of personal constructs used is an important characteristic differentiating individuals.

Bieri and Blacker (1956) have demonstrated that the number of personal constructs used is probably a general characteristic of the cognitive functioning of individuals. They found that people who use many personal constructs to differentiate between people they know well also use many categories to differentiate between nonhuman objects. People who use few personal constructs for people use few categories for nonhuman objects.

Personal constructs may take many forms, but the attribution process deals with some that are more "personal" than others. When a person assumes that his associate "intended" to hurt him by a certain remark, he is attributing a negative characteristic to him that is intensified by the belief that it was "intended." Where does the general concept of intention come from? Our most immediate knowledge of intentions is a personal thing deriving from our knowledge of our own intentions that lead us to specific behaviors. When we observe similar behaviors directed toward us by another, we match these behaviors with what we might do under similar circumstances. If the match is good, we are led to the assumption that a specific intention lay behind the act. Our personal knowledge of intentions is basically subjective and private, and we have no direct knowledge of the intentions of others. Yet we are more prone to judge others by the intentions that we infer from their acts than by the acts themselves.

The matching process that involves inferring intentions has a special characteristic that may be generalized to other attribution processes. Our personal knowledge about *our* intentions is immutable. We *know* why *we* do things. This characteristic of personal knowledge may provide the key to the most ellusive aspect of the attribution process, and the answer to the question posed earlier, How does a person "know" whether his explanation of behavior is the "right" explanation? Ultimately, the feeling of satisfaction that goes along with an explanation forms the criterion for acceptance of that explanation as opposed to others. Objective criteria may be sought by laymen and psychologists alike, but both probably base their real convictions on personal knowledge. As we saw in Chapter 8, Polanyi (1958) has built a strong case that even scientific decisions have this basis rather than the carefully objectified criteria most often presented to justify them.

This does not mean that empirical evidence is not weighed and considered, for evidence from the world forms part of personal knowledge. However, an important aspect that has been ignored in attempts to objectify science is the aspect of personal knowledge derived from personal experience, an aspect that may defy present objective measurement techniques.

In brief, one party to the matching process, the personal construct, derives in large part from personal experience and as a result is more certain to the person and more resistant to change. When the observed facts seem to fit very closely with personal constructs, the person will have a feeling of certainty about his explanation, and his attribution of characteristics to the observed person will be satisfying to him.

Little is yet known scientifically about such personal knowledge, but Kelly's Role Repertory Test and other techniques are beginning to increase our knowledge. The private aspect of personal knowledge is the starting point of the attribution process, the aspect that leads to the feeling of certainty. If a person is aware of an intention-behavior link in himself, i.e., has experienced a feeling of personal causation, he is more likely to attribute a similar intention to others who manifest the behavior. Thus the personal constructs utilized by a person should be intimately related to his own feelings of personal causation. Emphasis on self-knowledge should not, however, obscure the fact that starting with self-knowledge of intentions and resulting behavior, a person has ample opportunity in daily interaction to observe instances of similar behavior in others that serve to refine his personal constructs.

The *mismatch* between constructs and observed behavior confronts us with new problems. It is possible that the observer may find that the constructs he is using are inappropriate. Although he may feel certain that he explained a sequence of behavior by attributing an intention and hence a personality characteristic to the actor, he may find in further interaction that he was wrong. A trusting individual may join a back-biting group, attribute their initial kindness to genuine friendliness, and then find that he is suddenly "stabbed in the back." As a result, he may alter the category into which he places friendly behavior or he may develop the new category of "flatterer" if there is evidence that the friendly behavior was accompanied by an ulterior motive. As a result of such "broadening" experiences, the person may develop a larger repertoire of personal constructs.

Most often, mismatches or discrepancies result from unusual behavior. Having interacted with a person, the observer has tacitly noticed certain behaviors and has more or less consciously attributed them to certain characteristics of the observed person. In future interaction, the observer brings to the situation certain expectancies about the behavior of the other person that derive from characteristics attributed to him. The match, then, is between what is expected and what is observed. When the match is good and the person behaves as expected, interaction proceeds and the attribution process is undisturbed. It is when the match is bad that important changes occur. When unexpected behaviors occur, the observer must adjust his expectancies. A new and discrepant element has been added to his knowledge of the person, and this new bit of information may demand a change in the characteristics attributed to the person — the person may be seen in a new light. In short, unexpected behavior leads to a mismatch, and to the extent that this behavior is discrepant from the expected behavior, it will force changes in the observer's view of the person. In general, the more discrepant, unexpected, or non-common the behavior is, the more important it is in changing the person's knowledge about his acquaintance. Uncommon and unusual behaviors, therefore, tell us more about another person than common behaviors, assuming, of course, that they are characteristic of him and not just a result of some unusual circumstance not related to his personality.

Heider

Implicit in the theory underlying the attribution process is the assumption that a person in social interaction strives to improve the match between his expectancies, which derive from characteristics attributed to the person being observed, and the observed actions of the person. Heider

(1958), from whom many of the ideas concerning attribution derive, presents a balance model to be applied to interpersonal relations.[2]

In essence, Heider assumes that when a person likes another person, he attributes positive attitudes and characteristics to him. This forms a balanced state between the first person, the second person, and the attitude or characteristic. If, however, the first person likes the second but learns that he has a negative characteristic, the situation is unbalanced. Under these conditions the person will have a tendency to resolve the imbalance by reducing his liking for the person or by deciding that the negative characteristic is not so bad after all. This strain toward balance is basic to the theory.

Heider uses two concepts here that are important. The first is that any two things that are assumed to go together tend to be united in thought and expectancies. This process he calls *unit formation,* and it is the "process" in the "attribution process," since it joins the behavior and the attribute into a conceptual unit. Heider says, "Briefly, separate entities comprise a unit when they are perceived as belonging together. For example, members of a family are seen as a unit; a person and his deed belong together" (Heider, 1958, p. 176).

Heider's second important concept is that positive and negative sentiments may be held toward another person, his acts, or his attitudes. "A sentiment refers to the way a person p feels about or evaluates something. The 'something' may be another person, $o,$ or an impersonal entity $x.$ Sentiments may be roughly classified as positive and negative" (Heider, 1958, p. 174).

The concept of balance between units and sentiment includes the notion that imbalance induces a pressure toward change in the system. "The concept of balanced state designates a situation in which the perceived units and the experienced sentiments co-exist without stress; there is thus no pressure toward change, either in the cognitive organization or in the sentiment" (p. 176).

An example of the whole process is given by Heider as follows: "Let us suppose p likes $o,$ and p perceives or hears that o has done something,

---

[2]We have chosen Heider's theory for presentation because it is the direct antecedent of the concept of the attribution process. However, several other theoretical positions having similar elements make the basic assumption of a pressure toward harmony. The basic notion has affinities with the concept of drive reduction in learning theory (Hull, 1943). More closely related, however, are Festinger's theory (1957) of cognitive dissonance, Rosenberg and Abelson's (1960) analysis of cognitive balancing, Pepitone's (1964) concept of cognitive consistency, and Osgood and Tannenbaum's (1955) principle of congruity.

which we call *x; x* may be something *p* likes and admires, that which is positive for *p*, or *x* may be something which is negative for *p*. If *p* likes *o* and *o* does something positive, this situation is pleasant for *p;* it is fitting and harmonious. As a triad the situation presents a balanced case characterized by three positive relations: . . . However, if the liked *o* does something that is negative, imbalance results: the triad contains two positive relations. . . and one negative relation. . . . This is an unpleasant situation for *p*. Tension will arise and forces will appear to annul the tension" (p. 207).

The essence of Heider's theory that underlies the attribution process is contained in the above statements. The basic concepts of balance, sentiment, and unit formation emphasize the importance of mismatches that lead to unbalanced relationships. In the attribution process, these mismatches are between observed behavior and expectancies derived from characteristics attributed to the observed person. The final connection between attribution and unit formation is stated by Heider. "Attribution, the linking of an event with its underlying conditions, involves a kind of unit formation" (p. 89).

We started this section on the attribution process as a matching procedure with three questions and confronted directly the first two, namely, What is being matched with what?, and, What happens when a mismatch is encountered? The third question: Does the matching process affect the categories used by the person? has been answered in examining the first two questions. Clearly the categories change; personal constructs are formed, and they change in the course of interaction. The most important element producing change is the mismatch between expectancies derived from the categories and observed behavior.

LINKS BETWEEN ATTRIBUTION AND BEHAVIOR

The crux of the attribution process is the formation of the link between behavior and dispositional attributes, or in Heider's terms, unit formation. We cannot assume constant links because the same behavior may derive from different dispositions, and the same disposition may lead to different behaviors. It does little good (and may stop investigation) if we assume that all people have an innate capacity to infer dispositional attributes from behavior, yet people obviously are capable of making such inferences. The conditions under which such inferences are formed must be studied.

In developing the notion of unit formation, Heider relies heavily on the gestalt laws of perceptual organization. The basic concept is that of "belongingness" (a "unit" is formed between things that "belong" together). Unfortunately, "belongingness" is hard to define. Assuming that the laws of perceptual organization apply as well to cognitive organization, Heider lists *similarity, proximity, common fate, good continuation, set,* and *past experience* as factors in cognitive unit formation. This is a mixed bag, but all have been shown to be related to perceptual organization (cf. Koffka, 1935). It is not difficult to see how some of them might be important in categorizing people or behaviors. It is more difficult to see how each of them could be used to form a unit from a behavior and an attribute, from an act and a dispostion. Heider says, however, "Unit-forming factors particularly relevant to groupings involving persons can be seen in the following: Things that are made by a person, or that are his property, belong to him. Changes that are attributed to a person as effects of his action also belong to him in a certain sense" (Heider, 1958, p. 178). Certainly the word "belong" captures the relationship between a person and his act, but the concept remains essentially aloof from attempts of further analysis.

Definitions of concepts used to describe the feeling we have of a relationship between acts and dispositions seem to be unsatisfactory. To a certain extent this is probably attributable to the element of personal knowledge that enters into this feeling. Such knowledge is notoriously difficult to express in words, but this does not put it beyond the reach of scientific research. People can consistently make distinctions between situations in which they are highly confident of their inferences about a person's attributes, and situations in which they are not confident of them. By studying the conditions that lead to high confidence and comparing them to conditions that do not, much can be learned about the attribution process.

Jones and Davis (1965) set out to identify conditions under which there is a strong *correspondence* between acts and inferred dispositions, a strong feeling that the act and the disposition belong together, that the disposition leads to the act. The meaning of the word "correspondence" is easier to keep in mind if we note immediately that it is defined operationally in terms of the confidence a person reports in assigning a trait attribute to a person that he knows or has observed.

> *Correspondence* refers to the extent that the act and the underlying characteristic or attribute are similarly described by the inference. . . . The perception of a link between a particular intention or disposition and a particular action may therefore be called an attribute-effect linkage. . . . *Given an attribute-effect linkage which is offered to explain why an act occurred, correspondence increases as the judged value of the attribute departs from the judge's conception of the average person's standing on that attribute"* (Jones & Davis, 1965, pp. 223–224).

Although the last sentence is introduced as a "formal definition of the correspondence concept," it seems rather to spell out one of the major conditions related to the strength of a correspondent inference. Actually a formal definition of "correspondence" seems almost as elusive as a definition of unit formation. Illustrative examples are equally unenlightening, since they all appear so obvious — domineering action results from the underlying trait of dominance, and the inference that connects the two is "correspondent."

Jones and Davis are not satisfied with such empty definitions and immediately proceed to give us an operational definition and to spell out conditions under which variability in the operational measure will occur. The operational definition is contained in the following passage: "As a simple example of how the concept of correspondence can be put to use in a research setting, we may provide the perceiver with rating scales designed to measure the strength of the trait attributed to the actor and his confidence in making his rating. The perceiver's certainty that the actor is extreme on a trait which provides sufficient reason for the action's occurrence is, then, the level of correspondence of his inference" (p. 224).[3]

Lacking an independent criterion, we can at least concentrate on the conditions that lead both experimenter and subject to be confident in their judgments. By such an approach, we are confronting the fundamental phenomenon (the feeling of confidence) and have stopped searching for the will-of-the-wisp "certainty."

Jones and Davis have isolated the concepts of "non-common effect," "personalism," and "hedonic relevance" as important criteria leading to confidence in attribution (degree of correspondence). We have already touched on concepts similar to these. *Non-common effects* may take the form of unusual or unexpected results of behavior that are more important in gaining knowledge about another person than "common effects" that are expected; but Jones and Davis do not use "non-common" as a synonym for unusual. To say an effect is unusual leaves unspecified the context within which it may be considered unusual. "Unexpected in a specific context" becomes more precise. Jones and Davis, however, attempt to be very specific by evaluating the effects of behavior in the context of choice. If it can be determined what the person did *and* what he chose *not* to do, then the effects that resulted from the

---

[3]Note that this "operational definition" does not truly "objectify" the concept. Rather it is more in keeping with our discussion of operational analysis in Chapters 2 and 8 in that it succeeds in making specific communication about a personal state (confidence) possible.

chosen behavior and would not have resulted from the non-chosen behavior are assumed to be the crucial effects in the choice. Any effect that would have resulted from both chosen and non-chosen behavior (common effects to both) could not be crucial in determining the choice. Thus the effects that were non-common between the chosen and non-chosen behaviors give information about why the choice was made and hence about the attributes of the person.

Personalism is the Jones and Davis term that stresses the importance of assessing a person's intention. If someone directs a nasty comment to me he intends to hurt me; he levels a "personal" insult. If the nasty comment is impersonally directed, it is more difficult to assess the intention. *Hedonic relevance* is similar to Heider's concept of "sentiment." If an act has hedonic relevance for me, it carries either a negative or a positive implication for my well-being; it has good or bad consequences for me.

Unexpected Behaviors and Non-Common Effects

An experimental study by Jones, Davis, and Gergen (1961) was performed to test derivations from the theory of correspondent inferences with special relevance to the observation of non-common effects. The study tests a hypothesis that is central to two propositions. First, a person may draw inferences about another person without actually knowing him, but just from knowledge of his role. Second, when a mismatch occurs between expectations and observed behavior, the resulting inference from behavior should be more confidently held by the observer. The study can be seen as an example of the effects of inferences drawn from knowing the role that a person is expected to play. A comparison was made of persons acting as would be expected by their role (in-role behavior) with persons acting in a way that would not be expected by their role (out-of-role behavior). Of primary concern to us is the hypothesis that out-of-role behavior leads to more confident inferences about personal characteristics than in-role behavior.

One hundred and thirty-four male college students listened to prepared tape recordings of interviews in which the interviewee was aspiring to become either an astronaut or a submariner. In the course of the tape the interviewer first described characteristics of the ideal astronaut or submariner. The ideal astronaut was described as a person who was essentially a "loner" (inner-directed). In sharp contrast, the ideal submariner was described as a person who was essentially a person who liked other people in close contact (other-directed).

The second part of the tape comprised the actual interview during which the interviewee revealed something about himself. One of the interviewees who was an aspirant astronaut revealed himself to be a person who seemed to fit the description of the needed characteristics of the astronaut. The other aspirant astronaut revealed himself to be a person who did not seem to fit the description of the needed characteristics of the astronaut. In the first case, the interviewee manifested "in-role" behavior and in the latter he manifested "out-of-role" behavior. A similar contrast was developed in the two tape recordings of the interviews with aspirant submariners.

The basic independent variable was "in-role" *vs.* "out-of-role" behavior. The scheme devised allowed the experimenters to investigate identical behavior that was either in-role or out-of-role, since "in-role" behavior for the astronaut was "out-of-role" behavior for the submariner, and vice-versa.

The dependent variable of the experiment that is of most interest to us was the rating of the confidence with which the subjects attributed relevant traits to the interviewee. Each subject was asked to rate the interviewee on a series of traits (to engage in the attribution process) and to fill out a five-point confidence scale in which he stated how confident he was in his attribution. This measure of confidence is what Jones and Davis (1965) see as the operational form of their concept of correspondence.

The basic hypothesis of the experiment is that attributions based on observations of out-of-role behavior will be made with more confidence than attributions based on observations of in-role behavior. In the terms of the experiment, the astronaut who is other-directed should be rated with greater confidence than the astronaut who is inner-directed, whereas the submariner who is inner-directed should be rated with greater confidence than the submariner who is other-directed.

The results of the experiment unequivocally supported the hypothesis. Table 9.1 shows the mean confidence in attribution where a low score is lack of confidence. Observations of in-role behavior do not give the subjects as much confidence as do observations of out-of-role behavior.[4]

Jones and Davis' (1965) explanation using the concept of non-common inferences runs as follows:

> In-role behavior does not lead to confident, correspondent inferences because such behavior has multiple consequences and many of these are high in cultural

---

[4]We have confined our presentation to the data relevant to confidence. The reader is referred to the original article for evidence that the experimental manipulations worked, and for results from other dependent measures. Particularly interesting is the finding that in-role behavior is recalled with greater accuracy than out-of-role behavior.

TABLE 9.1
Mean Confidence of Ratings in the
Astronaut-Submariner Experiment[a]

Out-of-role behavior	In-role behavior
Other-directed astronaut	Inner-directed astronaut
$\bar{X} = 15.85$	13.55
$s = 2.22$	2.45
$N = 33$	33
Inner-directed submariner	Other-directed submariner
$\bar{X} = 14.97$	14.00
$s = 2.39$	2.19
$N = 37$	31

[a] Data supplied by Edward E. Jones, Duke University.

desirability. Most people want to avoid embarrassing others by not meeting their expectations, most people want to gain the rewards implicit in approval from authority figures, most people wish to manifest their intelligence by showing that they understand what is required of them, and so on. Each of these effects is a "plausible reason" for in-role behavior in the experiment just described. On the other hand, plausible reasons for out-of-role behavior (i.e., those with a reasonable degree of assumed social desirability) are comparatively scarce. One of the few noncommon effects of behavior at variance with role demands is the satisfaction of expressing one's true nature. This effect is also a possible accompaniment of in-role behavior, but in that case it exists in the choice circle along with many other effects. Since there are fewer noncommon effects in the astronaut-other and submariner-inner choices, the effect of "being oneself" forms the basis of a more correspondent inference in these conditions and the interviewee's behavior tends to be taken at face value (Jones & Davis, 1965, p. 236).

Personalism

A more motivationally relevant factor that is important in the attribution process is the intention of the actor to do harm or benefit to the perceiver. If the perceiver knows that an insult is meant for him personally, his reaction to the insulter will be strong as compared to the reaction to a similar statement that was impersonally made. This factor of intention of the actor is called *personalism* by Jones and Davis. When a person infers that an act or an insult is intentional, he is implicitly assuming that the actor purposely chose the action. The assumption of choice is an important aspect that increases the observer's confidence in his inference about personal characteristics of the actor.

There is very little experimental evidence to support the hypothesis that personalism (the inference of intention) affects the confidence of attribution. It would be easy enough to test using techniques developed in the study of aggression. Pastore (1952), for instance, found that frustration leads to aggression against the frustrater primarily when his action is seen as deliberately antagonistic (intentional or personal). Thus a person standing in the cold, waiting for a bus, is frustrated if a bus goes by without stopping for him, but his reaction to the frustration will differ according to the situation. If the bus is obviously overcrowded with no room for him, his reaction will be quite different from his reaction if the bus is obviously not crowded. In the latter case, he will infer that the bus driver deliberately passed him by. What would be needed to test the hypothesis under consideration would be a measure of the confidence with which the frustrated person would attribute characteristics to the bus drivers under the two conditions.

The bus driver example demonstrates that the inference that the action was dictated by nonintentional conditions (overcrowding) is important. In general, it may be hypothesized that if the observer can assume that the actor is not entirely responsible for his actions, the observer will be less upset by negatively relevant behavior. Using reasoning similar to this, Jones and de Charms (1958) hypothesized that an observer who was directed to take into account the past history of maladjustment of a person would be less punitive toward that person than toward a person with no past history of maladjustment, i.e., the former person could be "excused" but the latter must be held accountable for his actions. In the experiment, the subjects were evaluating prisoners of war who had been returned from Korea, and the action of the prisoners (giving information to the enemy) was not personally relevant to the observer-rater. Under these conditions, the opposite of what was hypothesized resulted. The prisoner who was presented as being maladjusted was treated more punitively and liked less than the well-adjusted prisoner.

Jones, Hester, Farina, and Davis (1959) refined the hypothesis using the concept of personalism and tested the dual hypothesis that if an observer is directly and intentionally derogated by another person, a maladjusted derogator will upset the person less than a well-adjusted one because he can assume that the attack of the maladjusted person is attributable to the maladjustment, but must conclude that the attack of the well-adjusted person cannot be reasoned away. He will, therefore, dislike the well-adjusted derogator more than the poorly adjusted one. An uninvolved bystander however, will like the well-adjusted person better because the attack is not relevant to himself, and the well-adjusted person is, in general, more appealing. The crucial difference between the reactions of the involved person and the bystander is that the attack is personally directed to the involved person — the critical variable in personalism. Evidence from the study designed to test these hypotheses clearly supports the inference that personalism is an important factor in determining reactions in interpersonal interaction.

Hedonic Relevance

"The hedonic relevance of an effect is a function of its motivational significance for the perceiver; does the particular action consequence promote or undermine the perceiver's values; does it fulfill or obstruct his purposes?" (Jones & Davis, 1965, p. 237).

Using this definition, Jones and Davis propose that as hedonic relevance to the perceiver increases, his attributions will be made with greater confidence (inferences will be more highly correspondent). The reasoning underlying this hypothesis involves the notion of conceptual categories that we discussed earlier in this chapter. Observed actions may be cognitively organized around affective categories. Things that are good for me are categorized together, and things that are bad for me are categorized together. In short, hedonic relevance is a major basis for cognitive categorization. If the actor is perceived to be doing something that is good for me, I will be confident of my inferences about him. The same is true if he is perceived to be doing something that is bad for me. When his acts are neutral to me, I will not be as confident of my attributions of personal characteristics to him.

There is little evidence to test this hypothesis directly. Several experiments have manipulated hedonic relevance (Jones & de Charms, 1957; Kleiner, 1960; Pepitone, 1950), but none measured confidence of attribution. We can, however, look at the way hedonic relevance has been manipulated and note its effect on trait ratings. Jones and de Charms (1957) asked small groups of subjects to work individually on an experimental task. All subjects eventually completed the task, but an experimental confederate who was thought by the subjects to be one of the group always failed. In the *individual fate* condition, the subjects won prizes by solving the problem, and the failure of the confederate was irrelevant to them. In the *common fate* condition, however, no subject received a reward unless all members, including the confederate, were successful. His failure, therefore, was extremely relevant to these other members. This manipulation was the variation of hedonic relevance.

In one half of the groups, the subjects were led to believe that failure on the part of the confederate was attributable to lack of ability, a characteristic which, after all, he could do nothing about. In the other half of the groups, the subjects were led to believe that the confederate's failure was attributable to lack of motivation, i.e., that he could have succeeded but that he did not care enough to try. As a result of this procedure, the subjects were given the characteristic (either lack of ability or lack of motivation) to which the failing behavior should be attributed. These experimental manipulations presented the subjects with a failing person who did not try or one who could not have succeeded even if he did try. The failure of the subject was hedonically relevant for one half of the subjects, by keeping them from getting their reward, and irrelevant for the other half of the subjects.

In this experiment, the variable of hedonic relevance strongly affected the subjects' evaluation of the confederate. When the confederate's failure resulted in no reward for all subjects (common fate condition) he was rated very low on such traits as "competent," "dependable," "likable," etc., *if* he was seen as not trying. When it was assumed that he lacked ability, he was not rated low on the same traits. When his failure had no effect on the rewards for other subjects (individual fate condition), their ratings of him were more or less neutral, even if he was seen as not trying. The data support the hypothesis that hedonic relevance is important in the attribution process; but whether it affects confidence of ratings remains untested.

In summary, Jones and Davis (1965) have taken definite steps to clarify conditions that increase confidence of attribution (perceived correspondence between acts and dispositions). Three important factors are *(a)* effects of the observed action that would not have occurred if the actor had chosen another act (non-common effects), *(b)* the perceived intention of the actor (personalism), and *(c)* the positive or negative consequences of the act for the perceiver (hedonic relevance). Such an analysis takes us into the realm of understanding what factors promote the feeling of certainty in attribution, venturing beyond the vague hypothesis that certain acts are somehow cognitively associated with specific dispositions.

Inferred Motives and Causes

Having discussed some of the aspects of gaining knowledge of others and the attribution process, we may now confront the most important aspect of this area from the point of view of motivation. The process by which we attribute *characteristics* to a person has much in common with the process by which we infer his *motives*. Frequently, the two are treated together and not clearly distinguished. Heider (1958), for instance, treats the inferences that a person is "trying," and the attribution of "ability" to that person, as resulting from similar processes. Jones and Davis (1965) treat "personalism" (the attribution of intention) as a subcategory of the general attribution process. For us, motivational inferences hold a place of special interest. This preeminence may derive from the importance of motivational inferences as contained in Heider's (1958) concept of the locus of causality; but we cannot avoid the implication that inferences concerning motives and intentions are more central to the issues involved in getting to know another person than is the attribution of traits such as dependability, intelligence, and politeness.

Men learn to distinguish between situations in which it can be assumed that a person is acting of his own accord, and situations in which he is coerced. In Heider's (1958) terms, this is the distinction between inferring that the locus of causality for behavior is internal to the actor, and inferring that it is external to the actor. In our terms, this is the distinction between seeing a person as an Origin and seeing him as a Pawn.

THE PERCEPTION OF PHYSICAL CAUSALITY

The historic roots of Heider's (1958) concept of locus of causality lie in Michotte's (1963) studies of the perception of physical causality that were first published in French in 1946. In light of our discussion of physical causality in the first section of this book and of our discussion in this chapter of perception *vs.* attribution and inference, it may seem strange to turn now to a study of the *perception of physical causality*. As in the case of para-mechanical analogies concerning the impact of motivation on learning noted in Chapters 1 and 4, we again find the notion of physical causality used as a starting place for studies of motivational phenomena. As such Michotte's work is of historic interest in its impact on the work of Heider (1958) and Thibaut and Riecken (1955a,b) that will be discussed. In this instance, however, the clear statement of the mechanical relationships may have helped to emphasize the inadequacy of the para-mechanical analogy by forcing Heider to stress the distinction between *internal* and *external* loci of causality, rather than set a mold whereby all internal loci were rejected because they did not conform to the analogy with physical causation.

Michotte

To study empirically the stimulus elements that lead to the inference of physical causation (or of motivation), the subject is used as an instrument that reports the phenomenological observation of causation (or motivation) as the psychologist observes stimulus variations in the environment of the subject. This method was used by Michotte (1963) in studying the inference of causality from the activity of physical objects. As he says, "In order to understand perception of causality, the first thing to do is to try to produce experimentally some characteristic perceptions of causation and to determine empirically their conditions" (quoted in Beardslee & Wertheimer, 1958, p. 382; all of the following quotations from Michotte in English are from this source). In a series of experiments, Michotte presented two simple square objects to his subjects. One of the objects moved at a uniform rate from the left hand side of the visual field toward the second object that was fixated by the subject. When the first object made contact with the second, the first object stopped and the second object moved away in the direction of motion of the first object at approximately the same speed.

"The result of this experiment is perfectly clear: the observers see object A push object B and *drive it, throw it forward, cast it, give it impulsion*. The perception is clear; it is *A that makes B proceed, that produces* its movement" (p. 384).

Thus, Michotte set up a simple experiment that reliably leads subjects to infer causation. He isolated two types of stimulus behaviors both of which lead to the causal inference. In one of these, A, the initially moving rectangle, upon contact with B, continues to move along with B in the same direction. This Michotte calls the carrying effect *(l'effet Entrainement)*. In a second situation, A appears to push B forward in what Michotte calls the launching effect *(l'effet Lancement)*. Michotte stresses the fact that he calls these *effects* in the same sense that physicists designate particular facts as effects. He says, "As a matter of terminology it helps to avoid any misunderstanding and to make it clear that it is a matter of a phenomenal given *sui generis*" (p. 385).

Possibly the most interesting phase of Michotte's series of studies is the demonstration that with a very slight change in the stimulus components, the inference of causation can be completely eradicated.

> The specific character of experienced causality is particularly well illuminated when one slightly modifies experiments 1 and 2 by introducing an interval of a fifth of a second or more between the two phases of the experiment (that is, between the moment object A joins object B and when B begins moving in turn, whether accompanied by A or not), and then directly compares the perceptions experienced with and without an interval.
>
> The presence of the interval makes the perception of causality disappear totally.
>
> The result of the comparison is striking, and all observers agree that the perceptions are radically different. On the one hand, there are two intrinsically linked events, of which one "gives rise to" the other; and on the other hand, two sharply

separate events which occur successively, and neither of which presents the slightest causal characteristics (p. 386).

We have here a simple demonstration of some of the stimulus components which lead to the causal inference. The critical aspect is the temporal sequence; any time lapse between the end of phase one (when A contacts B) and the beginning of phase two (when B begins to move) destroys the perception of causality. Temporal sequence has long been discussed in the area of causation and has led to the paradox that the cause must precede the effect. But, as seen here, the cause must also be in some sense concomitant with the effect.

Michotte feels that the result that "it is possible to make the perception of causality appear or disappear at will . . . permits the categorical exclusion of any attempt to reduce this perception to a 'projection' into things, to a result of the efficacy of our internal activities, or to a secondary 'interpretation' based on past experience and on acquired knowledge" (pp. 382–383). It is clear that the perception of causality apparently arises from specific stimulus elements in the enviroment, and may be eradicated by minute changes in these stimulus elements. It is not clear, however, why these experiments categorically exclude any interpretation based on past experience or acquired knowledge. It is logically possible that the subjects have learned to attribute causality to certain types of subtle temporal sequences and not to attribute it to others.

Piaget

An interesting possibility to consider is that people learn to attribute effects to chance rather than to causes. This possibility is in a sense the reverse of the argument presented by a Humian interpretation of the learning of causal inferences. Rather than isolate the stimulus elements that strongly lead to the causal inference and try to account for the learning of these, one might argue that the human being initially assumes a causal relationship between all temporally contiguous events in the environment. The problem then would be to isolate perceptual elements that lead to the learning that some things are "less causal" than others. There is some evidence that children at first assume a causal relationship between any two events that occur in contiguity.

Piaget (1955) finds that at an early age the child assumes a meaningful relationship between any two contiguous events in the environment; he has arrived at this conclusion by analyzing the questions asked by children at various ages. "The material on which we shall work consists of 1125 spontaneous questions asked of Mlle. Veihl over a period of ten months by Del, a boy between 6 and 7. . . . These questions were taken down in the course of daily talks lasting 2 hours; each talk was a sort of lesson by conversation, but of a very free character during which the child was allowed to say anything he liked. These talks had begun long before lists were made of the questions, so that the child found himself in a perfectly natural atmosphere from the start. Also, what is more important, he never suspected that his questions were being noted in any way" Piaget, 1955, p. 172).

After collecting the questions, Piaget set out to categorize them in some meaningful way. His first step was to concentrate on "why" questions and he found three large groups of children's "whys": *(a)* causal explanation, *(b)* motivation, and *(c)* logical justification. "Let us designate as *motivation* that sort of explanation which accounts, not for a material phenomenon, . . . but for an action or a psychological state" (p. 175).

Interestingly enough, Piaget finds a bit of a paradox in the questions of this child. On the one hand, before the age of 7 or 8 years (he has comparison data with other questions of older children) the concern of the child with causal relationships is very small, either with respect to physical objects or to psychological actions, i.e., motivation. One might conclude from this fact alone that here is strong support for the empiricists' notion that the human being learns to infer causal sequences and motivational antecedents by observing concomitant events in his environment. However, the paradox arises when we note that the questions Piaget has recorded seem to indicate that the child is little concerned about the causal relationships at this point not because he has no idea of causation or motivation, but precisely because the idea is so strong that he assumes it to be present and apparently feels that it is trivial to ask about it. What he does ask about, however, is intended to check what he has observed. Thus, his notion of causality is quite different from that of the adult. It is, in a sense, omnipresent, assumed between any two events. Thus, one might argue that what the child learns at about 6 years of age is when *not* to make causal inferences rather than when *to* make them.

One implication of Piaget's discussion is that some discrepancy or mismatch between the omnibus assumption of causality in the very young child and the actual events in the environment leads to the development of the distinction between causation and chance. This is the way many researchers feel that the idea of motivation has developed. Freud (1901) and McClelland (1951) would say that one of the main uses for the concept of motivation is to explain the exceptions that occur in behavior rather than to explain expected behavior. Here we have another example of a *mismatch* as discussed above. The tendency to assume a causal relationship between two events occurs very early, and the distinction between two events that occur together by chance and an event that is linked to another "causally" may develop over time. What is learned is *when not to attribute causation,* i.e., when to appeal to chance, rather than when to attribute causation.

The implication drawn from Piaget's data is that the causal concept appears very early in childhood. We have suggested in Chapter 1 that it may come from the universal experience of being a cause. Every child learns that his behavior can result in effects in his environment, and one of his major problems is to learn how to behave in such a way as to produce desired effects. It can be assumed that every human being has some concept of himself as an origin of changes in his environment—of himself as a *causal agent.* In addition, the child also learns that he cannot always produce the effects that he wants, and that often he is at the mercy of stronger agents that force him to do things that he does not want to do. From this personal knowledge, which may be unverbalized and originally derived from purely private subjective impressions, he forms knowledge of motivation in himself. The result is the formation of conceptual categories all of which are basically motivational, all of which hinge on the notion that a person *can* produce effects (Heider's concepts of "can" and "try"), and all of which are organized around affective consequences, good or bad results (Jones and Davis' "hedonic relevance").

It is but a short step from assuming such motivational categories from personal knowledge to postulating that these categories are used in gaining knowledge of other people, i.e., in the attribution process. If these assumptions are correct, we should find that the inference that a person is motivated is very important.

THE ATTRIBUTION OF MOTIVES

Heider (1958) stresses the situation in which one person perceives another person as the cause of an event. Thus, much of his work deals with person perception and phenomenal causality. He has isolated two factors that he feels are phenomenologically important in the perception of personal causality. These he calls personal and impersonal causality. The distinction is between the perception of personal causation and the perception of physical causation in interaction with inanimate objects of the physical world. "What we have designated as personal causality refers to instances in which *p* causes *x* intentionally . . . this has to be distinguished from other cases in which *p* is a part of the sequence of events. For example, *p* may cause *x* unintentionally merely because his physical or social being exerts some influence on the environment" (Heider, 1958, p. 100).

Two important aspects which he discusses in connection with personal causality are equifinality and local cause.

> . . . if I meet a person who has certain intentions in regard to myself—for instance, who wants to get me into a certain state—that means that my environment contains conditions that are convergently directed towards this state, and if the person has enough power, this state will sooner or later be brought about whatever I do. In short, personal causality is characterized by equifinality, that is, the invariance of the end and the variability of the means. . . .
>
> Yet this is not the only characteristic of personal causality, for we must distinguish the equifinality in this case from that which sometimes occurs in physical systems, for instance, a system like a pendulum or a marble in a bowl which, in the end, will always come to rest at the lowest point regardless of where it started. In the inorganic world where a particular end state may be enforced, the forces leading to the unitary effect are not controlled by any part of the system. There is no power hierarchy, no leader-led distinction between the parts, and the process is understood in terms of the whole system. On the other hand, in the case of personal causality, the invariant end is due to the person. Because the person controls the causal lines emanating from himself, he not only is the initial source of the produced change, but he remains the persistent cause. Here, if anywhere, one can speak of a local cause, the second characteristic of the causal network in personal causality (pp. 101–102).

In attributing personal causality, two major factors are seen as important by Heider. In order to assume that a person is causally responsible for an action, the perceiver usually infers that the person *(a)* has the ability to perform the action, and *(b)* was motivated to perform the action, i.e., tried. Thus, Heider develops the concepts of *can* and *try*. "The distinction between can and try is related to the distinction between learning and motivation in scientific psychology" (p. 109).

According to Heider, the inference that a person can, or has the ability, to perform an act derives from inferences about forces residing within the individual in interaction with forces from the environment. Thus the success of an act may be attributed to the fact that the person is highly skillful, or to the fact that the environment presents a very favorable setting for the act to succeed. Under some environmental conditions great skill is required or demanded for certain acts to be successful, whereas under other conditions very little skill is required to perform the same acts. The inference that skill is involved appears to be learned from past experience with variable environmental conditions and interaction with certain types of task. Trying is inferred from the instrumental activity engaged in by the subject; difficulty may be inferred from the intensity of the instrumental activity, plus success or failure in light of what the perceiver knows from past experience about the probability of success or failure in the task. If we know nothing about the task difficulty, we may infer from intense, but unsuccessful, instrumental activity either extreme task difficulty or extreme ineptness on the part of the actor. As soon as we have some notion about the general difficulty of the task we can infer something about the level of ability of the actor.

These inferences are valid only if we can assume a constant level of motivation, i.e., that the actor is trying to succeed in the situation. However, if we know that the task is moderately easy and the actor has the requisite ability to succeed and yet fails, we may infer that he was not trying, i.e., that his motivation was not high enough. In this instance at least, it is necessary to make the inference of ability before one can infer the level of motivation of the actor. Again the level of motivation is often inferred from the intensity of the instrumental activity of the actor.

The concept of trying also has a personal aspect and an impersonal aspect. The problem here is clearly a motivational one involving the inference of intention plus the inference of the origin of intention. Person A may engage in an activity because he himself wishes to do so, in which case Heider would say that the locus of causality is internal to the person; or he may engage in the action because he is asked, induced, or forced to do so by some other person in the environment, in which case the locus of causality is external to the person.

In summary, the concept of "try" that may be perceived as the result of an internal or external locus of causality is most important in forming inferences about motivation, and is most often inferred from instrumental activity. It should be noted that motivational inferences may often be made from good or bad consequences associated with goal attainment or the lack thereof. The concept of "can" that develops from inferences about personal and environmental forces is not directly the source of motivational inferences but interacts with the concept of "try" in leading to such inferences.

Effects of Willingness and Ability on the Invocation of Moral Sanctions

Schmitt (1964) has studied the effects of willingness and ability to perform an act on the *invocation of moral sanctions* in attempting to influence the person to perform an act. He presented his subjects with four different hypothetical situations, all of which might conceivably involve moral obligation. Briefly, the situation involved (a) the promise by an uncle to give a boy a job when he completed college, (b) the obligation of a father to send his son to college, (c) the obligation of a doctor to treat a child on Sunday when he was not working, and *(d)* the obligation of a friend to repay at a specific time $2000 borrowed a year earlier. Each of these four situations was presented in four different conditions in which the potentially obligated person was shown to have one of the four possible combinations of the two attributes—ability to perform the obligated act and willingness to perform the obligated act. The questionnaire devised to present these fictitious situations thus confronted each subject with sixteen slightly different situations developed out of each of the four basic ones, consisting of four in which the object of influence was willing and able to perform the act, four in which he was willing and unable, four in which he was able and unwilling, and four in which he was unable and unwilling. This constitutes a two-by-two design of willingness or ability that is analogous to Heider's notion of the concepts of "can" and "try."

As a first step in the experiment, Schmitt demonstrated that the independent variables of willingness and ability were perceived by subjects who were not used again in the second phase. In the second step of the procedure, different subjects were asked to fill out a five-point scale indicating the degree to which they felt the person in the situation was morally obligated to perform the act. In addition, they were asked to select from three possible statements the most appropriate one for the complainant to use in discussing the problem and in attempting to influence the behavior of the person. One of these three statements involved the invocation of moral sanctions. Thus in the case of the high-school graduate who wants his parents to pay for his college, subjects were to choose from the following: The boy could tell his parents *(a)* he is satisfied with their plans concerning his college education, *(b)* he feels they are morally obligated to give him a college education, or *(c)* he is not satisfied with their plans concerning a college education, but due to the circumstances he must accept them.

The results of this part of Schmitt's experiment are shown in Table 9.2. The percentage of situations in which moral obligation was invoked under each condition represents the answer to the question whether the complainant would invoke moral obligation or not. The median of the moral obligation scale refers to whether the subject himself felt that moral obligation was involved. Both of these dependent variables indicate the condition in which moral obligation is perceived to be involved most often is the one involving a person who has the ability but is unwilling to perform the act. The two factors of willingness and ability have an interactive effect that influences the subject's own feeling of moral obligation and what he expects the person in the situation to do.

These results from Schmitt's experiment demonstrate the effects of

TABLE 9.2
Invocation of Moral Obligation[a]

	Able		Unable	
	Percent of 104 situations in which moral obligation was invoked	*Median of moral obligation scale*	*Percent of 104 situations in which moral obligation was invoked*	*Median of moral obligation scale*
Willing	19 (N = 26)	.65 (N = 26)	9 (N = 26)	.32 (N = 26)
Unwilling	88 (N = 26)	3.65 (N = 26)	27 (N = 25)	1.00 (N = 25)

[a]Data adapted from Schmitt (1964).

ability and willingness factors, or in Heider's terms the concepts of "can" and "try," on the perception of a type of ethical requiredness. The fact that the results are primarily shown in the interaction between the two variables makes it clear that in studying the motivational variable of trying we cannot ignore the variable of ability—the concept of "can."

In a supplementary portion of Schmitt's experiment, he found some data relevant to Heider's concept of power. The power relationships were held constant in the situations discussed above. In a variant of the experiment given to other subjects, the person trying to influence the behavior was given power, or the ability to bring pressure to bear upon the recalcitrant person in the situation. Under such conditions the subject felt that the person trying to influence the behavior would first resort to the invocation of moral obligation, but if this were ineffective he would resort to his power in an attempt to force compliance. Schmitt argues that in a moral situation there may be a hierarchy of influence techniques, the first being the invocation of moral obligation, followed by attempts to wield power in the situation.

Two Aspects of the Concept of "Can": Internal and External Power

Heider (1958) defines power as the ability to influence the social and physical environment of another person. Power may derive from personal characteristics and/or a person's worldly possessions. Personal characteristics such as intelligence, skill, and confidence lead to power, but a person may be powerful because he has the wherewithal to deal effectively with the environment. What a man possesses (in the crassest sense this can be money) may strongly influence his power, especially in the social environment. Heider says, "Certainly a person's apparent self-confidence often influences our judgments of his abilities. . . . Moreover, social and legal status often affects what a person can and cannot do by determining the strength of the environmental forces. . ." (pp. 94–95).

Wilkins and de Charms (1962) have distinguished between internal and external sources of power in the following way: "Internal power will be considered power accruing to the individual *qua* individual. This type of power is perceived by others through the individual's personal mannerisms, traits, and expressed values. External power will be considered power accruing to the individual in accordance with the positions the individual holds and his possession of societally valued material objects or experiences" (Wilkins & de Charms, 1962, p. 440). In their experiment, Wilkins and de Charms studied the inferences about persons who were perceived as having the four possible combinations of internal and external power. Each of the eighty male subjects listened to one tape recording of an interview that presented information about a person relevant to his internal and external power. Each subject heard only one variant of the tape. Four tapes were used in which the interviewee presented a strong character with a deep voice and much confidence in answering questions (high internal-power stimulus person), or a weak character and a weak sounding voice with many hesitations in answering questions (low internal-power stimulus person). High and low external-power cues were manipulated by presentation of the socioeconomic status of the stimulus person, i.e., the high external-power person had many worldly goods, whereas the low external-power person had few.

The four types of internal and external power cues presented by the stimulus persons had strong and significant effects on the inferences drawn by the subjects about the stimulus persons. For brevity's sake, Wilkins and de Charms referred to the four types of stimulus persons as the "tycoon," namely, the high internal-power and high external-power stimulus person, the "go-getter," the high internal but low external stimulus person, the "decadent aristocrat," the low internal and high external stimulus person, and the "shiftless trash," the low internal and low external stimulus person. In evaluating these four types of stimulus persons, subjects filled out among other things an acceptance scale which presented thirty-two adjectives, each to be rated on a seven-point scale. This scale was similar to the semantic differential procedure developed by Osgood, Suci, and Tannenbaum (1957). Factor analysis of the results of the scale led to five factors, all of which were highly related to the different types of stimulus persons. Wilkins and de Charms

(1962) summarized the results of this part of their study and related it to Heider's discussion of power and the concept of "can" in the following two paragraphs:

> These results demonstrate that Subjects were quite sensitive to the characteristics of the stimulus persons and responded with typical cultural values. The "tycoon" was strong and dependable but obnoxious, closed-minded and unfriendly. The "go-getter" was strong, dependable, and friendly. The "decadent aristocrat" was evidently not seen as decadent. He was open-minded, non-obnoxious, and friendly. "Shiftless trash" was lowest on every scale except that he surpassed the "tycoon" slightly in open-mindedness and non-obnoxiousness.
>
> The data here reported clearly support Heider's contention that perceived power of a stimulus person may be derived from personal characteristics and/or social status of the stimulus person. In addition, these two types of power cues have strong effects on the reactions of subjects to the stimulus persons. . . . The two types of power cues are not necessarily perceived independently of each other. Thus the four combinations of external and internal cues evidently lead to four distinct types in the perception of the subjects with regard to such aspects as friendliness, sincerity, open-mindedness, and dependability (Wilkins & de Charms, 1962, p. 455).

The Perception of Social Causality

A person may be sensitive to both internal and external sources of power in evaluating the behavior of another, as seen in the Wilkins & de Charms experiment. In addition, he may see another's behavior as self or internally caused or motivated, or externally caused by influence or coercion. Thus the locus of causality for behavior, as well as that for power, may be perceived as either internal to the person or as lying outside the person. If person A is successful in influencing the behavior of person B, he may perceive the compliance on the part of B as a result of external influence attributable to himself. Or he may perceive that his influence attempt was not really effective but that person B complied because he wished to do so, i.e., that his behavior was internally determined. This interesting distinction between internally and externally perceived locus of causality in the influence situation has been studied by Thibaut and Riecken (1955a). In two different experiments, these researchers placed the subject in a setting in which he was asked to attempt to influence the behavior of two experimental confederates, who he thought were also subjects, by sending influence notes. In both cases, one experimental confederate was introduced to the subject as having high status relative to the subject's own status, while the other subject was introduced as having low relative status. This situation allowed Thibaut and Riecken to test the hypothesis that perception of social causality involves differential status. In the course of the experimental procedure, both experimental confederates complied with the request of the subject, and the subject was asked why he thought they complied as well as his general impression of them and their behavior. In this situation, Thibaut and Riecken were able to test their hypothesis about the relationship between a subject, X, and two confederates, Y and Z.

> We suggest that the main factors determining the two types of perceptual attribution are the *power* relations between X and Y and between X and Z. Suppose that: (1) X perceived that Y has relatively high power and that Z has relatively low power, (2) X sends the same (or equally) strong instrumental communications to Y and Z, (3) X perceives that both Y and Z comply with the communication, (4) in complying, Y and Z are not behaving as they would have been in the absence of the influence attempt. If the foregoing conditions are met X will tend to perceive the cause of Y's compliance as located "inside" Y (self-caused) and the cause of Z's compliance as located "outside" Z (i.e., a consequence of coercion by the induced force of X) (Thibaut & Riecken, 1955a, p. 115).

In this study, the independent variable is the perceived power of the confederate; the dependent variables are the perceived locus of causality for compliance, and the liking for the confederate. Thibaut and Riecken hypothesize that a confederate who complies for internal reasons will be liked better than one who complies because of coercion.

> We began by saying that X prefers Y to Z when X's communication is perceived to cause Y's compliance. We concluded by saying that X prefers Y to Z when X's communication is perceived not to cause Y's compliance. A moment's reflection . . . will show that the contradiction is only apparent. When an individual is confronted by a controllable and an uncontrollable other, he will tend to accept or prefer the controllable other, because of the relevance of control to goal locomotion. On the other hand, when both (or all) others show compliance, discriminations in acceptance will be made on some basis other than the instrumental capacities of the other for satisfying the individual's needs (p. 115).

In a situation in which subjects tried to influence the confederates to donate blood to the Red Cross, and in a situation in which subjects tried to obtain for their own use a dictionary from the confederates, Thibaut and Riecken confirmed the hypotheses that the higher status confederate was more often seen as complying for internal reasons while the lower status confederate was seen as complying for external reasons. In addition, confederates seen as complying for internal reasons were liked better than confederates seen as complying for external reasons. These results show differential effects of the same behavioral act if seen as internally as opposed to externally motivated, and the relationship between this perception of locus of causality and an affect variable, namely, liking for the subjects. Here we have another careful demonstration of subtle perceptual differences in perception of locus of causality that, coupled with difference in liking, might induce motivation within the subjects for different behavior *vis à vis* the two confederates. Such a demonstration would indeed give us an example of the effects of perception on motivation.

Surveillance and Trust

Strickland (1958) started with the notion that if a person obtains compliance from another person by use of power over him, the powerful person learns little about what the person will do when power is not applied. On the other hand, if compliance is obtained without the application of persuasive power, the person who complies has shown what he will do on his own when left alone. If a supervisor finds himself checking up on one worker, A, and leaving another, B, alone, the behavior of A may be assumed to be forced by the surveillance, but the behavior of B may be attributable to his own characteristics because nobody checked on him. In general, the more a person uses power to force compliance, the less he knows about how the person will act in the absence of coercive power.

Strickland hypothesized that the mere fact that a supervisor had checked up on one worker and had not checked up on another would strongly affect the supervisor's perception of the two workers and his attitudes and behavior toward them. Strickland devised specific hypotheses from the general proposition that a worker who had been consistently checked on (despite the fact that his work was adequate) would be perceived as motivated by the external force of the supervisor's checks. In contrast, a worker who had not been checked on (whose work was identical to the monitored worker) would be perceived as motivated by internal forces resulting from his own characteristics. Strickland devised a situation in which a supervisor was arbitrarily led to check on (monitor) one worker and leave the other alone, although he had no previous information that one was more reliable than the other. The worker output was adequate throughout for both workers. Strickland hypothesized that the supervisor would perceive the monitored worker as more externally motivated and less trustworthy than the nonmonitored worker. He further hypothesized that as a result of the perceived locus of causality for the worker's behavior, the supervisor would feel it necessary to keep checking up on the monitored subject and leave the nonmonitored subject on his own.

An experiment was devised in which a supervisor (the subject in the experiment) was given power to monitor one of two workers and to "dock" the worker's pay if he caught him falling below a stated minimum. If the worker's production fell below the minimum on a trial in which he was not monitored, the loss came out of the supervisor's pay. Thus the supervisor had to attempt to keep production up, but he could monitor only one worker after any one production period.

The experiment was arranged so that during the first half of the production periods (ten periods) the supervisor monitored worker A eight times and B only twice, yet both A and B produced adequately. After the first ten production periods the supervisor-subject, who had never actually seen the workers but only reports of their production, filled out a questionnaire measuring his trust of A and B and asking why he thought they had complied with adequate production, i.e., whether they had been forced or had done it on their own.

In part II of the experiment (ten more production periods), the supervisor again had to attempt to maintain the level of production, but now he was free to monitor either worker, but only one after any one period. In addition, he was given another task that made it difficult for him to monitor every time. As a result he was faced with a situation in which he had to think carefully about whom to monitor in order to keep production up. After these production periods, he again filled out a questionnaire.

The independent variable in the experiment was the differential monitoring of the workers in the first ten production periods. The dependent variables were (a) the perceived locus of causality for the worker's compliance to demands, (b) the supervisor's trust of the two workers, and (c) the number of times the supervisor monitored each worker in the last ten trials, when he was free to monitor either worker.

When all the subjects' responses were categorized as indicating that they perceived the workers' behavior as either internally or externally motivated, i.e., done of their own accord or forced, the results revealed that the monitored worker was more often seen as externally motivated, i.e., forced, than the nonmonitored worker. However, many subjects did not give responses that could be clearly considered attribution of internal or external causality. As a result, the tendency shown by those subjects who did give clear responses, though in the predicted direction, was not statistically significant.

The data were clear, however, in confirming that the monitored worker was trusted less than the nonmonitored worker. Only one subject out of 40 trusted the monitored worker more, 24 trusted the monitored worker less (as predicted), and 15 were unwilling to say that they trusted one more than the other. Statistical analysis confirmed the hypothesized relationship between monitoring and distrust. When forced to choose one of the two workers as the more "dependable," 35 out of 40 chose the nonmonitored worker, one chose the monitored worker, and four did not answer.

If the supervisor distrusted the worker who was consistently monitored in the first ten trials more than the other worker, it would be assumed that he would go on checking on him when free to monitor either (but not both) in the last ten periods. Here we encounter a differential prediction of actual behavior toward a person who is perceived as internally as opposed to a person who is perceived as externally motivated. The data confirm that the supervisors chose to monitor the originally monitored worker more often than the other worker in the last ten trials.

It is unfortunate that the results of the measure of perception of locus of causality are not statistically significant. Despite this lack, the experiment clearly demonstrates that when a person uses his power to obtain compliance he will tend to distrust the person who complies, and feel that it is necessary to continue using his power if it is critical that no break occur in the compliant behavior.

If we use Origin-Pawn terminology to replace perceived locus of causality, the Strickland experiment seems to indicate that if a person is perceived as a Pawn, the perceiver will tend to distrust his "real" motives and to feel compelled to continue treating him as a Pawn if it is critical that compliance be maintained. On the other hand, if a person is seen as an Origin in doing behavior that is desired by the perceiver, he will be trusted to continue doing it and the perceiver will not feel compelled to treat him as a Pawn.

In the Strickland experiment, mistrust was induced by the independent variable. Constant monitoring as required by the experiment left the supervisor with no evidence that the worker could be trusted. In a real life situation, a supervisor who felt that the worker could, in fact, be trusted to produce adequately could test him by leaving him on his own. Evidence from studies by Thibaut and Riecken (1955b), Wilkins and de Charms (1962), and Deutsch (1960) indicate that supervisors who rate high on authoritarian tendencies (Adorno, Frenkel-Brunswik, Levinson, and Sanford, 1950) would be most suspicious and least trusting, and would be more influenced by the power relationships in the situation than by any evidence that there were internal factors indicating that the worker was to be trusted. Such a supervisor might tend to create an atmosphere of suspicion, treating the worker as a Pawn and reducing his incentive to produce unless forced to do so.

Teachers' Perceptions of Causality

Another situation in which the theory of perceived locus of causality is of practical interest is the interaction between a teacher and his pupils. Johnson, Feigenbaum, and Weiby (1964) have reported an experiment similar to Strickland's in which the subjects were teachers given the task of teaching two children arithmetic concepts. The independent variable in the experiment of concern to us was change in performance. The performance of child A was always good, so that he constituted a constant comparison for the behavior of child B. The behavior of child B was varied for different teachers in two periods in which the child attempted arithmetic problems after they have been explained by the teacher. In the first period, child B always performed very poorly as compared to child A, who performed very well. In the second performance period, child B performed poorly for one-half of the teachers and well for the other half, thus forming a group in which child B's performance remained low, and a group in which his performance improved.

The experiment was designed to test the teacher's perception of the locus of causality for the behavior of child B. The results indicated that the teachers attributed change toward better performance to their own efforts, and attributed lack of change to the child's own characteristics. In addition, they rated their own teaching effort as more adequate when child B's performance improved than when no improvement occurred. This finding supports the contention that they felt that when they did an adequate job of teaching the locus of causality for change in performance was their teaching efforts, i.e., internal to them and not internal to the pupil or attributable to his greater effort.

Students' Feelings of Control

A study by de Charms and Bridgeman (1961) gives evidence of the feelings of the student toward a teacher (or a follower toward a leader) when the student feels that he can have some control in determining the course of events in the classroom situation. The major hypothesis of the study was that when a student attempts to alter the course of events by a direct influence attempt upon the teacher, compliance by the teacher signifies to the student that he can originate behavior to change the situation—have some control of his fate—rather than merely react to the teacher's demands like a Pawn. Compliance on the part of the teacher was hypothesized to lead to changes in the student's perception of the teacher, changes in the student's feeling of security in the situation, changes in the student's feeling of reciprocity *vis à vis* the teacher, and changes in the student's motivation to work for the teacher.

In a small groups laboratory de Charms and Bridgeman (1961) devised a classroom-type situation in which they could present standard tape recorded lectures and ask the subjects to listen with the two aims of learning the material and evaluating the lecturer, who they thought was present behind a one-way screen. During the course of the experiment, the subjects were informed that they were not performing well; then they were asked for suggestions to be given to the lecturer which might help them to perform better. The subjects arrived at a group decision to ask for a summary to the lecture. The lecturer responded to this request immediately, and, depending on the group, he verbalized either compliance or noncompliance. This constituted the independent variable of verbal compliance on the part of the lecturer. In addition, in the course of his next short lecture, he either gave a clear, ad-libbed summary or he did not, depending on the experimental condition. This constituted the second independent variable of behavioral compliance.

The dependent variables consisted of a questionnaire designed to test the subjects' perception of the lecturer on the dimensions of liking, motivation, competence, security, reciprocity, and three dimensions of Osgood's (Osgood et al., 1957) semantic differential, namely, potency, evaluation, and activity. This questionnaire was administered twice, once before the manipulation of the independent variables and once afterward, so that variance attributable to individual differences could be assessed by the covariance technique.

As a measure of the subjects' motivation to work for the lecturer, de Charms and Bridgeman devised a procedure at the end of the experimental session in which the experimenter said that this lecturer had a special task not connected with the formal procedures in which he (the lecturer) would like to have them cooperate. This comprised what was called the "odious task." The lecturer asked the subjects to write some "creative stories." Subjects were given several short sentences devised by Elizabeth French (1955) to measure achievement motivation. They were left alone in the room for ten minutes to write as much or as little as they cared to write. The measure of productivity (motivation) was simply the number of words written.

Analyses of covariance using factor scores showed significant changes attributable to the experimental manipulations on all of the dependent measures. It is clear that the subjects' perception of the competence and motivation of the lecturer was affected by his compliance, as were the subjects' feelings of security and reciprocity toward him. Table 9.3, for instance, presents the results of the evaluation scale drawn from Osgood et al. (1957) made up of items such as "good-bad," "like-dislike," etc. As predicted, when the lecturer clearly complied to the request he was liked better than when his compliance was ambiguous. Verbal compliance had a similar effect. Both of these main effects were highly significant in the analysis of covariance.

TABLE 9.3
Adjusted Means ($\bar{Y}'$) and the Analysis of Covariance
of the Evaluation Subscale

		Clear behavioral compliance	Ambiguous behavioral compliance	Total
Verbal Compliance	N	14	13	27
	$\bar{Y}'$	28.10	24.94	26.58
Verbal Noncompliance	N	10	14	24
	$\bar{Y}'$	24.86	21.05	22.64
Control	N	13	10	23
	$\bar{Y}'$	25.83	22.71	24.47
Total	N	37	37	
	$\bar{Y}'$	26.43	22.87	

Source of Variation	d.f.	$MS_{y.x}$	F	p
Verbal compliance	2	75.45	5.25	<.01
Behavioral compliance	1	198.5	13.80	<.0005
Interaction	2	20.1	—	
Residual	62	14.38		

[a] From de Charms and Bridgeman (1961).

Analyses of the other questionnaire subscales showed significant results demonstrating that verbal compliance affected the subjects' perception of the lecturer's competence and their feelings of security with him. When the lecturer clearly showed behavioral and not merely verbal compliance, he was seen as more potent and active. One of the scales even picked up a reaction to the lecturer's inconsistency when he verbalized noncompliance but demonstrated behavioral compliance — he said he would not do what they wished, but apparently he recanted and did do so. In this condition, he was seen as inconsistent. When he recanted, however, the subjects worked harder for him on the "odious task" than in any other condition.

In general, the results of this experiment demonstrate important effects of compliance on the part of the lecturer on the behavior of the group members. The effects appear most strongly in the realm of subjects' feelings of security and reciprocity in interaction with the lecturer. Such compliant leadership behavior induces inferences concerning the leader's competence and motivation and arouses motivation in the subjects. A leader who verbalizes his willingness to comply may have strong influence over the members' morale even if he does not show clearly that he is able to comply. He will be perceived as not consistent if his stated intentions are not consistent with his actions. If he states a negative intention, however, and then reverses himself in his actions, an "elation effect" appears in the subjects' motivation and willingness to work for him.

These results may be interpreted as showing that when group members feel that they have some freedom to control the situation—if they feel that they can be the origin of suggestions about how the group and the leader proceeds—their feelings toward the leader and willingness to work for him will be much more positive than if they feel that they have no say in the procedure and that they are treated like Pawns.

The Origin-Pawn Variable in Person Perception

De Charms *et al.* (1965) set out to test the importance of the Origin-Pawn variable in person perception. They presented a series of very short stories to their subjects. In each story, the hero was being influenced to do something by a persuasive agent that was sometimes a person, sometimes a group or organization. The persuasive agent was variously presented as being either very attractive or very unattractive to the hero. The subjects themselves were classified high or low on a scale that was assumed to be related to their feelings about themselves along the Origin-Pawn dimension—their feelings of power or powerlessness in many situations.[5] These three independent variables combined into a rather complex statistical design to test three basic hypotheses: I, ". . . the hero would be perceived more as an Origin when he was being persuaded by an agent that he liked and more as a Pawn when being persuaded by

---

[5]The scale was composed of the twelve items presented by Rotter, Seeman, and Liverant (1962) designed to measure feelings of control of fate or of being controlled by it. They refer to the variable as the perception of internal or external control of reinforcements, and to the scale as the internal-external (I-E) scale. Details of other research using this scale will be presented in Chapter 10.

an agent that he disliked, . . ."; II, ". . . a hero reacting to a large organization would be seen as more of a Pawn then a hero reacting to a small group or an individual"; and III, ". . . subjects who feel that they have internal control over the consequences of their own actions will perceive the hero as more of an Origin than subjects who feel external control over their own behavior" (de Charms *et al.,* 1965, pp. 244–245). These hypotheses and the independent variables were designed to test the effects of one situational variable, the type of persuasive agent (individual, small group, or large organization), one variable presented as internal to the hero (his liking for the persuasive agent), and one variable deriving from the personal knowledge of the subjects themselves (their feelings of power or powerlessness as measured by the I-E scale).

After reading each of seven very short stories, the subjects responded to a four-item scale designed to measure the Origin-Pawn variable. The items asked the subjects to estimate how free or constrained the hero would feel in the situation described in the story — how much like an Origin or like a Pawn he would feel.

The results of the study may be seen in Figure 9.1. All three inde-

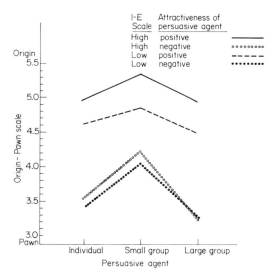

FIG. 9.1. Mean rating on the Origin-Pawn scale for subjects high and low on internal and external control (I-E) for various stimulus persons.

pendent variables were significantly related to perception of the hero along the Origin-Pawn dimension. Subjects who felt themselves to be powerful in controlling their own fate rated the hero as more of an Origin than subjects who felt relatively powerless. The hero who found the persuasive agent attractive was rated as more an Origin than the hero who found the agent unattractive. The type of group was significantly related to the Origin-Pawn variable, but not in the way that was hypothesized. Both the large organization and the individual were seen as constraining the hero more than the small group. This finding may have resulted from the fact that the small group may have been seen as exerting informal pressure, whereas the individual and the large organization may have been seen as wielding formal power to influence the hero.

Evidence from the study indicated that the Origin-Pawn variable, although not entirely independent of factors such as task-enjoyment, was accounting for significant variance not accounted for by a general positive orientation to the situation. As a first step, the study demonstrates that the Origin-Pawn dimension can be reliably used by subjects in a person perception experiment. Three quite different types of variables may affect the perception of a person as an Origin or as a Pawn. The major independent variables of this study, however, were rather gross, and much remains to be discovered concerning the characteristics of the hero, his station in life, etc., that affect the attribution of causality.

Summary

In this chapter, we have treated as a problem of concern for the motivation psychologist an area of research that is more often considered under the heading of social or person perception. The research reported is not well integrated with more traditional concerns of the psychology of motivation, but nevertheless it deals with a problem (motives inferred from behavior) that is of importance to motivation theory. As in the case of theories of motivation that developed out of learning theory, so with the problem of inferred motivation, the strictures of physicalism, operationism, and the objectivist dilemma have inhibited progress by discouraging the study of the influence of personal knowledge deriving from sources other than physical stimulus properties of the person. Like the para-mechanical analogy, the object perception analogy stands in the way of analysis of some of the most important aspects of gaining knowledge of other people's motives, desires, and intentions in social intercourse. Despite the influence of Michotte's work on the perception of physical causality, or perhaps because such work makes it clear that external loci of causation are inadequate to explain motivational inferences, recent research has begun to plumb the depths of the attribution process in general and of motivational inferences such as the perceived locus of causation for behavior or the Origin-Pawn variable. Such work can play an important role in the development of motivation theory based on the concepts of personal knowledge and personal causation and should in the future be more closely allied with other research in motivation.

Chapter 10

PERSONAL CAUSATION AND THE INTERNAL DETERMINANTS OF BEHAVIOR

Whether a man considers himself to be acting as an Origin or as a Pawn is the central issue for understanding the effects of personal causation in human motivation. When a person feels that he is an Origin, his behavior should be characteristically different from his behavior when he feels like a Pawn. This major hypothesis derives from our basic postulate that man's primary motivational propensity is to be effective in producing desirable changes in his environment. Thus we have reached the most fundamental aspect of human motivation—man's personal knowledge of his own motives.

There is an important difference between a man's knowledge of his own motives (the topic of this chapter) and a man's attribution of motives to other men (the topic of Chapter 9). The difference, and it is an enormous difference that lies at the center of all motivational theory, is in the source of knowledge about other people's behavior as opposed to personal knowledge about self. Our technical language may trap us into conceiving of the person as "perceiving," "feeling," or "experiencing" his own motives and behavior in the same way, based exclusively on external empirical inputs, that he "perceives" another person's behavior and attributes motives to him. With regard to self, we are almost forced to say "he perceives himself to be an Origin" when we mean something much more general than perception—something that may not be conscious, in the sense of reportable, and that may not be the result of any specific "experience" or "feeling." We mean something that is "known" in the broadest sense, without being at the same time in the forefront of consciousness or perception when it is affecting behavior. Such is the aspect of personal knowledge that we are seeking in motivation theory.

This is the unique "psychological" component of motivated behavior referred to in Chapters 1 and 8 that cannot be completely objectified and that will not yield to a strict behavioristic analysis. Needless to say, this quarry is an elusive beast, but we need not make a sacred cow, a mythical animal or even a ghost in the machine out of it. We must pursue it with the instruments of our science and look for observable differences in behavior under constrained and under free environmental conditions.

In pursuing this goal we must keep in mind another more familiar problem that has already beclouded the statement of the major problem of this chapter. The hypothesis in the first paragraph above relating the Origin-Pawn variable to behavior may be phrased in two slightly different ways that conceal an important difference in orientation. One could assume that some men are "Origins" and others are "Pawns," develop a typology and a measuring instrument, and go about studying the behavioral differences between the two types. This approach would constitute an extreme form of personality psychology emphasizing only the characteristics of the individual. At the other extreme, one could assume that all men are both Origins and Pawns depending entirely on the external circumstances that prevail in the situation. This extreme assumption would prompt a careful study of the external environmental conditions that induce Pawn vs. Origin "feelings" and their effects on behavior. The first approach (personality analysis) is associated with the overlap of Social with Clinical Psychology, while the second, often considered Experimental Social Psychology, derives from the more traditional experimental psychology. Although a cleavage between these two positions may exist in current writings, we shall try to mold both approaches into a more comprehensive statement regarding personal causation.

Our plan for the present chapter is to pursue the concept of "internal-external" as applied to the self, starting with a theory that attempts to derive a concept similar to the Origin-Pawn concept entirely from the instrumental-activity-reinforcement paradigm as discussed in Rotter's (1954) social learning theory. In moving from this attempt to "externalize" the more personal aspects we will quote a personal statement (Koch, 1956) rich in the flavor of personal knowledge of motivation. Contained in the personal statement are all the complexities and ambiguities along with the freshness and vitality of a phenomenological report. Our task is to use such a report as a springboard from which to derive essential characteristics of internally vs. externally motivated behavior. The major aspect that we shall pursue in detail is freedom vs. constraint. Freedom of choice implies commitment and self-involvement whereas constraint implies external influence. In the latter part of the chapter, we shall analyze these components as they relate to personal causation and the Origin-Pawn dimension and present evidence that they relate to behavior in tests of our major hypothesis as stated above.

The Instrumental-Activity-Reinforcement Paradigm

In learning theory terms, the goal of instrumental activity is reinforcement. Utilizing the instrumental paradigm, expectancy concepts, and an empirical definition of reinforcement, Rotter (1954) developed what has come to be known as "social learning theory." Within the framework of social learning theory, Rotter and his colleagues and students have developed and extensively researched the area of generalized expectancies for internal versus external control of reinforcement (cf. Rotter, Seeman, & Liverant, 1962; Rotter, 1966; Lefcourt, 1966). The similarity between the concept of internal control of reinforcement and the Origin concept is striking especially when the Rotter group use the phrase "internal locus of control" which is so similar to Heider's "internal locus of causality," the concept from which the Origin notion sprung. The emphasis on reinforcement and the instrumental paradigm, however, restricts the concept of control of reinforcements and directs attention primarily to the results of behavior (reinforcement) rather than to the behavior itself. Thus Rotter's theory appears to be securely within the objectivist and behaviorist tradition. A reinforcer is defined by Rotter as anything "that changes behavior in some observable way by either increasing or decreasing the potentiality of its occurrence" (Rotter, 1954, p. 112). He is not as restrictive, however, in his use of this definition as is Skinner. Rotter immediately moves on to distinguish between internal and external reinforcement.

> Internal reinforcement may be ideally defined as a subject's experience (or perception) that an event has occurred which has some value for him. That is, an event has occurred that is pleasant or unpleasant or that the subject expects will lead to a pleasant or unpleasant event. . . .
> External reinforcement is the occurrence of an event or act that is known to have predictable reinforcement value for the *group* or culture to which the subject belongs (Rotter, 1954, p. 112).

This attempt to go beyond the purely empirical definition of a reinforcer actually leaves the ultimate definition unclear. These attempts which try to broaden the empirical definition of reinforcement in order to include nonempirical aspects rob the concept of its status as the well-defined theoretical tool as used by Skinner. Unfortunately, it retains its prestige although it has become an omnibus explanation of dubious theoretical value. If we ask ourselves: Has an empirically established reinforcer been isolated and identified as the basis for all the instances cited of expectations of internal locus of control? — the answer is negative. This in itself is not as important as the fact that a "pleasant event" (the result of "internal reinforcement" according to Rotter) can never be reduced to objective outcomes of behavior, i.e., an empirically defined objective result of behavior *could not* be found in every case.

If one realizes that he is not on the firm objective ground of empirical reinforcement theory (like Skinner), but is using "reinforcement" loosely, then Rotter's concepts turn out to have much in common with the Origin and Pawn concepts.

> When a reinforcement is perceived by the subject as following some action of his own but not being entirely contingent upon his action, then, in our culture, it is typically perceived as the result of luck, chance, fate, as under the control of powerful others, or as unpredictable because of the great complexity of the forces surrounding him. When the event is interpreted in this way by an individual, we have labeled this a belief in *external control*. If the person perceives that the event is contingent upon his own behavior or his own relatively permanent characteristics, we have termed this a belief in *internal control* (Rotter, 1966, p. 1).

Although conceptually we take exception to Rotter's use of the concept of reinforcement, the internal-external (I-E) variable as used in research provides a body of evidence relevant to the Origin-Pawn variable. The Rotter group have dealt with both of the social psychological problems mentioned above, i.e., they have developed a questionnaire (the I-E scale) to measure expectancies as a personality variable, and they have investigated experimental situations that produce expectancies of internal versus external control (cf. Lefcourt, 1966).

Rotter (1966) presents the complete I-E scale along with impressive evidence for its reliability and discriminant validity. Results using the scale are summarized as follows:

> A series of studies provides strong support for the hypothesis that the individual who has a strong belief that he can control his own destiny is likely to *(a)* be more alert to those aspects of the environment which provide useful information for his future behavior; *(b)* take steps to improve his environmental condition; *(c)* place greater value on skill or achievement reinforcements and be generally more concerned with his ability, particularly his failures; and *(d)* be resistive to subtle attempts to influence him (Rotter, 1966, p. 25).[1]

[1]The studies demonstrating these findings are point for point *(a)* Seeman and Evans (1962), Seeman (1963); *(b)* Gore and Rotter (1963), Strickland (1965), Phares (1965); *(c)* Crandall, Katkovsky, and Preston (1962), Franklin (1963), Efran (1963), Rotter and Mulry (1965); *(d)* Crowne and Liverant (1963), Strickland (1962), Getter (1962), Gore (1962).

The similarity of the results with the I-E scale to those from the McClelland *et al.* (1953) measure of *n* Achievement is striking although Rotter (1966) suggests that the relationship between the two measures is probably not linear.

Studies of experimental situations have dealt primarily with complex learning under skill versus chance conditions.

> In its simplest form, our basic hypothesis is that if a person perceives a reinforcement as contingent upon his own behavior, then the occurrence of either a positive or negative reinforcement will strengthen or weaken potential for that behavior to recur in the same or similar situation. If he sees the reinforcement as being outside his own control or not contingent, that is depending upon chance, fate, powerful others, or unpredictable, then the preceding behavior is less likely to be strengthened or weakened (Rotter, 1966, p. 5).

In studies comparing chance and skill, Phares (1957) found evidence for the above hypothesis as did James and Rotter (1958), Rotter, Liverant, and Crowne (1961), Bennion (1961), and Blackman (1962) using resistance to extinction of expectancies.

In general, the studies of internal and external control constitute an impressive series. In our view, however, basing the "internal-external" concept on reinforcement is a barrier to confrontation with the basic issue of personal knowledge that is clearly implied by Rotter's stress on the perceived contingency between behavior and results. The important results of behavior are not always objectively measurable as hinted by Rotter's statement that the "internal" person "has a strong belief that he can control his own destiny" (Rotter, 1966, p. 25).[2]

The Personal Aspects of Motivated Behavior

We now wish to shift emphasis from the objective to the personal aspects of behavior. In order to do this in the most emphatic way, we will first set the stage with a personal document.

A Personal Statement

Koch (1956) has recorded a phenomenological description of his own personal feelings in connection with his intellectual activities. His descriptions of State A and State B encompass the expression of a man

---

[2]The weakness of the theory may show itself in the measure. As we saw in Chapter 9, "internals" as compared to "externals" on the I-E scale more often assume that other people are Origins (de Charms *et al.,* 1965); however, in two studies to be reported at the end of this chapter, the I-E variable does *not* relate to a person's own behavior when he is acting as an Origin or as a Pawn (Kuperman, 1967; de Charms *et al.,* 1965, unpublished). Based on the distinction made in Chapter 6 between extensity and intensity measures, we suspect that the most appropriate way to measure the Origin-Pawn variable is the technique of thought sampling, i.e., tapping spontaneously emitted thoughts, rather than eliciting controlled responses on a questionnaire such as the I-E scale.

when he feels himself to be a Pawn (State A) and of a man when he feels himself to be an Origin (State B).

State A (Pawn)

I am distractable, flighty, self-prepossessed, rueful over the course of my life and the value choices it has entailed. I feel depressed, continually drowsy, guilty about my purposelessness and general ineffectiveness. The world is a flaccid structure of neutral tone and value. My responses towards people are bumbling, inert, ineffective, rejective. There is evidence to suggest that I am unpleasant to live with. My self-image constricts into a small, desiccated thing: I am physically unattractive, devoid of color, wit, or style. An enormous distance seems to supervene between myself and my most prized values. I am aesthetically desensitized (relative to my image of myself); my system of tastes becomes cheapened and more tolerant. . . .

Under conditions of State A, creative or complex intellectual activity is first of all unlikely. Unfortunately, the conditions of life are such as frequently to demand that it occur. These "conditions" may be endogenously defined as, e.g., guilt, anxiety, or they may be pressures deriving from external agencies, e.g., deadlines, teaching obligations. Either of these classes of conditions can be characterized, if we follow conventional motivational logic, as defining *extrinsic* contexts for the performances that are called for. In other words, if such conditions are effective, *then* I will be working *in order to* relieve guilt, meet a deadline, get a promotion, please a friend. What is the performance like under these circumstances?

I rapidly pass over the fact that under such pressures one passes through innumerable resistances, escape detours, rationalizations, before getting into the problem situation. One may finally "get" or be impelled into the problem situation, but one never, as it were, "gets committed." Thinking is slow, rigid, disorganized, formless, and inelegant. Memory tends towards the "rote" and is saturated with spotty amnesia. Verbalization and writing is influent, stilted, imprecise, turgid — either overliteral or over-allusive — devoid of wit or flavor. Reading is slow, with much backtracking. The absolute ceiling with respect to the apprehension of complex relationships, the perception of subtle similarities and differences and of meaning nuances, the ability to filter the thought sequence through a complex assemblage of constraints — becomes suffocatingly low.

The unhappy fact about State A, at least for me, is that no manipulation of "extrinsic" conditions, or augmentation in the strength thereof, seems to improve matters much. One remains a prisoner to State A until it runs its course.

State B (Origin)

The central and decisive "mark" of State B is domination of the person by the problem context, or, better, by a certain direction defined by the problem context — a "diffuse" but absolutely compelling direction. All systems of personality seem "polarized" into the behavior; thus the personality is either integrated or, in a special sense, simplified, as you will. In State B, you do not merely "work at" or "on" the task; you have *committed yourself* to the task, and in some sense you *are* the task, or vice versa.

Perhaps one of the most remarkable properties of B is that thoughts relevant to the problem context seem to well up with no apparent effort. They merely present themselves. The spontaneity and fluency of ideation and the freedom from customary blockages seem similar to certain characteristics of the dream or certain states of near dissociation. As in these latter conditions, it is often difficult to "fix," hold in mind, the thoughts which occur. In fact, in State B, most of the "effortfulness" or "strain" encountered has to do not with the generation of ideas relevant to the problem context but with their decoding, fixing, or verbalization, and their selection and assemblage with respect to socially standardized requirements of communication. Effortful as such operations may be, verbalization, writing, reading, and all functionally significant breakdowns thereof are at a qualitatively different level from the A state of "affairs" (Koch, 1956, pp. 67–68).

The rich personal flavor of these descriptions may tend to exaggerate the differences in such a way as to make it seem hopeless to attempt to characterize distinctive aspects of the two states theoretically. The problem will not be solved easily and no complete solution is proposed here. For our purpose, however, there are two distinguishing aspects of the B state that stand out; *(a)* the total involvement of self, and *(b)* the lack of anxiety or threat. The crux of State A is its "in order to" quality, i.e., the instrumental quality of behavior that is engaged in only for the sake of obtaining an externally mediated goal.

INVOLVEMENT AND THE SELF

The psychology of ego-involvement has a long history (cf. Iverson & Reuder, 1956) but the involvement of self described by Koch in State B does not have the same character as that induced by so-called "ego-involving instructions" that essentially put the subject on trial. In State B, threat or compulsion of "ego-involvement" is absent and the self is more freely invested as in the state of commitment as discussed in Chapter 8. For this reason, we will use the phrase "self-investment" to try to distinguish this freer state of commitment from the customary threat produced ego-involving instructions used in experiments.

We must digress for a moment and mention an interesting paradox with regard to the self that is apparent in Koch's description. In State A, the self is involved in possible aggrandizement or debasement. It is critical that the boundaries of the self be set so that a positive outcome may be definitely attributed to the self and recognized by others. Success is mediated by the approval of an external source who must recognize the successful person. Important as the self is under these circumstances, the self-image becomes a "small, desiccated thing" during the instrumental activity. In State B by contrast, the self may be showing itself to great advantage and yet the self-image loses all importance. The boundaries of self are blurred and permeable, and the distinction between self and task is irrelevant. "You *are* the task." The Pawn must depend on his mentor to recognize him but the Origin derives satisfaction from the feeling of personal causation, whether recognized by anyone else or not. Confidence leads to the loss of self-consciousness in the Origin. This loss of self, though poorly understood, may be characteristic of a person when he has a strong sense of personal causation.

To follow the idea of loss of self too far is to run the risk of getting completely lost. Nevertheless, we shall note in passing that there may be some relationship between the concepts under discussion and the psychology of creativity. Loss of self is similar to Rugg's (1963) concept of "off-conscious" locus of creative imagination. The following quote from Kenneth Benne's editor's introduction to Part II of Rugg's (1963) posthumously published volume shows this relationship as well as summarizing Rugg's discussion of a process of knowing that is similar to personal knowledge.

> Among the differentia of the creative response, [Rugg's] construct of "transliminal" or "off-conscious" mind-body functioning proved to be central. In off-conscious functioning, the person lets things happen rather than tries to make them happen according to already known and cherished patterns of thought and habit. It is a state of relaxation from the dictates of external censorship or unconscious compulsion. It is a state of relaxation attained through a concentration of attention upon what is to be discovered or known. Yet the process of knowing involved is a coming to know through "inner" identification rather than through "external" categorization of that which is consciously observed—a process of discovery rather than one of logical verification (Rugg, 1963, pp. 133–134).

We shall let this digression stand as is and return now to our major theme.

THREAT VERSUS CHALLENGE

Motivation theories that stress external determinants inevitably concentrate on the threat of punishment or of the loss of reward. The challenge of mastering a situation is rarely considered. The negative emphasis has its roots in the Freudian concepts of regression in the face of threat and of reduction of stimulation to a state of low tension (cf. Chapter 3). The child is jarred out of a comfortable, safe, low tension state by the raw realities of the physical and interpersonal environment, but he never actively seeks a confrontation with a novel situation. The major focus of behavior during the disturbing episodes is to return (regress) to the pleasurable state of security. One way of dealing with a new situation that is forced on the child is for him to gain some mastery over it, but there is little value in the mastery itself other than the security that it produces. The emphasis is not on seeking situations to master but on relief in resolving an uncertain situation that was arbitrarily posed by a hostile environment.

The other side of the coin will be stressed here under the hypothesis that mastering an uncertain situation is valued for its own sake rather than merely for the relief that it produces. In the terminology of Chapter 3, we are saying that such phenomena cannot be accounted for entirely in terms of tension reduction. The arousal-jag proposal which seems implicit in some of Freud's writings and was proposed by Berlyne (1960) seems to go far in explaining the thrill of success in a very uncertain situation which clearly has some of the aspects of relief. If a person is forced against his will into a risky environment, relief may be produced by escape and combined with anxiety to form the major motivational components. The arousal-jag, however, does not seem adequate to account for behavior in which the person seems to attack problems in the environment with zest, apparently seeking uncertainty and change, and reveling in risky situations. The challenge-oriented, progressive, offensive, coping and mastering aspects as opposed to the threat-oriented, regressive, defensive, submitting aspects of behavior need further investigation and explanation.

Success in mastering the physical and interpersonal environment probably results more often from a tendency to strive for personal causation than it does from attempts to make the situation more secure. Behavior resulting from striving for personal causation may be sustained through repeated apparent "losses" of external rewards by the resulting feedback from the activity itself.

In order to understand this phenomenon, we must forego the temptation to look for an outcome or goal of instrumental activities. The instrumental paradigm has hidden within it the assumption that the instrumental activity is only put up with in order to attain the goal. The instrumental activity, then, cannot have positive appeal and is to be avoided unless it yields a concrete reward. We must try to school ourselves in the discipline of conceiving of certain activities, even some that demand great expenditure of energy, as sought for their own sake, as standing by themselves as desirable, without having to lean on the crutch of a desirable outcome. Play and games come closest to giving us the concept we need, and fun comes closest to describing the affective component. Some games are played "for their own sake," some games are played "to win," and some games are "serious," professional, and approach "work." All involve elements of displeasure and of tension; most have an outcome that is important but is not *all* important.

We have assumed that some behaviors are apparently done for their own sake, and that one class of behavior that appears to be done for its own sake is behavior resulting from striving for personal causation, behavior that results in environmental change that is controlled by the actor. *Of all possible behaviors that demonstrate a change effected by the actor, those will be preferred that result in maximum evidence of the effectiveness of the actor.*

INTRINSIC VERSUS EXTRINSIC MOTIVATION

What we have been discussing up to this point in this chapter often goes under the heading of the distinction between intrinsically versus extrinsically motivated behavior. Koch, for instance, was specifically addressing himself to the problem of "intrinsically regulated behavior" when he produced the personal statement quoted above. We have so far avoided the terms "intrinsic" and "extrinsic" because they are poorly defined and may tend to cloud the central issue. We are now prepared to introduce the terms as specifically related to the concept of personal causation. As a first approximation, we propose that whenever a person experiences himself to be the locus of causality for his own behavior (to be an Origin), he will consider himself to be intrinsically motivated. Conversely, when a person perceives the locus of causality for his behavior to be external to himself (that he is a Pawn), he will consider himself to be extrinsically motivated.

We are suggesting that the crux of the distinction between extrinsic and intrinstic motivation may lie in the knowledge or feeling of personal causation. The satisfaction deriving from the experience of personal causation is the satisfaction of having accomplished something by individual effort. The satisfaction of possession of objective rewards or results of the effort must be distinguished from the above. Conceptually, the distinction is important; practically, it is often difficult to make. Since objective rewards typically accompany individual accomplishment in the real world, the two types of motivation often lead to the same result. However, theoretically we may conceive of situations in which the two factors may be in opposition. It is in just such situations of interaction between extrinsic and intrinsic aspects in which the effects of striving for personal causation may be most clearly seen.

Interaction Between Intrinsic and Extrinsic Factors in Behavior

Common sense would lead to the prediction that behavior that leads to a sense of personal causation (intrinsic dimension) and at the same time is externally rewarded (extrinsic dimension) should result in the greatest satisfaction, i.e., the two aspects should summate. If such were the case, we might do very well with the assumption that the intrinsic dimension results from some type of internal reinforcement that acts like and summates with external rewards. Such a result would indicate no interaction between the intrinsic and the extrinsic dimensions.

If we assume, however, that a major factor in the intrinsic dimension is the desire for personal causation, then intrinsically motivating tasks are those in which the person feels that he is in control, that he originated the behavior (as an Origin) with the concomitant feelings of free choice and commitment. Introduction of extrinsic reward, however, places the person in a dependent position relative to the source of reward. To the extent that the person expects a reward for his task he is unfree and has not chosen the task for its own sake alone. The source of the reward is an external causal locus for his behavior. When rewards are important, dependence on the source of reward places a person in the position of a Pawn. Put in a more commonplace way, the highly paid employee is less free to dissent from the source of reward than the unpaid observer. The person with a golden egg must be careful not to kill the goose that laid it. Under such conditions, the goose can become a tyrant.

With regard to intrinsically preferred tasks, the addition of extrinsic rewards may reduce task motivation rather than enhance it. The motivation to perform a task undertaken originally as a result of the desire to demonstrate personal causation will suffer if an extrinsic reward is offered for task accomplishment. Conversely, the motivation to perform a task undertaken originally in order to obtain an extrinsic reward will be enhanced if the reward is withheld. In the light of reinforcement theory, these predictions sound ridiculous. On the one hand, if you find a man doing a good job without pay and decide to reward him, the predicted effect is that the quality of the job will deteriorate. On the other hand, if you offer to pay a man for a job and then renege on the pay, he will do a better job than if you paid him.

Ridiculous as these hypotheses may seem, there is some evidence to support them. Though scant, the evidence is strong enough to indicate the inadequacy of ignoring factors other than extrinsic rewards, and to encourage further investigation into interactions between intrinsic and extrinsic aspects of motivation.

The Effects of an Extrinsic Incentive on Intrinsically Motivated Behavior

Harlow *et al.* (1950) have presented a study of manipulatory behavior in monkeys that demonstrates that *(a)* monkeys learn to unfasten a puzzle device with no apparent extrinsic incentive, and that *(b)* after an extrinsic incentive is given for unfastening the puzzle the intrinsically motivated behavior deteriorates when the extrinsic incentive is subsequently removed.

Eight monkeys were used, all of which had a three-stage mechanical puzzle mounted for a period of 14 consecutive days in the cages in which they lived. For one-half of the monkeys (Group A), the puzzles were assembled; and for the other half (Group B), they were unassembled. Throughout the first 12 days, the puzzles were checked approximately 70 times to see if they had been assembled or disassembled. Each stage of the puzzle that was unfastened constituted one manipulation for the group with assembled puzzles; after each check, the experimenter re-assembled the puzzle. In no instance during the 12 days did the monkeys confronted with unassembled puzzles (Group B) fasten any of the devices. On days 13 and 14, five observations of five minutes each separated by one hour intervals were obtained. On the fourteenth day, two hours after the last five-minute observation in the home cage, the Group A monkeys were taken individually to a test cage where they had been previously trained to find raisins but had never seen the puzzle. The experimenter baited a puzzle that was identical to the one in their home cage with a raisin in the presence of the monkey and observed him for five minutes. Finally, the puzzle was reassembled without food while the animal watched and another five-minute observation was taken. Apparently, this last part of the experiment was not carried out with the Group B animals.

The first part of this experiment can be divided into the learning period of 12 days and the test period on days 13 and 14. During the learning period, the Group A monkeys were confronted with unbaited assembled puzzles and the Group B monkeys with unbaited unassembled puzzles. On the thirteenth and fourteenth day test periods, both groups were confronted 10 times with unbaited assembled puzzles and their responses were recorded. Group A monkeys had learned to disassemble the puzzle whereas Group B monkeys had not. Group A monkeys made 31 of a possible 40 solutions defined in terms of disassembling at least two of the three devices of the puzzle. Group B monkeys made only four solutions. Group A monkeys attained their solutions quickly, and made many fewer errors as defined as attacking a device out of sequence.

These results are taken by Harlow *et al.* (1950) as an indication of learning in the absence of extrinsic incentives. The authors suggest that the results be attributed to a manipulation drive and this is considered to be intrinsic motivation (Harlow, 1950). They note that the animals were hungry since they were tested before their daily feeding period, i.e., 14 to

22 hours after their last feeding. That the manipulation had been learned because of the hunger drive cannot be completely excluded as an explanation, but the authors think it unlikely. In a subsequent study, Harlow, Blazek, and McClearn (1956) demonstrated manipulatory motivation in infant monkeys before it could have been learned as instrumental to drive reduction.

The last part of the experiment confronted each Group A monkey twice with a baited puzzle, once in a cage where he had learned to find raisins and once in his home cage. Finally, the puzzle was reassambled, unbaited, and the monkey was observed. Adding the raisin constitutes the addition of an extrinsic incentive to an intrinsically motivated behavior. The introduction of the raisin interfered with efficient solution of the puzzle. When the raisin was placed under the hasp, the monkeys attacked the hasp directly; but, since it was the last device in the puzzle and could not be released until the other two devices were unfastened, such behavior was maladaptive. In addition, after the monkeys had once received the raisin for solving the puzzle, interest in manipulating the puzzle merely for the sake of manipulation seems to have greatly decreased.

The introduction of a reward apparently affects the subject's evaluation of the task itself. If the task has been performed without reward and a reward is introduced, the most obvious effect is for the subject to attempt to attain the reward with the least effort possible. Concentration on the goal may hamper task performance (as when the monkeys attacked the hasp directly rather than proceed through the sequence of devices in the order that they had learned previous to the introduction of the raisin). One of the effects of an extrinsic reward upon task behavior, then, is to focus attention on the reward and this effect may produce a deterioration of task performance.

The evidence from the last trial with the puzzle, again unbaited, indicated that the monkeys were much less prone to unfasten the puzzle than they were before the raisins had been introduced. Apparently, the intrinsic aspects of manipulation sufficed to sustain learning and persistent manipulation until the unfastening of the devices took on a instrumental aspect with the introduction of the raisin. With the raisin in place, the unfastening took on the "in order to" obtain food aspect. Once this had happened, the monkeys were much less prone to "play" with the puzzle for its own sake when there was no raisin to be gained. The puzzle game had become commercialized, the monkey was no longer an amateur, he would not work without pay. Play had turned into work, and the monkey was now dependent upon the experimenter to make the puzzle interesting to him by extrinsic means.

We have stressed the simple case of the monkeys and the raisin to make a point. The introduction of pay into play makes it work. The Origin who is committed to a course of action may lose some of his commitment and much of his freedom if he is offered too much praise and remuneration. He may become a Pawn to the source of the reward.

One further aspect of the experiment under consideration is interesting from the point of view of the concept of personal causation. The study gives a comparison of two situations in which one variable sufficed to produce intrinsic motivation in one group and not in the other. The authors fail to analyze the critical difference, namely that the Group A monkeys were confronted with assembled puzzles and the Group B monkeys with unassembled puzzles in the training period. None of the Group B animals ever fastened any of the devices. Manipulation in its broadest sense could include fastening, unfastening, or just playing with the puzzle. Apparently only unfastening was learned. In short, the manipulatory behavior discussed by Harlow is more specific than simple "monkeying" with gadgets in this case. It is unfastening elicited by an assembled puzzle and followed by a specific change in the environment. Persistent behavior results in learning how to "master" this situation. There are elements here of personal causation in the accomplishment of an environmental change. In the monkey, this behavior is only found in unfastening; in a higher organism, fastening the unassembled device might have been the result of a similar orientation to effect changes in the environment.

The Harlow et al. (1950) experiment illustrates the effects of adding an extrinsic incentive to an intrinsically motivated behavior pattern. The striking result is a deterioration of the intrinsically motivated behavior. The experiment gives a good example of learning as well as persistent behavior in the absence of extrinsic incentives, and provides an instance where rudimentary aspects of the concept of personal causation may be seen.

A Paradoxical Effect of Withdrawing an Extrinsic Incentive

We have not only hypothesized that adding an extrinsic reward may sully an intrinsically motivated behavior, but also that withdrawing a promised reward may enhance task performance. Weick (1964) invited 100 male college students to participate in an experiment for which they would receive experimental credit for a course in psychology. When the subjects arrived for the experiment one-half of them were informed by an elaborate procedure that they would not receive the experimental credit that they had been promised. This group comprised the No-Credit Group and the other half of the subjects were the Credit Group. The experimenter predicted that subjects in the No-Credit Group (as compared to the Credit Group) would work faster, accomplish the experimental task more efficiently, and rate it as more interesting. In short, they should show an enhancement of motivation as a result of being deprived of the extrinsic incentive that was used to get them there.

The subjects participated in a concept attainment task from which measures of speed and efficiency could be obtained and they rated the task and the experimenter at the end of the experiment. The task was one in which interest and probability of success increased as the subject increased his effort.

The results of the experiment confirm the hypotheses very strongly. Differences between the No-Credit and the Credit Group are highly significant on ten different measures of expended effort, task accomplishment, and goal setting. All of these measures indicate stronger motivation on the part of the No-Credit Group. In addition, the No-Credit Group rated the experiment more interesting than the Credit Group; but, as might be expected, they expressed greater dislike for the experimenter who had reneged on his promise of experimental credit.

The Weick experiment demonstrates the paradoxical effect of withdrawing a promised extrinsic reward. The subjects apparently show greater indication of intrinsic motivation and interest in the task after the promised reward is withdrawn. We have our example, but what is the explanation?

Two aspects of the experiment suggest the explanation that withdrawal of the extrinsic reward enhanced striving for personal causation in the No-Credit Group. First, it was made clear to the subjects in the No-Credit Group when it was announced that they would receive no credit that they were free to leave and that the choice to remain and participate was their own. They were treated like Origins with respect to whether they would participate or not. "Four out of the 54 subjects actually chose to leave. Of the 50 who remained, all indicated in the post-session interview that they felt free to leave, and that the choice had been their own" (Weick, 1964, p. 535). The No-Credit Group were treated more like Origins, the Credit Group more like Pawns.

The second aspect of the experiment that is important for a personal causation explanation is that the experimental task was intrinsically interesting. In fact, the author notes that as the subject expended more effort in solving the problems the task became more interesting and the subject got more feedback that he was effective in solving the problems. "In the present study, the task permits the subject to maintain considerable control over the outcomes that he receives. Expending greater effort on the concept-attainment task actually makes it more interesting and increases the probability of success. A task in which effort expenditure had no effect on the outcome might produce quite different results" (Weick, 1964, p. 539).

The No-Credit Group in the experiment apparently experienced the two major components that enhance striving for personal causation and make a person feel that he is the origin of his own behavior, namely, freedom and the opportunity for self-investment or commitment to the task.

In contrast to the above explanation, Weick's derivation of his original hypotheses and explanation of the confirming results stems from an entirely different orientation, namely, Festinger's (1957) theory of cognitive dissonance. The basic postulate of the theory is that when a person is confronted with two discrepant cognitive elements (beliefs, sentiments or accomplished facts) a state of dissonance will result and attempts will be made to reduce the dissonance by changes in beliefs. It is further hypothesized that changing a belief may have a significant effect on behavior. From these propositions Weick postulated that withdrawing the promised credit in the No-Credit Group would induce the subjects to dislike the experimenter. If they then chose to remain in the experiment as the experimenter desired them to, the fact that they were voluntarily doing something for the experimenter would be dissonant with their dislike for the experimenter. In order to reduce this dissonance they would be likely to change their attitude toward the experimental task in a positive direction so that the cognition that they had chosen to participate could be explained as a result of the attractiveness of the task and not the attractiveness of the experimenter who asked them to do it. It was hypothesized that dissonance reduction would enhance the attractiveness of the experimental task in the No-Credit Group but not in the Credit Group. The enhanced attractiveness in turn would affect the amount of effort expended on the task. "In summary, it is proposed that the choice to comply with a negatively valued task setter for no reward arouses cognitive dissonance and forces the subject to justify his continued association with the task setter. Initial task enhancement followed by high productivity constitutes a powerful avenue of dissonance reduction under these conditions" (Weick, 1964, p. 534).

The explanation in terms of personal causation is interesting as contrasted with the cognitive dissonance explanation in light of a discussion by Brehm and Cohen (1962). Their book amply demonstrates that cognitive dissonance theory cogently explains changes in attitudes. A few recent studies, of which Weick's is an example, have attempted to go beyond attitude change and take the step of predicting changes in task performance as a result of cognitive dissonance. Brehm and Cohen have argued that one of the factors which may produce cognitive dissonance is volition. If a person voluntarily chooses to do something distasteful, the cognition that he has done it is dissonant with the cognition that it is distasteful. Dissonance reduction can occur through the avenue of a changed attitude toward the task in the form of increased liking.

But Brehm and Cohen (1962) also assume that a person who feels that he is not in control of his own behavior suffers dissonance that he will attempt to reduce. "What may be involved here is the individual's feeling of control of his own behavior. We suspect that what the attempted coercion produced was strong individual differences in concern with and feeling of personal control. We shall call this conscious control of one's own behavior *volition*" (Brehm & Cohen, 1962, p. 201).

The experiments under discussion compared strong coercion with weaker coercion. The most obvious way to explain results in this case is to highlight the negative aspects of coercion and to assume that the subject will attempt to reduce them. But what about positive aspects of freedom and attempts to seek it out. In light of Brehm and Cohen's discussion of volition (the feeling of control, the dissonance explanation that stresses coercion), the personal causation, and the volitional dissonance explanations have much in common. Specifically, they both highlight the dimension of personal feelings of control. Dissonance theory must find dissonance, and therefore stresses the negative aspect of the *lack* of feeling of control. In this, it is similar to all theories that postulate reduction of a negative state. A state of reduced dissonance has no positive component, it is just less painful than a dissonance state. Strong coercion and the resulting powerlessness and lack of personal control would be unpleasant. The personal causation explanation, however, assumes a positive aspect. Freely chosen behavior is attractive in its own right.

Weick's dissonance explanation demands no consideration of intrinsically motivating aspects of the task. The personal causation explanation rests heavily on the assumption that striving for personal causation in an intrinsically interesting task is enhanced by freedom. Brehm and Cohen's suggestion that lack of volition leads to dissonance lies somewhere in between. A task that did not engage the subject's volition would not be attempted without coercion, but Brehm and Cohen slight the intrinsic quality of the task and stress the dissonance between volition and action.

Reduction and Enhancement of Freedom

Experimental manipulation of freedom is almost a contradiction in terms. Clearly it is easier to reduce freedom in the laboratory than to increase it. Reduction of freedom of choice is the major technique used by Brehm (1966) to demonstrate the motivational arousal that he calls psychological reactance. His technique creates conditions in which a person having lost a freedom once available to him is more of a Pawn than when the freedom was never available. In addition to Brehm's studies, three contrasting studies will be presented in which the attempt was to enhance freedom. The last two studies were specifically designed to study the Origin-Pawn variable experimentally.

PSYCHOLOGICAL REACTANCE —
THE EFFECTS OF BEING MADE A PAWN

In a recent book, Brehm (1966) reported a series of studies of people's reaction to reduction of their freedom. The following passage presents Brehm's basic hypothesis as well as an explanation of his use of "psychological reactance."

> . . . if a person's behavioral freedom is reduced or threatened with reduction, he will become motivationally aroused. This arousal would presumably be directed against any further loss of freedom and it would also be directed toward the re-establishment of whatever freedom had already been lost or threatened. Since this hypothetical motivational state is in response to the reduction (or threatened reduction) of one's potential for acting, and conceptually may be considered a counterforce, it will be called "psychological reactance" (Brehm, 1966, p. 2).

As an anecdotal example that captures the essence of his idea, Brehm suggests that a man, who normally plays golf on Sunday afternoon but occasionally chooses to putter in his workshop and feels that the choice is up to him, will experience reactance when his wife tells him that he must get out of the house and play golf because she is having a "hen" party. Psychological reactance in such a situation should result in an increased desire to stay home and a decreased attractiveness of golf. The critical factor is that his freedom of choice has been threatened.

Brehm presents evidence for the arousal of reactance when freedom is eliminated or threatened either by a personal or an impersonal source and when persuasive pressure is applied to change someone's attitude. As an example of personal elimination of freedom Hammock and Brehm (1966) report two similar experiments in which children were shown several desirable objects (candy bars in one case and toys in the other) and asked to rank them according to their desirability. The children were told that they would be given one of the objects and one-half of them were led to believe that they would have a choice between two gifts whereas the other half were not led to expect a choice. In all cases, an assistant arbitrarily gave them one gift without allowing a choice. The reactance effect was found in a subsequent ranking of all objects in that for the group who expected a choice but were not given that freedom the preference for the arbitrarily assigned gift dropped while preference for the denied alternative increased. For the no-choice group whose freedom had not been eliminated, the rank of the gift did not change. These effects were those predicted by the hypothesis that personal elimination of freedom of choice would arouse psychological reactance.

FREEDOM OF CHOICE

To feel strongly that one is the origin of his own behavior, one must also feel that it was up to him whether he did it or not. If he chose to act freely, he will locate the causation for the behavior within himself, and this will have important consequences for his behavior. But freedom is difficult to create. Capturing behavior which results from free choice presents formidable difficulties in the social psychology laboratory. A subject who comes to a psychological experiment has been drafted in some way that restricts his freedom, and it is typical for the subject (the very word implies constraint) to be ready to "subject" himself to the experimenter's wishes, and even to resist attempts to increase his freedom. He is in the hands of the experimenter, he expects to be treated as a Pawn, and he may dislike any redefinition of the situation in which he is forced to make choices and to be responsible for them.

Samples of subjects may differ according to the technique used to obtain them. For instance, volunteer subjects typically have stronger achievement motivation than do nonvolunteer subjects (Burdick, 1955), and the behavior of volunteers in the experiment may differ from the behavior of draftees. A comparison of persons who have freely chosen an activity (Origins) and persons who have been forced into it (Pawns) may show the effects of knowledge of personal causation on behavior. Any such comparison is relative, i.e., the Origin is only *more* free than the Pawn; no absolute distinction is implied.

In a study of volunteering, Green (1963) obtained subjects (1) who volunteered, (2) who volunteered and were then told that they actually had no choice, and (3) who did not volunteer but were drafted. These conditions constituted a major independent variable in the study and were operationalized in the following way. The experimenter went to several sections of a college course and asked for volunteers for an experiment. In half of the sections, the volunteers' names were collected; they were scheduled for the experiment and the experimenter left. In the other half, the names of volunteers were collected and then it was announced that all subjects were actually required to participate, i.e., they had all been drafted, whether they had volunteered or not. Thus groups of "volunteers," "drafted volunteers," and "draftees" were obtained.

Green argued that "volunteers are curious about and interested in the things that they are going to be asked to do," while nonvolunteers "do not volunteer because of a lack of interest in such things or an antipathy toward them" (p. 398).

In addition to interest, however, the groups should differ in locating the origin of their behavior either within themselves or in the experimenter. The feelings of responsibility for, and commitment to, the behavior should differ between the three groups. The volunteers chose to take part in the experiment; the draftees found that they had to take part; and the volunteer-draftees found, in effect, that they had to do what they had originally chosen to do. Volunteers and volunteer-draftees may have been similar as to interest and curiosity; volunteer-draftees and draftees may have been similar as to feelings of constraint, or reactance.

A questionnaire was used to ask subjects why they did or did not volunteer, but the results were not very illuminating. Enough of the volunteers suggested curiosity to encourage the experimenter that this might have been one of the differences between volunteers and draftees, although the responses were apparently so diffuse as to indicate that the questionnaire was not very reliable.

Green's dependent variable was a measure of the recall of incompleted versus completed tasks. The so-called Zeigarnik effect found in earlier experiments (Zeigarnik, 1927; Marrow, 1938; Lewis & Franklin, 1944) indicates, that, in general, subjects tend to recall more readily tasks that they have not finished than similar tasks that they have finished. Other studies (Glixman, 1949; Gilmore, 1954) have failed to obtain the Zeigarnik effect; and Green cites Atkinson (1955) as pointing out that subjects in the former studies were predominantly volunteers, whereas those in the latter were draftees. Green set out to determine if this difference was crucial in explaining different results of previous experiments. He gave his subjects twenty paper-and-pencil tasks that had been used in previous studies of the Zeigarnik effect, and allowed them to complete one-half of the tasks scattered through the list while he interrupted one-half. Immediately after the subjects had worked on the twenty tasks, he asked them to recall as many of them as they could. A ratio was formed of the number of interrupted tasks recalled, divided by the total number of tasks recalled. This ratio constituted the score on the dependent variable for each subject. If more interrupted tasks were recalled than completed tasks, as predicted by the Zeigarnik effect, the ratio would exceed .500; if more completed tasks were recalled, the ratio would be less than .500.

Table 10.1 presents the mean Zeigarnik ratios for the three groups of subjects. Although the differences are not large, they are in the direction predicted by Green, namely, most recall of interrupted tasks by volunteers (ratio >.500), and least by draftees (ratio <.500); the predicted trend reaches a significance of $p <.025$.

TABLE 10.1
Mean Recall Ratios[a]

Volunteers	Volunteer-Draftees	Draftees
$(N = 32)$	$(N = 32)$	$(N = 32)$
.533	.517	.480

[a]Ratio $= \dfrac{\text{Number of interrupted tasks recalled}}{\text{Total number of tasks recalled}}$; data from Green (1963).

The author interprets these data as confirming his hypothesis that the difference between conflicting results of some earlier studies was the result of the way subjects were recruited. The difference between volunteers and draftees which led to different recall ratios is speculatively attributed to a higher level of interest assumed to be characteristic of the volunteers.

No more penetrating analysis of the effects of volunteering is presented, since, as Green points out, volunteering may be done for many reasons, and the actual explanation of the Zeigarnik effect still eludes psychologists, despite a plethora of studies. We need not assume, however, that the reasons for volunteering actually accounted for the results. No matter what their reasons, they all did volunteer in two groups and did not in the third. The act of volunteering is an act of personal choice and commitment, and the reasons for it may become subordinated to the feeling of being committed to the experiment as a result of having originated the behavior that put them into the situation.

We would assume that a major difference between volunteers and draftees is the feeling in the latter of compulsion, or of being controlled from without—of being a Pawn. Differences in initial interest may contribute to differences between volunteers and draftees, but not to differences between volunteers and volunteer-draftees. Between these two groups, the major difference is that the volunteer-draftees may perceive their behavior in the experiment as more determined by the experimenter who has shown his power by allowing them to choose, but then indicating that the freedom implied by the choice was actually a sham. Such manipulation may well rob the subject of his feeling of being an Origin, and under such conditions he may feel less commitment and responsibility for his behavior in the experiment. In short, the volunteers should feel little constraint for they are doing what they chose to do for personal reasons of interest and the like. The volunteer-draftees should feel constrained for, after all, they found that they had no choice but were constrained to do something for which they had originally volunteered. The draftees, in addition to being constrained, were forced to do something that they had originally rejected for personal reasons.

The indications from the Green study are that the feeling of being an Origin, with its implication of commitment as operationalized in this case by volunteering, appears to foster the recall of incompleted tasks. Being an Origin enhances the recall of incompleted tasks because the Origin is involved in the tasks themselves. These tasks retain their interest because he has not yet overcome them. Being a Pawn enhances the recall of completed tasks because the constraint involved makes the relationship with the constraining force (the experimenter) more salient. The *struggle against* being treated as a Pawn must be directed toward the agent of constraint, and this can be done by demonstrating competence and thereby pleasing the experimenter. The completed tasks are recalled by the drafted Pawns because they impressed or pleased the experimenter.

INVOLVEMENT AND FREEDOM

In the Green experiment, the effects of interest and curiosity that may have led to volunteering, plus the fact that the volunteers freely chose to participate, should summate to increase commitment to, and self-investment in, the task. Another variable manipulated in the experiment was ego versus task orientation. As noted above, the psychological literature has used the phrase "ego-involvement" or "ego-orientation" in a way that usually means threat. Although discussions of ego-involvement often imply a positive approach to the task, operational manipulations almost always resort to a strong element of threat to self-esteem. Ego-involving instructions consist of telling the person that he is being evaluated, that the experimental task is actually a sensitive test of his ability, intelligence, etc., and that from the results the experimenter will be able to tell how good he is along some important dimension. Under these conditions, the person is constrained to work hard and do well if he is at all interested in the evaluations by the experimenter. His "self" is to be tested, his "self esteem" is threatened, and anxiety is invariably aroused. This is far from the type of involvement implied by the self freely investing his energies and interest in a task. Freedom is constrained rather than increased by ego-involving instructions, and the resulting behavior may be expected to show different characteristics from behavior resulting from free choice.

The Green study gives us a good example of the different results deriving from "ego-involving" instructions. The second independent variable in the study was a variation of subject orientation. Orienting instructions that were intended to produce ego-involvement were given to one-half of the subjects; task-orienting instructions, intended to make them concentrate on the task but not on an evaluation of themselves, were given to the other half of the subjects.

The ego-involving instructions were typical of those used in the large literature on ego-involvement and were modeled after an early "classic" in the area of ego-involvement studies by Marrow (1938). About the instructions, Green says, "A probable relationship between test performance and success in various professions was asserted and the experimenter added, 'Since you will probably be going into teaching or some professional field, you can see why we are interested in how successful you will be on these tests'" (p. 399).

The task-orienting instructions used the term "task" rather than "test" and stressed an interest in how people in general do on the tasks, rather than how the individual himself *did*. The importance of his total score was not mentioned. "We are interested in how rapidly and accurately each of these exercises can be completed. . ." (p. 399).

TABLE 10.2
Mean Recall Ratios[a]

	Volunteers	Volunteer-Draftees	Draftees	Total
Task orientation	.572	.554	.524	.550
Ego orientation	.493	.480	.437	.470
Total	.533	.517	.480	

[a] $\text{Ratio} = \dfrac{\text{Number of interrupted tasks recalled}}{\text{Total number of tasks recalled}}$; data from Green (1963).

The effects of these instructions upon the Zeigarnik ratio clearly demonstrate that "ego-involvement," as here manipulated, fosters the recall of completed tasks—the opposite of the effect of volunteering. Table 10.2 shows both effects. The orientation effect is significant beyond the .005 level of significance.

Evidently, ego-involvement has the opposite effect of volunteering in this situation as might be predicted if ego-involving instructions actually tend to constrain the subject and force him to show his ability under threat of negative evaluation. It is clear from this (and many other earlier studies show similar effects) that a person who chooses an activity freely and is committed to it cannot be said to be ego-involved in the sense that the term ego-involvement is used in experimental studies. (Ego-involvement stems from an external evaluative source; commitment, in the sense of personal investment of interest and energy, stems from an internal source.) Comparison of the means in Column 1 of Table 10.2 shows that the effect of having volunteered (a high ratio indicating predominant recall of incompleted tasks), is strongest under task-orienting instructions, and is greatly attenuated (actually below .500) under ego-orienting instructions. If we accept the Zeigarnik ratio as a sensitive indicator, it appears that ego-involvement actually interferes with the type of individual commitment that we see as related to free choice and personal investment.

Personal investment is to be distinguished from ego-involvement along the dimension of internal versus external locus of causality for behavior. The ego-involving instructions impose restraint from an external source that forces the subject to "produce or else." The subject will experience his own behavior as stemming from an external locus under these conditions. In the extreme, he will feel that he is a Pawn who must perform for the evaluator. Personal investment should result from a desire to engage in the behavior. The subject will experience his behavior as stemming from his own personal causation—he should feel that he is the origin of his behavior.

It is very difficult to conceive of experimental manipulations that will enhance the feeling of personal investment. The very idea that it can be induced in a subject by an external source is inimical to the notion that such investment stems from within the subject. For this reason very little can be found in the literature, whereas scores of studies of ego-involvement are available. The notion of "task-involvement" has been proposed by Asch (1952) in an attempt to distinguish an "objective interest" in a task from a "self-centered" orientation under ego-involvement. Task orientation for Asch implies interest in the task itself, which is a result of a need for an objective and productive relation to the environment. The stress is on interest in objects and activities; the implication is that task orientation is object-centered, ego orientation is self-centered. This distinction goes far to clarify an important orientation, but it seems to over-emphasize the subjective-objective distinction. Again we are led to the use of the word "personal." Personal investment is far from mere interest in objects and activities, for it implies a very personal "giving" of the self in the investment of energy.

TWO STUDIES DESIGNED TO MANIPULATE THE ORIGIN-PAWN VARIABLE

We can now turn to two studies (Kuperman, 1967; de Charms *et al.,* 1965, unpublished) specifically designed to induce in the subjects the feeling of being an Origin and of being a Pawn. The guiding idea behind the studies was that, when working as an Origin, subjects would feel more enjoyment and would show more personal investment in the task and in their own productions than when working as a Pawn. We learned much about manipulating the independent variable of the Origin-Pawn condition and the measurement of dependent effects by extensive pretesting conducted by Kuperman.

The extreme of inducing a feeling of complete freedom was impossible, especially in the laboratory. Failing this, it seemed probable that two degrees of constraint would be most effective. Kuperman had to tell his subjects what to do, but he could allow them much latitude in one case and little in another. It also became clear that they themselves should see the comparison, i.e., each subject should experience both degrees of constraint rather than have one group of subjects under one condition and another group under the other condition. The advantage of this (essentially using each subject as his own control) lies in the fact that all subjects are comparing the same things. A real comparison is involved. If subjects are asked for absolute judgments about one condition alone, each may have a private condition with which he is comparing the experimental condition. Thus the results are partially attributable to a variable factor that is unknown to the experimenter.[3]

The experiment was designed so that each subject performed similar tasks under both the Origin and the Pawn condition. The task was to build rather complex models from standard sets of Tinkertoys, a task that had been shown in pretests to be interesting, especially if the model included a gear arrangement that drove a shaft on which a fan could be placed. Kuperman systematically varied the attractiveness of the models built, but we shall not concern ourselves with this variable.

The basic problem was how to measure personal investment. Kuperman hypothesized that models built under the Origin condition would show greater quality than those built in the Pawn condition. Accord-

---

[3]This psychological fact is contained in the anecdote about the psychologist who, when asked, "How's your wife?" replied, "Compared to what?"

ingly, he took about one-third of the Tinkertoy pieces available to the subjects and rubbed them with dirt and generally soiled them and made them inferior to the other pieces. The plan was to count the number of inferior pieces used in each condition.

It was hypothesized that if the subject started one model under the Origin condition and one under the Pawn condition but did not complete either, he would tend to choose to complete the Origin model. This is the measure used in the studies of resumption of interrupted tasks, and pretests indicated that this was a usable measure.

The resumption criterion is an all-or-none variable and, as such, is not very sensitive. In an attempt to obtain a more sensitive measure, Kuperman allowed the subject to choose which model to resume, then asked him to complete both, and counted the number of additional pieces he added to each model when he was free to add anything he liked. He also measured how long the subject worked in completing each model.

In the course of pretesting, it seemed plausible that the degree of personal-investment in each model could be measured by forcing the subject to destroy one of the models. The hypothesis was that he would choose to destroy the Pawn model. The cost of complete destruction was prohibitive, but subjects were induced to dismantle one of the models.

The actual experiment was rather complicated since it had to control such things as which of the four models was built, which condition was experienced first, whether the partially completed Origin model was on the preferred side of the subject when he chose which to complete, and several other factors. These factors were controlled, but we shall ignore them here and concentrate on the major variables.

After the subject had practiced with the Tinkertoys so that when faced with building a model he would have some experience, he built one model under the Pawn condition and one under the Origin condition (ordinal position being controlled). In the Pawn condition, the subject was given a diagram to look at in building the model. After preliminary instructions to clarify the names of pieces, etc., the experimenter gave detailed instructions to the subject as to each step in the procedure, e.g., "1. Place one red rod in a center hole of a regular spool. 2. Place one blue rod in a radial hole of a regular spool" etc. There were approximately fifty instructions of this type for the Pawn model. The instructions proceeded in a way that arbitrarily avoided obvious next steps and prevented the subjects from attaining the final "gestalt" as long as possible. Subjects were not permitted to anticipate the instructions and they were given in a neutral tone.

The Origin condition attempted to create a feeling of freedom and self-directedness. The subject was given a picture of the model to be constructed and told to build the model as he saw fit and was left in privacy.

After having built both models (Phase I), one under Origin and one under Pawn conditions (ordinal position and model designs were counter balanced), the subject placed them across the room and returned to his table to fill out a questionnaire. Next the subject was told to go and get the model that he would like to work on further since neither model was complete in all details. The subject actually made a behavioral choice between the models thinking he could work on only one. When he had made the choice, however, he was informed that he would actually complete both models (Phase II). One-half of the subjects completed first the one they had chosen to complete, and the other half were instructed to complete the non-chosen one first and then to complete the chosen one.

The measures taken of completing the two models were the number of parts used and the time involved in Phase II. Subjects were free to elaborate and complete the models in any way that they wished, but they were instructed to plan what they wanted to do first because they would only be allowed to go to the parts table once and would have to get exactly the number of parts needed for their plan and not return. This procedure was an attempt to avoid an excessive amount of time in this phase.[4]

When both models were completed to the satisfaction of the subject, they were again placed across the room and he was asked to go and get one that he would then destroy. After the choice was made and recorded and before the model was destroyed, the subject was interrupted and told the experiment was over; questions were answered, and the subject was asked not to talk about the experiment.

The experiment produced two types of measures on 64 male college students. Questionnaires administered after each model was built and comparing them after both were completed asked the subjects (a) how free they felt, (b) how much like a Pawn they felt, (c) how much they enjoyed making each model, (d) how much they disliked making each model, (e) how motivated they felt to continue each model. Behavioral measures recorded during the experiment resulted in (a) number of defective parts used in initial building of each model (Phase I), (b) number of defective parts used in completing each model (Phase II), (c) total

---

[4]One pretest subject given unlimited time and parts spent the better part of an afternoon and built a model which nearly reached to the ceiling.

number of parts used in completing each model, *(d)* the model chosen for completion, *(e)* the model chosen to destroy.

Table 10.3 presents the data from the experiment in the serial order of the above-itemized measures. The questionnaire measures all produced results significant beyond the .001 level showing that subjects reported *(a)* feeling more free, *(b)* feeling less like a Pawn, *(c)* enjoying more, *(d)* disliking less, and *(e)* feeling more motivated to continue the Origin model as compared to the Pawn model.

TABLE 10.3

Frequency of Subjects Who Responded on Various
Measures Comparing Origin versus Pawn Conditions[a]

	Origin	*Pawn*	*Unclassified*[b]	χ^2	*p*
	Model				
I. Questionnaire measures ($N = 64$)					
a. Felt more free	60	2	2	52.4[c]	<.001
b. Felt more like Pawn	2	60	2	52.4	<.001
c. Enjoyed performance more	52	10	2	27.1	<.001
d. Disliked performance more	9	47	8	24.5	<.001
e. Felt more motivated to continue	46	10	8	21.9	<.001
II. Behavioral measures ($N = 64$)					
a. More defective parts in building (Phase I)	13	11	40	0.1	—
b. More defective parts in completing (Phase II)	32	13	19	7.2	<.025
c. Used more parts to complete	37	27	0	1.3	—
d. Chose to complete	36	28	0	0.8	—
e. Chose to destroy[d]	24	25	0	0.0	—

[a]Adapted from Kuperman (1967).
[b]Unclassified designates no preference on verbal responses and no difference on behavioral measures.
[c]All χ^2 corrected for continuity.
[d]Data available only on 49 subjects.

The results of the behavioral measures on the other hand, were completely negative. The only significant χ^2 in the second part of Table 10.3 shows that subjects, contrary to prediction, used more defective parts in completing the Origin model than in completing the Pawn model. It is hard to interpret this result, but in view of the fact that nearly two-thirds of the subjects showed no difference in using defective parts in the initial building, and nearly one-third of the subjects in the completion phase, it seems hardly worth speculating about.

In general, Kuperman was apparently successful in producing Origin versus Pawn feelings in his 64 male college students but unsuccessful in measuring any effects of the manipulations on behavioral measures designed to indicate personal investment in the Origin model. He reports also that the Rotter scale of expectancies of external versus internal control of reinforcement (adapted from Rotter *et al.*, 1962) was not related to any of the measures in the experiment.

Building on the experience of Kuperman's extensive pretesting, de Charms *et al.* (1965, unpublished) designed a very similar study attempting to increase the feeling of freedom in the Origin condition and to obtain more subtle behavioral measures of the effects of the Origin-Pawn manipulation. The Origin-Pawn models utilized both contained a gear mechanism that turned a shaft on which a fan could be placed. The subjects in both the Origin and Pawn conditions started with the gear mechanism and built the model around it. In the Pawn condition, explicit instructions were given for each step as in the Kuperman study.

In the Origin condition, every effort was made to create a feeling of freedom and self-directedness. The subject was given an identical gear to the one used in the Pawn condition, 50 assorted pieces, and told to build a model of his own design. Although he was restricted to 50 pieces, he could trade any of those he had for one on an open table of many pieces. The restriction to 50 pieces was explained as an effort to limit time spent and size of model. Once the subject was started building the Origin model, the experimenter left him alone in the room.

In trying to obtain more subtle behavioral measures of the effects of the Origin-Pawn manipulations *(a)* we refined Kuperman's measures of the quality with which the subject completed both models after the initial building under the experimental conditions, *(b)* we forced the subject to "borrow" a crucial part from one of the completed models rendering it inoperative (this was an attempt to refine Kuperman's "destroy" measure), and *(c)* we gave the models nonsense syllable names and measured the recall of the names one month later. With regard to these measures we hypothesized that *(a)* the Origin model would be more elegantly completed than the Pawn model, *(b)* the subject would "borrow" from and render inoperative the Pawn model, and *(c)* the subjects would recall the name of the Origin model more often than the name of the Pawn model.

These measures were operationalized in the following ways. Both of the models were built to near completion except that the shaft driven by the gear had nothing to turn. After building under the two conditions, the subject, with both models in front of him, was given two fans and asked to place them on the two models. One fan was clearly inferior to the other in that it was missing one blade. The measures taken were *(a)* which model he placed the fan on first, and *(b)* which model he put the complete fan on.

The "borrowing" measure actually came before the subject put the fans on the models. After the subject had built both the Origin and Pawn models (in the order required by the experimental design) to a point where they were both complete with the exception of placing a fan on the gear shaft, the models were placed across the room out of reach. He was then asked to build a simple rigid house from a diagram using parts supplied him. He was told that possibly the supply of pieces would be inadequate, and, if that were the case, he could "borrow" from one of the models across the room. In fact, each subject found himself one piece short and was forced to borrow from either the Origin or the Pawn model.[5]

During a familiarization period, the subject had worked with three models all of which had nonsense syllable names arbitrarily assigned to them and communicated to him on a card. An arbitrarily assigned nonsense syllable name of the Pawn model was communicated to the subject by a card also. After the subject had completed the Origin model, he chose a name for it from among five nonsense syllables. In all, he was exposed to nine nonsense syllables: one he chose for the Origin model, one assigned to the Pawn model, three for the practice models, and four which he rejected as the name for the Origin model.

After the experimental procedures, the subject answered a questionnaire designed to measure his comparative feelings about the Origin and Pawn models. The first question asked of the subject was which model he would choose to continue working on if he had more time and parts. (All models were designed in such a way that they could be added to and elaborated on). The remaining questionnaire items were scales on which the subject placed two marks, one indicating his rating of the Origin and one his rating of the Pawn model. The scales measured "success in building" (completely unsuccessful to completely successful), involvement (engrossed-detached), liking of *building* the model, feelings of freedom, and liking of the model itself.

Subjects were 64 male junior and senior students from physical science classes in a private high school. They were told that we were interested in estimates of time under varying conditions and were asked to make such estimates after each task. This device forestalled questions and minimized suspicion of manipulations. Subjects participated individually in the experiment.

---

[5]Procedures developed in pretests to make this part of the experiment plausible were used but need not concern us here. The "borrowed" piece was returned to the model by the experimenter before the subjects were given the fans to put on the shafts.

Approximately one month after the last subject participated, the experimenter returned to discuss the experiment with the class. Before doing so, however, he asked them to write on a card the nonsense syllable name of any of the models that they could remember in the order that they occurred to them.

The measures in this experiment can be divided into responses on the questionnaire, more strictly behavioral measures, and the recall measure. Some of the questionnaire items were checks on the adequacy of the manipulation of the independent variable, whereas others measured hypothesized effects of the manipulation.

We have stressed that working under Origin conditions, as compared to Pawn conditions, should be perceived as freer and should lead to more personal investment. Responses to the questionnaire reveal that we were highly successful in creating differential feelings along these dimensions in favor of the Origin condition. Table 10.4 indicates that 61 of 64 subjects felt freer, and 50 felt more involved in the Origin condition. These highly significant results may seem obvious, but they serve in demonstrating that the subjects actually did perceive the situation as we intended. The involvement result is important in its own right, and, as Ferguson (1962) pointed out, most ego-involvement studies fail to check on their manipulation. We can show, for instance, that often the subjects who did not conform to our hypotheses on other measures were subjects who reported more involvement in the Pawn model than the Origin. There were only 13 such subjects, however, so in general the manipulations were highly successful.

Stemming from the notions of personal investment, it was hypothesized that subjects would report that they liked building the Origin model better than the Pawn model. Table 10.4 shows a highly significant difference confirming this hypothesis. Furthermore, of the thirteen subjects who reported liking the Pawn model better, eight had also reported more personal investment in the Pawn model. These data are very consistent in indicating that the Origin-Pawn manipulation produced greater feelings of freedom and personal investment, and these conditions fostered a liking for building the Origin model. In the few instances in which manipulation failed to produce personal investment in the Origin model, subjects often reported liking to build the Pawn model best.

Our major interest was in their feelings *while building* each model, and the question just discussed stressed this. They were also asked which model *per se* they liked the best, the Origin or the Pawn. Here they showed no significant preference, indicating that they distinguished between pleasure in doing the task and liking of the final product.

One item on the questionnaire gave us a surprise. We had assumed (perhaps naively) that when asked about success, subjects would rate themselves most successful on the Origin model or at least on the one

TABLE 10.4
Frequency of Subjects Who Chose Origin
Versus Pawn Model on Various Measures[a]

	Origin	Pawn	Unclassified	O-P Comparison
I. Involvement rated higher	51	11	2[b]	$\chi^2 = 25.8, p < .0005$
Felt freer	61	3	0	$\chi^2 = 52.5, p < .0005$
Liked building best	42	13	9[c]	$\chi^2 = 14.0, p < .0005$
Liked model best	25	31	8[c]	$\chi^2 = 3.78$, n.s.
Success rated higher	12	49	3[d]	$\chi^2 = 22.4, p < .0005$
Choice to continue	53	9	2[e]	$\chi^2 = 31.19, p < .0005$
II. Fanned first	37	27	0	$\chi^2 = 1.5$, n.s.
Placed complete fan on	46	18	0	$\chi^2 = 12.25, p < .0005$
Borrowed from	47	17	0	$\chi^2 = 14.06, p < .0005$
III. Recalled only name of	40	3	21[f]	$\chi^2 = 31.8, p < .0005$

[a]From de Charms, Dougherty, and Wurtz study.
[b]Equal involvement
[c]Equal liking
[d]Equal success
[e]No answer
[f]Eight recalled both, eleven neither, two absent. Of the eight who recalled both, six recalled the Origin first.

they liked building best. This is far from the case. The large majority (49) *reported feeling more successful on the Pawn model.* This finding, plus the difference between liking to build and liking the product, indicates that the subjects were making fine distinctions between their answers on the questionnaire. In retrospect, it seems plausible that theory should not predict feelings of greater success on the Origin model. Success implies an external evaluation of the end product; and any such ego-involving orientation was carefully avoided during the experiment. When asked about "success," the subjects probably tried to take an objective evaluative point of view and said, quite reasonably, that the carefully experimenter-designed model they built as a Pawn was, in the end, more successful than their own (Origin) model that was conceived on the spur of the moment.

The subjects were never asked to resume actual work on one of the two models, both of which were incomplete in that they had no fan. Strictly speaking, then, we have no behavioral measure of resumption.

We do have results from a questionnaire item that asked which they would choose to continue if permitted. The results are very strongly in the direction predicted. Fifty-three out of sixty-four subjects chose to continue the Origin model.

When given a complete and incomplete fan and asked to put one on each of the models, subjects showed a slight tendency to complete the Origin model first, but this was not a significant finding. What was highly significant was that 46 of them put the complete fan on the Origin model, thus choosing to complete it in a more elegant way than the Pawn model.

The data contained a second surprise. We had assumed that personal investment in the Origin model would lead subjects to borrow from the Pawn model, but the results indicate that a highly significantly greater number (47) borrowed from the Origin model. It is possible that the Pawn model was considered as the experimenter's and the Origin model as the subject's (some referred to it as "mine"), and therefore they felt that they could borrow more freely from their own. In addition, the original hypothesis was that subjects would avoid complete destruction of the Origin model, but the experimental condition was far from that. They merely had to take the most available piece, since any piece could be traded for any other (this was arranged so that availability would not be a factor, but tended to make the manipulation artificial). Our best guess is that the Pawn model was associated more with the authority of the experimenter and thus avoided when borrowing.

Perhaps the most striking results come from the recall measure. It will be remembered that subjects encountered nine nonsense syllables during the experiment. One of these was arbitrarily assigned by the experimenter to the Pawn model and one was chosen by the subject to be applied to the Origin model. Thus the subjects had more commerce with the two assigned to the experimental models. An average of 2.6 syllables were recalled by the subjects, although many of these were incorrect guesses. The data presented in Table 10.4 consider only correct recalls and only the two critical syllables for the Origin and Pawn models.[6] Forty subjects recalled the Origin but not the Pawn syllable, while only three recalled the Pawn but not the Origin syllable. This result clearly indicates the effects of the Origin-Pawn variable on recall and is consistent with, but much more striking than, Green's (1963) results with volunteers and draftees.

Of the eight subjects who recalled both the Origin and Pawn name, six listed the Origin name first. This is consistent with an early finding by Pachauri (1935) who demonstrated that incompleted tasks were not only

---

[6]Since syllables assigned and presented for choice were rotated systematically, the results cannot be attributed to outstanding characteristics of one syllable.

recalled in greater numbers than completed tasks, but were also recalled first chronologically, in a Zeigarnik-type experiment.

The results of this experiment strikingly demonstrate the effects of the manipulation of the Origin-Pawn variable. The experiment indicates that feelings of freedom and personal investment can be manipulated in the laboratory. In addition, the manipulation strongly affects liking of the task, choice to continue working, choice to complete the model elegantly, and recall of names associated with the model. All of these measures favored the model built under the Origin condition and all were chosen as indicators of a general positive affect invested in the product of work conducted under the Origin condition compared with work under the Pawn condition.

The two unexpected results were that the subjects reported feeling more successful on the Pawn model than on the Origin and that the subject chose to borrow from the Origin rather than the Pawn model, thus rendering it incomplete. These findings may be the result of associating the Pawn model with the authority of the experimenter. The idea of "success" implies external evaluation of the objective product rather than the feeling of personal success that the subject may have felt in building. This interpretation is supported by the evidence that the subjects liked building the Origin model best, but did not report liking the objective product more than the Pawn model.

Summary

We started this chapter with the hypothesis that the behavior of a person who feels that he is an Origin should be different from that of a person who feels that he is a Pawn. We noted that a man's knowledge of his own motivation implied in the phrase "feels like an Origin or Pawn" is not a simple perception of a stimulus, but a total experience and that not only can it be induced by environmental conditions, but also a person may have a tendency toward, or predominance of, Origin or of Pawn "feelings" that may be measured and constitute a personality characteristic.

Rotter's social learning theory has resulted in a measure and in considerable research that touches on a variable that is similar to the Origin-Pawn variable, called the "expectancy for internal versus external control of reinforcements." This approach borrows on the prestige of the objective definition of reinforcement, but when dealing with expectancies the theory dilutes the definition and loses its "objective rigor."

Koch's (1956) phenomenological description of his own states of motivation led us to hypothesize a relationship between the Origin-Pawn concept and the concepts of intrinsically and extrinsically motivated behavior. Extrinsically motivated behavior appears to be behavior done "in order to" reach an extrinsic reward. In such a situation, the person may be a Pawn to the mediator of the reward. Intrinsically motivated behavior, like Origin behavior, seems to involve freedom and self-investment. Here a distinction between ego-involvement and self-investment becomes necessary. Some paradoxical effects of the interaction between intrinsically and extrinsically motivating situations were noted as an indication that the two factors do not necessarily summate.

The final section of the chapter presented evidence for the effects of freedom or the loss of it and the Origin-Pawn variable on behavior.

Chapter 11

WE CAN KNOW MORE
THAN WE CAN TELL

In this chapter, it would be nice if we could tie everything together in a nice neat little package; but that is not possible. It has never been the aim of the book to present a new theory complete or incomplete. Rather we have tried to discuss some old problems in order to understand the present status of the concept of motivation. In an intensive study of the concept with special reference to human motivation and behavior, it has become clear that *the concept of motivation has no place in a strictly objective science of behavior.* This is so because, try as we may, *we can never completely objectify the concept of motivation.*

This conclusion leaves us with the major dilemma to which we admit no compromise. Either we pursue the goal of a completely objective science of behavior and renounce the concept of motivation, or we pursue the concept of motivation and renounce the goal of complete objectivity. The first alternative has been admirably set forth by Skinner, although other less pure behavioristic approaches have muddied the water with compromises. This book, spurred by some recent discussions by scientific philosophers, notably Bridgman and Polanyi, has tried to consider the case for a science of psychology that accepts personal states and personal knowledge as prime data and faces the fact that they can never be completely objectified.

Too often attempts in this direction are taken as a complete rejection of all that is implied by the phrase "a science of behavior." Too often the alternative is couched in terms of humanistic values and moralistic preachments and smacks of a return to the pre-Darwinian notions of man as a unique being. We have tried to avoid this adoration of our own kind. In tracing motivational phenomena to the concept of personal causation

355

and in postulating that man is not a stone, a machine, nor a mere animal, but an Origin, we have tried to emphasize what seems to us an elemental fact. *Man conceives of himself and of other human beings as loci of causality*. This is basic to man's knowledge of other persons as distinct from his knowledge of men as objects, as organisms, as things. In obtaining knowledge of other men, a man starts with a unique source of knowledge about himself. It is this source of knowledge that differentiates the study *by* man *of* man as a psychological being, as a subject, from the study *by* man of any thing else in the world.

The physical sciences first developed in an atmosphere of uncritical acceptance of the attribution of causality to the physical world, and, in macro-mechanics, the assumption works tolerably well. The search for empirical evidence for the attribution of causality was, however, fruitless, and empirical science has been puzzled by the problem ever since. On the one hand, the attribution of causality was often useful and compelling; but, on the other hand, it seemed incompatible with the basic tenets of scientific epistemology.

With the tremendous growth of psychology in the twentieth century and its emulation of scientific method, the analogy between physical causation of the movement of objects and the psychological motivation of human behavior seemed obvious. The more the psychologist pressed for objective knowledge of man, however, the more he was impressed by the necessity to question the concept of motivation, much as the physical scientists had come to question the concept of causation. *Causation turned out to be an inadequate concept upon which to base the concept of motivation.* In fact, the concept of causation proved itself to be an elusive concept in any context.

Man's knowledge of himself as motivated is the source from which his concept of causation comes; therefore, to seek to understand human motivation by analogy to physical causation is to seek an explanation of the more basic concept from the less basic one. Once this is accepted as a basic premise, psychological theories that have attempted to reduce motives to causes can be seen in the context of objectivism and physicalism that has strongly influenced psychology. The roots of these positions can be traced to Cartesian Dualism and the physicalistic resolution of the psychophysical dilemma with its implications of a para-mechanical conception of causation. This context is basically inimical to the study of the first-person subject and can only result in a psychology of the third-person as object—a behaviorism. The concept of motivation is central to the former and has no place in the latter. Behavioristic attempts to deal with motivational phenomena either *(a)* reduce to operational definitions, such as the empirical definition of reinforcement, that are rigorous until one attempts to generalize them, or *(b)* introduce into the machine a ghost who experiences "satisfaction." But to call this satisfaction self- or internal-reinforcement fails to rescue the theory from the realm of the first-person subjective and to resolve the paradox by failing to reduce all terms to objective physical operations.

There is no need to review in detail the sections of the book, but it may be worthwhile to note that the major concepts used as tools suffer from inadequate conceptualization of their personal aspects. Thus "reinforcement" loses its rigor when it takes on the connotation of pleasant or of self-reinforcement; "affect" cannot be adequately conceived in purely physical and physiological terms and is insufficient to explain human behavior when construed as a stimulus which impels action; "achievement motivation" apparently cannot be completely reduced to rules for counting objective things, but in the end may be contained in an operational analysis of "introspectional words in the private mode." Not only are our concepts and language inadequate at present to capture the essence of motivational phenomena, but our reliance on dated concepts in the physical sciences, most conspicuously the para-mechanical conception of causation, has led to a conceptual framework that tends to blind us to the primary source of knowledge that we have in studying human beings — our personal knowledge. As a result, we try to avoid assuming that other people are like us because such an assumption is clearly false in studying inanimate objects.

The inadequacy of our language and concepts is most apparent in dealing with the phenomena of human motivation. In this realm more than any other ". . . we know more than we can tell" (Polanyi, 1966, p. 4). The "more" that we know comes from personal knowledge, a source of knowledge that must be tapped for scientific purposes. In this book, we have tried to emphasize this need for techniques of validating personal knowledge and making it reliable as an adjunct to, not as a substitute for, the techniques we have already devised for obtaining knowledge of objective facts. We have tried to point in a direction that may facilitate advancement of this goal, but we are aware that we have not solved many problems or presented any new theory that may lead to solutions. We can attempt to end the book gracefully by acknowledging that the results of our thinking are inelegant and inadequate to comprehend the intricacies of the problem of human motivation. We felt that the problems needed to be raised, and we take comfort in Maslow's suggestion that "what needs doing, is worth doing even though *not* very well" (Maslow, 1966, p. 14).

REFERENCES

Adorno, T. W., Frenkel-Brunswik, E., Levinson, D. J., & Sanford, R. N. *The authoritarian personality*. New York: Harper & Row, 1950.

Allport, G. W. *Becoming: Basic considerations for a psychology of personality*. New Haven, Conn.: Yale University Press, 1955.

Alpert, R. Perceptual determinants of affect. Unpublished master's thesis, Wesleyan University, 1953.

Alpert, R., & Haber, R. N. Anxiety in academic achievement situations. *Journal of Abnormal and Social Psychology*, 1960, **61**, 207–215.

Angier, R. P. The aesthetics of unequal division. *Psychological Review*, 1903, **4**, (Mongr. Suppl.), 541–561.

Anscombe, G. E. M. *Intention*. Oxford: Blackwell, 1957.

Aronoff, J., & Litwin, G. H. Achievement motivation training and executive advancement. Unpublished paper, Harvard University, 1966.

Aronson, E., & Carlsmith, J. M. Performance expectancy as a determinant of actual performance. *Journal of Abnormal and Social Psychology*, 1962, **65**, 178–182.

Asch, S. E. *Social psychology*. Englewood Cliffs, N.J.: Prentice-Hall, 1952.

Atkinson, J. W. *Studies in projective measurement of achievement motivation*. Ann Arbor, Mich.: University Microfilms, 1950. Vol. X, No. 4, Publ. No. 1945. (Abstract)

Atkinson, J. W. Explorations using imaginative thought to assess the strength of human motives. In M. R. Jones (Ed.), *Nebraska symposium on motivation*. Lincoln: University of Nebraska Press, 1954.

Atkinson, J. W. The achievement motive and recall of interrupted and completed tasks. In D. C. McClelland (Ed.), *Studies in motivation*. New York: Appleton, 1955.

Atkinson, J. W. Motivational determinants of risk-taking behavior. *Psychological Review*, 1957, **64**, 359–372.

Atkinson, J. W. (Ed.) *Motives in fantasy, action, and society*. Princeton, N.J.: Van Nostrand, 1958.

Atkinson, J. W., Bastian, J. R., Earl, R. W., & Litwin, G. H. The achievement motive, goal-setting, and probability preferences. *Journal of Abnormal and Social Psychology*, 1960, **60**, 27–36.

Atkinson, J. W., & Feather, N. T. (Eds.) *A theory of achievement motivation*. New York: Wiley, 1966.

Atkinson, J. W., & Litwin, G. H. Achievement motive and test anxiety conceived as motive to approach success and avoid failure. *Journal of Abnormal and Social Psychology*, 1960, **60**, 52–63.

Atkinson, J. W., & McClelland, D. C. The projective expression of needs: II. The effect of different intensities of the hunger drive on thematic apperception. *Journal of Experimental Psychology*, 1948, **38**, 643–658.

Atkinson, J. W., & O'Connor, P. Neglected factors in studies of achievement-oriented performance: Social approval as an incentive and performance decrement. In J. W. Atkinson, & N. T. Feather (Eds.), *A theory of achievement motivation*. New York: Wiley, 1966.

Atkinson, J. W., & Reitman, W. R. Performance as a function of motive strength and expectancy of goal attainment. *Journal of Abnormal and Social Psychology,* 1956, **53**, 361–366.

Attneave, F. Some informational aspects of visual perception. *Psychological Review,* 1954, **61**, 183–193.

Attneave, F. Physical determinants of the judged complexity of shapes. *Journal of Experimental Psychology,* 1957, **53**, 221–227.

Austin, J. L. *How to do things with words.* Cambridge, Mass.: Harvard University Press, 1962.

Bakan, D. Clinical psychology and logic. *American Psychologist,* 1956, **11**, 655–662.

Bare, J. K. The specific hunger for sodium chloride in normal and adrenalectomized white rats. *Journal of Comparative and Physiological Psychology,* 1949, **42**, 242–253.

Bayley, N. A study of the crying of infants during mental and physical tests. *Journal of Genetic Psychology,* 1932, **40**, 306–329.

Beach, F. A. The descent of instinct. *Psychological Review,* 1955, **62**, 401–410.

Beardslee, D. C., & Wertheimer, M. (Eds.). *Readings in perception.* Princeton, N.J.: Van Nostrand, 1958.

Beebe-Center, J. G. *The psychology of pleasantness and unpleasantness.* Princeton, N.J.: Van Nostrand, 1932.

Beebe-Center, J. G., Black, P., Hoffman, A. C., & Wade, M. Relative per diem consumption as a measure of preference in the rat. *Journal of Comparative and Physiological Psychology,* 1948, **41**, 239–251.

Bellak, L. The concept of projection. *Psychiatry,* 1944, **7**, 353–370.

Bem, D. J. An experimental analysis of self-persuasion. *Journal of Experimental and Social Psychology,* 1965, **1**, 199–218.

Bennion, R. C. Task, trial by trial score variability of internal versus external control of reinforcement. Unpublished doctoral dissertation, Ohio State University, 1961. (Cited in Rotter, 1966.)

Bennis, W. G., Schein, E. H., Berlew, D. E., & Steele, F. I. *Interpersonal Dynamics: Essays and readings on human interaction.* Vol. III. Homewood, Ill.: Dorsey Press, 1964.

Bergman, G., & Spence, K. W. The logic of psychophysical measurement. *Psychological Review,* 1944, **51**, 1–24.

Berkeley, G. (1709). An essay towards a new theory of vision. In A. C. Fraser (Ed.), *The works of George Berkeley.* Oxford: Clarendon Press, 1871.

Berlyne, D. E. Novelty and curiosity as determinants of exploratory behavior. *British Journal of Psychology,* 1950, **41**, 68–80.

Berlyne, D. E. A theory of human curiosity. *British Journal of Psychology,* 1954a, **45**, 180–191.

Berlyne, D. E. An experimental study of human curiosity. *British Journal of Psychology,* 1954b, **45**, 256–265.

Berlyne, D. E. Conflict and information-theory variables as determinants of human perceptual curiosity. *Journal of Experimental Psychology,* 1957, **53**, 399–404.

Berlyne, D. E. *Conflict, arousal, and curiosity.* New York: McGraw-Hill, 1960.

Berlyne, D. E. Uncertainty and epistemic curiosity. *British Journal of Psychology,* 1962, **53**, 27–34.

Berlyne, D. E. Motivational problems raised by exploratory and epistemic behavior. In S. Koch (Ed.), *Psychology: A study of a science.* Vol. 5. New York: McGraw-Hill, 1963.

Bernard, C. *Lecons sur les propriétés physiologiques et les alterations pathologiques des liquides de l'organisme.* Vols. I & II. Paris: Ballière, 1859.

Bexton, W. H., Heron, W., & Scott, T. H. Effects of decreased variation in the sensory environment. *Canadian Journal of Psychology,* 1954, **8,** 70–76.

Bieri, J., & Blacker, E. The generality of cognitive complexity in the perception of people and inkblots. *Journal of Abnormal and Social Psychology,* 1956, **53,** 112–117.

Blackman, S. Some factors affecting the perception of events as chance determined. *Journal of Psychology,* 1962, **54,** 197–202.

Bogdonoff, M. D., Klien, R. F., Estes, E. H., Jr., Shaw, D. M., & Back, K. W. The modifying effect of conforming behavior upon lipid responses accompanying CNS arousal. *Clinical Research,* 1961, **9,** 135.

Boring, E. G. *A history of experimental psychology.* (2nd ed.) New York: Appleton, 1950.

Bradford, L., Gibb, J. R., & Benne, K. D. *T-Group theory and laboratory method.* New York: Wiley, 1964.

Brehm, J. W. *A theory of psychological reactance.* New York: Academic Press, 1966.

Brehm, J. W., & Cohen, A. R. *Explorations in cognitive dissonance.* New York: Wiley, 1962.

Brentano, F. C. (1874). *Psychologie vom empirischen standpunkte.* Leipzig: Meiner, 1924–1925.

Bridgman, P. W. *The logic of modern physics.* New York: Macmillan, 1927.

Bridgman, P. W. *The way things are.* Cambridge, Mass.: Harvard University Press, 1959.

Brodbeck, A. J. An exploratory study on the acquisition of dependency behavior in puppies. *Bulletin of the Ecological Society of America,* 1954, **35,** 73.

Brown, D. R. Stimulus-similarity and the anchoring of subjective scales. *American Journal of Psychology,* 1953, **66,** 199–214.

Brown, J. S. Problems presented by the concept of acquired drives. In J. S. Brown *et al.* Eds.), *Current theory and research in motivation: A symposium.* Lincoln: University of Nebraska Press, 1953. Pp. 1–21.

Brown, J. S. *The motivation of behavior.* New York: McGraw-Hill, 1961.

Brown, N. O. *Life against death.* New York: Random House, 1959.

Brown, R. *Social psychology.* New York: Free Press, 1965.

Brownell, M. H., & Goss, A. E. Stimulus-response analysis of inferences from projective test behavior. *Journal of Personality,* 1957, **25,** 525–538.

Bruner, J. S., & Postman, L. Tension and tension-release as organizing factors in perception. *Journal of Personality,* 1947, **15,** 300–308.

Bruner, J. S., & Postman, L. Symbolic value as an organizing factor in perception. *Journal of Social Psychology,* 1948, **27,** 203–208.

Bruner, J. S., Shapiro, D., & Tagiuri, R. The meaning of traits in isolation and in combination. In R. Tagiuri & L. Petrullo (Eds.), *Person perception and inter-personal behavior.* Stanford, Calif.: Stanford University Press, 1958.

Bugelski, R. Extinction with and without sub-goal reinforcement. *Journal of Comparative Psychology,* 1938, **26,** 121–134.

Bunge, M. *Causality.* Cambridge, Mass.: Harvard University Press, 1959.

Burdick, H. A. The relationship of attraction, need achievement and certainty to conformity under conditions of a simulated group atmosphere. Unpublished doctoral dissertation, University of Michigan, 1955.

Burris, R. W. The effect of counseling on achievement motivation. Unpublished doctoral dissertation, University of Indiana, 1958.

Campbell, B. A. The fractional reduction in noxious stimulation required to produce "just noticeable" learning. *Journal of Comparative and Physiological Psychology*, 1955, **48**, 141–148.

Campbell, B. A., & Kraeling, D. Response strength as a function of drive level and amount of drive reduction. *Journal of Experimental Psychology*, 1953, **45**, 97–101.

Cannon, W. B. *Bodily changes in pain, hunger, fear, and rage.* (Rev. ed.) New York: Appleton, 1915.

Cannon, W. B. *The wisdom of the body.* New York: Norton, 1932.

Carnap, R. The methodological character of theoretical concepts. In H. Feigl & M. Scriven (Eds.), *Minnosota studies in the philosophy of science.* Minneapolis: University of Minnesota Press, 1956. Pp. 38–76.

Carr, H. A. *Psychology, a study of mental activity.* New York: Longmans, Green, 1925.

Cassirer, E. *Determinism and indeterminism in modern physics.* New Haven, Conn.: Yale University Press, 1956.

Chisholm, R. M. Sentences about believing. *Proceedings of the Aristotelean Society*, 1955–1956, 123–148.

Clark, R. A. The projective measurement of experimentally induced levels of sexual motivation. *Journal of Experimental Psychology*, 1952, **44**, 391–399.

Cofer, C. N., & Appley, M. H. *Motivation: Theory and research.* New York: Wiley, 1964.

Condillac, E. B. (1754). *Traité des sensations.* Paris: Hachette, 1893.

Crandall, V. J., Katkovsky, W., & Preston, A. Motivational and ability determinants of young children's intellectual achievement behaviors. *Child Development*, 1962, **33**, 643–661.

Cronbach, L. J., & Meehl, P. E. Construct validity in psychology tests. *Psychological Bulletin*, 1955, **52**, 281–302.

Crowne, D. P., & Liverant, S. Conformity under varying conditions of personal commitment. *Journal of Abnormal and Social Psychology*, 1963, **66**, 547–555.

Dashiell, J. F. A quantitative demonstration of animal drive. *Journal of Comparative Psychology*, 1925, **5**, 205–208.

Dashiell, J. F. *Fundamentals of objective psychology.* Boston: Houghton, 1928.

Davis, R. C. Somatic activity under reduced stimulation. *Journal of Comparative and Physiological Psychology*, 1959, **52**, 309–314.

de Charms, R. The effects of individual motivation on cooperative and competitive behavior in small groups. Unpublished doctoral dissertation, University of North Carolina, 1956.

de Charms, R., & Bridgeman, W. J. Leadership compliance and group behavior. Technical Report No. 9, 1961, ONR Project Nonr 816 (11), Washington University, St. Louis, Missouri.

de Charms, R., Carpenter, V., & Kuperman, A. The "origin-pawn" variable in person perception. *Sociometry*, 1965, **28**, 241–258.

de Charms, R., & Davé, P. N. Hope of success, fear of failure, subjective probability, and risk-taking behavior. *Journal of Personality and Social Psychology*, 1965, **1**, 558–568.

de Charms, R., Dougherty, K., & Wurtz, S. Unpublished manuscript, Washington University, 1965.

de Charms, R., & Moeller, G. H. Values expressed in American children's readers: 1800–1950. *Journal of Abnormal and Social Psychology*, 1962, **64**, 136–142.

de Charms, R., Morrison, H. W., Reitman, W. R., & McClelland, D. C. Behavioral correlates of directly and indirectly measured achievement motivation. In D. C. McClelland (Ed.), *Studies in motivation.* New York: Appleton, 1955.

Deutsch, M. Trust, trustworthiness, and the *F* scale. *Journal of Abnormal and Social Psychology*, 1960, **61**, 138–140.

Dollard, J., & Miller, N. E. *Personality and psychotherapy: An analysis in terms of learning, thinking and culture.* New York: McGraw-Hill, 1950.

Efran, J. S. Some personality determinants of memory for success and failure. Unpublished doctoral dissertation, Ohio State University, 1963. (Cited in Rotter, 1966.)

Elliot, O., & King, J. A. Effect of early food deprivations upon later consummatory behavior in puppies. *Psychological Reports,* 1960, **6,** 391–400.

Engel, R. Experimentelle Untersuchungen uber die Anhangigkeit der Lust und Unlust von der Reizstarke beim Geschmacksinn. *Archiv für die Gesamte Psychologie,* 1928, **64,** 1–36. (Cited by Woodworth, 1938.)

Eriksen, C. W. Figments, fantasies, and follies: A search for the subconscious mind. In C. W. Eriksen (Ed.), Behavior and awareness: A symposium of research and interpretation. *Journal of Personality,* 1962, **30,** (2), 1–26.

Escalona, S. K. The effect of success and failure upon the level of aspiration and behavior in manic-depressive psychoses. *University of Iowa Studies in Child Welfare,* 1940, **16,** 199–302.

Farber, I. E. Response fixation under anxiety and non-anxiety conditions. *Journal of Experimental Psychology,* 1948, **38,** 111–131.

Feather, N. T. The relationship of persistence at a task to expectation of success and achievement related motives. *Journal of Abnormal and Social Psychology,* 1961, **63,** 552–561.

Feather, N. T. Mowrer's revised two-factor theory and the motive-expectancy-value model. *Psychological Review,* 1963, **70,** 500–515.

Fechner, G. T. *Einige Ideen zur Schopfungs-und Entwicklungsgeschichte der Organismen.* Leipzig: Breitkopf & Hartel, 1873.

Feigl, H., & Scriven, M. (Eds.) *Minnesota studies in the philosophy of science.* Vols. I & II. Minneapolis: University of Minnesota Press, 1956–1958.

Fenichel, O. *The psychoanalytic theory of neurosis.* New York: Norton, 1945.

Ferguson, E. D. Ego-involvement: A critical examination of some methodological issues. *Journal of Abnormal and Social Psychology,* 1962, **64,** 407–417.

Festinger, L. A theoretical interpretation of shifts in level of aspiration. *Psychological Review,* 1942, **49,** 235–250.

Festinger, L. *A theory of cognitive dissonance.* Stanford, Calif.: Stanford University Press, 1957.

Finan, J. L. Quantitative studies in motivation: I. Strength of conditioning in rats under varying degrees of hunger. *Journal of Comparative Psychology,* 1940, **29,** 119–134.

Fink, R. Horatio Alger as a social philosopher. Introduction to Alger, H. *Ragged Dick and Mark, the match boy.* New York: Collier, 1962.

Fisher, A. E. The effects of differential early treatment on the social and exploratory behavior of puppies. Unpublished doctoral dissertation, Pennsylvania State University, 1955. (Cited in Scott, 1963.)

Fiske, D. W., & Maddi, S. R. (Eds.) *Functions of varied experience.* Homewood, Ill.: Dorsey Press, 1961.

Flavell, J. H. *The developmental psychology of Jean Piaget.* Princeton, N. J.: Van Nostrand, 1963.

Franklin, R. D. Youth's expectancies about internal versus external control of reinforcement related to *N* variables. Unpublished doctoral dissertation, Purdue University, 1963. (Cited in Rotter, 1966.)

Freeman, G. L. *Introduction to physiological pychology.* New York: Ronald Press, 1934.

Freeman, G. L. *The energetics of human behavior.* Ithaca, N. Y.: Cornell University Press, 1948.

French, E. G. Some characteristics of achievement motivation. *Journal of Experimental Psychology*, 1955, **50**, 232–236.

French, E. G. Motivation as a variable in work-partner selection. *Journal of Abnormal and Social Psychology*, 1958, **53**, 96–99.

Freud, A. *The ego and the mechanisms of defense.* London: Hogarth Press, 1936. (Republished: New York, International Universities Press, 1946.)

Freud, S. (1900). The interpretation of dreams. In A. A. Brill (Ed. and transl.), *The basic writings of Sigmund Freud.* New York: Random House, 1938. Pp. 179–549.

Freud, S. (1901). The psychopathology of everyday life. In A. A. Brill (Ed. and transl.), *The basic writings of Sigmund Freud.* New York: Random House, 1938.

Freud, S. (1905a). Three essays on the theory of sexuality. In J. Strachey (Ed.), *The complete psychological works of Sigmund Freud.* Vol. VII. London: Hogarth Press, 1953.

Freud, S. (1905b). Psychopathic characters on the stage. In J. Strachey (Ed.), *The complete psychological works of Sigmund Freud.* Vol. VII. London: Hogarth Press, 1953.

Freud, S. (1908). The poet and day-dreaming. In *Collected papers of Sigmund Freud.* Vol. IV. (J. Riviere, transl.) London: Hogarth Press, 1959.

Freud, S. (1915a). Instincts and their vicissitudes. In *Collected papers of Sigmund Freud.* Vol. IV. (J Riviere, transl.) London: Hogarth Press, 1949.

Freud, S. (1915b). Instincts and their vicissitudes. In J. Strachey (Ed.), *The complete psychological works of Sigmund Freud.* Vol. XIV. London: Hogarth Press, 1957.

Freud, S. (1916). Wit and its relation to the unconscious. In A. A. Brill (Ed.), *The basic writings of Sigmund Freud.* New York: Random House, 1938.

Freud, S. (1920). Beyond the pleasure principle. In J. Strachey (Ed.), *The complete psychological works of Sigmund Freud.* Vol. XVIII. London: Hogarth Press, 1955.

Freud, S. (1924). The economic problem of masochism. In J. Strachey (Ed.), *The complete psychological works of Sigmund Freud.* Vol. XIX. London: Hogarth Press, 1961.

Getter, H. Variables affecting the value of the reinforcement in verbal conditioning. Unpublished doctoral dissertation, Ohio State University, 1962. (Cited in Rotter, 1966.)

Gibson, J. J. *The perception of the visual world.* Boston: Houghton Mifflin Company, 1950.

Gilmore, J. L. Recall of success and failure as a function of subjects' threat interpretations. *Journal of Psychology*, 1954, **38**, 359–365.

Glixman, A. F. Recall of completed and incompleted activities under varying degrees of stress. *Journal of Experimental Psychology*, 1949, **39**, 281–295.

Goffman, E. *The presentation of self in everyday life.* New York: Doubleday, 1959.

Goldstein, K. *The organism: A holistic approach to biology derived from pathological data in man.* New York: American Book, 1939.

Gore, P. M. Individual differences in the prediction of subject compliance to experimenter bias. Unpublished doctoral dissertation, Ohio State University, 1962. (Cited in Rotter, 1966.)

Gore, P. M., & Rotter, J. B. A personality correlate of social action. *Journal of Personality*, 1963, **31**, 58–64.

Gosling, J. Mental causes and fear. *Mind*, 1962, **71**, 289–306.

Goss, A. E., & Brownell, M. H. Stimulus-response concepts and principles applied to projective test behavior. *Journal of Personality*, 1957, **25**, 505–523.

Green, D. R. Volunteering and the recall of interrupted tasks. *Journal of Abnormal and Social Psychology*, 1963, **66**, 397–401.

Grice, G. R., & Davis, J. D. Effect of irrelevant thirst motivation on a response learned with food reward. *Journal of Experimental Psychology*, 1957, **53**, 347–352.

Grossman, M. I. Integration of current views in the regulation of hunger and appetite. *Annals of the New York Academy of Science,* 1955 **63,**76–89.

Guthrie, E. R. *The psychology of human conflict: The clash of motives within the individual.* New York: Harper & Row, 1938.

Guthrie, E. R. *The psychology of learning.* (Rev. ed.) New York: Harper & Row, 1952.

Guttman, N. Operant conditioning, extinction, and periodic reinforcement in relation to concentration of sucrose used as reinforcing agent. *Journal of Experimental Psychology,* 1953, **46,**213–224.

Gwinn, G. T. The effects of punishment on acts motivated by fear. *Journal of Experimental Psychology,* 1949, **39,**260–269.

Haber, R. N. Discrepancy from adaptation level as a source of affect. *Journal of Experimental Psychology,* 1958, **56,**370–375.

Halpin, A. W. *Theory and research in administration.* New York: Macmillan, 1966.

Hamilton, J. A., & Krechevsky, I. Studies on the effect of shock upon behavior plasticity in the rat. *Journal of Comparative Psychology,* 1933, **16,**237–253.

Hamilton, W. *Lectures on metaphysics and logic.* Edinburgh: Blackwood, 1859.

Hammock, T., & Brehm, J. W. The attractiveness of choice alternatives when freedom to choose is eliminated by a social agent. *Journal of Personality,* 1966, **34,** 546–554.

Harlow, H. F. Learning and satiation of response in intrinsically motivated complex puzzle performance by monkeys. *Journal of Comparative and Physiological Psychology,* 1950, **43,**289–294.

Harlow, H. F. The nature of love. *American Psychologist,* 1958, **13,**673–685.

Harlow, H. F. The heterosexual affectional system in monkeys. *American Psychologist,* 1962, **17,**1–19.

Harlow, H. F., Blazek, N. C., & McClearn, G. E. Manipulatory motivation in the infant rhesus monkey. *Journal of Comparative and Physiological Psychology,* 1956, **49,** 444–448.

Harlow, H. F., & Harlow, M. K. Social deprivation in monkeys. *Scientific American,* 1962, **207,**136–146.

Harlow, H. F., Harlow, M. K., & Meyer, D. R. Learning motivated by a manipulation drive. *Journal of Experimental Psychology,* 1950, **40,**228–234.

Harlow, H. F., & McClearn, G. E. Object discrimination learned by monkeys on the basis of manipulation motives. *Journal of Comparative and Physiological Psychology,* 1954, **47,**73–76.

Harriman, A. E., & MacLeod, R. B. Discriminative threshold of salt for normal and adrenalectomized rats. *American Journal of Psychology,* 1953, **66,**465–471.

Harvey, O. J., & Clapp, W. F. Hope, expectancy, and reactions to the unexpected. *Journal of Personality and Social Psychology,* 1965, **2,**45–52.

Healy, W., Bronner, A., & Bowers, A. *The structure and meaning of psychoanalysis.* New York: Knopf, 1930.

Heathers, G. L., & Arakelian, P. The relation between strength of drive and rate of extinction of a bar-pressing reaction in the rat. *Journal of General Psychology,* 1941, **24,** 243–258.

Hebb, D. O. *The organization of behavior.* New York: Wiley, 1949.

Hebb, D. O. Drives and C. N. S. (Conceptual nervous system). *Psychological Review,* 1955, **62,**243–254.

Heckhausen, H. *The anatomy of achievement motivation.* New York: Academic Press, 1967.

Heider, F. Social perception and phenomenal causality. *Psychological Review*, 1944, **51**, 358–374.

Heider, F. *The psychology of interpersonal relations.* New York: Wiley, 1958.

Helson, H. Adaptation-level as frame of reference for prediction of psychophysical data. *American Journal of Psychology*, 1947, **60**, 1–29.

Helson, H. Adapatation level theory. In S. Koch (Ed.), *Psychology: A study of a science.* Vol. I. New York: McGraw-Hill, 1959.

Heron, W., Doane, B. K., & Scott, T. H. Visual disturbances after prolonged perceptual isolation. *Canadian Journal of Psychology*, 1956, **10**, 13–18.

Hess, E. H. The relationship between imprinting and motivation. In M. R. Jones (Ed.), *Nebraska symposium on motivation.* Lincoln: University of Nebraska Press, 1959. Pp. 44–77.

Hess, E. H., & Polt, J. M. Pupil size as related to interest value of visual stimuli. *Science*, 1960, **132**, 349–350.

Hess, E. H., & Polt, J. M. Pupil size in relation to mental activity during simple problem solving. *Science*, 1964, **143**, 1190–1192.

Hilgard, E. R. *Theories of learning.* (2nd ed.) New York: Appleton, 1956.

Hilgard, E. R. Motivation and learning theory. In S. Koch (Ed.), *Psychology: A Study of a science.* Vol. V. New York: McGraw-Hill, 1963.

Holt, E. B. *Animal drive and the learning process.* New York: Holt, 1931.

Horenstein, B. Performance of conditioned responses as a function of strength of hunger drive. *Journal of Comparative and Physiological Psychology*, 1951, **44**, 210–224.

Horowitz, R. A. N Achievement "correlates" and the executive role. Unpublished honors thesis, Harvard College, 1961.

Hull, C. L. Knowledge and purpose as habit mechanisms. *Psychological Review*, 1930, **37**, 511–525.

Hull, C. L. Goal attraction and directing ideas conceived as habit phenomena. *Psychological Review*, 1931, **38**, 487–506.

Hull, C. L. The goal gradient hypothesis and maze learning. *Psychological Review*, 1932, **39**, 25–43.

Hull, C. L. The concept of the habit-family-hierarchy and maze learning: Part I. *Psychological Review*, 1934, **41**, 33–54.

Hull, C. L. *Principles of behavior.* New York: Appleton, 1943.

Hume, D. (1740). *A treatise of human nature.* London: Clarendon Press, 1888.

Hunt, J. McV. Motivation inherent in information processing and action. In O. J. Harvey (Ed.), *Motivation and social interaction.* New York: Ronald Press, 1963. Pp. 35–94.

Hunt, J. McV., & Quay, H. C. Early vibratory experience and the question of innate reinforcement value of vibration and other stimuli: A limitation on the discrepancy (burnt soup) principle in motivation. *Psychological Review*, 1961, **68**, 149–156.

Hunt, W. A. Anchoring effects in judgment. *American Journal of Psychology*, 1941, **54**, 395–403.

Igel, G. J., & Calvin, A. D. The development of affectional response in infant dogs. *Journal of Comparative and Physiological Psychology*, 1960, **53**, 302–305.

Iverson, M. A., & Reuder, M. E. Ego involvement as an experimental variable. *Psychol. Reports*, 1956, **2**, 147–181.

James, W. *The principles of psychology,* Vol. II. New York: Holt, 1890.

James, W. H., & Rotter, J. B. Partial and 100% reinforcement under chance and skill conditions. *Journal of Experimental Psychology*, 1958, **55**, 397–403.

Johnson, T. J., Feigenbaum, R., & Weiby, M. Some determinants and consequences of the teacher's perception of causation. *Journal of Educational Psychology,* 1964, **55,** 237–246.

Jones, E. E., & Davis, K. E. From acts to dispositions. The attribution process in person perception. In L. Berkowitz (Ed.), *Advances in experimental social psychology.* Vol. II. New York: Academic Press, 1965.

Jones, E. E., Davis, K. E., & Gergen, K. J. Role playing variations and their informational value for person perception. *Journal of Abnormal and Social Psychology,* 1961, **63,** 302–310.

Jones, E. E., & de Charms, R. Changes in social perception as a function of the personal relevance of behavior. *Sociometry,* 1957, **20,** 75–85.

Jones, E. E., & de Charms, R. The organizing function of interaction roles in person perception. *Journal of Abnormal and Social Psychology,* 1958, **57,** 155–164.

Jones, E. E., Hester, S. L., Farina, A., & Davis, K. E. Reaction to unfavorable personal evaluations as a function of the evaluator's perceived adjustment. *Journal of Abnormal and Social Psychology,* 1959, **59,** 363–370.

Jones, E. E., & Thibaut, J. W. Interaction goals as bases of inference in interpersonal perception. In R. Tagiuri & L. Petrullo (Eds.), *Person perception and interpersonal behavior.* Stanford, Calif.: Stanford University Press, 1958.

Jordan, T. E., & de Charms, R. The achievement motive in normal and mentally retarded children. *American Journal of Mental Deficiency,* 1959, **64,** 457–466.

Kant, I. (1781). *Critique of pure reason.* (F. M. Miller, transl.) New York: Macmillan, 1949. Pp. 432–458.

Karsten, A. Psychische Sättigung. *Psychologische Forschung,* 1928, **10,** 142–254.

Kelley, H. H. Attribution theory in social psychology. In D. Levine (Ed.), *Nebraska symposium on motivation.* Lincoln: University of Nebraska Press, 1967.

Kelly, G. A. *The psychology of personal constructs.* New York: Norton, 1955.

Kenny, D. T. The contingency of humor appreciation on the stimulus-confirmation of joke-ending expectations. *Journal of Abnormal and Social Psychology,* 1955, **51,** 644–648.

Kiesow, F. Sur la methode pour etudier les sentiments simples. *Archives Italiennes de Biologie,* 1899, **32,** 159–164.

Kleiner, R. J. The effects of threat reduction upon interpersonal attractiveness. *Journal of Personality,* 1960, **28,** 145–156.

Klinger, E. Fantasy need achievement as a motivational construct. *Psychological Bulletin,* 1966, **66,** 291–308.

Koch, S. Behavior as "intrinsically" regulated: Work notes towards a pre-theory of phenomena called "motivational." In M. R. Jones (Ed.), *Nebraska symposium on motivation.* Lincoln: University of Nebraska Press, 1956.

Koch, S. Psychology and emerging conceptions of knowledge as unitary. In T. W. Wann (Ed.), *Behaviorism and phenomenology.* Chicago: University of Chicago Press, 1964. Pp. 1–46.

Koffka, K. *Principles of Gestalt psychology.* New York: Harcourt-Brace, 1935.

Kolb, D. A. Achievement motivation training for underachieving high-school boys. *Journal of Personality and Social Psychology,* 1965, **2,** 783–792.

Kubzanski, P. E. The effects of reduced environmental stimulation on human behavior: A review. In A. D. Biderman & H. Zimmer (Eds.), *The manipulation of human behavior.* New York: Wiley, 1961. Pp. 51–95.

Kuperman, A. Relations between differential constraints, affect, and the origin-pawn variable. Unpublished doctoral dissertation, Washington University, 1967.

Lamprecht, S. P. Empiricism and epistemology in David Hume. *Studies in the History of Ideas,* 1925, **11,** 221–252.

Lasker, H. M. Factors affecting responses to achievement motivation training in India. Unpublished honors thesis, Harvard College, 1966.

Lazarus, R. S., Baker, R. W., & Mayer, J. Personality and psychological stress. *Journal of Personality,* 1957, **25,** 559–577.

Lefcourt, H. M. Internal versus external control of reinforcement: A review. *Psychological Bulletin,* 1966, **65,** 206–220.

Lehmann, A. *Hauptgesetze des menschlichen Gefühlslebens.* Leipzig: Reisland, 1892.

Lewin, K., Dembo, T., Festinger, L., & Sears, P. S. Level of aspiration. In J. McV. Hunt (Ed.), *Personality and the behavior disorders.* New York: Ronald Press, 1944. Pp. 333–378.

Lewis, H. B., & Franklin, M. An experimental study of the role of the ego in work: II. The significance of task-orientation in work. *Journal of Experimental Psychology,* 1944, **34,** 195–215.

Lewis, S. *Babbitt.* New York: Harcourt-Brace, 1922.

Lilly, J. C. Mental effects of reduction of ordinary levels of physical stimuli on intact healthy persons. *Psychiatric Research Reports,* 1956, **5,** 1–9.

Lindsley, D. B. Psychophysiology and motivation. In M. R. Jones (Ed.), *Nebraska symposium on motivation.* Lincoln: University of Nebraska Press, 1957. Pp. 44–105.

Lindzey, G., & Kalnis, D. Thematic apperception test: Some evidence bearing on the "hero assumption." *Journal of Abnormal and Social Psychology,* 1958, **57,** 76–83.

Littig, L. W. Effects of motivation on probability preferences. *Journal of Personality,* 1963, **31,** 417–427.

Litwin, G. H. Achievement motivation, expectancy of success, and risk-taking behavior. In J. W. Atkinson & N. T. Feather (Eds.), *A theory of achievement motivation.* New York: Wiley, 1966.

Lorenz, K. Z. Der kumpan in der umwelt des vögels. *Journal für Ornithologie,* 1935, **83,** 137–214, 289–413. (Cited in Hunt, 1963.)

Lowell, E. L. A methodological study of projectively measured achievement motivation. Unpublished master's thesis, Wesleyan University, 1950.

Luchins, A. S. Mechanization in problem solving. The effect of *Einstellung. Psychological Monographs,* 1942, **54,** No. 248.

Luckhardt, A. B., & Carlson, A. J. Contributions to the physiology of the stomach: XVII. On the chemical control of the gastric hunger mechanism. *American Journal of Physiology,* 1914, **36,** 37–46.

Lumsdaine, A. A. Conditioned eyelid response as mediating generalized finger reactions. *Psychological Bulletin,* 1939, **36,** 650.

McArthur, C. C. The effects of need for achievement on the content of TAT stories; a re-examination. *Journal of Abnormal and Social Psychology,* 1953, **48,** 532–536.

McCall, R. B. Stimulus change in light-contingent bar-pressing. *Journal of Comparative and Physiological Psychology,* 1965, **59,** 258–262.

McClelland, D. C. *Personality.* New York: W. Sloane Associates, 1951.

McClelland, D. C. The psychology of mental content reconsidered. *Psychological Review,* 1955a, **62,** 297–302.

McClelland, D. C. Some social consequences of achievement motivation. In M. R. Jones (Ed.), *Nebraska symposium on motivation.* Lincoln: University of Nebraska Press, 1955b.

McClelland, D. C. Methods of measuring human motivation. In J. W. Atkinson (Ed.), *Motives in fantasy, action and society.* Princeton, N. J.: Van Nostrand, 1958.

McClelland, D. C. *The achieving society.* Princeton, N. J.: Van Nostrand, 1961.

McClelland, D. C. Toward a theory of motive acquisition. *American Psychologist,* 1965a, **20,** 321–333.

McClelland, D. C. N achievement and entrepreneurship: A longitudinal study. *Journal of Personality and Social Psychology,* 1965b, **1,** 389–392.

McClelland, D. C. Longitudinal trends in the relation of thought to action. *Journal of Consulting Psychology,* 1966, **30,** 479–483.

McClelland, D. C., & Atkinson, J. W. The projective expression of needs. I. The effect of different intensities of the hunger drive on perception. *Journal of Psychology,* 1948, **25,** 205–232.

McClelland, D. C., Atkinson, J. W., Clark, R. A., & Lowell, E. L. *The achievement motive.* New York: Appleton, 1953.

McClelland, D. C., Clark, R. A., Roby, T. B., & Atkinson, J. W. The projective expression of needs. IV: The effect of the need for achievement on thematic apperception. *Journal of Experimental Psychology,* 1949, **39,** 242–255.

McClelland, D. C., Rindlisbacher, A., & de Charms, R. Religious and other sources of parental attitudes toward independence training. In D. C. McClelland (Ed.), *Studies in motivation.* New York: Appleton, 1955.

MacCorquodale, K., & Meehl, P. E. On a distinction between hypothetical constructs and intervening variables. *Psychological Review,* 1948, **55,** 95–107.

McGeoch, J. A. *The psychology of human learning.* New York: Longmans, Green, 1942.

McGeoch, J. A., & Irion, A. L. *The psychology of human learning.* New York: Longmans, Green, 1952.

Maddi, S. R. Affective tone during environmental regularity and change. *Journal of Abnormal and Social Psychology,* 1961, **62,** 338–345.

Mahone, C. H. Fear of failure and unrealistic vocational aspiration. *Journal of Abnormal and Social Psychology,* 1960, **60,** 253–261.

Malcolm, N. Behaviorism as a philosophy of psychology. In T. W. Wann (Ed.), *Behaviorism and phenomenology.* Chicago: University of Chicago Press, 1964. Pp. 141–155.

Mandler, G., & Cowen, J. E. Test anxiety questionnaires. *Journal of Consulting Psychology,* 1958, **22,** 228–229.

Margenau, H. *The nature of physical reality.* New York: McGraw-Hill, 1950.

Marlowe, D. Relationships among direct and indirect measures of the achievement motive and overt behavior. *Journal of Consulting Psychology,* 1959, **23,** 329–332.

Marrow, A. J. Goal tensions and recall: I and II. *Journal of General Psychology,* 1938, **19,** 3–35, 37–64.

Martin, B. Reward and punishment associated with the same goal response: A factor in the learning of motives. *Psychological Bulletin,* 1963, **60,** 441–451.

Maslow, A. H. *Motivation and personality.* New York: Harper & Row, 1954.

Maslow, A. H. Deficiency motivation and growth motivation. In M. R. Jones (Ed.), *Nebraska symposium on motivation.* Lincoln: University of Nebraska Press, 1955.

Maslow, A. H. *Toward a psychology of being.* Princeton, N. J.: Van Nostrand, 1962.

Maslow, A. H. *The psychology of science.* New York: Harper & Row, 1966.

Masserman, J. H. *Principles of dynamic psychiatry.* Philadelphia: Saunders, 1946.

Mead, G. H. *Mind, self and society.* Chicago: University of Chicago Press, 1934.

Meehl, P. E. On the circularity of the law of effect. *Psychological Bulletin,* 1950, **47,** 52–75.

Meier, G. W., Foshee, D. P., Wittrig, J. J., Peeler, D. F., & Huff, F. W. Helson's residual factor versus innate S-R relations. *Psychological Reports,* 1960, **6,** 61–62.

Melton, A. W. Learning. In W. S. Monroe (Ed.), *Encyclopedia of educational research.* New York: Macmillan, 1941.

Meyer, L. B. *Emotion and meaning in music.* Chicago: University of Chicago Press, 1956.

Michotte, A. *The perception of causality.* New York: Basic Books, 1963.

Miller, N. E. Analysis of the form of conflict reactions. *Psychological Bulletin,* 1937, **34,** 720. (Abstract)

Miller, N. E. Studies of fear as an acquirable drive. I: Fear as motivation and fear-reduction as reinforcement in the learning of new responses. *Journal of Experimental Psychology,* 1948a, **38,** 89–101.

Miller, N. E. Theory and experiment relating psychoanalytic displacement to stimulus-response generalization. *Journal of Abnormal and Social Psychology,* 1948b, **43,** 155–178.

Miller, N. E. Learnable drives and rewards. In S. S. Stevens (Ed.), *Handbook of experimental psychology.* New York: Wiley, 1951.

Miller, N. E. Experiments on motivation: Studies combining psychological, physiological and pharmacological techniques. *Science,* 1957, **126,** 1271–1278.

Miller, N. E. Liberalization of basic S-R concepts: Extensions to conflict behavior, motivation and social learning. In S. Koch (Ed.), *Psychology: A study of a science.* Vol. II. New York: McGraw-Hill, 1959. Pp. 196–292.

Miller, N. E. Some reflections on the law of effect produce a new alternative to drive reduction. In M. R. Jones (Ed.), *Nebraska symposium on motivation.* Lincoln: University of Nebraska Press, 1963. Pp. 65–112.

Miller, N. E., & Dollard, J. *Social learning and imitation.* New Haven, Conn.: Yale University Press, 1941.

Moelk, M. Vocalizing in the house-cat: A phonetic and functional study. *American Journal of Psychology,* 1944, **57,** 184–205.

Montgomery, K. C. The relation between exploratory behavior and spontaneous alternation in the white rat. *Journal of Comparative and Physiological Psychology,* 1951, **44,** 582–589.

Montgomery, K. C. Exploratory behavior as a function of "similarity" of stimulus situations. *Journal of Comparative and Physiological Psychology,* 1953a, **46,** 129–133.

Montgomery, K. C. The effect of the hunger and thirst drives upon exploratory behavior. *Journal of Comparative and Physiological Psychology,* 1953b, **46,** 315–319.

Montgomery, K. C. The effect of activity deprivation upon exploratory behavior. *Journal of Comparative and Physiological Psychology,* 1953c, **46,** 438–441.

Montgomery, K. C. The role of the exploratory drive in learning. *Journal of Comparative and Physiological Psychology,* 1954, **47,** 60–64.

Montgomery, K. C. The relation between fear induced by novel stimulation and exploratory behavior. *Journal of Comparative and Psychological Psychology,* 1955, **48,** 254–260.

Montgomery, K. C., & Monkman, J. A. The relation between fear and exploratory behavior. *Journal of Comparative and Physiological Psychology,* 1955, **48,** 132–136.

Montgomery, K. C., & Segall, M. Discrimination learning based upon the exploratory drive. *Journal of Comparative and Psychological Psychology,* 155, **48,** 225–228.

Morgan, C. T. *Physiological psychology.* New York: McGraw-Hill, 1943.

Morgan, C. T. Physiological mechanisms of motivation. In M. R. Jones (Ed.), *Nebraska symposium on motivation.* Lincoln: University of Nebraska Press, 1957. Pp. 1–35.

Morgan, H. H. A psychometric comparison of achieving and nonachieving college students of high ability. *Journal of Consulting Psychology,* 1952, **16,** 292–298.

Moruzzi, G., & Magoun, H. W. Brain stem reticular formation and activation of the EEG. *Electroencephalography and Clinical Neurophysiology,* 1949, **1,** 455–473.

Moss, F. A. Study of animal drive. *Journal of Experimental Psychology,* 1924, **7,** 165–185.

Moulton, R. W. Effects of success and failure on level of aspiration as related to achievement motives. *Journal of Personality and Social Psychology,* 1965, **1,** 399–406.

Mowrer, O. H. On the dual nature of learning: A reinterpretation of "conditioning" and "problem solving." *Harvard Educational Review,* 1947, **17,** 102–148.

Mowrer, O. H. *Learning theory and personality dynamics: Selected papers.* New York: Ronald Press, 1950.

Mowrer, O. H. *Learning theory and behavior.* New York: Wiley, 1960a.

Mowrer, O. H. *Learning theory and the symbolic processes.* New York: Wiley, 1960b.

Mowrer, O. H., & Aiken, E. G. Contiguity vs. drive-reduction in conditioned fear: Temporal variations in conditioned and unconditioned stimulus. *American Journal of Psychology,* 1954, **67,** 29–38.

Mowrer, O. H., & Lamoreaux, R. R. Avoidance conditioning and sign duration — a study of secondary motivation and reward. *Psychological Monographs,* 1942, **54.**

Mowrer, O. H., & Miller, N. E. A multi-purpose learning-demonstration apparatus. *Journal of Experimental Psychology,* 1942, **31,** 163–170.

Mowrer, O. H., & Solomon, L. N. Contiguity vs. drive-reduction in conditioned fear: The proximity and abruptness of drive-reduction. *American Journal of Psychology,* 1954, **67,** 15–25.

Muenzinger, K. F. Motivation in learning. I: Electric shock for correct response in the visual discrimination habit. *Journal of Comparative Psychology,* 1934, **17,** 267–277.

Munsinger, H., & Kessen, W. Uncertainty, structure, and preference. *Psychological Monographs,* 1964, **78,** (Whole No. 586), 1–24.

Munsterburg, H. *Die Willenshandlung,* Freiburg in Breisgau: J. C. B. Mohr, 1888.

Murray, H. A. *Thematic apperception test manual.* Cambridge, Mass.: Harvard University Press, 1943.

Murray, H. A. *Explorations in personality.* London and New York: Oxford University Press, 1938.

O'Connor, P., Atkinson, J. W., & Horner, M. Motivational implications of ability grouping in schools. In J. W. Atkinson & N. T. Feather (Eds.), *A theory of achievement motivation.* New York: Wiley, 1966.

Olds, J. A preliminary mapping of electrical reinforcing effects in the rat brain. *Journal of Comparative and Physiological Psychology,* 1956, **49,** 281–285.

Olds, J., & Milner, P. Positive reinforcement produced by electrical stimulation of septal area and other regions of rat brain. *Journal of Comparative and Physiological Psychology,* 1954, **47,** 419–427.

Osgood, C. E. *Method and theory in experimental psychology.* London and New York: Oxford University Press, 1953.

Osgood, C. E., Suci, G. J., & Tannenbaum, P. H. *The measurement of meaning.* Urbana: University of Illinois Press, 1957.

Osgood, C. E., & Tannenbaum, P. H. The principle of congruity in the prediction of attitude change. *Psychological Review,* 1955, **62,** 42–55.

Pachauri, A. R. A study of gestalt problems in completed and interrupted tasks. *British Journal of Psychology,* 1935, **25,** 365–381, 447–457.

Parsons, T. *Essays in sociological theory: Pure and applied.* Glencoe, Ill.: Free Press, 1949.

Pastore, N. The role of arbitrariness in the frustration-aggression hypotheses. *Journal of Abnormal and Social Psychology,* 1952, **47,** 728–731.

Pepitone, A. Motivational effects in social perception. *Human Relations*, 1950, **3**, 57–76.

Pepitone, A. *Attraction and hostility*. New York: Atherton Press, 1964.

Peters, R. S., McCracken, D. J., & Urmson, J. O. Symposium: Motives and causes. *Aristotilian Society*, 1952, 139–194 (Suppl. 26).

Pfaffman, C., & Bare, J. K. Gustatory nerve discharge in normal and adrenalectomized rats. *Journal of Comparative and Physiological Psychology*, 1950, **43**, 320–334.

Phares, E. J. Expectancy changes in skill and chance situations. *Journal of Abnormal and Social Psychology*, 1957, **54**, 339–342.

Phares, E. J. Internal-external control as a determinant of amount of social influence exerted. *Journal of Personality and Social Psychology*, 1965, **2**, 642–647.

Piaget, J. De quelques formes de causalité chez l'enfant. *Annee Psychologique*, 1925, **26**, 31–71.

Piaget, J. *The child's conception of the world*. New York: Harcourt-Brace, 1929.

Piaget, J. *The child's conception of physical causality*. New York: Harcourt-Brace, 1930.

Piaget, J. *The origins of intelligence in children*. (M. Cook, transl.) New York: International University Press, 1952.

Piaget, J. *The language and thought of the child*. New York: Meridian, 1955.

Pitts, C. E. Affective arousal to music as a function of deviations in perceived complexity from adaptation level. Unpublished doctoral dissertation, Washington University, 1963.

Polanyi, M. *Personal knowledge*. Chicago: University of Chicago Press, 1958.

Polanyi, M. *The tacit dimension*. New York: Doubleday, 1966.

Postman, L. The experimental analysis of motivational factors in perception. In J. S. Brown, *et al.* (Ed.), *Current theory and research in motivation: A symposium*. Lincoln: University of Nebraska Press, 1953. Pp. 59–108.

Premack, D. Toward empirical behavior laws. I. Positive reinforcement. *Psychological Review*, 1959, **66**, 219–233.

Reitman, W. R. Motivational induction and the behavioral correlates of achievement and affiliation motives. *Journal of Abnormal and Social Psychology*, 1960, **60**, 8–13.

Ricciuti, H. N. The prediction of academic grades with a projective test of achievement motivation. I. Initial validation studies. Princeton, N. J.: Educational Testing Service, 1955.

Ricciuti, H. N., & Sadacca, R. *The prediction of academic grades with a projective test of achievement motivation. II. Cross validation at the high school level*. Princeton, N. J.: Educational Testing Service, 1955.

Richter, C. P. A behavioristic study of the activity of the rat. *Comparative Psychological Monographs*, 1922, **1**, 1–55.

Richter, C. P. Animal behavior and internal drives. *Quarterly Review of Biology*, 1927, **2**, 307–343.

Rosen, B. C. The achievement syndrome. *American Sociological Review*, 1956, **21**, 203–211.

Rosenberg, M. J., & Abelson, R. P. An analysis of cognitive balancing. In M. J. Rosenberg *et al.* (Eds.), *Attitude, organization and change*. New Haven, Conn.: Yale University Press, 1960.

Rotter, J. B. *Social Learning and Clinical Psychology*. Englewood Cliffs, N.J.: Prentice-Hall, 1954.

Rotter, J. B. Generalized expectancies for internal versus external control of reinforcement. *Psychological Monographs*, 1966, **80**.

Rotter, J. B., Liverant, S., & Crowne, D. P. The growth and extinction of expectancies in chance controlled and skilled tests. *Journal of Psychology*, 1961, **52**, 161–177.

Rotter, J. B., & Mulry, R. C. Internal versus external control of reinforcement and decision time. *Journal of Personality and Social Psychology,* 1965, **2,** 598–604.

Rotter, J. B., Seeman, M., & Liverant, S. Internal versus external control of reinforcements: A major variable in behavior theory. In N. F. Washburne (Ed.), *Decisions, values and groups.* Vol. 2. New York: Macmillan, 1962.

Rugg, H. *Imagination.* New York: Harper & Row, 1963.

Russell, B. (1918). *Mysticism and logic.* London: Penguin, 1953.

Ryle, G. *The concept of mind.* New York: Barnes & Noble, 1949.

Saidullah, A. Experimentelle Untersuchungen uber den Geschmacksinn. *Archiv für die Gesamte Psychologie,* 1927, **69,** 475.

Saltzman, I., & Koch, S. The effect of low intensities of hunger on the behavior mediated by a habit of maximum strength. *Journal of Experimental Psychology,* 1948, **38,** 347–370.

Sanford, R. N. The effects of abstinence from food upon imaginal processes: A further experiment. *Journal of Psychology,* 1937, **3,** 145–159.

Schachtel, E. G. *Metamorphosis.* New York: Basic Books, 1959.

Schachter, S., & Singer, J. Cognitive, social, and physiological determinants of emotional state. *Psychological Review,* 1962. **69,** 379–399.

Schmitt, D. R. The invocation of moral obligation. *Sociometry,* 1964, **27,** 299–310.

Scott, J. P. Critical periods in behavioral development. *Science,* 1962, **138,** 949–958.

Scott, J. P. The process of primary socialization in canine and human infants. *Child Development Monographs,* 1963, **28.**

Sears, R. R. Experimental studies of projection: I. Attribution of traits. *Journal of Social Psychology,* 1936, **7,** 151–163.

Seeman, M. Alienation and social learning in a reformatory. *American Journal of Sociology,* 1963, **69,** 270–284.

Seeman, M., & Evans, J. Alienation and learning in a hospital setting. *American Sociological Review,* 1962, **27,** 772–782.

Selltiz, C., Jahoda, M., Deutsch, M., & Cook, S. W. *Research methods in social relations.* New York: Holt, 1959.

Sheffield, F. D., Roby, T. B., & Campbell, B. A. Drive reduction versus consummatory behavior as determinants of reinforcement. *Journal of Comparative and Physiological Psycology,* 1954, **47,** 349–354.

Sherrington, C. S. *The integrative action of the nervous system.* New York: Scribners, 1906.

Sherwood, J. J. Self-report and projective measures of achievement motivation. *Journal of Consulting Psychology,* 1966, **30,** 329–337.

Shipley, W. C. An apparent transfer of conditioning. *Journal of General Psychology,* 1933, **8,** 382–391.

Siegel, P. S. The relationship between voluntary water intake, body weight loss, and number of hours of water privation in the rat. *Journal of Comparative and Physiological Psychology,* 1947, **40,** 231–238.

Skinner, B. F. *The behavior of organisms: An experimental analysis.* New York: Appleton, 1938.

Skinner, B. F. *Science and human behavior.* New York: Macmillan, 1953.

Skinner, B. F. Behaviorism at fifty. In T. W. Wann (Ed.), *Behaviorism and phenomenology.* Chicago: University of Chicago Press, 1964. Pp. 79–108.

Smith, C. P. The influence of testing conditions on need for achievement scores and their relationship to performance scores. In J. W. Atkinson & N. T. Feather (Eds.), *A theory of achievement motivation.* New York: Wiley, 1966.

Spiegelberg, H. Report on the first workshop in phenomenology at Washington University. Unpublished manuscript, Washington University, 1965.

Spitz, R. A., & Wolf, K. M. Anaclitic depression; an inquiry into the genesis of psychiatric conditions in early childhood. *Psychoanalytic Study of the Child,* 1946, **2,** 313–342.

Stouffer, S. A., Guttman, L., Suchman, E. A., Lazarsfeld, P. F., Starr, S. A., & Clausen, J. A. *Measurement and prediction. Studies in social psychology in World War II.* Vol. IV. Princeton, N. J.: Princeton University Press, 1950.

Strickland, B. R. The relationships of awareness to verbal conditioning and extinction. Unpublished doctoral dissertation, Ohio State University, 1962. (Cited in Rotter, 1966.)

Strickland, B. R. The prediction of social action from a dimension of internal-external control. *Journal of Social Psychology,* 1965, **66,** 353–358.

Strickland, L. H. Surveillance and trust. *Journal of Personality,* 1958, **26,** 200–215.

Terwilliger, R. F. Pattern complexity and affective arousal. *Perceptual and Motor Skills,* 1963, **17,** 387–395.

Thibaut, J. W., & Riecken, H. W. Some determinants and consequences of the perception of social causality. *Journal of Personality,* 1955a, **24,** 113–133.

Thibaut, J. W., & Riecken, H. W. Authoritarianism, status, and the communication of aggression. *Human Relations,* 1955b, **8,** 95–120.

Thorndike, E. L. *The psychology of learning.* Vol. 2. *Educational psychology.* New York: Teachers College, 1913.

Titchener, E. B. *A textbook of psychology.* New York: Macmillan, 1909–1910.

Tolman, E. C. *Purposive behavior in animals and men.* New York: Appleton, 1932.

Tomkins, S. S. *Affect, imagery, consciousness.* Vol. 1. New York: Springer, 1962.

Troland, L. T. *The fundamentals of human motivation.* Princeton, N. J.: Van Nostrand, 1928.

Valins, S. Cognitive effects of false heart-rate feedback. *Journal of Personality and Social Psychology,* 1966, **4,** 400–408.

Valins, S. Emotionality and information concerning internal reactions. *Journal of Personality and Social Psychology,* 1967a, **6,** 458–463.

Valins, S. Emotionality and autonomic reactivity. *Journal of Experimental Research in Personality,* 1967b, **2,** 41–48.

Van Ostrand, D. Reactions to positive and negative information about the self as a function of certain personality characteristics of the recipient. Unpublished master's thesis, University of Colorado, 1960.

Vogel, W., Baker, R. W., & Lazarus, R. S. The role of motivation in psychological stress. *Journal of Abnormal and Social Psychology,* 1958, **56,** 105–112.

Wada, T. An experimental study of hunger in its relation to activity. *Archives of Psychology, New York,* 1922, **8,** (57), 1–65.

Wann, T. W. (Ed.) *Behaviorism and phenomenology.* Chicago: University of Chicago Press, 1964.

Wang, G. H. The relation between "spontaneous" activity and oestrus cycle in the white rat. *Comparative Psychological Monographs,* 1923, **2** (6).

Warden, C. J. *Animal motivation: Experimental studies on the albino rat.* New York: Columbia University Press, 1931.

Warren, H. C. *Dictionary of psychology.* Boston: Houghton, 1934.

Warren, R. P., & Pfaffman, C. Early experience and taste aversion. *Journal of Comparative and Physiological Psychology,* 1959, **52,** 263–266.

Watson, J. B. Psychology as the behaviorist views it. *Psychological Review,* 1913, **20,** 158–177.

Webb, W. B. The motivational aspect of an irrelevant drive in the behavior of a white rat. *Journal of Experimental Psychology*, 1949, **39**, 1–14.

Weick, K. E. Reduction of cognitive dissonance through task enhancement and effort expenditure. *Journal of Abnormal and Social Psychology*, 1964, **68**, 533–539.

Weiner, I. H., & Stellar, E. Salt preference of the rat determined by a single stimulus method. *Journal of Comparative and Physiological Psychology*, 1951, **44**, 394–401.

White, R. W. Motivation reconsidered: The concept of competence. *Psychological Review*, 1959, **66**, 297–333.

Wilkins, E. J., & de Charms, R. Authoritarianism and response to power cues. *Journal of Personality*, 1962, **30**, 439–457.

Winterbottom, M. R. The relation of need for achievement to learning experiences in independence and mastery. In J. W. Atkinson (Ed.), *Motives in fantasy, action and society*. Princeton, N.J.: Van Nostrand, 1958.

Wisdom, J. *Problems of mind and matter*. London and New York: Cambridge University Press, 1934.

Wundt, W. *Vorlesungen über Menschen und Thierseele*, 1863.

Wundt, W. *Grundzüge der physiologischen Psychologie*. (5th ed.) Vol. II. Leipzig: Engelmann, 1874.

Yamaguchi, H. G. Drive as a function of hunger. *Journal of Experimental Psychology*, 1951, **42**, 108–117.

Yoshioka, J. G. Weber's law in the discrimination of maze distance by the white rat. *University of California Publications in Psychology*, 1929, **4**, 155–184.

Young, P. T. *Motivation of behavior: The fundamental determinants of human and animal activity*. New York: Wiley, 1936.

Young, P. T. The role of hedonic processes in motivation. In M. R. Jones (Ed.), *Nebraska symposium on motivation*. Lincoln: University of Nebraska Press, 1955. Pp. 193–238.

Young, P. T. The role of affective processes in learning and motivation. *Psychological Review*, 1959, **66**, 104–125.

Young, P. T. *Motivation and emotion: A survey of the determinants of human and animal activity*. New York: Wiley, 1961.

Young, P. T., & Asdourian, D. Relative acceptability of sodium chloride and sucrose solutions. *Journal of Comparative and Physiological Psychology*, 1957, **50**, 499–503.

Young, P. T., & Chaplin, J. P. Studies of food preference, appetite and dietary habit: (X) Preferences of adrenalectomized rats for salt solutions of different concentrations. *Comparative Psychological Monographs*, 1949, **19**, 45–74.

Young, P. T., & Falk, J. L. The relative acceptability of sodium chloride solution as a function of concentration and water need. *Journal of Comparative and Physiological Psychology*, 1956, **49**, 569–575.

Young, P. T., & Greene, J. T. Quantity of food ingested as a measure of relative acceptability. *Journal of Comparative and Physiological Psychology*, 1953, **46**, 288–294.

Young, P. T., & Shuford, E. H., Jr. Intensity, duration, and repetition of hedonic processes as related to acquisition of motives. *Journal of Comparative and Physiological Psychology*, 1954, **47**, 298–305.

Zeigarnik, B. Uber das Behalten von erledigten und unerledigten Handlungen. *Psychologische Forschung*, 1927, **9**, 1–85.

Ziehen, T. *Leitfaden der physiologischen Psychologie*. (10th ed.) Berlin: Jena: G. Fischer, 1914.

Zimbardo, P. G., & Montgomery, K. C. The relative strengths of consummatory responses in hunger, thirst, and exploratory drive. *Journal of Comparative and Physiological Psychology*, 1957, **50**, 504–508.

Author Index

377

Subject Index